To Doug & Missy:

Kill a commie!
for mommy! ☺

Best wishes
[signature]
May 28 2011

SUBVERSION
INC.

How Obama's ACORN Red
Shirts are Still Terrorizing and
Ripping Off American Taxpayers

Matthew Vadum

WND Books

SUBVERSION, INC.
WND Books

Published by WorldNetDaily
Washington, D.C.

WRITTEN BY MATTHEW VADUM
JACKET DESIGN BY MARK KARIS
INTERIOR DESIGN BY NEUWIRTH & ASSOCIATES, INC.

WND Books are distributed to the trade by:
Midpoint Trade Books
27 West 20th Street, Suite 1102
New York, NY 10011

WND Books are available at special discounts for bulk purchases. WND Books, Inc.
also publishes books in electronic formats. For more information,
call (541-474-1776) or visit www.wndbooks.com.

First Edition

ISBN: 978-1-935071-14-3

Library of Congress information available

Printed in the United States of America

10 9 8 7 6 5 4 3 2 1

To my Aunt Bonnie, who knew I would be a writer long before I did and encouraged me when it was the last thing on my mind, and to my father who taught me the importance of language.

"Radicals are most adept at breaking the necks of conservatives."
SAUL ALINSKY, *Reveille for Radicals*

Contents

CONTENTS

Preface

IN THIS BOOK I've tried to prove that whatever you've heard about ACORN, in reality, the group is far, far worse. It celebrates and promotes the worst pathologies in society in an effort to kill the American experiment in self-governance.

Rumors of its death have been greatly exaggerated. The group declared bankruptcy at the end of 2010, but its leaders acknowledge that they are building a new network of activist groups to continue ACORN's work undermining American institutions.

ACORN is like a "boiler room" sales operation. Once the authorities get wind of it, it moves and assumes a new name while it seeks out fresh victims. Long before two conservative activists captured ACORN employees on video offering to assist in the creation of a brothel for pedophiles, ACORN insiders knew the game plan. They predicted, correctly, that whenever the group's day of reckoning finally came, ACORN wouldn't stay dead for long.

ACORN was not, as its defenders insist, a victim of its own success. It didn't grow so quickly that it failed to adopt sensible business practices. It wasn't singled out for persecution by Fox News. It wasn't a bunch of well-intentioned liberals who made a few mistakes that could happen to anyone. Sure, there were some decent people in the organization who wanted to help the poor, but when they deviated from the group's Marxist leaders they were kicked out.

ACORN is part political group, part crime syndicate, part terrorist organization. Much of the time it operates outside the legitimate political process, waging war against the framework of society.

ACORN is in the business of subverting the American system, so what Americans saw on the undercover videos released in 2009 was just another day at the office at ACORN.

If I were to write about every aspect of ACORN that fascinated me, the book would be 2,000 pages long (or maybe longer). I hope other researchers and writers pick up the beat and begin excavating more ACORN-related scandals. A 40-year-old group with 400,000 members is bound to have thousands more stories of crime and corruption.

After studying ACORN intensely for three years, I've barely scratched the surface of America's most dangerous, devious political group. I couldn't possibly cover every destructive thing ACORN has ever done, so in this book I've tried to highlight the most important things.

But there is so much about ACORN that has yet to be explored.

Matthew Vadum
Washington, D.C.
January 2011

Prologue:
Bringing Down the System

HOW MANY DEAD Republicans does it take to satisfy the bloodlust of ACORN founder Wade Rathke?

We'll never know, because the FBI thwarted the attack planned by his allies on the 2008 Republican national convention. It's impossible to determine how many American lives were saved that September day in St. Paul, Minnesota, because Rathke's progressive comrades-in-arms were caught before they could incinerate innocent Americans who disagreed with them politically.

This attempt by radical left-wing anarchists to kill delegates and police and to shut down the nation's democratic process didn't enrage Rathke, chief architect of President Barack Obama's favorite community organizing group. On the contrary, five months later Rathke wrote a blog post without a single word of criticism for the perpetrators.

The planned murder and mayhem didn't interest him at all. What really drove ACORN's patriarch *nuts* was that a fellow radical leftist, a member of his own political camp, had dared to work with the government to fight left-wing thuggery. On his Chief Organizer blog, Rathke denounced FBI informant Brandon Darby, formerly a fellow America-hating radical community organizer, for helping to disrupt the attack: "It seemed so, how should I say it, '60s?"

"One thing to disagree, but it's a whole different thing to rat on folks, or, even worse, as some now allege, to try and mousetrap people," Rathke wrote. "Why in the age of Bush did we need to go back to the 60's and the Darth Vader times again?" Rathke continued, nostalgically gazing into his navel. "I'm not sure exactly what may have happened. Darby is suddenly not talking, but this is all both sketchy and creepy, and I want there to be different rules of engagement in the Age of Obama." (The entire blog post is available in Appendix C.)[1]

Human life, pain and suffering, the possibility of civil disorder, the sanctity of the American electoral process—all were less important to Rathke than protecting terrorists who shared his vision for America. Rathke must also have been incensed that the attack came so soon after the Democrats' national convention, which had highlighted community organizers and what they do to the communities they target. And it must have made his blood boil that the terrorist attack failed at a Republican convention whose star attractions subjected his chosen profession to pitiless ridicule.

The GOP convention that nominated John McCain and Sarah Palin faithfully followed the fifth rule of power tactics according to community organizing guru Saul Alinsky, one of Rathke's inspirations: *Ridicule is man's most potent weapon.* Ridicule "is almost impossible to counterattack," Alinsky taught. During the proceedings in St. Paul, prominent Republicans such as former New York City mayor Rudolph Giuliani relentlessly mocked the vocation of community organizing. As Giuliani said of candidate Obama, "On the other hand, you have a resume from a gifted man with an Ivy League education. He worked as a community organizer. *What?*" Giuliani said, interrupted by loud laughter, hoots, and hollers. "He worked—I said—I said—okay, okay. Maybe this is the first problem on the resume. He worked as a community organizer." And Rathke was no doubt deeply offended by Palin's taunt that being "a small-town mayor is sort of like a 'community organizer,' except that you have actual responsibilities."

Adding insult to injury, informant Darby had previously thumbed his nose at ACORN on Rathke's home turf of New Orleans. A co-founder of Common Ground, a nonprofit relief agency that won national acclaim for helping Crescent City residents rebuild their lives in the wake of 2005's Hurricane Katrina, Darby refused to submit to ACORN.

This is a particularly serious offense in the world of leftist empire-building. Official ACORN policy calls for competing groups to be co-opted, or if that proves impossible, destroyed. The Association of Community Organizations for Reform Now, born in 1970 out of fading '60s-era radicalism, is only interested in community organizations that promote its firebrand agenda using its extreme methods. According to Darby, who in recent years has renounced his youthful anti-American radicalism, ACORN threatened and intimidated Common Ground:

> When you didn't do what ACORN wanted, all of a sudden nonprofits, other people started to do political attacks against you, claiming that you were a white supremacist, claiming that you were like a missionary coming in on a white horse trying to have the white man help the black people, trying to reinforce the notion that blacks can't help themselves, and these are the kinds of innuendoes, subtleties, and political attacks that would occur.[2]

In 2002 ACORN put the hurt on San Francisco's Outer Mission Residents Association. It bussed in activists from out of town to disrupt OMRA events. "ACORN members then began showing up at some neighbors' homes, and in one case jabbed a person in the chest," a newspaper reported. OMRA objected to ACORN's practice of charging fees for community events. One OMRA member paid by check to attend one event and then found that ACORN had used the check information to withdraw money from his bank account for meetings he did not attend.

ACORN also broke up community meetings with local officials. San Francisco parking chief Fred Hamdun said one meeting that ACORN targeted was "the most abusive meeting I've ever subjected myself and my staff to, ever." OMRA leader Steve Currier said ACORN was "spreading terror at community meetings, trying to muscle established neighborhood groups out of the way."[3]

This viciousness is standard operating procedure for ACORN, inspired by Saul Alinsky, the Chicago thug whose paean to ruthlessness, *Rules for Radicals*, is the community organizer's bible.

Like all elite community organizers, Rathke is an Alinsky devotee.

Rathke first put his unique skill set to use as a professional agitator for the violent Students for a Democratic Society in the 1960s. SDS experimented with radicalizing inner cities through community organizing and published a newsletter called *Firebomb*. The group was home to terrorist bombers Bernardine Dohrn and Bill Ayers, who later helped Barack Obama launch his political career with a fundraiser in their living room. Rathke further honed his gangster skills in ACORN's parent organization, the infamous National Welfare Rights Organization.

Leftists who abandon their faith are demonized by their former co-religionists. Relentless attacks on Greenpeace co-founder Patrick Moore and former radical David Horowitz continue to the present day, decades after they moved rightward. This is because on the Left there is a presumption of good intentions—even on the part of terrorists who happen to be in the same political camp. As left-wing talk radio host Thom Hartmann told this right-leaning writer: "My left-wing crazies are better than your right-wing crazies."

Hartmann explained:

Your right-wing crazies are incited to violence based on fear and hate of people because of whom they are, because they're gay, because they're Catholic, because they're Jewish, because they're black, because they're Hispanic. And our left-wing crazies are incited to violence because they're trying to create a better world. They're trying to save the environment in the case of the eco-terrorists. They're trying to end the Vietnam War in the case of the Weather Underground. They're trying to bring about civil rights in the case of the Symbionese Liberation Army and some of the other black terrorist groups that were operating in the 1970s.[4]

To the Left, violent acts are worthy of praise as long as they promote desirable ends, especially if aimed at the other side. Riots aren't the work of antisocial criminals; they're praiseworthy examples of the people expressing their will.

Internationally known "small-c" communist* author Naomi Klein openly called for violence at the 2004 Republican convention, urging protesters to bring the Iraq War to the streets of New York City. The Canadian writer wasn't ostracized by the Left after her outrageous statement; if anything, her public stature has only grown since 2004. And she remains true to her view, praising the June 2010 riots at the G20 summit in Toronto.

If right-wing terrorists plotted to attack a Democratic National Convention, whoever foiled the conspiracy would be immortalized in film,

---

* An important note on terminology: When I refer to anyone as a *small-c communist* I mean that the person is sympathetic to communism but is not a member of the Communist Party USA (or similar American parties such as the Revolutionary Communist Party and the Socialist Workers Party). Former radical David Horowitz prefers the phrase "neo-communist," by which he appears to mean roughly the same. As I see it, communism is a political movement whose adherents believe that markets are fundamentally unjust and that physical force should be used to attain a classless society. When the legitimate political process allows it to achieve its goals, ACORN supports American-style democracy. When it doesn't, ACORN steps outside the legitimate political process and uses physical force and intimidation. *Socialist* is not a strong enough adjective to describe ACORN. ACORN is not a debating society. It is not a collection of coffee klatch bohemians pontificating about making the world better. ACORN is about taking action to tear down the American system.

Besides, is socialism much different from communism? Karl Marx thought of socialism as a necessary weigh station on the road to the supposed utopia of communism. Socialism versus communism is a never-ending debate in academic circles, and it is one that is too involved to get into here. (Fellow ACORN chronicler Stanley Kurtz agonizes over the definition of socialism in his wonderful recent book *Radical-in-Chief.* It is so unnecessary.) Suffice it to say that socialists and communists all want government or the collective to be master. They all subscribe to bad, un-American ideas, are all in the same ideological camp, and all tend to believe that the ends justify the means. In ideological terms, there is no bright line dividing socialism from communism.If a government nationalizes an industry does it really matter whether that government was elected or seized power by force? The fundamentals are more or less the same.

Does referring to ACORN as small-c communist imply the group wanted to set up a Soviet-style totalitarian state? Of course not, but the group's leaders reject the core values of American society. Such radicals marginalize adversaries by calling them crazy when they point a finger at communists, as if communists were figments of someone's fevered imagination. "In a stunning demonstration of the power or propaganda, accusing someone of having been a Communist makes *you* the nut," Ann Coulter opined at page 192 of *Treason: Liberal Treachery from the Cold War to the War on Terrorism*, Crown Forum, 2003. No doubt ACORN and its allies will use the same tactic in an attempt to discredit this book. So be it. ACORN is what it is.

literature, and song as a savior of democracy. Radical Hollywood director Oliver Stone would fund a movie project with his own money. But left-wing terrorists attacking Republicans? Reactions on the Left would range from indifferent yawns to cries of "they got what they deserved!"

According to the nation's entertainment-media complex, social justice-oriented terrorism isn't ugly and anti-American, it's praiseworthy and hip. So it should come as no surprise that anarchists Bradley Neil Crowder and David Guy McKay, the would-be GOP convention bombers that Darby stopped, are in the process of being rehabilitated by the Left while serving time in prison. Crowder received a 24-month prison term after cutting a deal with prosecutors. McKay got 48 months.

And what did this praiseworthy and hip pair do? They assembled eight Molotov cocktails, mixing the gasoline in their bottles with oil "so it would stick to clothing and skin and burn longer," according to Darby. They also brought to St. Paul 35 homemade riot shields made from stolen traffic barrels to help demonstrators block streets and prevent delegates from reaching the convention.[5]

Early on, Crowder and McKay became a cause célèbre for the Left, dubbed the Texas Two. A documentary film about them is under way titled—you guessed it—*Better This World*, thanks to an HBO Documentary Films Fellowship. No doubt there will be more praise heaped on them as they ascend to the Left's pantheon of social justice champions, joining cop killer Mumia abu Jamal, Lynne Stewart, Bill Ayers, Bernardine Dohrn, and Leonard Peltier. To be clear, ACORN had nothing to do with the GOP convention attack planned by Crowder and McKay, but like Bobby Seale's Black Panther Party and George Wiley's NWRO, it comes from the same tradition of violent activism. And it's only a matter of time before Rathke stars as the hero in a Hollywood movie that no one will go to see.

In real life, Rathke's star turn at ACORN is over, just as ACORN itself has collapsed under the weight of its own destructive and illegal methods. His successor as chief ACORN organizer, former squatter and actress Bertha Lewis, was never really in control from the time she became CEO in mid-2008 until the organization went bust in November 2010. Although ACORN's membership included people of all races, the politically correct white leftists in senior management wanted someone of color to be their public face. Lewis was the puppet of national executive director Steve Kest and his younger lobbyist brother Jon, ACORN insiders say. Whites' domination of the upper echelons of the organization generated racial resentment within ACORN. "What you have is a plantation mentality working here," said former ACORN official Coya Mobley. "What you have here is a plantation owner having your plantation workers out there working."[6]

Lewis received some unwanted publicity in April 2010 when her paranoid rant before the Young Democratic Socialists found its way onto YouTube. YDS is the youth arm of the radical and misleadingly named Democratic Socialists of America (DSA), which is closely tied to the Congressional Progressive Caucus, a group of more than eighty left-wing Democratic lawmakers in the last Congress. In the video, Lewis gives a rambling speech in which she praises radicalism and harshly criticizes conservatives and corporations.

Although ACORN leaders, like all Alinskyites, typically resist the socialist label because they realize the term carries a negative connotation in American culture, Lewis openly embraced socialism. "First of all let me just say any group that says, 'I'm young, I'm democratic, and I'm a socialist,' is all right with me," Lewis said.

Lewis said to applause that the Tea Party movement, a grassroots reaction against Big Government, was a "bowel movement in my estimation" that is associated with "racism."

Lewis also seemed to predict that America would soon enter a period of violent upheaval. "Right now we are living in a time which is going to dwarf the McCarthy era," she said. "It is going to dwarf the internments during World War II. We are right now in a time that is going to dwarf the era of Jim Crow and segregation."

She may have also warned of a coming race war—or *something*.

Get yourselves together. Get strong. Get big. And get in this battle. Get in this battle because again, it's all about money. How this country works. All that we have in this country, and the fact that this fear of a black planet, that's being played out, in the United States today, the future of our country, is people of color. And how that's going to change our psyche and our economics. This is why folks are grabbing so hard to change the economic paradigm because we gettin' ready to have a majority country of people of color. And the fear of a black planet is real.

Fear of a Black Planet is a 1990 album by the hip-hop band Public Enemy, which is known for its militant, racially charged lyrics. The album contained a song called "Fight the Power." (A transcript of the entire speech is available in Appendix D.)

This wasn't Lewis's first rant about race. She lied to host Lou Dobbs on CNN in April 2009, declaring that Arizona sheriff Joe Arpaio had claimed to be a member of the Ku Klux Klan. In fact, what Arpaio said was that left-wing activists often accused him of being racist, as if he were a Ku Klux Klan member, when he attempted to enforce U.S. immigration laws. The sheriff said the insults did not bother him.

Lewis refused to back down from her malicious, counterfactual assertion, which is not surprising because when confronted, ACORN officials routinely lie, lie, and lie some more.[7] For example, according to ACORN, there's no such thing as voter fraud, though undermining the electoral process has long been one of the organization's chief objectives and voter fraud helped to set the stage for ACORN's downfall.

Fearmongering seems to be one of Lewis's special skills. In her YDS speech, she told the audience unnamed forces are "coming after you." They are "going to be brutal and repressive. They've already shown it to you," she said. "Organize. Get out into the street. You really have got to circle the wagons. This is not rhetoric or hyperbole. This is real."

"Immigration," said Lewis, "is the next big battle."

"Immigration, immigration, and immigration," she said. "And the reason that this is so important is, you know, here's the secret."

Whispering, Lewis said, "We're getting ready to be a majority-minority country. *Shhhhh.* We'll be like South Africa. More black people than white people. Don't tell anybody."

Radical, relentless, and loose with the truth. That is the legacy of ACORN.

ONE

Burn, Baby, Burn:
ACORN's Radical Origins

THE 1960s WAS a decade that gave birth to so many monstrous, ugly things. Despite baby boomers' unlimited nostalgia for the era, it was, in the words of historian Paul Johnson, "America's suicide attempt."[8] The radical rallying cry of the period was, "Burn, baby! Burn!"—the chant of rioters in the Watts neighborhood of Los Angeles during six devastating days in August 1965, when 34 people were killed and more than 3,000 arrested. It was a time when radical leftists who had long aspired to destroy the American "system," which they saw as oppressive, exploitive, sexist, racist, and imperialist, finally became a political force to be reckoned with. The radical so-called New Left muscled in on parts of the political establishment in the 1960s, then finished the job by taking over the Democratic Party and nominating George McGovern for president in 1972. These children from the Age of Aquarius rejected American values then, and reject them now as they dominate the Obama administration, which is shaping up to be the most radical presidency in American history. Obama may have only been a little boy in the 1960s but he now eagerly embraces the values of that decade. The era gave birth both to the non-violent civil rights movement and to groups violent in varying degrees, including Students for a Democratic Society (SDS), its splinter group the Weather Underground Organization (WUO), and the National Welfare Rights Organization (NWRO) that spawned an ACORN from which much evil has grown. These radicals have deliberately conflated civil rights with wealth redistribution to cover their tracks and bask in the glow of the civil rights movement. Their tale is a false narrative long overdue for debunking.

It was out of the nihilistic 1960s that the small-c communist Association of Community Organizations for Reform Now was born. ACORN poses as a civil rights group but it is nothing of the sort. It is a group committed to tearing down America in order to transform it into something unrecognizable. The story of ACORN is the story of the planned decline of the United States that is now in progress. It is the story of revolutionary Marxists Richard Cloward, Frances Fox Piven, and Saul Alinsky, who developed disruptive antisocial strategies and tactics aimed at destroying the American system from within. Cloward, Piven, and Alinsky were admirers of the criminal underworld (Alinsky even gave financial advice to the Chicago mob). Wade Rathke, the trio's loyal disciple, built ACORN from nothing as its first chief organizer and ruled his empire of destructive activism with an iron first for nearly four decades—until his own corruption brought him down. Most ominously, the story of ACORN is the story of Barack Obama, who worked for the operation, trained its organizers, and reveled in its radical, un-American values.

ACORN is a strange, complex political creature with tentacles that slither into the highest levels of the United States government, the Democratic Party, corporate America, the labor movement, the non-profit world, the media, foreign governments, and academia. More than four decades ago during a dangerous period of upheaval from which America barely escaped, ACORN gestated in the womb of the NWRO, a single-issue group focused on so-called welfare rights. NWRO created ACORN in 1970 as an experiment in multi-issue advocacy, while pioneering many of the thuggish tactics ACORN uses today. Its members stormed and terrorized welfare offices in order to extract more and more benefits from governments. NWRO, which

hated fallen civil rights leader Martin Luther King for not being sufficiently radical, took no prisoners and neither has ACORN. ACORN
learned everything from Cloward, Piven, and Alinsky, who played a
critical role in the organization, and in other groups with similar objectives. They were not mere theorists but activists involved in the radical
movement as a means of putting their various strategies for attacking
the American system into practice. Cloward and Piven, who developed
the elegantly simple model for politicoeconomic subversion that bears
their names, were so close to ACORN that they wrote the foreword to
Organizing the Movement: The Roots and Growth of ACORN, a 1986 book
by ACORN's first staff organizer, Gary Delgado. ACORN, they wrote,
"is very much a creation of the halcyon days of the 1960s, and the *zeit-
geist* of that period has continued to influence the young organizers
who successively flocked to the ACORN banner."[9]

Cloward, who died in 2001, and his wife, Piven, worked with and
advised ACORN throughout their lengthy careers. Even today Piven
is a member of ACORN subsidiary Project Vote's board of directors[10]
and a member of the advisory board of ACORN's journal, *Social Policy*.[11] ACORN was so indebted to Cloward that when he was stricken
with lung cancer in 2001, the group helped to put together a tribute
for him. Said ACORN stalwart Madeleine Adamson:

> I hate to begin a tribute to one of our foremost public intellectuals
> with a borrowed advertising slogan, but I can't get this one out of
> my mind: 'When Richard Cloward talks, organizers listen.' Since
> the late 1950s, when he argued that juvenile delinquents were pur-
> suing the American dream by the only avenues open to them, Rich-
> ard has continually presented a challenging view of social problems
> along with creative strategies to solve them. With his partner, Fran
> Piven, he was the instigator of the 'break the bank' strategy that
> helped launch the Welfare Rights Organization. I had the pleasure
> and privilege of working in association with him over a number of
> years. Combining the best of academics and activism, he has made
> an extraordinary contribution to social change organizing over the
> past four decades.[12]

That's an understatement.

NWRO was founded in 1966—the same year Cloward and Piven's seminal article "The Weight of the Poor" was published. NWRO grew out of a merger between Alinsky's flagship rabble-rousing organization, the Industrial Areas Foundation (IAF), "and the civil rights movement, sparked by a 1965 organizer training program that brought together veteran organizers Saul Alinsky, Warren Haggstrom, and Fred Ross to build an 'on the streets' community organization model through the Syracuse University School of Social Work."[13] Cloward and Piven acknowledge they "were intimately involved in the affairs of NWRO: we participated in discussions of strategy, in fund-raising efforts, and in demonstrations. We were strong advocates of a particular political strategy—one stressing disruptive protest rather than community organization . . ."[14]

What's the difference between ACORN and the Weather Underground, infamous for its firebombing rampage in the late 1960s and '70s? Answer: not as much as you might think. Both failed to find support at the ballot box and chose to implement their agendas by force. The difference is largely a matter of degree, strategy, and tone rather than political ideology. ACORN comes out of the same cluster of violent New Left groups such as Students for a Democratic Society that rioted at the 1968 Democratic national convention and spilled American blood during the "Days of Rage" of 1969 in an effort to undermine the U.S. war effort in Vietnam. It is no coincidence that SDS also tried its hand at organizing the poor in the early 1960s. SDS leader Todd Gitlin, now a professor of journalism and sociology at Columbia University, said, "The poor know they are poor and don't like it; hence they can be organized so as to demand an end to poverty and the construction of a decent social order." The SDS project, ERAP, which was pronounced *ee-rap* and stood for Economic Research and Action Project, was started with a $5,000 grant from the United Auto Workers. "ERAP, by getting off the campuses and into the ghettos, would get to the grass roots, get to where the people are," writes radical scholar Kirkpatrick Sale. "There we can listen to them, learn from them, organize them to give voice to their legitimate complaints, mobilize them to demand from the society the decent life that is rightfully theirs."[15] SDS members also helped to create a group in Boston called Mothers for Adequate Welfare (MAW).[16]

Weather Underground bomber Bill Ayers, who recently retired as an education professor at the University of Illinois at Chicago, summed up his group's philosophy: "Kill all the rich people. Break up their cars and apartments. Bring the revolution home. Kill your parents." When eight-and-a-half-month pregnant Hollywood actress Sharon Tate and her baby were brutally murdered by the Manson family cult in 1969, Ayers's now-wife Bernardine Dohrn squealed with delight. Today a law professor—of all things—at Northwestern University, Dohrn said it was a virtuous revolutionary act for Tate's assailants to shove a fork into her belly. So it made perfect sense when Ayers, an unreconstructed anti-American revolutionary Marxist, became a strong supporter of ACORN after he left firebombing behind to poison the minds of the young. In his post-terrorist career, he's never missed an opportunity to direct foundation grants to his favorite radical advocacy group.

Whatever differences they might have had in terms of tactics and doctrine, all these extremist groups from the 1960s sought to overthrow "the system." They all wanted to exterminate American capitalism, though they disagreed on how to do it and what exactly should replace it. Because ACORN doesn't pursue its goals through rational discussion or the democratic process, it is incorrect to think of ACORN as a mere advocacy organization. Reformed 1960s radical David Horowitz, a former Black Panther Party supporter and *Ramparts* magazine editor, describes ACORN "as a neo-communist ground force." ACORN is "a classic communist front group" which is "the army for the agenda of its elitist leadership which aims to destroy the capitalist system," he said in an interview.

ACORN can't always hide its nihilistic desire for destruction. In a strange detour into Internet-based merchandising, the group printed pricey posters featuring kitsch art by one of its lawyers, Steve Bachmann, that reflect ACORN's values. One poster honored German Marxist Walter Benjamin. His quotation, "There is no document of civilization which is not at the same time a document of barbarism," accompanied a portrait of the philosopher who died in 1940. Another poster depicted socialist Kurt Weill, a German-American composer. The Weill portrait is accompanied by a quotation attributed to another Marxist, playwright Bertolt Brecht: "Now all you cultured folk who want to lead us and teach us to refrain from major wrongs, the first thing you must do is stop and feed us. When we have eaten try your righteous songs." One poster celebrated ACORN's home-invading squatters.[17]

NOT A CIVIL RIGHTS GROUP:
THE SHOCK TROOPS OF THE LEFT

President Obama's favorite activist organization is no fringe group. In tongue-in-cheek remarks, ACORN court historian John Atlas declared:

> I am here to warn you about the most powerful, most dangerous organization in the country. An organization that has been accused of stealing a presidential election, has been blamed for causing the subprime crisis. It's been accused of embezzling millions of dollars, of misusing federal funds, of having relations with a prostitute, as well as engaging in widespread voter fraud and intimidation, intimidating banks and insurance companies to give them money, and this is all true. It's all documented.

Atlas's punchline was that he was really talking about the Republican Party. The audience at a leftist confab in summer 2010 roared with laughter. The irony was that Atlas's Alinskyite ridicule was a more or less accurate sketch of ACORN's 40-year history.[18]

ACORN was forced to regroup in early 2010 after a series of scandals drove it to the brink of bankruptcy, and decided to go underground until after the 2010 midterm elections. Transferring bank accounts and personnel, it dissolved its national structure and had its state chapters incorporate themselves separately under different names. The staff and offices for the new organizations were largely unchanged. However, in November 2010, after the Democrats suffered the worst midterm election defeat in more than half a century—a devastating repudiation of the liberal agenda—ACORN announced it was filing Chapter 7 bankruptcy and closing its doors.

The final nail in the coffin for ACORN was a series of hidden camera videos shot by conservative activists James O'Keefe and Hannah Giles. Giles posed as a prostitute. O'Keefe posed as her pimp. They had no difficulty getting ACORN employees across America to offer advice on illegal activities. ACORN workers offered helpful hints on getting a government grant to establish a brothel, importing illegal alien child prostitutes, and evading taxes.

The videos began airing September 10, 2009 on Andrew Breitbart's Big Government website and on Glenn Beck's TV show. Within days the Census Bureau and the IRS severed ties to ACORN. Lawmakers demanded investigations and Congress passed a bill stripping ACORN of federal funding. Donors who stuck with the group through previous scandals began to jump ship. With their videos, O'Keefe and Giles accomplished what 10,000 op-eds and years of media coverage of ACORN's persistent election fraud schemes failed to do: put ACORN out of business.

At its height, ACORN claimed 400,000 members. These shock troops of the Left have been intimately involved in passing and protecting legislation harmful to America. ACORN has lobbied relentlessly for the Community Reinvestment Act, National Voter Registration Act (also known as the "Motor Voter" law), minimum wage laws, and so-called living wage laws. It played a key role in promoting Obamacare. Its massive fraud-plagued voter drives helped elect Democrats nationwide. President Obama even put a former ACORN fundraiser, David F. Hamilton, on the federal bench.[19] ACORN has been both feared and respected by Democratic officeholders across America. Its ties to the labor movement, particularly the radical, thuggish Service Employees International Union (SEIU), helped ACORN drive the political conversation on the activist Left.

SEIU, incidentally, was involved in discussions with now impeached Illinois Gov. Rod Blagojevich over whom he planned to appoint to Barack Obama's Senate vacancy in that state. ACORN affiliates even took credit for Blagojevich's election.[20]

ACORN wins elections for the Left. It gets Democratic voters to the polls—whether living or dead. ACORN is effective in part because of its PAL programs. PALs are Precinct Action Leaders who are recruited from local neighborhoods and trained to build neighborhood networks. Each volunteer participant in PAL programs creates and services a list of about 100 family, friends, and others in the local community. The PALs make sure everyone is registered, informed, and ready to vote.

Although ACORN is being liquidated in bankruptcy court, its legacy of destruction and deceit remains with us as a lesson, a warning, and a continuing menace to American legal, political, and economic institutions. ACORN has portrayed itself as a well-intentioned poor people's group similar to crusading civil rights groups of the 1960s. It is better thought of as a lynch mob whose rage is strategically directed at undermining the foundations of the American republic.

The image ACORN tries desperately to hold onto is that of a public-spirited organization in pursuit of a fuzzy abstraction known as social justice. ACORN boasts of registering the poor to vote and encouraging citizen involvement in morally uplifting projects and community development. It claims to have spurred production of affordable housing, protected tenants' rights, and kept unjustly exploited borrowers in their homes. ACORN presents itself as fighting for the rights of immigrants, utility ratepayers, and workers—though it ignores labor laws and ferociously attacks those who try to unionize ACORN workers.

Yet looking through the lens of history at this recent casualty of its own hubris and criminality, what we see is a corrupt army of looters that sustains itself with plunder. Blackmail and vote manufacturing are its major profit centers. With its members dressed in bright red shirts, ACORN organizes aggressive in-your-face protests against business people and public officials. ACORN goes to their homes, frightens their children, wrecks their lawns, and dumps garbage on their property. ACORN breaks into foreclosed homes and illegally seizes them. ACORN occupies bank offices demanding donations and forcing them to lend money to the constituencies they claim to represent. ACORN coerces corporations into signing so-called community benefits agreements, or CBAs, in which the businesses offer conditional surrender to ACORN. Once a business waves the white flag and agrees to pay the group tribute, the shakedowns never stop. Vicious harassment of a target is standard operating procedure in what organizers call an "action."

Although leftists like to consider this violent anti-establishment approach used against businesses to be a form of civil disobedience, that is a misnomer: civil disobedience is by definition an act aimed at a government. What ACORN and its many imitators practice is piracy aimed at undermining the economic system while enriching the perpetrators. The money ACORN liberates from businesses is reinvested in other projects aimed at bringing change to America that most Americans do not want.

Opposed to the profit motive and capitalism in general, ACORN pushes for more government control including gun control, a government monopoly in healthcare and an open door immigration policy. It supports a big raise in the federal minimum wage and so-called "living wage" laws enacted by states and cities. ACORN wants more funding for urban public schools, and wants federal and state laws guaranteeing paid sick leave for all full-time workers. The group claims to fight for affordable housing and rails against foreclosures and "predatory" lending, even while the small-c communist predators at ACORN demand that banks make loans destined to default.

ACORN claims to live by the old adage that if you give a man a fish, you feed him for a day, but if you teach a man to fish, you feed him for a lifetime. If only ACORN were that charitable and public-spirited! ACORN doesn't teach anyone how to fish: it breeds artful dodgers, teaching people how to steal fish from their neighbors, whether through stealth or open confrontation. This mobocratic species of self-help is the essence of so-called "social justice," itself a particularly un-American concept that rests upon a pathological hatred of material inequality. The pursuit of this holy grail of social justice serves as the justification for a never-ending war that ACORN helps the nonproductive elements of society wage against the productive.

A historical snapshot also gives us the image of ACORN as an international extortion and election fraud conglomerate. When the group isn't busing schoolchildren to the nation's capital to protest proposed tax cuts, it's campaigning to expand the size and scope of government, raising the dead from cemeteries and leading them to the voting booth, and promoting the so-called Fairness Doctrine in order to bludgeon conservative-dominated talk radio by demanding equal airtime for liberals. Like Obama associates Jeremiah Wright, Michael Pfleger, Jesse Jackson Sr., and Al Sharpton, ACORN activists try to build a perverse kind of community solidarity through the corrosive rhetoric of class warfare and racial conflict.

ACORN devotees vilify the group's critics, calling them mean-spirited, intolerant haters of the poor who fear minority groups. Opponents are routinely denounced as evil right-wingers conspiring to deprive the poor of what's owed them. This vitriol is to be expected because in the hierarchy of progressive activist groups, ACORN sits atop Mount Olympus, unassailable because its motives are viewed as pure. It may have flaws but to its faithful supporters, the fact that it is so regularly attacked by conservatives and Republicans is evidence the group must be doing something right.

What ACORN's celebrity donors such as Bruce Springsteen,[21] Roseanne Barr, and Barbra Streisand don't know—or are unwilling to admit—is that ACORN is a multi-million dollar international conglomerate devoted to undermining democracy and the capitalist system. Not a good thing for millionaire entertainers to be associated with. They may also be blissfully ignorant of the fact that ACORN was founded not to teach self-reliance, but to encourage poor people to hop on the welfare rolls. By overloading the system or "breaking the bank," the Cloward-Piven Strategy held, radical change would come to America.

ACORN founder Wade Rathke was fascinated by the Cloward-Piven Strategy of orchestrated crisis. Cloward and Piven became Rathke's mentors.[22] Rathke created ACORN on behalf of his then-employer, the National Welfare Rights Organization, which was co-founded by Cloward and Piven to carry out their strategy of upheaval and the agenda of welfare entitlement. ACORN's official "People's Platform" is essentially a *Communist Manifesto* for America's community organizers. Although the Framers got by with an elegantly simple 52-word preamble to the U.S. Constitution, the 1990 version of the more than 7,000-word People's Platform opens with this ponderous prose:

> We stand for a People's Platform, as old as our country, and as young as our dreams. We come before our nation, not to petition with hat in hand, but to rise as one people and demand.
>
> We have waited and watched. We have hoped and helped. We have sweated and suffered. We have often believed. We have frequently followed.
>
> But we have nothing to show for the work of our hand, the tax of our labor. Our patience has been abused; our experience misused. Our silence has been seen as support. Our struggle has been ignored.
>
> Enough is enough. We will wait no longer for the crumbs at America's door. We will not be meek, but mighty. We will not starve on past promises, but feast on future dreams.
>
> We are an uncommon people. We are the majority, forged from all minorities. We are the masses of many, not the forces of few. We will continue our fight until the American way is just one way, until we have shared the wealth, until we have won our freedom.
>
> This is not a simple vision, but a detailed plan.
>
> Our plan is to build an American reality from the American rhetoric, to deliver a piece of the present and the fruits of the future to every man, to every woman, to every family.
>
> We demand our birthright: the chance to be rich, the right to be free.

Our riches shall be the blooming of our communities, the bounty of a sure livelihood, the beauty of homes for our families with sickness driven from the door, the benefit of our taxes rather than their burden, and the best of our energy, land, and natural resources for all people.

Our freedom is the force of democracy, not the farce of federal fat and personal profit. In our freedom, only the people shall rule. Corporations shall have their role; producing jobs, providing products, paying taxes. No more, no less. They shall obey our wishes, respond to our needs, serve our communities. Our country shall be the citizens' wealth and our wealth shall build our country.

Government shall have its role: public servant to our good, fast follower to our sure steps. No more, no less. Our government shall shout with the public voice and no longer to a private whisper. In our government, the common concerns shall be the collective cause.

We represent a people's platform, not a politician's promise.

We demand the changes outlined in our platform and plan. We will work to win. We will have our birthright. We will live in richness and freedom. We will live in one country as one people.[23]

The only sentence that matters here is this: "We will continue our fight until the American way is just one way, until we have *shared the wealth*, until we have won our freedom." [emphasis added] Everything else in the platform is subordinate to the goal of sharing the wealth of Americans through redistributionist policies.

This platform remained alive and well at ACORN, which created a new kind of tax preparation service based on the assumption that Americans have a "right" to welfare. Think of it as H&R Block for subversives. The group and its allied entities help people claim the Earned Income Tax Credit (EITC), a "refundable" tax credit that is welfare by another name. ACORN's goal is not to help Americans in need but to increase governmental burdens.

ACORN violated its own People's Platform. The Employment Policies Institute found that the group violated "more than one in four of its own guiding principles." ACORN supports the right of all workers to organize but has illegally fired and illegally interrogated its own employees who tried to unionize. ACORN says all employees should be guaranteed a decent minimum annual income yet ACORN organizers were typically paid $18,000 a year for 54-hour weeks. ACORN says all workers have a "fundamental right" to workplace safety but it routinely sent employees to work alone evenings in dangerous neighborhoods. Some female ACORN workers were sexually assaulted while performing this work.[24]

ACORN's abusive attitudes towards its own workers prompted one ACORN employee to write this satirical help-wanted ad:

Immediate Openings. Have you always wanted to be a martyr? ACORN is currently hiring community organizers to dedicate their lives at the expense of everything else for a least a year for a minimum of 54 hours a week. Job duties include door knocking by yourself to sign up members (sometimes at night); developing leadership; planning meetings, protests and rallies; running campaigns and fundraising. Working for ACORN is a position of privilege, so if you are single, young, can go for weeks without a paycheck, and you think you have what it takes, call us at 555-ACORN. Fluency in Spanish and the willingness to neglect your own well-being a plus.[25]

URBAN TERRORISM

Even in its downfall, ACORN remains America's best known, most accomplished urban terrorist organization.

Since he founded the innocuous-sounding Neighborhood Assistance Corporation of America (NACA) in 1988, Bruce Marks has been doing the same things ACORN does. A skilled practitioner of Saul Alinsky's antisocial techniques, Marks proudly—and accurately—calls himself an "urban terrorist."[26]

Marks is more forthright—some would say more hotheaded—than ACORN founder Wade Rathke who studiously avoids ideological labels of any kind. Rathke generally tries to paint a big happy face on his Marxism. Like any evasive Alinsky disciple, Rathke conceals his true beliefs. He's said he's "just good at what I do—moving an agenda for low- to moderate-income people to take back what's rightfully ours." When Rathke is asked to explain what "rightfully theirs" means, he replies with a smile, "Why, everything!" Of ACORN he's said, "Our membership aren't out there in the clouds somewhere saying this is the way the world should look in 100 years. Our philosophy is very closely related to our membership's daily life experience. There's no ideology that instructs what we do. People make decisions and they start moving."[27]

What they do when they try to bring about political change by frightening people amounts to terrorism.

Terrorism is activity intended to frighten, demoralize, or neutralize an enemy—in other words, a variety of psychological warfare. It is, according to Merriam-Webster, "the systematic use of terror especially as a means of coercion." ACORN's weapon is people. Its target is "the system." Terror and intimidation are the means to its politico-economic ends. Not every ACORN campaign involves violence, but almost all involve an attempt to intimidate a target into making a concession. ACORN doesn't necessarily aim for bloodshed, but if a few perceived enemies of the poor get roughed up from time to time, no tears are shed at ACORN headquarters.

The Weather Underground and ACORN are in the same broad category of political organizations. Weathermen wanted to frighten and kill people, while ACORN opted for a softer version of terrorism using angry mobs instead of explosives. The Weathermen made no effort to conceal their hatred of America and its institutions, while ACORN sugar-coated its poison in order to appear as a reform-minded champion of American values. Though they had different goals—WUO wanted a full-blown American Communist state while ACORN had a more vague, less defined end-goal—they are part of the same continuum of terrorist groups. WUO is at one end of the continuum, while ACORN is closer to the other.

Some may say defining ACORN as an urban terrorist group is harsh or unfair. Since the 9/11 attacks, terrorism has been associated in the public mind with horrific life-ending atrocities. Yet terrorism doesn't consist exclusively of crashing airplanes or planting time bombs or the random spraying of crowds with machine-gun fire. It's not always about bloodshed and explosions.

Those who disagree with the description of ACORN as a terrorist group need to heed the agenda-setting ultra-leftist Noam Chomsky, once called "arguably the most important intellectual alive" by the *New York Times*. The *Chicago Tribune* noted that "a survey of a standard reference work, the Arts & Humanities Citation Index, found that over the last dozen years Chomsky was the most often cited living author. Among intellectual luminaries of all eras, Chomsky placed eighth, just behind Plato and Sigmund Freud."[28] On the Right, among those few who know his work, he is reviled. David Horowitz calls him "the ayatollah of anti-American hate."[29]

Chomsky serves on the board of advisors for *Social Policy*, ACORN's journal edited by founder Wade Rathke. Chomsky accepts the U.S. military's definition of terrorism: "the calculated use of violence or the threat of violence to attain political or religious ideological goals through intimidation, coercion, or instilling fear."[30] Clearly, ACORN is a terrorist group, measured by any reasonable standard, including that used by Chomsky and the federal government.

In an August 2010 interview, Chomsky said he's still "willing to accept the U.S. government definition of terrorism." In response to the question, "Wasn't what ACORN practiced arguably a form of terrorism?" Chomsky took umbrage at the line of inquiry and suggested we change the subject.

That's like saying, isn't moving in front of the line, suppose there's a line waiting in a store and you push somebody aside and take their place in the line, is that the same as throwing people into gas chambers? Well, at some abstract enough level it is, but the question doesn't make any sense. If you want to use the government definition as I do then let's start by talking about the huge crimes of terrorism like those that you and I pay for if we pay taxes.

Chomsky said there was no point in discussing whether ACORN's tactics constituted terrorism because whatever bad things ACORN may have done they were "miniscule as compared to the regular actions of public relations organizations of corporations and so on, and certainly government."

When asked if he approved of ACORN's "tactics of intimidation such as storming banks," and "using people to occupy banks and surrounding corporate CEOs' homes with noisy protesters," he replied, "A demonstration? I might be in favor of it or not. It depends what the circumstances were. But whatever it was you might also ask how it compared with the crimes that were being committed by the banks and the corporate executives. This is not necessarily justifying the tactic but putting it in context."

Chomsky said in his view "a bank may be within its legal rights when it deludes poor people into taking subprime mortgages, but that's destroying their lives and also bringing down the financial system. Now maybe the right answer to that isn't surrounding somebody's home—in fact, I don't think it is—but that's a far more serious injustice than what you're describing."

In fact, Chomsky rejected the suggestion that ACORN played a role in convincing banks to hand out these doomed subprime mortgages through its protest tactics.

> That's part of the standard right-wing propaganda. What it means is that ACORN and others were trying to improve the conditions, were trying to get banks to meet the social responsibility of paying some attention to people who don't have the means to obtain decent living standards. That doesn't mean you do that by deluding them into taking subprime mortgages which you know are going to collapse so you bet on their collapse.

Here's a translation of Chomsky's comments: Whatever ACORN did was nothing compared to what the banks did, and besides, ACORN was only pressing banks to observe their moral duty to lend money to poor people regardless of their ability to pay. The banks had it coming to them anyway because they were acting like criminals and tricking poor people into taking out subprime mortgages. Whatever its faults, ACORN was only trying to help, so lay off these wonderful, if flawed, crusaders for social justice, you mean-spirited conservative.

Read on. Much of the rest of this book refutes Chomsky's nonsense.

TWO

Intimidation on the Left: ACORN's "Fascism"

ACORN'S ANTI-DEMOCRATIC, UN-AMERICAN activities are not legitimate political advocacy protected by the First Amendment. They cry out for prosecution under federal racketeering laws. Such tactics are "a form of fascism," former Speaker of the House Newt Gingrich (R-GA) said in an interview. "It's the kind of thing that the Italian and German fascists and the Soviet Communists used routinely, and it's the fundamental disruption of people's rights." He added, "I regard ACORN as an opportunistic collection of people who earn a living being disruptive and destructive and intimidating on behalf of their allies, many of whom are certainly socialists."

One of those professional disrupters is former Chicago ACORN leader Madeline Talbott. A master of the bank shakedown, she's bragged about "dragging banks kicking and screaming" into questionable loans.[31] Talbott thought highly of Barack Obama's organizing work in the Windy City and invited him to lecture her staffers. She also led a mob attack on the Chicago City Council during a "living wage" debate. ACORN demonstrators "pushed over the metal detector and table used to screen visitors, backed police against the doors to the council chamber, and blocked late-arriving aldermen and city staff from entering the session." Six people, including a defiant Tal-bott, were led away in handcuffs.[32]

Gingrich himself had a taste of ACORN's stormtrooper tactics in 1995, when about 500 ACORN activists took over the Washington Hil-ton, forcing Gingrich to cancel a speech to 2,500 county commission-ers. Demonstrators chanting "Nuke Newt!" grabbed the microphone and commandeered the head table, then cheered when the speech was cancelled.[33]

"ACORN is part of the enforcement wing and the intimidation wing of the left," Gingrich said. "And because the elite media is so biased towards the left they routinely fail to cover and connect the dots, just as they [fail to] do with union intimidation tactics and with the New Black Panthers intimidation. Intimidation by the left is seen as social justice by left-wing reporters and editors. If anything comparable were happening on the Right it would be a page one national story every-day." The media won't condemn thug tactics on the Left because it views the activists as "innocent angels seeking deeply to create a bal-anced and fair America in the face of capitalist intimidation," he said.

In his opinion it was a strategic blunder for Palin and Giuliani to mock community organizing at the 2008 Republican national con-vention. The mockery was "not helpful" because "it trivialized Obama and Obama is not a trivial person," Gingrich said. "Obama is the most serious radical threat to traditional America ever to occupy the White House." It would have been better if Republican leaders "had got-ten up and said, here is what he was teaching, and they had taken the audience through five principles of Alinsky." Such a discussion "would have sobered the country. It wasn't a funny thing. It was a pro-found insight into how radical Obama is."

Republican Mike Huckabee is another of many Republican office-holders to be terrorized by ACORN. In 1998, while governor of Arkansas, Huckabee prepared to deliver a speech on civil rights. Like Gingrich he was silenced by hundreds of screaming ACORN activ-ists armed with bullhorns who stormed a Little Rock hotel confer-ence room and drove him away. "They surrounded not only the outer walls, but then, much to the dismay of the state troopers who were with me, they then mounted the stage," said Huckabee, who cut the speech short and left abruptly. "It was a very tense moment. It was totally unnecessary."[34]

During the anti-Huckabee demonstration, Johnnie Pugh, head of ACORN's Arkansas chapter, seized the microphone. "We want justice," she said. ACORN is "trying to get the bills paid and make a living wage and welfare reform is not working." ACORN members chanted "The people united will never be defeated," "Justice for welfare; Huckabee don't care," and "We're fired up; we're not going to take it no more." A dozen ACORN activists ran after Huckabee. Some jumped on the governor's car and pounded on it as others attempted to prevent him from leaving.[35] When Arkansas State Police investigated to determine if the demonstrators had broken any laws, Pugh called the probe "retaliation" and a "witch hunt." She even threatened to hit Huckabee again with more in-your-face protests. "The squeaky wheel gets the grease," she said.[36]

Radicals believe their goals warrant criminal means and "can be relied on to lie, steal votes and justify murder when committed by their political friends . . . because they are engaged in a permanent war whose goal is the salvation of mankind," according to Horowitz. "In this context, restraint of means can easily seem finicky."[37] ACORN's violence-inciting techniques still flourish, practiced out in the open by organized labor and countless other radical groups. AFL-CIO president Richard Trumka, an ACORN ally, is unashamedly pro-thuggery. He told members of the United Mine Workers in Illinois to "kick the shit out of every last" worker who violated the sanctity of his picket lines.[38]

The outrageous behavior tolerated by police today would have landed a person in jail earlier in America's history. Political incitements to riot, which occur almost exclusively on the Left, fail to move law enforcement. Why? Because as a society we have gradually become inured to these evil tactics. It is "defining deviancy down," to borrow a phrase coined by Daniel Patrick Moynihan to discuss the process by which society grows accustomed to antisocial behavior, rationalizing it away over time and redefining it: "[T]he amount of deviant behavior in American society has increased beyond the levels the community

can 'afford to recognize' and that accordingly we have been redefining deviancy so as to exempt much conduct previously stigmatized,
and also quietly raising the 'normal' level in categories where behavior is abnormal by any earlier standard." Moynihan warned ominously
that "we are getting used to a lot of behavior that is not good for us."[39]

Early twentieth-century Americans were horrified by anarchist and
labor union-initiated violence. Many labor organizations at the time
were revolutionary terrorist groups. They killed people, incited riots,
and fomented rebellion. But over time corporations and governments
began to ignore the cardinal rule: don't negotiate with terrorists.
They took a short-term perspective, deluding themselves into believing they were buying peace by caving in to terrorists' demands, all in
the hope of gaining market share or a few extra votes on Election Day.
The left-wing, pro-radical media has played a role too, lulling Americans into complacency by telling them nothing's wrong. Leftists using
ACORN-style tactics are portrayed as well-intentioned mainstream
activists, noble crusaders for social justice who have everyone's best
interest at heart. Activists may get out of hand every once in a while,
according to journalists, but they mean well. (Of course when patriotic Tea Party activists, alarmed that America is being transformed
into a socialist state by the nation's Community Organizer-in-Chief,
express their well-founded concerns by merely booing a few congress-
men and holding protest rallies, the media labels them heel-clicking
fascist storm troopers. If there's one thing the Left cannot tolerate, it
is diversity of opinion and freedom of speech.)

Americans have become so desensitized to in-your-face protest and
shakedown tactics that ACORN's jackboot activism, which rightly horrified society in past years, hardly registers today. Unless ACORN or
its lawless brethren in the so-called progressive movement are wreck-
ing front lawns, obstructing businesses, burning bankers in effigy, or
chasing politicians from a stage, such groups are boring to Americans. Maybe that's why, in the words of former ACORN national board
member Marcel Reid, it took "a half-naked 20-year-old" to spark the
nationwide backlash that erupted against the group in 2009.[40] Without the undercover videos publicized by media entrepreneur Andrew

Breitbart and talk show host Glenn Beck showing ACORN employees offering advice on establishing an illegal brothel employing underage Salvadoran girls,[41] Americans' concern about the group's persistent lawbreaking might never have reached a fever pitch that forced Congress to defund the group in September 2009, beginning its final slide into bankruptcy. ACORN was only conducting business as usual, but the videos provided graphic evidence that the group's business was not only unsavory but illegitimate.

Yet there are still those delicate softheaded souls who rhapsodize about the primacy of good intentions, asserting that whatever ACORN's faults, it has managed to help some people. Joe Conason, a reliable excuse-generator for the Left, maintains that even though "ACORN is not immune to the pathologies that can afflict institutions" in the nation's poorest communities, the group has "a history of honorable service to the dispossessed and impoverished."[42] It is true ACORN may have helped some people somewhere, but at what cost? Terrorist groups and revolutionary organizations frequently provide social services to their constituencies for propaganda—or if you prefer, *public relations*—value. The Black Panther Party provided free breakfasts for school children. Such programs may help the people they serve, but that's not why the programs exist. The goal is to build and maintain support for the group's radical program, that is, to win the hearts and minds of the people.

Looking at more current examples, Hezbollah in Lebanon maintains a "vast network of social services." The group provides "schooling, medical care, and welfare" to its constituencies. It also maintains a "radio station and satellite television station."[43] Hamas in Palestine devotes much of its budget to "an extensive social services network." It "funds schools, orphanages, mosques, healthcare clinics, soup kitchens, and sports leagues," and "[a]pproximately 90 percent of its work is in social, welfare, cultural, and educational activities."[44]

In an unusual moment of moral clarity, left-leaning TV pundit Bill Maher grasped this idea that terrorist groups hand out goodies to buy support: "You can't give Hamas credit for starting a widows and orphans fund when their day job is creating widows and orphans."[45] ACORN too prides itself on bringing "benefits" to its members, recognizing a basic principle of human nature: if you give people things, they tend to like you—so much they may even ignore your transgressions.

ACORN deliberately targets corporations and government officials, labeling them as enemies of the poor. It uses force to prevent banks from conducting business. It starts riots in order to bring its targets to their knees. It blackmails its corporate victims. It's a selective kind of urban terrorism perhaps, consisting partly of surgical strikes against specific targets as opposed to the population as a whole, but it's still terrorism.

Rutgers political science professor Heidi Swarts, author of a sympathetic book on ACORN, counsels that smart community organizers should avoid giving themselves away by using telltale radical vocabulary. Words that are standard fare among Marxist academics, such as *racism, sexism, classism, homophobia,* and *oppression,* are seldom used by organizers because they are part of extreme "ideological movements beyond the experience of most of their members."[46] But that radicalism is surely there. Describing one ACORN national convention, Swarts notes that "[t]he opening exercises" are "an expressive ritual designed to produce collective excitement that would build shared identity and commitment." ACORN uses songs and chants to reinforce identity and boost morale.[47] ACORN songs typically contain three recurring themes: ACORN's growing power, the solidarity of "the people," and a definition of the group's enemies.[48] There is "ACORN Marches On," which is sung to the tune of the "Battle Hymn of the Republic":

Mine eyes have seen the glory when the people stand as one.
We have scattered all the bureaucrats and put them on the run.
But even with our list of wins our work has just begun.
The ACORN marches on.

There's Republicans, there's Democrats, I don't know which is worse,
Cuz the elephants they kill my job; the donkeys kill my purse.

Well, it's time to take those fossil groups and pack them in a hearse.

As ACORN marches on.

And there is the "ACORN Marching Song," which is sung to the tune of the "Caisson Song" ("over hill, over dale . . ."):

In our cities, in our states,
We're the ones that pay the freight,
But the rich folks go rolling along.

Keep us divided, whites from blacks,
Moderate and poor on different tracks.

And the rich folks go rolling along.[49]

Are these harmless fighting songs like a college football team might use, or are they incitements meant to keep an army of radicals on its toes?

RATHKE ENDORSES TERRORISM

ACORN founder Wade Rathke is usually quite careful in public. He soft-pedals his radicalism with positive-sounding phrases such as "citizen wealth" and "participatory democracy," but from time to time even a master manipulator like Rathke slips up. His essay "Tactical Tension" is a case in point. It dates back to mid-2001 when the Left was in a stupor. Liberal and radical activists were angry and demoralized because their would-be savior, Democratic candidate Al Gore, had just barely lost the presidency to George W. Bush. Although there has never been any credible evidence that Republicans stole the election, it became an article of faith on the Left that the GOP had cleverly carried out a coup d'etat and deprived the American people of their rightful president. Many on the Left had high hopes for Gore after Bill Clinton tacked toward the political center and now those hopes were dashed.

To this perceived affront to democracy, Wade Rathke offered his comrades a declaration of war. His militant rant is very revealing.[50] He comes across more Rev. Jim Jones than Rev. Martin Luther King. He begins it with what for him is a flowery but instructive preamble:

Sometimes the silence itself is deafening. The daily din of CNN: full of sound and no fury. Headlines are narcotizing the daily news with show and spectacle. A full scale revolution being waged almost virtually and without real struggle. An entire country kidnapped and sold for cheap ransom. An entire people—our people—after a generation of work—force-fed a perversion of democracy as hollow as a doughnut. Thieves in three piece suits or jurist's robes prattling endlessly an ideology of class, while we wait on our ass. Watchwords of warning no longer have the same meaning: accommodation, stability, "a place at the table," "making a difference," "doing a deal," "staying in the game," whatever! For what one wonders? Tomorrow not only comes after today, but can also be lost today!

Rathke argues that the Left is losing and needs to get more aggressive. "We need an edge, some harder steel on the rim," he writes. "If some day we want to make more just laws, then today we may have to just learn to break more laws." In a "wish list," he includes "[t]actics that include civil disobedience and political defiance" and "[t]actics that include extra-legal activity."

He praises the rioters in Seattle during the 1999 World Trade Organization meeting as "progressive forces." Their civil disturbances were "a colorful, exciting, smoky, hazy amalgamation of helmeted police, broken glass, and righteous rage." He continues admiringly, "Dispersed affinity groups operating on 'street' consensus [were] making a range of tactical decisions and holding ground in a way that made the momentum of the actions impossible to immobilize in spite of rain, gas, and cops."

Rathke then attempts a delicate rhetorical balancing act, denouncing violent tactics in general while at the same time advocating specific examples of it: "We do not embrace violence, quite the contrary, but we need to create chemistry containing the elements of more explosive combinations in order to create more force and power through the equations of action and reaction that we push to the target." Despite this perfunctory condemnation of violence that fosters an illusion of respectability, the rest of the essay is filled with explicit endorsements of violent and illegal tactics. He praises the violent Black Panther Party of the 1960s and longs for some computer hackers to come to the aid of the labor movement.

> Crazy, computer viruses are started by young kids around the world or hackers bored out of their skulls that live right down the street. As union organizers we are still doing 8 point difficulty dumpster dives for alpha lists of employees, when theoretically some good geeks could tap in, load up, and download the whole thing and throw it over our transom window. What a waste of talent when such a huge contribution could be made to the labor movement.

"Simply put, why isn't there more 'monkey wrenching' in our world? Where is our Earth First!" he writes. Monkey-wrenching is a form of eco-terrorism or *ecotage* (eco-sabotage) that consists of harming the economic interests of those who are perceived threats to the environment. It might be arson, destruction of crops or sport utility vehicle dealerships, bombing, or tree-spiking, in which an activist drives metal rods into trees in order to prevent them from being cut down for commercial use. Tree-spiking has led to the injury and death of lumberjacks.[51]

It further enrages Rathke that some of ACORN's targets have not only defended themselves but have dared to fight back. ACORN's founding Intimidator-in-Chief, whose stock-in-trade is thuggery, denounces these acts of self-defense as "intimidation." Some targets filed lawsuits against ACORN "designed to sap resources and chill membership organized campaigns," he huffs.[52]

AN UN-AMERICAN IDEA OF DEMOCRACY

ACORN's methodological ancestors are pirates. Around the time the Thirteen Colonies began their revolutionary rumblings, pirates also professed a strong belief in democracy, electing their own leaders as they looted targets on the high seas.[53] That pirates believed in democracy does not absolve them of their crimes, which they may have rationalized as redistributive acts of social justice. The key difference between ACORN's modern day pirates and the eighteenth-century variety is that today's antisocial activity is rewarded with governmental and corporate grants instead of dancing the hempen jig.

To take the focus off their support for redistributionism, which is widely despised in America, many radical groups including ACORN try to dress their beliefs up in more acceptable clothing. These groups conspicuously exhibit a false reverence for "democracy." In so doing they mock democracy as the idea is understood by most Americans. They are not inspired by a method of governance. They are excited at the prospect of reordering society with the help of capitalism-hating agitators. They want to rip apart America and then stitch it back together to fit their own design. Presidential friend Bill Ayers of the now-defunct Weather Underground Organization acknowledged he had "decided that I was committed to being a part of what I thought was going to be a really serious and ongoing rebellion, upheaval, that had the potential of not just ending the [Vietnam] war but of overthrowing the capitalist system and put[ting] in its place something much more humane."[54] Today Ayers fancies himself an education reformer even though he wishes to use schools not to educate, but to indoctrinate in an effort to foment revolution. Co-editor of a textbook titled, *Teaching for Social Justice: A Democracy and Education Reader* (New Press, 1998), Ayers considers himself a champion of democracy, just as Karl Marx, V.I. Lenin, and Leon Trotsky did before him. He considered himself to be a crusader for democracy as he was bombing the Pentagon too.

Although in retrospect Ayers has criticized some of his past statements as foolish, his core beliefs haven't changed. His hatred of America burns just as bright today as when his terrorist cell plotted to use dynamite to murder military officers at a dance in Fort Dix, New Jersey in 1970. "This society is not a just and fair and decent place," he said in 2001. "The pundits all pat themselves on the back: 'God, what a great country.' . . . It makes me want to puke."[55] In what must have been the worst case of bad timing in history, Ayers denounced the U.S. in a profile that ran in the *New York Times* on Sept. 11, 2001. "I don't regret setting bombs," he said. "I feel we didn't do enough."[56]

What exactly did Ayers mean? According to *Bringing Down America* author Larry Grathwohl, the Weather Underground made plans to kill the one-tenth of the U.S. population they expected would turn out to be "diehard capitalists" incapable of reeducation. Grathwohl is a Vietnam War veteran who, after fighting Communists abroad, decided to fight them at home. After returning to America having served in the U.S. Army's 101st Airborne Division, Grathwohl took it upon himself to infiltrate the group. Incredibly, very little has been written about what the Weather Underground planned to do to America if it seized power.[57]

Even today Ayers refuses to disavow violent tactics. "I never denounced what we did and the reason is, because in the context of those times and what was going on I actually think that we were very restrained and I've always thought that and I still think it. I think the most violent force then and even more violent today is the U.S. government."[58]

ACORN'S ROOTS

ACORN and other leftist groups trace their lineage to the 1962 Port Huron Statement, formulated at a United Auto Workers camp in Port Huron, Michigan. The UAW union has long underwritten radicalism that Americans find repugnant.[59] Although today the document is best known as the lead-up to a punchline from the 1998 movie *The Big Lebowski*, it is, in fact, a serious manifesto of radical students disillusioned with America. The declaration, composed largely by radical leftist Tom Hayden, later a California state lawmaker and a one-time husband of Viet Cong enthusiast Jane Fonda, asserted the American system was beyond redemption and reform, hopelessly mired in racism, militarism and nihilistic materialism. It declared that "[t]he allocation of resources must be based on social needs" and that "public utilities, railroads, mines, and plantations, and other basic economic institutions should be in the control of national, not foreign, agencies."[60] It became the founding document of Hayden's radical group Students for a Democratic Society, an organization that grew out of the League for Industrial Democracy, which, in turn, was originally named the Intercollegiate Socialist Society. The great radical agitator Saul Alinsky acknowledged he trained SDS members as community organizers.[61]

This Magna Carta of the so-called New Left called for greater worker control over the economy and for so-called participatory democracy. The problem is that to radical leftists the word *democracy* has a very different meaning than most Americans assign to it. Pushing a perverse, un-American political agenda, radicals have twisted the meaning of the word beyond all recognition so that to them it's something approaching the Marxist concept of the "dictatorship of the proletariat." They use it to describe something more akin to the system of governance during the French Reign of Terror and Communist China's Cultural Revolution in which angry mobs made their own law through ACORN-like "actions," meting out social justice on the heads of those unlucky enough to get in their way. Seize a house, burn a business to the ground, lynch a government official considered to be a servant of the oppressive capitalist status quo. To them democracy is Marxist mobocracy. And it's only *true* democracy if they prevail. If they lose, it's not democracy: the capitalists stole the election or took advantage of the people because they suffer from a mass "false consciousness."

American politicans who openly self-identify as socialists are usually doomed to fail. (ACORN supporters such as self-described socialist Sen. Bernie Sanders of Vermont, are anomalies.) So radicals try to associate themselves with American values such as fair play and "democracy" because they know a brazen appeal for a workers' revolution isn't going to resonate with the public. To them *democracy* becomes a code word for socialism. To this end, some leftists have tried to rebrand socialism as economic democracy. Before the Age of Obama, socialist Princeton professor Cornel West, an ACORN ally and advisor on Obama's campaign team, wrote *Democracy Matters: Winning the Fight Against Imperialism*, which holds that the U.S. is under the control of racist, patriarchal, authoritarian fundamentalists. West hails democracy as a concept but also calls himself a "progressive socialist," writing that "Marxist thought is an indispensable tradition for freedom fighters." When West visited leftist strongman Hugo Chavez's Venezuela in 2006, he praised its government, which has nationalized industries, jailed and murdered its opponents and threatened the United States. West went, he said, "to see the democratic awakening taking place." By "democratic awakening," he meant the transmogrification of Venezuela into a socialist state. In other words, if radical leftists don't end up with the political result they want, it can't possibly be real democracy.[62]

ACORN's president in the late 1970s, Steve McDonald, summed up ACORN's philosophy, tying democracy to redistributionism. "Seventy percent of the population is low- or moderate-income people," he said. "We want a real democracy. We want our piece of the pie."[63] It's no mistake that the extreme anti-capitalist news program on Pacifica Radio, "Democracy Now!" uses democracy in its name. Host Amy Goodman routinely interviews guests like Bolivia's communist president Evo Morales, who declared on the show, "Capitalism is the worst enemy of humanity," and called for its destruction.[64] "She's a communist," said former 1960s radical David Horowitz, who like Goodman also avoided the word communist in his self-description when he was younger, preferring the phrase "revolutionary Marxist." Asked what he thought radicals meant when they use the term *democracy*, he said radicals nowadays would never admit an affinity for dictatorship of the proletariat-style democracy. "They don't think that clearly; they wouldn't cop to that," Horowitz said in an interview. "They would tell you about participatory democracy and workers' councils." It's also important to remember that Communist countries such as the Soviet Union enthusiastically embraced democracy in theory even while they held sham elections. Even today Stalinist North Korea's official name is the *Democratic* People's Republic of Korea.

But Americans reject democracy as defined by radicals. Typically Americans use the word democracy as shorthand for America's stability-promoting institutions, the same "democratic" culture that Alexis de Tocqueville described in his classic study, *Democracy in America.* They mean the rule of law and basic standards of fairness, such as legal due process and an ability to seek redress of grievances, that Americans take for granted and enjoy every day. When they refer to the American electoral process, they refer implicitly to indirect democracy and not to direct democracy, an approach to governance that rightly horrified the Framers of the Constitution. James Madison and the delegates to the 1787 convention in Philadelphia feared direct democracy (meaning that citizens actually make governmental decisions themselves rather than electing others to represent them) because they knew it would encourage the majority to oppress the minority.

As for Students for a *Democratic* Society, at the end of the 1960s it splintered into factions. One bloc eventually became the violent Weather Underground Organization. The Weathermen embraced terror as a tool of socioeconomic and political change and became enamored of explosives. After getting off criminal charges on a legal technicality, two of the group's leaders, would-be mass murderers Bill Ayers and Bernardine Dohrn, decided to poison the minds of the young by turning them against the American system. The unrepentant totalitarian leftists became members of the faculties of, respectively, University of Illinois at Chicago and Northwestern University School of Law. Ayers, who while serving on the board of the Woods Fund of Chicago with Barack Obama helped to steer grants to ACORN, taught students how to indoctrinate their future pupils. Dohrn, his wife, teaches students how to use the law to achieve the left-wing abstraction known as social justice.

A BIPARTISAN ACORN

ACORN hasn't always been universally reviled on the Right.

Marcel Reid, a member of ACORN's national board from October

2005 to late 2008, learned about ACORN when conservative talk show host and author Laura Schlessinger recommended the group as a housing resource in her book, *Ten Stupid Things Women Do to Mess Up Their Lives.*[65] The myth that Republicans oppose ACORN only because the group registers and mobilizes Democratic voters is a useful lie that ACORN propagates for recruiting purposes and to maintain control over its membership. The truth is that the Republican Party did not initiate a war against ACORN; ACORN declared war on the Republicans.

Although ACORN has always been closer ideologically to Democrats, in its early days it reached out to both major political parties. It was only during the national ascendancy of Ronald Reagan, who in 1979 presciently called ACORN "dangerous" on a radio talk show,[66] that ACORN began to put itself firmly in the Democratic camp. Naturally, ACORN hated Reagan, a strong advocate of limited government, with a passion and successfully used his presidency as a fundraising tool.

In fact it was a Republican who got ACORN into the voter registration business and gave the group a helpful early injection of cash. Liberal Republican Arkansas Gov. Winthrop Rockefeller met with ACORN in 1970 to ask the group for help with voter registration and get-out-the-vote efforts. Rockefeller and Wade Rathke got along so well that when Rathke noticed the governor had monogrammed cowboy boots with their shared initials—W.R.—he suggested they swap boots.[67]

Gov. Rockefeller was an easy mark for Rathke. In 1970 Rathke created ACORN's first front group as part of an effort to dupe Rockefeller into carrying out ACORN's policy agenda. In Arkansas, he hired the son of a widely respected local preacher to create Citizens for the Abolition of Poverty. It was "a model for 'neutralizing the opposition,'" according to Gary Delgado, the first organizer Rathke hired at ACORN. Using this newly formed front group, ACORN led a successful campaign exaggerating the state's poverty. ACORN had its front group issue a press release denouncing "the inhumanity of a state where children are forced to sleep on the floor." It was emotionally manipulative, demagogic nonsense, but the powers that be fell for it. The campaign led to Rockefeller creating a new state agency called Furniture for Families, which collected and distributed used furniture.[68]

The naïve Rockefeller then attempted to co-opt ACORN for his own purposes—and failed. The governor thought paying ACORN to register and mobilize black voters would help his reelection effort but he ended up financing his own demise. Rockefeller sent ACORN $3,000 in cash in a brown paper bag. ACORN kept the money and registered Democrats.[69] "[T]hey thought we were going to register Republicans," Delgado snickers, but "[w]e did not register a single Republican voter in that election. However, we did use those resources early on to build the organization . . . that money enabled us to hire our first additional organizer after me."[70] After it became clear that Democratic challenger Dale Bumpers had ousted Rockefeller, Rathke took his leaders to the winner's victory party. "It's free food, plenty of contacts, and it looks like we backed a winner all along," Rathke rationalized. Because Rockefeller's payment had been in cash, he couldn't very well demand an accounting. Metaphorically, Rockefeller's was the first head ACORN placed over its mantle.[71]

By 1979 ACORN had decided it would be useful to embarrass Republicans across the nation. As part of a campaign aimed at high-profile party officials, the group disrupted a GOP fundraising meeting in Memphis in September 1979. ACORN conducted actions against meetings of the Republican Regional Platform Committee hearings in Iowa, Missouri, and Pennsylvania. On July 31, 1979, a year out from the Republicans' Detroit convention, 30 ACORN members laid siege to the Detroit Convention Bureau to harass city officials. ACORN pressured then-Sen. John Tower (R-TX), who chaired the GOP platform committee, to agree to allow it to address that committee in Detroit. ACORN scored a propaganda coup when it conducted a high-profile tour of the "real Detroit," that provided 50 Republicans, 25 ACORN members, and 30 journalists an up-close look at the worst parts of the city. It was a waste, ACORN maintained, for so much money to be spent on the GOP convention when so much work remained to be done in Detroit's neighborhoods.[72] Ironically, at that time the Motor City was already in an advancing state of urban decay, thanks largely to the kind of left-wing policies ACORN advocates.

SHOWING DEMOCRATS WHO'S BOSS

In 1976 ACORN began its campaign to take over the national Democratic Party. Not all ACORN officials were sold on the idea at first.
They protested that taking control of the party was "not the business of a community organization." But by 1977 a compromise was
reached under which ACORN would run committed delegates for
the conventions of both national political parties. For the time being,
ACORN had decided to focus on the issues and refrain from endorsing specific candidates.[73] This restraint was to be short-lived.

After ACORN's 1979 convention in St. Louis, it set out to increase
its clout within the Democratic Party. Local chapters were urged to
push adoption of the People's Platform, a radical declaration of war
on capitalism and limited government. Members of the ACORN People's Platform Committee (APPC) pledged to reach out to church,
civil rights, women's, and labor groups for endorsements. ACORN
adopted an inside/outside strategy, according to Gary Delgado.

> The inside strategy was one of co-optation: ACORN organizers and
> leaders were encouraged to talk with sympathetic party delegates,
> opportunistic candidates, and members of the Democratic Social-
> ist Organizing Committee (DSOC), who, after years of hard work,
> had managed to capture a quarter of the seats on the Democratic
> platform committee. DSOC was helpful in ascertaining where there
> might be support for the ACORN platform and in assessing the
> Association's ability to elect delegates to state and local conventions.

The outside strategy involved using the "three I's" approach
against less-than-cooperative Democratic Party members. According to Delgado, the three I's are "identify, isolate, and ice." ACORN
knew it couldn't use an inside strategy against the Grand Old Party so
it choose to rely mostly on confrontation tactics in its dealings with
the Republican apparatus. ACORN also used its clout with organized
labor to advance its plan against Democrats and frequently looked
to small-c communists for inspiration. ACORN's St. Louis head orga-

nizer Dan Cantor wrote a telling strategic memo that viewed his group's relationship with labor through a Marxist lens and urged tactics that would push both ACORN and organized labor further left. He also quoted a Marxist philosopher who demanded the end of capitalism. "The more that labor realizes it doesn't really have power on the hill, and the more they realize that capitalism ignores OSHA [the Occupational Safety and Health Act], then the more they are driven back to the grassroots level where militant stands might be taken." Cantor continued:

> These are not revolutionary times, so neither the unions nor ACORN are revolutionary organizations . . . though labor is heavily invested in the mythology of labor/management cooperation, the labor movement is objectively on our side. We cannot do away with their worldview but we can . . . create situations that change the way discourse is conducted by opening things up for our own member-ship and theirs [in a way] that moves both organizations to a more radical plane. Gortz [sic] calls it pushing for non-reformist reforms, and it means raising demands and programs that do not accommo-date themselves to the capitalist system, though their implementa-tion does not in itself mean the downfall of the system.[74]

Although Cantor and Delgado misspelled his surname, surely they were referring to Andre Gorz, an Austrian-born Marxist theorist who died in 2007. Gorz wrote about many of the same issues that ACORN concerned itself with. "Let us make no mistake about this," wrote Gorz. "[W]age-labour has to disappear and, with it, capitalism." Gorz believed that capitalism was destroying itself by "producing the conditions for its own transcendence." He urged likeminded people "to seize upon those conditions and think through the transition" to another system entirely. "[W]e have to maximize the number of paths 'out of capitalism,'" he wrote. Like Richard Cloward and Fran-ces Fox Piven, Gorz supported the idea of the government guarantee-ing a minimum annual income for all members of society. Also, like Cloward and Piven, he expressed contempt for workfare programs, such as those President Clinton signed into law, claiming such programs "stigmatize the unemployed as incompetents and scroungers, whom society is entitled to force to work—for their own good."[75]

ACORN kept the pressure on Democrats by humiliating them in public. The group interrupted two of First Lady Rosalyn Carter's speeches, staged a sit-in at the office of DNC chairman John White, and planted wooden representations of ACORN's "planks" in the lawn of a high-ranking party official in St. Louis.[76] By 1984, ACORN had abandoned all pretence that it was nonpartisan. That year it formally endorsed the community organizer and shakedown artist extraordinaire Jesse Jackson for president. The group went even further, running Jackson's insurgent Democratic campaign in New Hampshire. ACORN was also deeply involved with the campaign in Arkansas and Michigan.[77]

More recently ACORN only gave lip service to nonpartisanship. To protect the coveted tax-exempt tax status of its affiliates, ACORN claimed to be community-oriented and officially nonpartisan. Yet it celebrated the most left-wing urban politicians and endorsed Democratic Party candidates. If it's ever endorsed a Republican, that endorsement is well-hidden. When Glenn Beck asked ACORN spokesman Scott Levenson to name one Republican ACORN has endorsed, Levenson couldn't come up with a single name.[78]

During the 2008 election campaign, ACORN chief organizer Bertha Lewis offered an impassioned endorsement of Obama on YouTube. In the video posted by one of ACORN's partisan vehicles, the Working Families Party of New York, Lewis exclaims: "If you live in New York there's one more simple thing you can all do to help ACORN: vote for the community organizer Barack Obama on the Working Families Party ballot line . . . Voting for Barack is good but voting for him on the Working Families Party line is better. Vote change like you mean it, people."[79]

In February 2008, ACORN Votes, which is ACORN's national political action committee, endorsed Obama for president. Maude Hurd, ACORN's national president, said the then-senator was "the candidate who best understands and can affect change on the issues ACORN cares about like stopping foreclosures, enacting fair and comprehensive immigration reform, and building stronger and safer communities across America." Obama understands the issues facing low- and moderate-income people, said Alicia Russell, ACORN's western regional representative. "He's on the same level as we are, and sees our issues as we do." Texas ACORN president Toni McElroy lauded Obama, embracing his call for "fundamental change in our economy to protect homeowners and neighborhoods from the scourge of foreclosures that is sweeping communities across Texas."

In 2008, Anita MonCrief, who worked for ACORN affiliate Project Vote and in the Strategic Writing and Research Department (SWORD) of ACORN's political operations division from 2005 to early January 2008, said ACORN served unofficially as an appendage of the Democratic Party in the 2008 election cycle. ACORN used cash in order to conceal some of its financial transactions. "It has always been a Democrat operation," she told World Net Daily. "They've never made any secrets about who they support. Their political action committees are usually set up to support these Democratic candidates." During voter registration drives ACORN told voters not to support Republican candidates, she said. MonCrief, who was fired by ACORN, testified in a Pennsylvania court in 2008 that the Obama campaign gave a list of "maxed out" campaign donors to Project Vote to allow it to seek contributions from those donors. The idea was that donors who had already contributed the legal limit could secretly give more money to the Obama cause by donating to ACORN, which Obama considered to be an arm of his campaign.[80] This could be a violation of election laws.

New York Times reporter Stephanie Strom, who had done some fine investigative articles on ACORN, had the "maxed out" donors story but her editors told her to spike it. The newspaper went on record six months *after* the election to admit that just before Election Day it killed the politically sensitive news story. In a snarky column the Old Gray Lady's "public editor" Clark Hoyt used the word "nonsense" to describe the allegations of impropriety leveled against ACORN and the Obama campaign. Hoyt rejected the idea that the story might have been "a game-changer in the presidential election" and downplayed the potential illegalities, calling them "technical violations of campaign finance law."

We can only wonder what the *New York Times* would have done if it had gained information that Republican presidential candidate John McCain's campaign had committed technical violations of campaign finance law. Oh wait; no we don't. The newspaper did publish a blog item about the DNC's allegation that McCain's campaign had illegally procured a loan[81]—a highly technical possible violation of campaign finance law. In addition, the paper was only too willing to imply in a February 21, 2008, story that McCain was having a romantic affair with a female lobbyist three decades his junior. The charge, based on anonymous sources supposedly working for McCain, ultimately proved groundless and the newspaper retracted the allegation long after the election was over. The *Times* disingenuously claimed that it had never intended to suggest that the lobbyist "had engaged in a romantic affair with Senator McCain."[82]

MonCrief announced in July 2010 that she planned to file a complaint with the FEC over the Obama campaign's improper coordination with ACORN in the 2008 election cycle.[83]

Minnesota ACORN endorsed Democrat Al Franken in his 2008 U.S. Senate campaign against Republican incumbent Norm Coleman. ACORN endorsed Democrat Kweisi Mfume in his unsuccessful 2006 primary run for the U.S. Senate against Ben Cardin, the eventual winner; and ACORN's PAC endorsed Rep. Chaka Fattah (D-PA) when he ran unsuccessfully for mayor of Philadelphia against Michael Nutter in 2007. ACORN's 2005 annual report identifies as allies Los Angeles mayor and former community organizer Antonio Villaraigosa, also a Democrat, and Rep. Maxine Waters (D-CA).

It is worth noting that Waters considered the Los Angeles riots of 1992 to be a shining example of participatory democracy. She called the disturbances a "rebellion" and said they were caused by Republican tax cuts. "The Reagan-Bush administrations have taken away programs that have been very helpful, very empowering," the congresswoman said. "In addition to that, the recession and the tax policies that are allowed for the exportation of jobs to Third World countries for cheap labor—all have caused us to come to the point where we are today—desperation, hopelessness. I lay the blame squarely at the foot of Bush and Reagan."[84]

Another ACORN video on YouTube that used Capitol Hill as a backdrop didn't bother showing a single Republican lawmaker. The video called "ACORN Grassroots Democracy Campaign," showcases a parade of congressional Democrats as its allies, including strategist and CNN contributor Paul Begala, Senators Sherrod Brown (D-OH) and Robert P. Casey Jr. (D-PA), and Representatives Dennis Kucinich (D-OH), Donna Edwards (D-MD), Barney Frank (D-MA), and Brad Miller (D-NC).

Casey is a particularly outspoken supporter of ACORN. He praised the group for stepping in and trying "to help families, to be their advocate, to be their voice . . . because as important as it is here in Washington to pass legislation in the House and the Senate—that's obviously important—but we cannot do this alone."[85]

It's ironic that Sen. Pat Leahy (D-VT) made a cameo appearance in the 2008 Batman movie, *The Dark Knight.* "We're not intimidated by thugs," his character growls at the villain. In real life Leahy is in league with thugs. The longtime ACORN ally was one of just seven U.S. senators to vote against depriving ACORN of federal funding after the group's criminal inclinations were captured on video in 2009. The other six ACORN enablers in the Senate who refused to stand up for taxpayers were self-described socialist Bernie Sanders (I-VT), Casey, Sheldon Whitehouse (D-RI), Kirsten Gillibrand (D-NY), Majority Whip Dick Durbin (D-IL), and Roland Burris (D-IL) who took over Obama's seat after he became president.[86]

Some Democratic lawmakers give money to ACORN. Senators Herb Kohl (D-WI) and John Kerry (D-MA) each gave ACORN's Project Vote subsidiary $25,000 in the 2004 election cycle, according to internal ACORN documents provided by inside ACORN sources. Rep. Jerrold Nadler (D-NY) has given the Working Families Party of New York at least $66,600 since 2002.[87]

Massachusetts Gov. Deval Patrick, a lawyer who was a national co-chairman of Obama's presidential campaign, represented the Clinton era Justice Department in support of ACORN in *ACORN v. Edgar*, a 1995 ballot access case in which Obama was ACORN's lead attorney. In April 2008, the Democratic governor steered a $33,000 grant through the Massachusetts legislature for ACORN Housing.

At an April 2007 banquet celebrating New York ACORN's 25th anniversary, keynote speaker Bill Clinton praised ACORN effusively. On his way past Wade Rathke's table, he bragged that in his 2007 book about philanthropy, "I gave ACORN a big wet kiss."[88] Indeed, in the book titled *Giving*, Clinton lauded ACORN's work in post-Hurricane Katrina New Orleans, which included strong-arming residents into claiming EITC benefits. The former president recommends ACORN to readers. "If you're interested in policy changes that would strengthen the middle class and help poor people work their way into it, you can contact . . . ACORN, which organizes low-income people for economic empowerment . . ."[89]

Speaking at ACORN's 2006 national convention, Hillary Clinton looked back fondly on her memories of ACORN's early days in Arkansas. It was a love fest. After noting that she founded a group called Arkansas Advocates for Children and Families that dealt with many of the same issues ACORN focused on, she hailed ACORN as a group of vision. "I thank you for being part of that great movement, that progressive tradition that has rolled across our country." Quoting Martin Luther King Jr., Clinton said, "Let's move it forward, let's be drum majors for justice."[90]

On ACORN's silver anniversary in 1995, a slew of financial institutions and politicians expressed their support for—or perhaps their fear of—ACORN by purchasing ads in the *ACORN Member Handbook—25th Anniversary Edition*. Among the better known of the 80 banks, credit unions, and savings and loans expressing solidarity with ACORN on this occasion were Bank of America, Chase Manhattan, Chemical Bank, Comerica, Provident Bank, and Riggs Bank of Washington, D.C.

Three big city mayors bought ads praising ACORN: Dennis W.

Archer of Detroit, Thomas Menino of Boston, and Sharon Sayles Belton of Minneapolis. Archer in particular felt the need to osculate ACORN's posterior, writing, "We're proud to support your tireless struggle to improve conditions for America's low and moderate income families. ACORN has made a huge difference in the quality of life and now there's a new era of cooperation between City government and your efforts to provide affordable housing. Keep on pushing us to do our part and here's to the next 25 years of making it better."

ACORN broke in Menino even before he was inaugurated in 1993. About 15 ACORN members stormed the office of the Boston mayor-in-waiting with signs reading "After School Programs Not Gangs" and "The people united will never be defeated." At the time Menino grumbled, saying, "I think this was a set-up."[91] But the activists must have trained Menino well because he became a steadfast ACORN ally afterward. Even with all the adverse publicity the group received in 2008 and 2009 the mayor still saw fit to reward ACORN national president Maude Hurd with an appointment to Boston's Living Wage Advisory Committee in early 2010.[92]

Though Republican ties to ACORN have been few and relatively tenuous by comparison, there are some GOP officeholders who have collaborated with ACORN. Since ACORN's creation in 1970, all Republican HUD secretaries—including former Sen. Mel Martinez (R-FL), Alphonso Jackson, and 1996 vice presidential candidate Jack Kemp—worked with ACORN to varying degrees. Some Republican federal lawmakers and governors have played ball with ACORN too.

After working with ACORN to promote the loosening of immigration laws, Sen. John McCain (R-AZ) exposed himself to charges of hypocrisy during the third presidential debate in 2008. Jousting with ACORN loyalist Obama, McCain accused the group of being "on the verge of maybe perpetrating one of the greatest frauds in voter history in this country, maybe destroying the fabric of democracy." ACORN wasted no time pointing out McCain's apostasy. The senator's attacks on ACORN "are puzzling given his historic support for the organization and its efforts on behalf of immigrant Americans,"

ACORN announced in a press release. The group noted that "[a]s recently as February 20, 2006, Senator McCain was the keynote speaker at an ACORN-sponsored Immigration Rally in Miami, Florida, at Miami Dade College—Wolfson Campus." ACORN chief organizer Bertha Lewis noted gleefully that "[m]aybe it is out of desperation that Senator McCain has forgotten that he was for ACORN before he was against ACORN." It was a devastating repartee to a man who felt uncomfortable attacking his former allies.[93]

When he was still a Republican in 2008, Florida Gov. Charlie Crist and his chief elections officer, Secretary of State Kurt S. Browning, both rejected McCain's condemnation of ACORN. When reporters asked the governor if he objected to ACORN being active in Florida elections, he replied, "no." Browning concurred.[94] Crist also signed into law an ACORN-backed bill that restored the voting rights of more than 100,000 ex-convicts.[95]

In 2008, California Gov. Arnold Schwarzenegger signed into law an ACORN-backed bill making it more difficult for mortgage lenders to foreclose. At the bill-signing ceremony he allowed Oakland's radical mayor Ron Dellums to speak. A longtime ACORN ally, Dellums thanked ACORN by name for promoting the legislation.[96] In 2009, Minnesota Gov. Tim Pawlenty called for state funding of ACORN to be cut off,[97] but two years earlier he signed into law an anti-predatory lending bill ACORN played a role in drafting.[98] In 2004, then-Massachusetts Gov. Mitt Romney signed into law an ACORN-backed bill that cracked down on the subprime lending industry.[99] So while Republican connections are relatively few, ACORN has made itself heard and felt on the Right. Still, the organization has been far more closely allied with the Democrats ever since presidential candidate Ronald Reagan told the world the unvarnished truth about its tactics and objectives.

[THREE]

Messy and Misleading: ACORN's Mysterious Structure

ACORN IS A nonprofit version of Enron, the infamous failed energy company that imploded under the pressure of hopelessly confusing, misleading, and illegal accounting practices. The ACORN network has developed a tangled, deliberately complex mess of inter-locking directorates and who-knows-how-many affiliated tax-exempt groups that routinely swap seven-figure checks that has long cried out for a probe under federal racketeering laws. Philanthropy databases indicate that the network took in at least $107 million from founda-tions from 1993 to 2008. The ACORN network has also received at least $79 million in federal funds, yet, as of November 2009, owed more than $2.3 million in back taxes. (See Table of Federal Grants to ACORN at page 211.) At that time, the liens were preventing ACORN from selling its old headquarters, a former funeral home at 1024 Elysian Fields Avenue in New Orleans. The asking price was $835,000, but presumably the nearly $1.3 million in pending tax liens would be sufficient to frighten away prospective buyers.[100] The total amount ACORN has received from state and local governments over the years is an open question.

No one knows how large the entire ACORN network's budget is.

ACORN leaders have given conflicting accounts of its size. In October 2009, chief organizer Bertha Lewis said ACORN had an "average budget" between "$20 [million] and $25 million a year for everything, all of the offices combined."[101] ACORN national president Maude Hurd indicated in a reference manual that ACORN's budget in 2008 was $50 million.[102] Wade Rathke claimed ACORN's annual budget was more than $100 million.[103] Of course, Lewis, Hurd, and Rathke may all have been playing word games. By "ACORN" they may have been referring to the whole far-flung network of affiliates or solely to the lead corporate entity, that is, to the nonprofit corporation called the Association of Community Organizations for Reform Now Inc. (Federal Employer Identification Number 72-0481941) that refuses to seek tax-exempt status from the IRS in order to conceal its shady financial dealings. ACORN allies Peter Dreier and John Atlas wrote in 2008 that "ACORN and its affiliates have an annual budget of over $100 million."[104]

Although ACORN claims to practice "participatory democracy" in which members govern the organization, the claim is a farce. "It's not participatory," former radical David Horowitz said in an interview. "Wade Rathke is the lifetime ruler. How's that participatory democracy? It's like all communist organizations: the dictatorship of the elite." ACORN is indeed highly autocratic. National by-laws vest authority in elected local, state, and national representatives who in theory carry out the will of members. However, the national chief organizer has total authority in the hiring and firing of employees. After quitting, Nevada ACORN chairman William Brookerd complained in 1979, "If the leadership at any level insists on pursuing their priorities over staff priorities, they are 'democratically' exorcised from the leadership." Of course, all membership dues are forwarded to ACORN's headquarters.[105]

One of the reasons that determining ACORN's actual budget is difficult is that corporate shakedown payments and donations do not always appear in databases. Also, tracking housing and community development grants administered by the U.S. Department of Housing and Urban Development (HUD) is difficult. HUD often distributes the money to states and localities, which then allot the funds to many different nonprofit groups. Getting a total financial picture would require enlisting an army of Freedom of Information Act requesters. HUD, by the way, ought to stand for Department of Homewrecking and Utopian Development. The federal department has long been a partner with ACORN and other radical groups that use the nation's poor and inner-city communities as laboratory rats in social engineering schemes.

All the ACORN-affiliated entities in the network are tightly controlled from the top through overlapping boards of directors and large intra-network financial transfers. Founder Rathke designed it that way so he could exercise complete authority over every little fiefdom in his empire of activism. ACORN "may be the most brilliantly orchestrated criminal organization set up in many a year," said one ACORN insider. When you study how ACORN is set up, "you realize just how bright Wade Rathke and his brother Dale were."

Former ACORN official Charles Turner said ACORN should be investigated for racketeering because it is "a continuing criminal enterprise." Speaking on behalf of a reform group called ACORN 8, Turner said, "We believe the way the money has been moved around, they've been laundering money, they've been using the mails to defraud. They've been using federal dollars as well as our membership money to support themselves, their friends, elected officials in other places and we don't understand why Congress won't investigate."[106]

Before ACORN declared bankruptcy in late 2010, the vast ACORN empire had included ACORN Housing Corp. Inc. (arranged mortgages), ACORN Institute Inc. (leadership training for activists), WARN (Wal-Mart Alliance for Reform Now, which supported organizing unions in Wal-Mart stores), Living Wage Resource Center (tracked efforts by cities and states to raise the minimum wage above the federal standard), two "social justice" radio stations in Arkansas and Texas, Project Vote (voter registration and mobilization), Service Employees International Union (SEIU) Locals 100 (Arkansas, Louisiana, Texas) and 880 (Illinois, Indiana), Site Fighters (fought "big box" chains such as Wal-Mart and Target), and American Institute for

Social Justice (published *Social Policy* magazine with ACORN Institute Inc. and the Organizers' Forum). It also operated a handful of "social justice" high schools in New York and California.

OBAMA'S CAMPAIGN COVERS UP TWO DECADES
OF TIES TO ACORN

As the 2008 election heated up, Republicans seized on Obama's deep, longstanding connection to ACORN, a group he trained organizers for, worked for, and represented in court. In September 2008, ACORN began receiving a mountain of bad publicity relating to nationwide allegations of election fraud. Having a community organizer running for the White House was in a sense a curse for ACORN because it brought an unprecedented level of scrutiny to all its shady enterprises. The Obama campaign launched an aggressive disinformation campaign that was eagerly received by the mainstream media.

One of the campaign's media minions, *Huffington Post* writer Seth Colter Walls, eagerly conveyed the lies of the Obama campaign. After jousting online with conservative commentator Seton Motley over Obama's links to ACORN, Walls wrote up a news story having done little if any actual research. Walls simply accepted the word of campaign spokesman Ben LaBolt that Obama's ties to ACORN were ephemeral at best. The new president later rewarded LaBolt, known for his pugnaciousness, by making him an assistant White House press secretary. The accusations of Obama's close relationship to ACORN were "smoke and mirrors," LaBolt said. "The fact is, Barack Obama was never an employee of ACORN, he never served as an ACORN organizer or an ACORN trainer. As an attorney, he successfully challenged Governor Edgar to enforce the federal Motor Voter law, making sure voting was as accessible for Illinois residents as the law required." LaBolt's prevarications were echoed in an official campaign website called Fight the Smears that offered to keep visitors up to date on "right wing smears" against Obama.

Walls then indicated that the Obama campaign "[b]roadly" admitted that "Obama represented a coalition of groups that sued Illinois Gov. Jim Edgar in order to get the state to implement the federal 'Motor-Voter' voting access law." After noting that the administration of longtime ACORN ally Bill Clinton later joined the lawsuit, Walls wrote in an evasive, lawyerly fashion that "Obama aides say he wasn't 'representing' ACORN individually, but as part of a larger coalition."[107]

This claim, that ACORN wasn't being represented *individually* employs the kind of nonsensical reasoning that gets tossed around in a college seminar on postmodernist literature. Either Obama represented ACORN or he didn't. The "complaint for injunctive and declaratory relief" dated January 11, 1995, that initiated the lawsuit in the U.S. District Court for the Northern District of Illinois identifies ACORN, along with one other group and four individual voters as plaintiffs in the action. The only person to sign the document was Obama himself, then a lawyer with the Chicago law firm Davis, Miner, Barnhill & Galland. Obama is identified under the signature line near the end of the document as "One of the Attorneys for Plaintiffs."[108] Clearly, Obama represented ACORN in the suit.

LaBolt left out another lawsuit in which Obama represented ACORN. In 1994 Obama acted in *Buycks-Roberson v. Citibank Federal Savings Bank*, a case in which the group pressured the bank to increase lending to marginally qualified minority applicants "in a race neutral way." ACORN settled out of court.[109]

Obama was also a member of a minor socialist party in Illinois called the New Party. The party was created with the help of the Marxist organization Democratic Socialists of America (DSA), and endorsed Obama when he ran for Illinois state senate.[110] Rutgers professor Heidi Swarts notes that ACORN was "a major force behind" the New Party,[111] which ACORN's Dan Cantor and Zach Polett worked to strengthen in the 1990s.[112]

Some time later bloggers noticed an article that linked Obama to ACORN and to Project Vote and also made clear that the two entities were joined at the hip. The 2004 article, "Case Study: Chicago—The Barack Obama Campaign," was by Toni Foulkes, a Chicago-based member of the ACORN national board who is now a Chicago alderman. It appeared in the Winter 2003/Spring 2004 issue of *Social Policy*, which at the time was an official publication of ACORN's American Institute for Social Justice.

In the article, Foulkes makes a series of admissions that demonstrate that Obama's ties to ACORN went way back. She wrote that when Obama worked for Project Vote in 1992, running a highly successfully voter drive in Chicago that helped to elect Sen. Carol Moseley Braun (D-IL), Project Vote was a part of the ACORN network. Foulkes's account clearly establishes connections that the Obama campaign insisted didn't exist. Although in the heat of the 2008 presidential campaign Obama's defenders attacked Foulkes as unreliable, she appears to be completely truthful, though she has a problem recalling dates.

According to her account, ACORN first "noticed" Obama when he was organizing poor people on Chicago's south side through the church-based Developing Communities Project (DCP). "He was a very good organizer," she wrote. The future president ran DCP from 1985 to 1988.

As Foulkes noted, Obama's ties to ACORN actually go back to the 1980s. The election of hard-left candidate Harold Washington as mayor of Chicago in 1983 inspired Obama to relocate to the Windy City in 1985. It was that move that helped put Obama on ACORN's radar screen. "The Harold Washington coalition was led by an alliance of Chicago communists, socialists and 'community activists,'" according to researcher Trevor Loudon. As early as 1993, Obama joined Progressive Chicago, a sister group of the ACORN-linked New Party that was key to electing Washington. Progressive Chicago was created by New Party members Madeline Talbott of Chicago ACORN and labor activist Dan Swinney.

ACORN and SEIU played an outsized role in Progressive Chicago, which described itself in its literature as "a renewal of the old Harold Washington coalition; activists and academics; women; unemployed and union; gay and straight; community organizations and churches; African American, Latino, Asian, native American and white; seniors and people with disabilities; low income and middle income; west and south side . . ." Among key Progressive Chicago leaders were: Talbott (who worked with Obama in Project Vote); Swinney; ACORN's Ernestine Whiting; then-SEIU Local 880 (an ACORN affiliate) president Bessie Cannon; SEIU Local 880 head organizer Keith Kelleher (husband of Talbott); and DSA member Danny Davis, a radical who is now a Democratic congressman representing part of Chicago.[113]

Foulkes wrote that after ACORN spent so many years getting to know Obama, it was only "natural for many of us to be active volunteers in his first campaign for State Senate and then his failed bid for U.S. Congress in 1996 [sic]." In fact Obama ran for the Illinois state senate in 1996 and lost his bid to wrest the Democratic nomination away from U.S. Rep. Bobby Rush (D-IL) in 2000. The upshot? "By the time he ran for U.S. Senate [in 2004], we were old friends."

Foulkes continued, "When he returned from law school, we asked him to help us with a lawsuit to challenge the state of Illinois' refusal to abide by the National Voting Rights Act, also known as motor voter." While it is true that Obama did return to Chicago after graduating from Harvard Law School in 1991 and that Obama did represent ACORN in *ACORN v. Edgar*, the lawsuit wasn't launched until 1995.

Having somehow gotten it into her head that *ACORN v. Edgar* preceded the Moseley Braun voter drive, she then wrote that after Obama won the court case he "went on to run a voter registration project with Project VOTE in 1992 that made it possible for Carol Moseley Braun to win the Senate that year. Project VOTE delivered 50,000 newly registered voters in that campaign (ACORN delivered about 5,000 of them)."

Foulkes adds that since the Moseley Braun campaign "we have invited Obama to our leadership training sessions to run the session on power every year, and, as a result, many of our newly developing leaders got to know him before he ever ran for office." In early October 2008, as media coverage of ACORN election fraud scandals intensified, ACORN removed the smoking gun of an article from the *Social Policy* website. After a fortnight of unrelenting criticism in the blogosphere, as of October 18, 2008, the article had been restored.[114]

Obama repaid ACORN's loyalty by sending foundation grant

money its way. From at least 1999 through 2001, Obama and Bill Ayers, who launched Obama's political career at a fundraiser in his living room, were on the board of the Woods Fund of Chicago together. In that period, the Woods Fund gave a $45,000 grant for "community development" to Chicago ACORN. The charity also gave two grants to Chicago ACORN as "fiscal agent" for the American Institute for Social Justice, ACORN's leadership school. The first such grant for $75,000 for "social and human services" was dated 2001 while Obama and Ayers sat on the board, but the second ($70,000) was dated 2002, after Obama had left the board. That grant was also designated for "social and human services."[115]

From 1995 to 1999, Obama headed the Chicago Annenberg Challenge (CAC), an education foundation that was the brainchild of Ayers. Obama stayed on its board until 2001, disbursing funds to ACORN and other radical groups.[116] The Grassroots School Improvement Campaign (GSIC) took in $75,000 from CAC in 1997. GSIC was a partnership between Chicago ACORN, eight Chicago schools, Cross City Campaign for Urban School Reform, and the Small Schools Workshop. As Aaron Klein and Brenda J. Elliott reported,

> The Small Schools Workshop, created in the nineties, is co-directed by Ayers and Mike Klonsky. In 1968 Klonsky was Students for a Democratic Society national chairman and a "demonstration organizer." In his post-SDS days Klonsky formed "the October League (Marxist-Leninist) and Communist Party (Marxist-Leninist), part of the new communist movement that emerged in the 1970s." Ayers and Klonsky, both communists, were consultants for Mayor Richard M. Daley's "agenda for public schools."[117]

Whenever Obama got involved in charity management, the funding of radicalism inevitably followed.

Obama himself made no secret of his ties to ACORN before the group became a political liability in 2008. At the Heartland Democratic Presidential Forum, a conference for community organizing groups including ACORN, Senator Obama announced that he would meet with the radical groups assembled during his first 100 days as U.S. president. He said, "Before I even get inaugurated, during the transition, we're going to be calling all of you in to help us shape the agenda. We're going to be having meetings all across the country with community organizations so that you have input into the agenda for the next presidency of the United States of America."

John Fund of the *Wall Street Journal* noted that when Obama filled out a questionnaire listing supporters of his 1996 Illinois state senate run, he listed ACORN first: "[I]t was not an alphabetical list." Years later when Obama made it to the U.S. Senate, he pushed ACORN's priorities, becoming the Senate's "leading critic of Voter ID laws, whose overturn was a top Acorn priority."[118]

In late 2007, Obama told an ACORN audience: "I've been fighting alongside ACORN on issues you care about my entire career. Even before I was an elected official, when I ran Project Vote voter registration drives in Illinois, ACORN was smack dab in the middle of it, and we appreciate your work."

During the 2008 primaries, the Obama presidential campaign engaged ACORN's notorious get-out-the-vote machine to do its dirty work against then-contender Hillary Clinton. ACORN's work may have made all the difference in the battle between the two Alinskyite contenders for the presidency: among delegates to the Democratic nominating convention, Obama won 1,766 elected delegates, barely edging out Clinton who won 1,639 delegates.[119] The Obama campaign disguised its $832,598 payment to ACORN affiliate Citizens Services Inc., describing the sum in a Federal Election Commission filing as covering "polling, advance work and staging major events." In fact, the campaign hired CSI for voter mobilization services (also known as GOTV—"get out the vote"). After the deception was revealed, the Obama campaign filed an amended report with the Federal Election Commission admitting it hired ACORN. "CSI appears to have been a front to funnel payments to ACORN for campaign advance work," noted author Michelle Malkin.[120]

Although statements issued by political parties in the heat of battle often need to be taken with a grain of salt, the GOP correctly nailed Obama for the cover-up. "Barack Obama's failure to accurately report his campaign's financial records is an incredibly suspicious situation that appears to be an attempt to hide his campaign's interaction with a left-wing organization previously convicted of voter fraud," said Blair Latoff, a spokeswoman for the Republican National Committee. "For a candidate who claims to be practicing 'new' politics, his FEC reports look an awful lot like the 'old-style' Chicago politics of yesterday."

Jim Terry, chief public advocate for the Consumers Rights League, which tracks ACORN, said CSI's participation in the Obama campaign was suspicious. "All of this just seems like an awful lot of money and time spent on political campaigning for an organization that purports to exist to help low-income consumers," he said.

"ACORN has a long and sordid history of employing convoluted Enron-style accounting to illegally use taxpayer funds for their own political gain," he said. "Now it looks like ACORN is using the same type of convoluted accounting scheme for Obama's political gain."[121]

CSI also took in another "suspiciously large payment" that raises questions about "what kind of work this purportedly non-partisan, non-profit offshoot of ACORN is doing," Malkin reported. In early 2009, left-wing activist group Ohio Citizen Action reported making a payment of $907,808 to CSI for canvassing and $590,526 for "campaign consulting."

"That's some gold-plated get-out-the-vote and consulting services right there," Malkin opined. "The scheme has all the appearances of another left-wing slush fund for Democrat satellites exploiting non-profit status and skirting campaign finance laws."

OBAMA'S HISTORY WITH PROJECT VOTE

Obama's ties to ACORN go back at least to 1992, the year he directed voter registration for ACORN affiliate Project Vote.

It's unclear how much, if any, contact President Obama had with ACORN after moving into the White House. "It's kind of irrelevant," said Newt Gingrich. "He is *their* president. He knows everything he needs to know. They don't need to talk to him. He's them."

But the issue of Obama's relationship to ACORN was a subject of heated debate and furious spin-doctoring during the presidential campaign. Desperate to erase Obama's nearly two decades of ties to ACORN, the campaign claimed in 2008 that Project Vote was not part of ACORN in 1992.

Aware of the history-altering stakes, Project Vote founder Sanford A. Newman helped the campaign run interference. Newman used lawyerly, evasive wording as he claimed in a letter to the editor that ran in the *Wall Street Journal* that Project Vote was not part of ACORN in 1992:

> John Fund's "Obama's Liberal Shock Troops" (op-ed, July 12) has some facts wrong. The historic nonpartisan drive to increase voter participation that Barack Obama led in 1992 wasn't for the Association of Community Organizations for Reform Now, but for Project Vote—of which I was the national director in 1992.
>
> Instead of accepting far more prestigious and better paying offers, Mr. Obama accepted a grueling job with Project Vote for a meager salary. He believed so much in the democratic process that he even gave up the contract for publication of his book, not knowing whether he would ever find another publisher. He brought a broad spectrum of community organizations into that effort, conducting what remains the most successful nonpartisan voter drive in Illinois history.
>
> Project Vote remains a separate organization today. Indeed, it wasn't until after Mr. Obama's tenure had ended that it began to conduct projects more frequently with Acorn than with other community-based organizations.
>
> Both Project Vote and Acorn should be proud that their efforts have increased voting. Acorn should also be proud of its other work, including winning minimum-wage increases and helping lead the fight against predatory lending and unfair foreclosures.
>
> Mr. Obama's willingness to sacrifice because of his deep commitment to strengthening the democratic process is something that all Americans should applaud regardless of their party or politics.
>
> Sanford A. Newman
> Takoma Park, Md.[122]

As Dana Carvey's Church Lady character used to say on *Saturday Night Live*: Well, isn't that *convenient?*

FactCheck.org, a project of the Annenberg Public Policy Center of the University of Pennsylvania, interviewed Newman and cast doubt on his version of events. The watchdog website noted that despite Newman's statements, "after law school, Obama may have had contact with ACORN when he directed a Chicago registration drive for Project Vote in 1992."[123]

Further research reveals that ACORN was, in fact, part of Project Vote's voter registration coalition in 1992. Project Vote announced in an October 5, 1992, press release that in New York City it had worked with ACORN and the New York Public Interest Group to add "more than 90,000 voters" to the voter rolls.[124] At some point, Voting for America Inc., which today is Project Vote's formal corporate name, acquired the "Project Vote" trademark.[125]

ACORN apologist John Atlas continues the cover-up the Obama campaign initiated. In his history of ACORN, *Seeds of Change*, he misleadingly writes that "within a decade" of the 1992 voter drive that helped elect Moseley Braun, "Project Vote would join ACORN's family of organizations." At the same time, Atlas acknowledges that in 1992 "Local 880 and ACORN saw a chance to flex their political muscle when Cook County's recorder of deeds, Carol Moseley Braun asked Talbott and Kelleher to play a major role in her voter registration and get-out-the-vote efforts in her run for the U.S. Senate."[126]

But Atlas's statements are problematic. Service Employees International Union (SEIU) Local 880 was an official affiliate in the ACORN network when Obama ran Project Vote's drive in 1992. Moreover, Atlas's acknowledgement that Moseley Braun asked "Talbott and Kelleher"—that would be Madeline Talbott and her husband Keith Kelleher of Chicago—to help her campaign with voter registration and voter mobilization efforts further points to official ACORN involvement. Both Talbott and Kelleher were national ACORN leaders at the time. Kelleher was head of SEIU Local 880.

ACORN's fingerprints were all over Project Vote in 1992. As the evidence of close collaboration between these technically separate organizations continues to mount, it becomes less important whether a piece of paper exists somewhere officially connecting the two. Of course, neither ACORN nor Project Vote has ever made public any legal documentation to support its claim about when the two organizations became formally entangled. Besides, affiliation is a funny thing. It's a fairly flexible concept. To affiliate is to bring into close association. If I say we're affiliated today, we're affiliated. If I say tomorrow we're not affiliated, we're not affiliated.

To say that Obama worked for Project Vote but didn't work for ACORN is nothing but word games. There is no wall of separation between the two. On registration and mobilization campaigns, ACORN and Project Vote work together to the point where it is difficult, if not impossible, to tell the difference. They share staff, office space, and money.

Whether the ties were formal or informal, evidence overwhelmingly demonstrates that when Barack Obama worked for Project Vote in 1992, it was part of the ACORN network. Or as Stanley Kurtz concluded, "despite his denials in 2008, Obama's 1992 Project Vote alliance was deeply entangled in ACORN's broader organizing work."[127]

PATRICK GASPARD

President Obama isn't the only longtime ACORN operative working in the White House. There's also the low-profile Patrick Gaspard who holds the title of White House political affairs director, one of the titles Karl Rove held in President Bush's White House. Evidence suggests that years before he joined the Obama administration, Gaspard was ACORN boss Bertha Lewis's political director in New York.

How do we actually know Gaspard, who shuns the public spotlight and scarcely appears in Nexis searches, was Lewis's right hand man? Because Gaspard's employment with ACORN was acknowledged by no less an authority than ACORN founder Wade Rathke himself. Rathke wrote May 16, 2009, at his blog:

Tell me that 1199's former political director, Patrick Gaspard (who was ACORN New York's political director before that) didn't reach out from the White House and help make that happen, and I'll tell you to take some remedial classes in "politics 101."

The "before that" time period Rathke is referring to is 2003 when Gaspard was executive vice president for political and legislative affairs for Service Employees International Union Local 1199 (United Healthcare Workers East). According to publicly available disclosure documents, Gaspard registered as a federal lobbyist for SEIU on October 22, 2007. The registration and subsequent disclosures indicate he lobbied Congress on SCHIP, the State Children's Health Insurance Program.[128] It's also worth noting that of all the entries in Bertha Lewis's rolodex, a copy of which this writer gained possession of in 2009, the entry for Gaspard is the most extensive.

Of course, the lines between ACORN and radical left-wing SEIU become fuzzy in places. Until late 2009, SEIU Locals 100 and 880 were part of the ACORN network of organizations. Local 100 in New Orleans is headed by Rathke. Longtime ACORN insider Keith Kelleher headed SEIU Local 880 in Chicago, which has since been swallowed up by a larger unit within SEIU. Kelleher remains involved in labor organizing, though inside ACORN sources say he's no longer involved with ACORN.

Gaspard's ties to ACORN, SEIU, and Lewis go back at least to 1989, when he volunteered for the David Dinkins mayoral campaign in New York City. In 2003, he became acting field director for Howard Dean's presidential bid. He was national field director in 2004 for America Coming Together, a now-defunct get-out-the-vote operation that received a $775,000 fine for campaign finance abuses. In 2006, Gaspard was acting political director for SEIU International. In 2008, Gaspard worked as national political director for the Obama campaign followed by a stint as associate personnel director for the Obama-Biden transition team. As the old Washington saying goes, politics is personnel. Who knows how many administration officials were put in place by Gaspard with direct input from ACORN's Bertha Lewis? It boggles the mind.

Gaspard also worked for New York's Working Families Party, an appendage of ACORN. Lewis is a co-founder of that party—which endorsed Obama in 2008—and has close ties to Rep. Jerrold Nadler (D-NY) who was most reluctant to have the House Judiciary subcommittee he chaired investigate ACORN. In 2009, Nadler invented the incredibly creative argument that legislative language aimed at depriving ACORN of federal funding constituted an unconstitutional "bill of attainder." Perhaps singling out the mafia for a federal funds cutoff would be unconstitutional too in his eyes.

As news of Gaspard's involvement with ACORN spread, Rathke changed his blog entry. Where he had written that Gaspard worked for New York ACORN, he inserted two new sentences: "This line used to contain a reference to Patrick Gaspard working for NY ACORN. This is untrue, he never worked for ACORN."[129]

But Rathke wasn't able to shove all evidence tying Gaspard to ACORN down the memory hole. If Gaspard isn't tied to ACORN, why did he sign a letter to the editor of the *Nation* magazine (dated July 2, 2001) on behalf of the Working Families Party of New York? The party is part of ACORN, according to ACORN's website which in 2009 confirmed that in 1998, "ACORN members spearhead[ed] formation of the Working Families Party, the first community-labor party with official ballot status in New York state in more than 50 years." In Lewis and Gaspard's letter, they spell out how closely intertwined are ACORN, the Working Families Party, and SEIU Local 1199:

> Doug Ireland's offhand comments about the Working Families Party's role in the upcoming municipal elections in New York City were inaccurate and hurtful ("Those Big Town Blues," June 4). He wrote that the WFP "could have played a role in recruiting Council candidates" but did not because the progressive unions took no initiatives and ACORN was distracted by its fight against the Edison Corporation.
>
> Speaking for two affiliates of the WFP—ACORN and SEIU/1199—I say that this is dead wrong. We have been involved in a marvelous WFP-initiated process that has included scores of neighborhood

and borough meetings, a remarkable series of interviews with more than 100 potential candidates, worksite presentations on the issues by WFP workplace captains, the ongoing recruitment of neighbor-hood captains and much more. We had more than 1,000 people at a WFP mayoral forum and have won concrete commitments on our living-wage bill from candidates across the city. Until the WFP, there was no group trying to pull together a community-labor-religious coalition to move ideas, people, money and energy in contests from Nassau County to Niagara Falls.

The WFP slate for this year's city elections will have more union members, community activists and progressives than any slate in memory. We hope Nation readers will vote for, work for and send money to all the WFP endorsed WFP endorsed candidates for pri-maries and the general election.

Bertha Lewis, ACORN, WFP

Patrick Gaspard, SEIU State Council, WFP[130]

Internal ACORN documents obtained by this writer show Gaspard gave ACORN $40,000 before he joined the Obama administration. While Gaspard worked as an executive vice president of SEIU Local 1199, he gave ACORN $15,000 in 2007 and $25,000 in 2008. That's an awfully large tithe for someone who made $111,894 in 2007 and who has a wife and two children. The $111,894 figure comes from an SEIU 1199 tax return. (If salary and deferred benefits are combined, the total is $151,869.) Moreover, Gaspard hails from New York which has a crushing tax burden, especially for individuals earning six-figure salaries—and he lived in the upscale neighborhood of Park Slope, Brooklyn.

It is entirely possible that the $40,000 Gaspard handed over to ACORN was SEIU money. In the scheme of things, it doesn't matter whether the lefty lucre belonged to Gaspard or SEIU. What matters is the fact that Gaspard handed over the money to ACORN. Given Gaspard's longstanding links to ACORN, it's not at all surprising that Scott Levenson, a lobbyist and spokesman for ACORN, dropped by the White House in March to visit with his former co-worker. The purpose of the meeting was not disclosed.[131] (At press time, the DNC had just announced Gaspard would become its executive director.)

Another New Yorker in the Obama administration, secretary of Housing and Urban Development Shaun Donovan, also has close ties to ACORN. Before taking office Donovan was New York mayor Michael Bloomberg's housing development commissioner. He worked closely with ACORN for five years on several projects.[132]

"Perhaps no administration official has had more interaction with Acorn than" Donovan, according to the *New York Times*. Reinforcing the newspaper's point, ACORN chief organizer Bertha Lewis praised the HUD secretary. "We grew to respect him, and he grew to respect us," she said.[133]

Roll Call, a Washington, D.C. newspaper that covers Capitol Hill, reported Lewis admitted "ACORN has friends in high places for the first time in a long time." Lewis acknowledged "that she has particularly good relationships with Housing and Urban Development Secretary Shaun Donovan and with Patrick Gaspard, the White House political director."[134]

For eight months in 2010, HUD stonewalled this writer's Freedom of Information Act request that sought correspondence between Donovan and ACORN. Eventually HUD replied that no such correspondence existed. This is next to impossible to believe given the longstanding close relationship between Donovan and ACORN.[135]

FOUR

The Poor as a Weapon:
ACORN's Cannon Fodder

WHEN BARACK OBAMA was a little boy surrounded by parents and grandparents and mentors sympathetic to communism, like-minded people were building ACORN's parent organization, the National Welfare Rights Organization. Armed with tax dollars, left-wing extremists Richard Cloward, Frances Fox Piven, and Saul Alinsky were at play in the 1960s, wreaking havoc on society in an effort to induce revolutionary change. All three of these relatively obscure figures labored to create NWRO along with a vast constellation of tax-supported groups determined to destroy the American society they loathed. Changes in federal social policy in the early 1960s helped to lay the groundwork for this artificial activism and the welfare-related unrest it caused. President Lyndon Johnson's "unconditional war on poverty in America," really should have been called an unconditional war on American values.

Johnson unveiled the massive redistributionist plan in his first State of the Union address, providing a ready-made platform for agitation. Kennedy-era social programs were enlarged and "provide[d] the vehicles through which the black ghettos mobilized to demand government services," Cloward and Piven wrote.[136] They used taxpayer resources in an effort to turn American society upside-down and the government encouraged their adventures in social engineering. During that period the federal government laid the foundation for the creation of ACORN. The War on Poverty gave taxpayers' money to community groups in order to encourage them to agitate against the status quo. In a sense, America declared war on itself and funded so-called participatory democracy-oriented groups to do the fighting.

The larger spending programs spurred poor blacks to activism and created a new leadership structure in the inner cities, according to Cloward and Piven. Some of the federal money went directly to local groups as political patronage. "[G]hetto groups were encouraged by federal policymakers to use these funds to create organizations and to press their own interests, especially in the arena of municipal services and politics." This, in turn, stimulated demand for more government spending as taxpayer dollars became a kind of ever-increasing subsidy for pro-Big Government activism.[137]

Howard Phillips, now head of the Conservative Caucus, a public policy organization in suburban Washington, D.C., was acting director of the federal Office of Economic Opportunity (OEO) in 1973 under President Nixon. Phillips recalled in an interview that the OEO was created by the Johnson administration "to implement the policies of assorted left-wing activists, notable among them a fellow named Michael Harrington." Harrington, who died in 1989, was a revolutionary Marxist theorist and activist and a committed Trotskyist. He joined the Socialist Party in 1953, rising to the post of national party chairman, which he held from 1968 to 1972. Scholars identify his 1962 book, *The Other America*, as the catalyst for the War on Poverty.[138] Harrington also founded the misleadingly named *Democratic Socialists of America* (DSA), a U.S. affiliate of the Socialist International. The DSA "are all neo-communists," David Horowitz said in an interview. "By 'neo' I mean that they would say Soviet Communism was bad, they would probably say they're against a dictatorship of the proletariat. Like Khrushchev they're critical of past Communists."

While at OEO Phillips followed the work of Cloward and Piven "closely because they were two of the ideological architects of much of what OEO was doing," he said.

Cloward and Piven never missed an opportunity to undermine civil society and slam the American way of life. They denounced "the strident American belief in individualism."[139] In 2009, Piven critiqued the supposedly unfair allocation of wealth in American society. "We've become a very unequal society where some people own everything and live lavishly. The concentration of wealth, and the concentration also of consumption, is quite astonishing."[140] At a 2009 radicals' conference called "Class in Crisis," Piven made it clear that her main objection to Karl Marx's *Communist Manifesto* was only that it was too vague to achieve radical social transformation. "Our model could be the *Manifesto* but the *Manifesto*, the *Communist Manifesto*, was really too general for the purposes that we need to put the strategic work to today," she said. "We need to study in a way that the *Manifesto* did not, could not, how people can be organized in the face of a more dispersed character of contemporary sites of labor. We need new forms of organization."[141] Both Cloward and Piven were members of the Trotskyist-founded DSA. Piven is not only a member of DSA—she's an honorary chairman of the group[142]—and Cloward was a member until his death in 2001.[143] When Cloward died, the DSA magazine *Democratic Left* bragged about his achievements. "Richard had the unusual ability not only to generate political ideas about social movements, but also to turn these ideas into action," writes his friend Ken Grossinger, who worked for ACORN-allied SEIU and is on the editorial board of ACORN magazine *Social Policy*.[144] "He raised money to finance organizers and organizations to advance movement strategies," Grossinger writes.[145]

SAUL ALINSKY INFLUENCED THE WAR ON POVERTY

Phillips said community organizing guru Saul Alinsky was also "a huge influence on OEO and its key employees." Alinsky, Phillips noted, "was of the view that society could be remade by community activism." He gave copies of Alinsky's how-to guide to Marxist revolution, *Rules for Radicals*, "to a great many people so that they would understand what I was up against, and I pointed out that he dedicated the book to Lucifer whose ideology was akin to that of Mr. Alinsky." Alinsky may not have joined DSA, which wasn't created until the 1980s, or the Communist Party USA for that matter, but he was sympathetic to the party's revolutionary goals. As Horowitz writes:

> Although he was never formally a Communist and did not share their tactical views on how to organize a revolution, his attitude towards the Communists was fraternal, and he saw them as political allies. In the 1969 'Afterword' to his book *Reveille for Radicals* he explained his attitude in these words: "Communism itself is irrelevant. The issue is whether they are on our side . . ."[146]

The agency where Phillips worked came out of the Economic Opportunity Act (EOA) of 1964, the centerpiece of President Johnson's War on Poverty. The War on Poverty itself was a part of the massive left-wing social engineering experiment known as the Great Society. President John F. Kennedy's brother-in-law, Sargent Shriver, wrote the EOA statute and became the first director of the OEO. The law "provided for job training, adult education, and loans to small businesses to attack the roots of unemployment and poverty." Many of the EOA-created programs still exist today, including VISTA (Volunteers In Service To America), now known as AmeriCorps VISTA, Job Corps, and Head Start.[147]

The EOA introduced a doctrine known as "maximum feasible participation." The idea was that the government-funded groups spawned by the law were supposed to try to involve the poor in activism aimed at changing society. The idea had "revolutionary implications" because "it involved a redistribution of power," according to academic Lillian B. Rubin. "The idea of 'maximum feasible participation' has captured the imagination of the urban poor, with the force of an idea whose time has come; it will not die," Rubin prophetically predicted in 1969.[148]

According to Phillips, in everyday practice "maximum feasible participation" meant encouraging more people to receive government benefits such as welfare. "OEO was a major proponent of government intervention in the economy and welfare," he said. "The way to fight poverty in their view was to expand government subsidies to elements of the population."

"What OEO did was fund some 10,000 organizations employing several hundred thousand people who worked to radically transform the policies of the United States without reference to either elections or congressional action," Phillips said. "When I became director I had already served as an assistant to the director who at that point was Frank Carlucci, who funded some of the most extreme activities subsidized by the agency."

Before rising to the post of OEO director, Phillips closely observed in the field how programs that the agency funded worked. He saw radical Students for a Democratic Society organizers "working in the field with immigrants and I saw many of the outrageous activities being put forward and I became determined that I would strive to become the director of the agency and then in that role I would use my authority to veto or halt as much of the outrageous funding as possible."

Phillips resolved to cut off funding of left-wing advocacy groups that the $3-billion agency supported with taxpayer money.[149] One of the groups he pushed away from the overflowing teat of government was ACORN, he said. Phillips zeroed out ACORN's funding "for the same reason I defunded the others, because they were involved in activities that were not just unwise, but corrupt and destructive." At that time, ACORN was promoting governmental redistribution of wealth and "promoting activities at the grassroots level which in my view were inimical to the best interests of the country."

Phillips said that the group, whose acronym at that early stage in its life stood for *Arkansas* Community Organizations for Reform Now, "caused me great concern and whether it was a pittance or pound or a great amount, it was not something the federal government ought to have been funding." ACORN and the organizations OEO funded, including the National Welfare Rights Organization that spawned ACORN, "were really accountable only to themselves and they employed some 500,000 people who were actively involved in efforts to remake American society."

Phillips fought with one of his predecessors as OEO director, Frank Carlucci, over subsidizing leftist activities. Carlucci later served as defense secretary under President George H.W. Bush. Phillips said he "had many an argument with Mr. Carlucci who was a strong proponent of these entities." Phillips recalled a conversation he had with former Vice President Richard Cheney, who at the time was an aide to Carlucci at OEO.

> Dick said to me, "Howard, I am sure glad you're getting this job because you'll do things that we wouldn't dare do." And unfortunately that was the case. They were afraid to take on the left-wing entities because those entities had powerful allies in the media and the special interest world and indeed I was subject of a great deal of enmity in the media and elsewhere and there were dozens of lawsuits brought against me by organizations which I defunded.

Indeed the Phillips appointment was not well received by liberals. Sensing that his arrival at OEO foreshadowed an attempt to dismantle the agency, left-wing lawmakers launched an offensive, filing a lawsuit challenging his appointment. The suit was led by a corrupt liberal lawmaker, Sen. Harrison A. Williams Jr. (D-NJ), who left office after being convicted in the "Abscam" bribery scandal in 1982. Sen. Walter Mondale (D-MN), who later became Jimmy Carter's vice president, and Sens. Claiborne Pell (D-RI) and William Hathaway (D-ME) also participated in the lawsuit.[150]

Some time after Phillips left OEO it was abolished, but the programs it administered lived on, transferred elsewhere in the federal government. "It was like a cancer which instead of being eradicated was cut into pieces and spread far and wide," he said. Ironically, Phillips noted, the conservative President Ronald Reagan funded a radical community group in Massachusetts. Around 1983, as Reagan was "quite properly" using military force to overthrow Bernard Coard's brutal Communist dictatorship in Grenada, millions of taxpayer dollars were flowing to Action for Boston Community Development (ABCD), which was an OEO grantee, Phillips said. ABCD was headed for 40 years by Coard's brother Robert Coard, who died in 2009. Not surprisingly, the left-wing governor of Massachusetts, longtime ACORN and Obama ally Deval Patrick, attended the funeral.[151] "So on one hand [Reagan] was fighting Communism in Grenada but he was subsidizing it in the United States," said Phillips. Reagan "may not have been aware of it prospectively, but he was aware of it retroactively because I did bring it to his attention."

THE TRANSFORMATIVE POWER OF VIOLENCE

Like Alinsky, Cloward and Piven believe the ends justify the means. Piven says she favors the strategic use of violence if it advances the cause. "I have considerable respect for nonviolence but I don't treat it as inevitably a necessary rule." She respects nonviolence because it "helps to protect the protesters" from being accused of using violence which brings a strong response from the authorities. "Probably unless you have a good reason for breaking the window, probably you shouldn't do that *unless it's a big part of your strategy.*"[152] [emphasis added]

Cut through the scholarly-sounding mumbo jumbo of leftist professors Richard Cloward and Frances Fox Piven, and it becomes apparent they believe America's real problem is that it doesn't have enough of the right kind of violence: socially, economically, politically disruptive violence. Although they go to great lengths to conceal or downplay this brutal perspective in order to make their ideas more socially palatable, it is clear from their work that they believe violence carries in it the possibility of redemptive societal transformation. Violence that disrupts the business of governments and corporations is key to bringing dramatic change to America, they argue. Strategic disruption—the power "to shut it down" Piven calls it—has served the labor movement well, Piven says.[153]

Cloward and Piven were impressed by the disorder caused by the Great Depression and by the potential for revolutionary change that marked those stressful times. "Economic distress had produced unprecedented disorder and the specter of cataclysmic disorder," they wrote approvingly in one book. In the 1930s, revolutionary violence seemed just around the corner. They quote Rep. Hamilton Fish, Jr. (R-NY) who warned that "if we don't give [security] under the existing system, the people will change the system. Make no mistake about that." Collectively these developments "signaled political disaffection on a scale unparalleled in the American experience," they wrote, no doubt salivating. "The people were turning against their leaders and against the regime—against [President Herbert] Hoover, against business, even against 'the American way.'"[154]

Excited at the prospect of helping to turn Americans against the American way, Cloward and Piven developed various strategies that sought to replicate the disruptions of the 1930s. Disruptive activism such as community organizing helps to motivate the poor to act for change—but it's not easy work, Piven notes. "The power potential at the bottom, in particular, is not automatically expressed," she says. "A lot of strategic work has to be done to realize that power." People without power "have to come to recognize that they are important, that they are making contributions."[155]

CALLING IT CRIME IS A SYMPTOM OF YOUR BOURGEOIS PREJUDICES, COMRADE

Tellingly, in 1965 Cloward argued that America didn't have a crime problem—it had a *law* problem. Laws enforcing an unjust social order were oppressing the poor, he claimed. "The problems are being greatly exaggerated," he said. "The American people are more lawful today than ever before." A month after the statement, Cloward visited Philadelphia to address a peace corps gathering. After the speech ended about 10 p.m. he visited a bad neighborhood. "The area in which Doctor Cloward was wandering at 1:30 a.m. is a particularly lawless section of the city," according to a 1965 memorandum from the FBI's Philadelphia field office. "It is difficult to understand why he was permitted to walk alone in such a notorious section of the city." While he toured a rough part of town, two "Negroes" bummed a cigarette off him. Cloward was then shot from behind as he walked away. A 22-caliber bullet was removed from his shoulder at Temple University Hospital. "The fact that I got hurt doesn't mean we are in the midst of a crime wave," said Cloward, his appreciation of criminals undiminished. "The vast majority of people are law abiding citizens," he added, frustrated. Perhaps he would have shrugged were it not for the fresh bullet hole the oppressed victims of American society made in his shoulder.[156]

Cloward and Piven adhere to a classic Marxist analysis of capitalist society that holds criminals blameless for their crimes. In a nutshell, that topsy-turvy intellectual tradition contends that crime is merely a matter of perspective. There is no such thing as individual responsibility. If the poor do it, it cannot be crime because in a capitalist society like America, law is an instrument of system-reinforcing oppression directed at poor people. It follows that the American system is a fraud that inflicts harm on low-income Americans, according to Cloward. Capitalism is a cruel hoax. "Day after day we pick up a newspaper and its big stories are about the so-called welfare fraud and not about the income distribution fraud, and not about the wealth concentration fraud," he writes.[157] Poor people are by definition oppressed, controlled, and kept in their place by the sinister, inhumane system comprised of markets and the rule of law. (Whether poor people have job skills or other factors relevant to advancement in a market-based economy never seems to enter into the Marxist calculus.)

In a 1960 book he co-wrote with Lloyd Ohlin, *Delinquency and Opportunity: A Theory of Delinquent Gangs*, Cloward argued that capitalism created criminals. He rejected the eminently sensible then-dominant view that criminals are irresponsible, antisocial individuals. Cloward instead argued that poor inner-city youth were only rationally pursuing their own self-interest when they committed crimes. Delinquency was caused by poverty, which denied would-be criminals opportunities

for economic advancement. Dr. Cloward's all-too-predictable prescription was massive spending on social programs. Although coated
with the veneer of science, there was nothing scientific about the
book: it was pure Marxism—like the rest of Cloward and Piven's work.

Cloward and Ohlin tried to put their "'opportunity theory' into practice on the Lower East Side of Manhattan, with the creation of a project
called Mobilization for Youth to help youth gang members on their own
terms."[158] Mobilization for Youth (MFY), which Cloward co-founded in
1961, "became the programmatic model for the federal War on Poverty
and pioneered community action programs and the anti-poverty legal
services."[159] Cloward met Frances Fox Piven at Mobilization for Youth
and she became his partner in domestic subversion for the rest of his
life.[160] Incidentally, MFY was a hotbed of Communist activity, according
to the FBI. "[O]ur files contain references to communist affiliations of
several of the members of that organization," the bureau indicated in
a 1965 internal memorandum. However, the document indicates the
FBI had no evidence "reflecting that the Communist Party has specifically instructed its members to infiltrate" the group.[161]

To Cloward and Piven, when a poor person commits a crime it is
a justifiable act of rebellion worthy of sympathy, if not support. It is
both a cry for help and for revolution. In a book titled *Poor People's
Movements: Why They Succeed, How They Fail*, the two academics decry
the tendency of society to apply "the pejorative labels of illegality and
violence" to describe "defiance by the lower classes." Using these
"labels" glosses over the fact that the poor are trapped in "a structure of political coercion inherent in the everyday life of the lower
classes."[162] Criminals are either misunderstood, freedom fighters, or
perhaps both, according to the antisocial activists. Even the process
by which public officials are elected is part of a clever capitalist conspiracy designed to control and pacify the poor. "The electoral system
is another modern, and especially a capitalist, phenomenon," they
write. In the past, discontent "was signaled primarily by disorder in
the streets, [but] the electoral system is designed to channel it into
the voting booth."[163] In other words, as Cloward and Piven saw it, the
electoral system violates the democratic rights of the poor by stifling

their expression of dissent, even if that expression sometimes takes the form of violence.

CLOWARD:
"A MAJOR UPHEAVAL" NEEDED TO TRANSFORM AMERICA

The poor have every reason to revolt, according to Cloward. They would benefit more than other groups "from a major upheaval in our society."[164] The poor make progress only "when the rest of society is afraid of them."[165] The 1960s was an ideal time to proceed because in that decade "[m]any of the poor had apparently come to believe that a society which denied them jobs and adequate wages did at least owe them a survival income," Cloward and Piven wrote.[166]

Writing three years before "The Weight of the Poor" was published, Cloward and Piven wrote that society can be made to fear the poor if they use disruptive tactics in an effort to bring down the system. Such tactics

are intended to command attention and to win concessions by the actual trouble they cause in the ongoing operations of major institutions—by interfering with the daily business of city agencies or with the movement of traffic or the profits of businessmen. Such disruptions cause commotion among bureaucrats, excitement in the media, dismay among influential segments of the community, and strain for political leaders. When people sit in, or refuse to pay the rent, they are breaking the rules. This means that effective disruption depends on the ability of leaders to induce people to violate norms of conduct that are ordinarily deeply ingrained. Somehow the normal pieties, must be overcome. Moreover, to break the rules ordinarily involves some danger; people must be induced to run the risk of provoking coercive and repressive forces.[167]

Whether the poor people involved in the disruptive activities get hurt is of little consequence to Cloward and Piven. The poor are cannon fodder for their revolution.

CLOWARD AND PIVEN'S CALL TO ARMS:
"THE WEIGHT OF THE POOR"

Cloward and Piven were inspired by Leon Trotsky's metaphorical war against bureaucrats as they devised their break-the-bank strategy for ushering in radical change. This "Cloward-Piven Strategy," a name used in a 1970 *New York Times* article to describe the approach, "had a simple radical appeal" and was "wildly successful, especially in New York City."[168] The Cloward-Piven Strategy relies on strategic disruption, or what Piven calls the power "to shut it down." This power is nothing new. It has been the basic tool of the labor movement ever since the first worker walked off the job. But the labor movement didn't traditionally try to disrupt systems by overwhelming them with impossible demands. Unions often lacked ulterior motives. Focusing on the short term, they wanted to win a better deal for their members, not overthrow the American system of government. The use of the disruptive power outside labor disputes and for subversive purposes, as Cloward and Piven called for, was a significant strategic innovation for the radical Left. NWRO, ACORN, and countless other radical groups have followed the Cloward-Piven Strategy in order to promote a revolutionary transformation of American society.

It is clear from the body of their work that Cloward and Piven delight in attacking the welfare system, which they regard as an evil appendage of the capitalist system. They also despise the welfare regime because they consider it demeaning. Their contempt for America's relief architecture is a sentiment not shared by most Americans today and it was definitely not shared by the public in the 1960s. The dominant view then and now is that those who are dependent on taxpayers for support have little standing to complain about the system. This is not to say that Americans lack compassion, but there are limits. Whether welfare is demeaning to recipients is not the foremost concern of most Americans. They are far more concerned that welfare recipients take steps to become self-sufficient. Most Americans would probably view any petty humiliations built into the welfare apparatus as the cost recipients must pay for making society support them. Beggars cannot be choosers.

Ironically, decades of leftist activism and propaganda have destigmatized welfare somewhat and this cannot be a good thing for a free, productive society. Making it easy for nonproductive people to become drains on the public purse, long a goal of ACORN, is in itself a profoundly inhumane, antisocial act. Benjamin Franklin's summing up of the prevailing American sentiment of his day holds just as true in our own: "I think the best way of doing good to the poor, is not making them easy in poverty, but leading or driving them out of it."

Cloward and Piven raged against the welfare system, but not because they embraced the homespun all-American common sense of Franklin. They believed the relief regime was designed to bribe the poor into acquiescence in order to prevent them from overthrowing capitalism. "[P]ublic benefits have been designed to placate unrest among the poor and to deflect any political articulation of this unrest," they write.[169] They considered it morally unconscionable for society to discourage applicants from applying for relief. They denounced the welfare system, which "serves to celebrate the virtue of all work, and deters actual or potential workers from seeking aid."[170]

The relief policies of the capitalist welfare conspiracy were designed not only "to mute civil disorder" but also "to reinforce work norms." One of the ways the welfare system controls the poor is by granting relief "on condition that they behave in certain ways and, most important, on condition that they work." The primary function of poor relief programs is

> to regulate labor, and they do that in two general ways. First, when mass unemployment leads to outbreaks of turmoil, relief programs are ordinarily initiated to absorb and control enough of the unemployed to restore order; then, as turbulence subsides, the relief system contracts, expelling those who are needed to populate the labor market.[171]

The welfare system, which Cloward and Piven abhorred, "entrenches and reinforces" the "powerlessness" of the poor.[172] They believed it had to be destroyed and replaced with a guaranteed income scheme which paid Americans to sit on the couch, eat junk food, and watch TV soap operas all day. That Cloward and Piven were willing to condemn millions of people to government dependency, to trap them and generations of their descendants for life in a system they themselves considered loathsome and miserable, all in the hope that it might lead the poor to violently rise up and bring about a socialist counter-revolution in America, tells you all you need to know about their moral code.

Ironically, Cloward and Piven were striving to implement a policy idea advanced by someone from the other end of the political spectrum. The idea of a guaranteed, taxpayer-support annual income scheme was espoused in the 1950s by famed conservative economist Milton Friedman, who somehow fantasized that it would curb the appetite of the welfare state. It was Friedman's "only bad" idea, writes David Frum.

> He wanted to abolish all government assistance to individuals—no more minimum wage, no more unemployment insurance, no more old-age pensions, no more public housing, no more welfare, no more survivors' payments to widows, no more disability benefits— and replace it with a government guarantee that everyone in need would be topped up to a decent minimum . . . If you earned nothing, you'd get a cheque for $3,000. If you earned $1,500, you'd get an additional $1,500. If you earned $3,001, you were on your own.

President Richard Nixon flirted with the guaranteed income proposal and tested it in an experiment in Portland, Oregon, in 1969. In practice it was a disaster and Nixon abandoned the idea. The problem is that "when the government appears to cease to stigmatize non-work—if, in fact, it formally endorses the proposition that non-work may well be a rational economic choice—it will lure into non-work thousands of self-respecting, low-income people who might otherwise have been appalled by the thought of taking a handout."[173]

On this issue, Cloward and Piven, who were not economists, had more common sense than Friedman. They understood the economics of incentives. They knew that welfare was a narcotic that robbed people of ambition and promoted a host of social pathologies—and yet they wanted to push welfare on the poor.

PACKING THE WELFARE ROLLS

Cloward and Piven's model of political and economic subversion called upon activists to pack the welfare rolls in order to spread dependency, bankrupt the government, and cause uprisings against the capitalist system. According to Richard Poe:

> This was an example of what are commonly called Trojan Horse movements—mass movements whose outward purpose seems to be providing material help to the downtrodden, but whose real objective is to draft poor people into service as revolutionary foot soldiers; to mobilize poor people en masse to overwhelm government agencies with a flood of demands beyond the capacity of those agencies to meet. The flood of demands was calculated to break the budget, jam the bureaucratic gears into gridlock, and bring the system crashing down. Fear, turmoil, violence and economic collapse would accompany such a breakdown—providing perfect conditions for fostering radical change.[174]

Cloward and Piven counseled that instead of using the state to buy off the poor with government handouts, activists should work to undermine the welfare system in an effort to bring about its collapse, which would spark a political and economic crisis that would shake America to its core. As the poor rebelled, then "the rest of society" would give in to their demands, Cloward reasoned. "Disruptive tactics" were the only means by which low-income people could exert "effective political influence." Using the language of the looter, Cloward explained that the strategy was a smash-and-grab approach to redistribution. "Our strategy always was, grab what you can and run like hell," he said. And never let a good crisis go to waste. "Ours was much more of a guerrilla strategy. Hit the centers, drive up the rolls, take advantage of the times to get something for people while you can." Cloward and Piven outlined their plans to give the fledgling welfare rights movement a major boost in an article titled "The Weight of the Poor: A Strategy to End Poverty." The essay was a runaway success on the Left. Cloward boasted to the *New York Times* that the magazine that published it sold an unprecedented 30,000 reprints.[175]

Cloward and Piven's more than 6,000-word article appeared May 2, 1966, in the pages of *The Nation*.[176] They acknowledged their goal was government-directed "income redistribution" and claimed if their strategy were carried out, "a political crisis would result that could lead to legislation for a guaranteed annual income and thus an end to poverty." Another side benefit would be that those activist groups packing the welfare rolls would earn the loyalty of new welfare recipients, some of whom themselves would join in the fight by becoming active in organizing. "If organizers can deliver millions of dollars in cash benefits to the ghetto masses, it seems reasonable to expect that the masses will deliver their loyalties to their benefactors," they wrote.

Many Americans, they noted, were eligible for welfare but were not receiving it: "The discrepancy is not an accident stemming from bureaucratic inefficiency; rather, it is an integral feature of the welfare system which, if challenged, would precipitate a profound financial and political crisis." They noted disapprovingly that only about 50 percent of those eligible for welfare were actually on the rolls because the system discouraged people from signing up. Puffed up with contemptuous indignation, they mocked responsible Americans for not being enthusiastic about welfare as a concept. Society "is wholly and self-righteously oriented toward getting people off the welfare rolls." They proposed ignoring the public's abiding distaste for government dependency and making a crisis happen by proceeding with "a massive drive to recruit the poor *onto* the welfare rolls." [emphasis in original] President Johnson's Great Society effort wasn't enough. It was a "feeble," pork-barrel response to society's ills that served only "to reinforce the allegiance of growing ghetto constituencies to the national Democratic Administration," they opined.

Cloward and Piven seethed that welfare systems attempted to keep expenditures low "by failing to inform people of the rights available to them; by intimidating and shaming them to the degree that they are reluctant either to apply or to press claims, and by arbitrarily denying benefits to those who are eligible." Welfare drives in large cities would turn the situation around by forcing "action on a new federal program to distribute income, eliminating the present public welfare system and alleviating the abject poverty which it perpetrates." A series of campaigns to get more people on the welfare rolls and to encourage current recipients to squeeze every last penny from the system "would produce bureaucratic disruption in welfare agencies and fiscal disruption in local and state governments." This in turn would "generate severe political strains, and deepen existing divisions among elements in the big-city Democratic coalition: the remaining white middle class, the white working-class ethnic groups and the growing minority poor." In order to prevent the Democratic Party's electoral coalitions from coming apart, "a national Democratic administration would be constrained to advance a federal solution to poverty that would override local welfare failures, local class and racial conflicts and local revenue dilemmas." This attack on local bureaucrats, coupled with "the collapse of current financing arrangements," would generate "powerful forces" that would push "for major economic reforms at the national level."

Cloward and Piven were offended that policymakers were responsive to the electorate and that they dared to attach strings to welfare payments in order to encourage recipients to improve their lives. It was "oppression" that welfare recipients could be required to better themselves by attending literacy classes and receiving medical or vocational rehabilitation. Conditioning benefits violates the "civil liberties" of the poor. Guaranteeing "the right to income" would eliminate such "pervasive oppression," they wrote. The ignorance of poor people about their welfare "rights" could be remedied through a "massive educational campaign." Brochures could be drafted, advertisements could be made in newspapers and broadcast on the radio and "[l]eaders of social, religious, fraternal and political groups in the slums should also be enlisted to recruit the eligible to the rolls." Because the campaign is aimed at informing people "of their legal rights under a government program," it would be perceived as "a civic education drive" which "will lend it legitimacy," they wrote.

Welfare rights organizers will have to push the system to the brink, they continued. Organizers will have to threaten legal action and follow through. Volunteer lawyers would be needed to help with only some of the legal cases. "[M]ost cases will not require an expert knowledge of law, but only of welfare regulations; the rules can be learned by laymen, including welfare recipients themselves (who can help to man 'information and advocacy' centers)." [parenthetical statement in original] Any potential welfare recipients' resistance to going on the dole could be overcome with "organized demonstrations to create a climate of militancy." Organized mass protests and in-your-face confrontations would help to remove the stigma associated with receiving welfare and motivate the poor to rise up and seize what society owed them. As the crisis deepened, the mass media could be used "to inform the broader liberal community about the inefficiencies and injustices of welfare" and to promote "a new federal income distribution program." They noted that organizations funded by the federal government under the War on Poverty could be used to advance the strategy. "[W]hether they participate or not, they constitute a growing network of resources to which people can be referred for help in establishing and maintaining entitlements. In the final analysis, it does not matter who helps people to get on the rolls or to get additional entitlements, so long as the job is done."

A political movement should be forged out of this welfare rights organizing push using "cadres"—a Communist term meaning "professional revolutionaries"—of "aggressive organizers" from churches, the civil rights movement, and "militant low-income organizations like those formed by the Industrial Areas Foundation (that is, by Saul Alinsky), and from other groups on the Left," they wrote. [parenthetical statement in original] Although past poor people's movements had failed, the new strategy would succeed because it promised quick cash for new welfare recipients. "This is a point of some importance because, whereas America's poor have not been moved in any number by radical political ideologies, they have sometimes been moved by their economic interests," they wrote. Union leaders, they noted, recognize that their power is "almost entirely" dependent on their ability "to provide economic rewards to members." Rent strikes in Northern cities appealed to tenants not because they endorsed "radical ideologies," but because the "tenants have been attracted by the promise that housing improvements would quickly be made if they withheld their rent."

The Cloward-Piven Strategy was also economical, they wrote. "[O]ne need not ask more of most of the poor than that they claim lawful benefits." Large organizations would not be needed to keep the strategy going because it would keep moving forward on its momentum. "Once eligibility for basic food and rent grants is established, the drain on local resources persists indefinitely." The welfare crisis created by the strategy would "produce dramatic local political crisis, disrupting and exposing rifts among urban groups." It would also promote racial conflict within the Democratic Party's coalition and this would be helpful in advancing the cause, they wrote. "Group conflict, spelling political crisis for the local party apparatus, would thus become acute as welfare rolls mounted and the strains on local budgets became more severe." Because welfare costs are usually shared between the federal, state, and local governments, the "crisis in the cities would intensify the struggle over revenues that is chronic in relations between cities and states." Cities would likely be unable to get bailouts from their state governments and the federal government would have to come to their rescue. "[A] federal income program would not only redeem local governments from the immediate crisis but would permanently relieve them of the financially and politically onerous burdens of public welfare." Localities should be delighted to have welfare provision responsibilities taken off their hands because it "generates support from none and hostility from many, not least of all welfare recipients," they wrote.

Not everyone on the Left was enamored of the Cloward-Piven Strategy when it was first revealed. Former Marxist Ron Radosh, the nation's foremost expert on Communist traitors Julius and Ethel Rosenberg, attended a presentation Piven gave on the strategy in the 1960s. "I remember her saying in this presentation that everybody should register for welfare and remember the response of the people at that talk was we all thought she was nuts—and remember we were on the left," Radosh said in an interview. "We thought that that was the most destructive, crazy thing that we'd ever heard." In the end it didn't matter whether Radosh and other leftists approved of the approach. The flooding-the-welfare-rolls strategy didn't need a lot of academic support. It would flourish as long as the poor could be duped into serving as pawns.

INSPIRED BY TROTSKY:
THE SIGNIFICANCE OF THE PHRASE
"THE WEIGHT OF THE POOR"

Why would two American academics pick such an unusual name, "The Weight of the Poor," for the most important article of their lives, a call to arms for a quintessentially un-American revolution? Could it be because they were inspired by, and even followers of, the blood-thirsty Communist Leon Trotsky, who coined the phrase?

It's a truly odd-sounding title for a *cri de coeur*, especially since most Americans are inclined to think the word *weight* in this context refers to the burden the poor place on society. (An informal survey of a dozen people confirmed my suspicion—only one gave an unexpected answer.) In fact, *weight* in this case refers to the *influence* or *power* of the poor. Throughout the seminal article, Cloward and Piven describe how the weight of the poor may be used as a battering ram against the welfare system, and by extension, against the American system itself.

In a fascinating non-coincidence, the phrase "the weight of the poor," appears in a tract written by Bolshevik leader Trotsky in the early days of Communist Russia.[177] This is significant because Trotsky was arguably an ideological purist: a Communist's Communist. During the Russian Civil War, he "was surpassed by none in his advocacy of dictatorial ruthlessness and authoritarianism. He frankly defended every means of violence and intimidation for the compelling end of revolutionary victory."[178] Trotsky was an outspoken supporter of terrorism as a tactic in the revolutionary struggle. He argued that Communists who reject "terrorism in principle" weren't real Communists.[179]

Although differentiating totalitarian mass murderers such as Trotsky and Joseph Stalin on minor doctrinal points is largely an exercise in futility, like discussing how Adolf Hitler and Joseph Goebbels might have differed in drafting press releases, it seems fair to say that Trotsky's rigid utopian fanaticism was rejected by the Soviet Communist establishment. Stalin, as monstrous as he was, was arguably less radical than the ultra-leftist Trotsky, whose followers were sometimes known by the pejorative terms "Trotskyites" or simply "Trots." Stalin favored the "Socialism in One Country" model and was content to focus on building the revolution in the USSR so that it could serve as an inspiration to revolutionaries worldwide. But the even more fanatical Trotsky wanted change, and like the Association of Community Organizations for Reform *Now*, he wanted it *now!* Trotsky favored "permanent revolution" that spread beyond the Soviet Union's borders, setting the entire world on fire in the process. "Lenin referred to people like that as suffering from an infantile disorder," former Communist Party USA (CPUSA) recruiter Eugene Genovese said in an interview.

To an extent, the various factions that competed for power in the USSR after Lenin's death in 1924 made up rationalizations to justify their positions as they went along. "Basically it was a struggle for power in the Soviet Union and when that happens you begin to invent all sorts of *isms*, and the Trotskyists became the anti-Stalinist Communists as it were," said Genovese, a scholar of slavery and the American South who became a conservative late in life. During and after the Stalin-Trotsky power struggle, the U.S. Communist Party was controlled by Stalinists, including, at the time, Genovese. The Stalinists and the Trotskyists "fought each other tooth and nail," he said. "We were a lot stronger than they were but they were very well organized and even though their numbers were small they were very effective in certain areas [such as] the trade union movement and on the campuses." Said Genovese, "I wouldn't say I was scared of them but I certainly respected their abilities. I didn't underestimate them."

In 1940, years after he lost out in the power struggle with Soviet dictator Joseph Stalin, Trotsky was assassinated on Stalin's orders.

Another principal difference between Stalin and Trotsky was how they viewed bureaucrats. Trotsky bemoaned the rising power of what in his view was the meddlesome bureaucracy of the Soviet state. Bureaucrats, in Trotsky's view, were preventing true socialist so-called democracy, that is, what Karl Marx called the "dictatorship of the proletariat," from coming into being. In the *Platform of the Joint Opposition*, Trotsky complained in 1927 that the *weight*, or influence, of the poor, who were the very reason for carrying out the Communist revolution, was being diminished in the Communist Party:

> The League of Communist Youth in the country is more and more losing its proletarian and poor peasant support. Its cultural and economic work in the country has for its main object the development of individual farms. The relative *weight of the poor* is systematically falling everywhere in the general composition of the rural branches, in the active membership, in the nucleus of party members. Along with the continual diminishing of the influx of young town workers, the League is filling up in the countryside with middle and well-off peasant youth.[180] [emphasis added]

Trotsky, who had been Soviet minister of war and head of the Red Army, urged that "war" be "waged by the workers and farm-hands with the support of the poor peasants, and with the alliance of the middle peasants against our own kulaks, new bourgeoisie, bureaucrats . . ."

Trotsky used the word *weight* in the sense of *power* or *influence* elsewhere in the essay too. He criticized "[t]he Stalin course," which would lead "to a lowering of the relative weight of the socialist element." He wrote of "a lowering of the relative weight of the proletariat in Soviet society," and of "a reduction in the relative economic weight of the middle peasant." He wrote also of the "relative economic weight" of the "co-operating peasantry," of a desire to augment "our relative weight in world economy," and of "an increased activity and weight of the proletariat in all the institutions and organs of the Soviet State without exception."

Having been exiled from the Soviet Union, Trotsky hated everything having to do with Stalin, including his bureaucrats. In Trotsky's view, they were preventing social progress by not allowing the Communist revolution to move forward to its next glorious stage. In *The Revolution Betrayed*, published in 1937, Trotsky denounced the bureaucracy, "which strangles the workers' movement in capitalist countries." Emphasizing his argument, he wrote, "The name of that social guild which holds back and paralyzes all the guilds of the Soviet economy is—the bureaucracy." He criticized the bureaucracy for "its intermediary and regulating function, its concern to maintain social ranks, and its exploitation of the state apparatus for personal goals."[181]

"In bourgeois society," that is, in such places as America, Trotsky might have meant, "the bureaucracy represents the interests of a possessing and educated class, which has at its disposal innumerable means of everyday control over its administration of affairs," he wrote. The bureaucracy in the USSR was "Thermidorian," a reference to the Thermidorian Reaction, a revolt that brought the most extreme phase of the French Revolution to its conclusion. The rant continued:

As a conscious political force the bureaucracy has betrayed the revolution. But a victorious revolution is fortunately not only a program and a banner, not only political institutions, but also a system of social relations. To betray it is not enough. You have to overthrow it. The October revolution has been betrayed by the ruling stratum, but not yet overthrown. It has a great power of resistance, coinciding with the established property relations, with the living force of the proletariat, the consciousness of its best elements, the impasse of world capitalism, and the inevitability of world revolution.

Surely Cloward and Piven hated the bureaucrats enforcing what they considered to be the capitalist system's oppressive welfare system at least as much as Trotsky hated Stalin's bureaucrats. Even though they didn't state it explicit in "The Weight of the Poor," they must have viewed welfare case workers as the enemy because those bureaucrats did what Cloward and Piven viewed as dirty work. Like a gangster who explains to you "it's strictly business" before he slits your throat, their hatred was not personal, but political. To borrow the words of Saul Alinsky, they must have hated "these individuals not as persons but as symbols representing ideas or interests . . . inimical to the welfare of the people."[182]

Recall the supposed horrors Cloward and Piven catalogued in "The Weight of the Poor" as they condemned "the inefficiencies and injustices of welfare." Welfare systems keep costs low by failing to advise people of their rights. They shame the poor into inaction and arbitrarily reject claims. They oppress welfare recipients and deprive them of their "civil liberties." Bureaucrats say no to people and offer new arrivals from other cities bus tickets to go back to where they came from. It is their job to trim the welfare rolls, not to help people.

Anyone with Cloward and Piven's beliefs isn't likely to harbor warm feelings for bureaucrats—and they didn't. In an article titled "The Professional Bureaucracies," published six years after "The Weight of the Poor," they open fire on bureaucracies and sound very much like Trotsky while doing it. It's Trotsky versus Stalin, American-style, but without the intrigue and ice-axes. "The growth of the bureaucracies of the welfare state has meant the diminished influence of low-income people in public spheres," they write. They complain that federal social programs "permit bureaucratic usurpation of power" and extend "bureaucratic control" over poor people. "The professional bureaucracies represent a new system of public action, only occasionally subject to electoral control." This undue control over the poor is exercised by "the bureaucracies, and the professional associations linked to the bureaucracies," which are controlled by "middle-class groups."[183]

CLOWARD AND PIVEN:
KEEP BLACK AMERICANS IN THEIR PLACE

Cloward and Piven also made it clear they believed that black Americans could be used to help precipitate the crisis they needed to overthrow the system. They argued that blacks hated bureaucrats and that that hatred could be leveraged to an advantage. Like Saul Alinsky, the two radical Marxists looked down on liberals for shunning aggressive, disruptive tactics aimed at changing society. They wrote that as low-income blacks began protesting in the early 1960s, liberals felt poor blacks ought "to seek redress like proper Americans, informing themselves about the institutional practices which are the source of their grievances, negotiating with institutions and disciplined pressure at the polls . . . We think this argument wrong. The disruptive tactics used by blacks were in fact their only resource for political influence."[184] Echoing a sentiment expressed by radical lawyer William Kunstler—defender of the Chicago Seven antiwar protesters, accused of crossing state lines to incite riots at the 1968 Democratic National Convention—they write that growing numbers "of the black poor view police, firemen, teachers, public-welfare workers and other city employees as their oppressors." The services the police provide, in particular, "take on the character of an army of occupation in the ghetto." The welfare state itself is racist and white social workers use it to perpetrate a kind of genocide-by-bureaucracy against blacks, they argue: "In education and public welfare, the effects of cleavage between white staff and black recipients are even more pervasive and tragic, for by blocking and distorting the delivery of these services white staffs virtually fix the life chances of the black poor."[185]

In discussing race, Cloward and Piven sound at times like they ought to be donning Black Panther uniforms and raising their arms in a clenched-fist salute. Cloward and Piven claim that blending in with white society would, in a sense, make blacks Uncle Toms in America, which the professors considered to be irretrievably racist. "One day an interpretation of American racism will be written, and it will say that White supremacy ultimately succeeded because the African

American was led to believe that he could have no reality, no identity, except as a reflection of whites," they wrote. It is necessary "to protect the African American from the devastating effects of American racism by building black pride, black solidarity, and black power."[186]

To build this "black power," blacks should stay in urban ghettos and turn them into political power bases. In a telling essay titled, "The Case Against Urban Desegregation," they wrote, "If the African American is to develop the power to enter the mainstream of American life, it is separatism—not integration—that will be essential to achieve results in certain institutional arenas." The black American would be better off "consolidating his power within the central city" in order to "have some impact on the environment of the ghetto itself." Blacks have to "organize as a bloc." Achieving "effective separatist power" would not be accomplished by arguing "the ghetto must be dispersed."[187]

Racial integration, they argued, is meaningless without redistribution. Physical desegregation would actually block blacks from being integrated "in the institutional life of this society." Integration has to be viewed "not as the mingling of bodies in school and neighborhood but as participation in and shared control over the major institutional spheres of American life." This can only be achieved by "developing communal associations that can be bases for power—not of dispersing a community that is powerless." The breakdown of the family and other social problems in the black community won't be helped by integration. Instead, mountains of money have to be thrown at the black ghettos and black power must be promoted in order to prevent the black minority from being submerged in the white majority. Moreover, it was a "myth," they wrote, that racial integration efforts were "bringing better housing to the negro." Activists should forget about integrating black neighborhoods and instead try to bring more government money to the ghetto. "[A]lthough schools that are racially and economically heterogeneous are probably superior, removing class inequities in the quality of teachers and programs is also an important goal—and a far more realistic one." Even "huge rebuilding programs" would probably not advance desegregation, they wrote.[188]

For Cloward and Piven, naming the essay "The Weight of the Poor" made perfect sense. It was more than a witty, clever, cryptic tribute to Trotsky; it was a revolutionary incitement against the American system dedicated to a revolutionary Communist they must have admired. Sharing Trotsky's visceral hatred of bureaucrats who stand in the way of social progress, Cloward and Piven created an urban terrorist group, NWRO, to execute their plan to destroy the welfare system and usher in an era of socialism in America. Theirs was a made-in-America approach to radical agitation that played on Americans' distrust of government and government's handmaids, the bureaucrats. Most Americans would find it difficult to get upset with an activist group for giving bureaucrats and social workers hell—such actions might even resonate to an extent with right-wingers and other Americans otherwise unsympathetic to ACORN. Americans certainly weren't likely to flood their congressional representatives' offices with angry telephone calls because bureaucrats were being mistreated.

Nowadays, as commentator Glenn Beck opines on the Cloward-Piven Strategy routinely on his TV and radio shows,[189] Americans are righteously incensed. "Cloward and Piven," said Beck, "sought to hasten the fall of capitalism by overloading the government with a flood of impossible demands, thus pushing society into crisis and economic collapse, forcing a complete overhaul of the way our government redistributes income—also known as forcing as many people on welfare as possible."[190] Radical leftists cannot abide being exposed and ridiculed, so now Piven and *The Nation* are playing dumb, as if the strategy described in "The Weight of the Poor" had been aimed narrowly at welfare reform, instead of at a socialist transformation of society. Piven describes Beck's lectures as "silly" and "not accurate." Instead of addressing the allegations, she smears Beck, vilifying him as a supposed racist and demagogue.

In his view, the reason for all sorts of developments in American society over the last 40 years are in that article that you have there. And in fact, that article was as much a reflection of things that were already happening in the society as it was plan, a design. It was partly a plan or a design, but it was a design that tried to take into account, to register, accounts that were already unfolding in the late 1960s. But, even taking that into account, that article—in his diagram he attributes the, all sorts of developments, from ACORN to Obama to the financial crisis to these ideas, to an article published in a little magazine. He's looking for a scapegoat. The idea is to say that everything would be nice in American society if it wasn't for these Columbia professors. He always calls us Columbia professors. If it wasn't for their nasty scheming, no financial crisis. Can you think of anything sillier than to attribute the financial crisis to an article published in a low-circulation magazine in 1966? So, it's an old technique of right-wing ideologues, finding a scapegoat, somebody preferably who is not a farmer, an intellectual, and attributing things that go wrong in American society to somebody who's foreign or dark-skinned or an intellectual.[191]

The historical record reflects the fact that Cloward and Piven bragged for years about the destructive, transformative impact that their strategy would have on America. Their writings also demonstrate that they were shrewd observers of history and as such were surely aware that once those forces are unleashed they cannot be easily controlled. Their assertion that their goal was merely to replace welfare programs with a guaranteed annual income scheme is simply not believable. These apostles of depravity fervently wanted to unleash chaos on America. They said so over and over and over again.

Confronted with actual evidence of Cloward and Piven's malice, the best response Richard Kim, a senior editor at *The Nation*, can muster is to ridicule and defame Beck for letting Americans know about this "crap," as he puts it. "All of this, of course, is a reactionary paranoid fantasy," he writes. Tracking all the steps Cloward and Piven took to carry out their plan is "looniness" and like "a Scooby-Doo comic mystery." Those who believe in the Cloward-Piven Strategy are racist, he suggests: "Racial and class resentments, however, are never far from the surface, no matter which subject is slotted into the great Cloward-Piven conspiracy machine." The strategy itself, as described by Tea Party supporters is a "fun-house-mirror version of Naomi Klein's Shock Doctrine theory," Kim writes, referencing an actual professional conspiracy theorist's paranoid fantasy that is widely believed on the Left and wholly unsupported by facts. And the Tea Party itself is chock full of bad, desperate, crazy people, he writes, describing the movement as "an uneasy conclave of Ayn Rand secular libertarians and fundamentalist Christian evangelicals; it contains birthers, Birchers, racists, xenophobes, Ron Paulites, cold warriors, Zionists, constitutionalists, vanilla Republicans looking for a high and militia-style survivalists." Kim, who must believe his magazine's readers are as dumb as a bag of hammers, advances the nonsensical argument that Cloward and Piven couldn't possibly have wanted to overthrow capitalism because "the words 'capital' and 'capitalism' never appear in their article." (*Eureka!* he may have cried out as he wrote the latter words.) Kim also gets in a dig against David Horowitz, accusing him of coining the term, "Cloward-Piven Strategy," to describe what he called the two academics' "strategy of forcing political change through orchestrated crisis." In fact, as discussed earlier in this book, the *New York Times* used the expression four decades ago.[192]

FIVE

Maximum Eligible Participation: ACORN's Welfare Strategy

A CORN FOUNDER WADE Rathke wants to use the Internet and other modern technology to implement the Cloward-Piven Strategy. He has renamed it the "Maximum Eligible Participation" Solution, which is a variation of "maximum feasible participation" from the War on Poverty.

In his book, *Citizen Wealth: Winning the Campaign to Save Working Families,* Rathke devotes an entire chapter to the plan, hailing "Cloward and Piven's exciting call to arms." With pride he notes that the National Welfare Rights Organization that they created and he worked for caused "a flood tide from its work that allowed many boats to rise, including the level of participation in government assistance programs."

Under Rathke's leadership, ACORN vigorously pushed its low-income membership and members of the public to claim the misnamed Earned Income Tax Credit (EITC). It's welfare with a feel-good name. The only advantage of the EITC over traditional welfare handouts is that, arguably, it does not provide a disincentive for work. Claimants have to be working and file a tax return with the IRS in order to claim it. ACORN is especially proud of a welfare scheme it enacted in Washington State. The group led a successful campaign in 2008 to enact a "Working Families Credit" in the state, the first state-level EITC in a state that doesn't have an income tax. Thanks to ACORN's agitation, all New England states except Connecticut that have an income tax have a state EITC.[193]

President Clinton served as a pitchman for the fraud-ridden EITC program at an ACORN press conference:

> Can you imagine working all week and instead of cashing your paycheck, you rip it up? If you earn under $35,000 a year and you're not claiming your Earned Income Tax Credit, then you're doing just that—throwing away your hard-earned money. The main idea of EITC is still the old idea of the American Dream, that if you work hard and play by the rules, you ought to have a decent life, and a chance for your children to have a better one. I hope this initiative helps more Americans achieve their dreams and reaches those Americans whose lives were shattered by last year's hurricanes.[194]

Of course, it never occurred to ACORN and Clinton that the American Dream isn't supposed to be based on welfare or special interest-driven tax loopholes.

Rathke urges a new drive to get Americans on relief. "[I]t is hard to believe that we cannot assemble the troops to mount a campaign for maximum eligible participation that harvests the opportunities and dollars already available if we could achieve full utilization of existing programs," he writes.

In an interview with DailyKos blogger Robert Ellman, Rathke complains bitterly that Americans are not getting all the government benefits to which they are legally entitled. Ellman unwittingly lays bare the entitlement mentality that so many on the far Left possess. The blogger asks if the "lack of participation" in food stamps, Medicaid, and the State Children's Health Insurance Program (S-CHIP), all of which many eligible people are not claiming, is "a failure of government, political will, or a culture that demonizes poor people?" Rathke responds, "Once again you've hit the trifecta."

The system is "still criminalizing poor people, requiring fingerprints in states like Florida and Texas and California," he says. "For even simple welfare applications and food stamp applications, we are going out of our way . . . to make it almost easier to do anything in the world other than get benefits that people are legally entitled to." Technology should be employed "to make sure everything that's legally entitled to people actually finally gets to people." There is no reason not to do this, Rathke argues.

> Why we're forcing everybody to fill out a million forms, come up with a million different pieces of paper when we could do almost all of it through computers, do it quickly, verify it, keep the records, you know, in PDFs or scanned documents or whatever. There's a lot of people who know how to do this more than you and I, but this could be a huge breakthrough in eligibility.

Rathke asks, "Why not have computers in grocery stores and community centers—and they are in many libraries now—and in churches and synagogues so that people in working communities have easy access to the software to apply for these benefits." Many states now give welfare recipients a plastic credit card-like card so they "can get the food stamps on a card so it's less stigmatizing," he adds.[195]

Rathke should be delighted that even without his high tech encouragement to abandon the work ethic, more Americans than ever are on food stamps. In June 2010 as the unemployment rate was close to a 27-year high, a record 41.3 million Americans received Supplemental Nutrition Assistance Program subsidies. This is more than one eighth of the entire U.S. population, a leap of 18% from a year before. In 2011, the number of recipients is expected to climb to 43.3 million.[196]

USING THE WEIGHT OF THE POOR
IN THE ELECTORAL SYSTEM

Strictly speaking, the Cloward-Piven Strategy refers only to the break-the-bank welfare strategy unveiled in "The Weight of the Poor." But

Cloward and Piven plotted other disruptive assaults on the American system aimed at overthrowing the existing order by overwhelming governmental systems with impossible demands. Among conservative political junkies the phrase "Cloward-Piven" has become shorthand for such antisocial enterprises.

Unlike packing the welfare rolls, registering voters isn't on its face a subversive activity aimed at overwhelming the system. Registering voters seems like a noble, public-spirited activity. But Cloward and Piven found a way to give it a subversive tinge. They formulated a plan to swamp voter rolls with low-income people in order to eat away at the limited government underpinnings of the republic. The theory was that the newly registered poor would start voting to take wealth away from those who earned it. The proposal reinforces the timeless wisdom of libertarian curmudgeon H.L. Mencken that "every election is a sort of advance auction of stolen goods." Cloward and Piven explained their approach in an article titled "Toward a Class-Based Realignment of American Politics: A Movement Strategy," that ran in ACORN's magazine, *Social Policy*, in 1983. The two professors might as well have named it "The Weight of the Poor—Part Two."

Their strategy was to enroll "massive numbers of new voters," but only those that would push the Democratic Party to port:

[E]nlisting millions of new and politicized voters is the way to create an electoral environment hospitable to fundamental change in American society. An enlarged and politicized electorate will sustain and encourage the movements in American society that are already working for the rights of women and minorities, for the protection of the social programs, and for transformation of foreign policy. Equally important, an enlarged and politicized electorate will foster and protect future mass movements from the bottom that the ongoing economic crisis is likely to generate, thus opening American politics to solutions to the economic crisis that express the interests of the lower strata of the population . . . The objective is to accelerate the dealigning forces already at work in American politics, and to promote party realignment along class lines.

In other words, Cloward and Piven wanted to compound and unleash class-based antagonisms in order to promote radical change. They noted that nonvoters tend to be concentrated at the lower end of the socioeconomic scale and are more likely than average Americans "to be dependent on various welfare state programs." In the words of Jesse Jackson during his ACORN-endorsed presidential run in 1984, the unregistered poor were "rocks lyin' around."[197] The academics hoped the strategy would be so successful that it would drive the Democratic Party even further to the Left, bringing back radical leftists who had long grumbled about the party's perceived centrist positions. If this happened, "the retreat by some groups on the left to a third-party alternative would no longer be necessary."[198]

Another factor spurred Cloward and Piven to act: their distaste for Ronald Reagan. When Reagan, whose all-American mom-and-apple-pie antipathy to Big Government helped get him elected, became president in 1981, Cloward and Piven described his ascension in Marxist terms. The Reagan administration and its allies in big business "declared a new class war on the unemployed, the unemployable, and the working poor."[199] Reagan's "attack on welfare state programs is highlighting concrete issues of urgent concern to large numbers of nonvoters." For example, welfare recipients' alarm that their checks might be taken away could be used to force them to become politically involved by voting.[200]

Cloward and Piven urged that the welfare state apparatus be used to destroy the American system. They urged that welfare recipients, who are naturally inclined to support political candidates promising to steal the wealth of productive members of society and redistribute it to the poor, be registered to vote in the same welfare offices where they leech off society. In other words, put them on the voter rolls while they stand in the food stamp lines or pick up welfare checks—the precise moment in which they are most resentful towards the society many of them blame for their failure in life.

OBAMA ENDORSED CLOWARD AND PIVEN'S APPROACH

When he worked for ACORN's Project Vote affiliate in 1992, Barack Obama endorsed the Cloward-Piven plan. "All our people must know that politics and voting affects their lives directly," he was quoted saying in a newspaper column written by the late Vernon Jarrett, father-in-law of Obama White House senior advisor Valerie Jarrett. "If we're registering people in public housing, for an example, we talk about aid cuts and who's responsible," Obama said.[201]

There is no way to overstate just how profoundly antisocial and un-American the Cloward-Piven voter registration strategy is. It is akin to the government handing out taxpayer-purchased burglary tools.

In 1984, conservative activist and OEO veteran Howard Phillips said the plan seemed viable because Great Society programs had "created a vast army of full-time liberal activists whose salaries are paid from the taxes of conservative working people." William I. Greener III, a Republican National Committee spokesman, said at the time that such welfare waiting room voter drives would cause a public backlash. "If social workers are registering while on their tax-paid jobs to achieve partisan advantage for one party or candidate, that's something that voters, as taxpayers, will view dimly."[202] Unfortunately Greener was proven wrong: some conservatives and Republican operatives may have cared, but Americans for the most part didn't. Indeed, many Americans welcomed the convenience of a fast-food approach to voter registration—whether at the welfare office or the department of motor vehicles—and so Cloward, Piven, ACORN, and its allies won that battle.

In their 1983 *Social Policy* article, Cloward and Piven marveled at how the welfare system made it easy for them to undermine the American way of life. "The newly created terrain of the welfare state provides the ideological and organizational opportunities to facilitate voter registration on a vast scale," they noted. Welfare agencies have access to "large numbers of nonvoters who are otherwise dispersed and difficult to reach." With the Reagan administration pushing pro-business policies "in the midst of an economic crisis," the time was "ripe for issue-oriented drives among the millions of unregistered clients of the welfare state who can plainly be told that the corporate-Republican alliance is determined to make deep slashes in the income-support programs, and that the Democratic party will not fight back vigorously unless its ranks are augmented by social-program beneficiaries." One can almost picture Cloward and Piven rubbing their hands together in anticipation as they write this: "[T]he organizing networks of the welfare state offer the opportunity for registration drives of unprecedented magnitude, since it brings together millions of people. They congregate in its lines and in its waiting rooms, and it is there that they can be efficiently registered."[203]

Conspicuously absent in the article was the hostility they expressed toward bureaucrats in "The Weight of the Poor." Ever adaptable, Cloward and Piven must have realized that some bureaucrats could become allies in the fight to undo America. Social workers (they called them "human-service workers") could be enlisted in the effort to place welfare recipients on the voting rolls. In a feat of cognitive dissonance only the most committed intellectuals could pull off without their heads exploding, suddenly not all social workers were bureaucrats. The authors introduced a dichotomy that was not present in "The Weight of the Poor:" distinctions between management bureaucrats and worker bureaucrats. Those running the welfare agencies were *bad* bureaucrats and their subordinates were *good* bureaucrats. The good bureaucrats were human-service workers, those well-intentioned souls who were the "natural allies" of welfare recipients because "workers and clients both have stakes in the social programs." They explained that:

Millions of human-service workers regularly interact with tens of millions of nonvoters in hospital social-service departments, day-care centers, settlement houses, local development corporations, family service agencies, senior-citizen centers, Supplemental Security Income offices, unemployment offices, welfare waiting rooms, public housing projects, and in scores of other agencies. There are other institutions that provide similar linkages. Unions of low-wage workers are an obvious example, for leaders can use the union apparatus to reach members who depend on welfare state benefits. The thousands of churches in the ghettoes and barrios involve millions of people, and the ability of church leaders to induce them to register and vote by making economic rights the rallying cry is probably enormous. Nevertheless, it is human-service workers who are the most strategically placed.[204]

Human-service workers already "think of themselves as politically powerless," but with Reagan in the White House they felt particularly vulnerable as their jobs could be "wiped out, and their clients driven into greater misery," Cloward and Piven opined. These workers could become the vanguard of a new revolution.

In tens of millions of everyday transactions, they can warn clients about the social-program cuts and the longer-term dangers of the corporate solution, and they can distribute registration forms while making issue-oriented but nonpartisan appeals about the importance of registering and voting. Because of the sheer growth of the welfare state, in other words, human-service workers—*more than any other single group*—now have the capacity to set forces in motion leading to a class-based political realignment.[205]

PROJECT VOTE FLOODS VOTER ROLLS
WITH WELFARE RECIPIENTS

Cloward and Piven also single out for praise ACORN's Project Vote subsidiary, which they describe as a group that registers the poor "in public-housing projects where the Reagan Administration rent rises are being felt, and in other locations where people are gathered by the numerous programs of the welfare state." Project Vote's "registration strategy exploits two of the three organizing opportunities afforded by the growth of the welfare state: the issues raised by the attack on the social programs, and the way the social programs concentrate nonvoters." Project Vote leverages the anger of the poor by sending out volunteer voter registrars in cities on the day that food stamp recipients get their vouchers by mail.

> As lines begin to form at the banks and check-cashing centers, the volunteers distribute fliers dramatizing past and pending cuts in the food stamp program, pass out voter registration forms, and warn that food stamp benefits will be lost unless people register and vote . . .These tactics make it possible for a small group of volunteers to register hundreds of people in a day.[206]

Sanford Newman, founder of ACORN affiliate Project Vote, freely admitted Project Vote's work helped the Left almost exclusively. "While our work is nonpartisan, it is realistic to assume that upward of 90 percent of the people we register on unemployment and other social service distribution lines will oppose politicians who have supported cuts in the programs on which they rely," he said. "They are likely to vote Democratic in most instances."[207]

Republicans noticed the efforts of Project Vote and the groups that adopted its voter registration model. In 1984, Texas GOP chairman George W. Strake voiced concerns about a policy that used state taxpayer resources to register people who were likely to vote for Democrats. Then-Texas Gov. Mark White, a Democrat, issued an order that state workers "while discharging their regular duties," had to offer to register people applying for welfare benefits. "Everybody who's eligible should be registered, but here they are using taxpayers' money to register predominantly Democrats," said Strake. "There are not a lot of Republicans in the welfare lines."[208]

Cloward and Piven also argued their approach could help the Left's efforts to undermine U.S. national security. The misnamed "peace movement" could proselytize welfare recipients to agitate against the government. They could be approached because "[t]he link between the social-program cuts and the military buildup has become obvious." If the Reagan administration could be "prevented from cutting the income-maintenance programs, the bloated military budget will have to give way." Nonproductive Americans could become the bulwark of a new strategy aimed squarely at the Pentagon. "By turning to the waiting rooms of the welfare state as voting registrars, peace activists can intensify resistance to militarization."[209]

Cloward and Piven didn't wait for others to move forward with their subversive voter registration strategy. Around the time they wrote their article for *Social Policy*, Cloward, Piven, and former NWRO organizer Hulbert James created Human Service Employees Registration and Voter Education Fund (Human SERVE) as a lobbying vehicle in the early 1980s. Human SERVE, ACORN, and Project Vote all "set to work lobbying energetically" for the National Voter Registration Act of 1993, commonly known as the Motor-Voter law.

Along the way, Human SERVE and Ralph Nader's U.S. Public Interest Research Group (PIRG) backed a bill sponsored by longtime ACORN ally Rep. John Conyers (D-MI) "to provide for voter registration for Federal elections on all regular business days and at the polls on Election Day," and an accompanying measure to allow voting registration by postcard.[210]

Cloward and Piven attended the White House ceremony in which President Bill Clinton signed the bill into law. Piven gave a brief speech and Clinton hailed Project Vote by name as a group "for whom the goal of full voter participation has been a durable and lasting dream." Curiously, it was Clinton's first major legislative priority even though he "had just won an election in which the country had seen the largest increase in voter turnout in a generation," writes *Wall Street Journal* columnist John Fund. "Nonetheless, President Clinton declared a 'crisis' in civic participation and proceeded to ram the proposed law through Congress."[211]

Fund argues that the law leads to voter fraud by forcing states to register on the spot "anyone entering a government office to renew a driver's license or apply for welfare or unemployment compensation." Voter registrars were forbidden to ask even for proof of U.S. citizenship or identification. States were also forced to allow mail-in voter registration, which made it easy for troublemaking activists to place false names on the rolls without any human contact with a government official. States were also under orders not to purge the dead, criminals, or people who moved from the voter rolls for a minimum of eight years. Since its enactment, the Motor-Voter law has "fueled an explosion of phantom voters," Fund writes. "Perhaps no piece of legislation in the last generation better captures the 'incentivizing' of fraud . . . than the 1993 National Voter Registration Act."[212] For this, we have Cloward, Piven, and ACORN to thank.

Some writers have suggested the actions of ACORN and other Alinsky-inspired organizations that adhere to the Cloward-Piven Strategy of manufactured crisis helped to cause the 2007–2008 meltdown on Wall Street. Certainly radical activists have had their eyes on the financial markets for a long time. A cheeky conservative might even argue that the crisis on Wall Street is a kind of Reichstag fire—metaphorical kin to the blaze set by Nazis and blamed on the Communists that helped Hitler consolidate power—but unlike Germany in 1933, this time communists really are the arsonists.

Certainly it is not difficult to imagine Cloward and Piven embracing the Community Reinvestment Act (CRA), a financial affirmative action law enacted during the Carter administration. The CRA outlawed "redlining" and forced banks to issue home mortgages to people in poor communities regardless of their ability to repay. It also gave community groups like ACORN the opportunity to blackmail banks that failed to do their bidding.

Evidence is elusive at this point that Cloward and Piven were actually involved in the enactment of this law. Piven did, however, make it clear in early 2010 that she favored ACORN's tactics aimed at destabilizing America's financial system. During the Great Depression, she noted, many Americans didn't leave their farms or homes when they were evicted. "They resisted, and when they resisted, the mayors issued orders for a moratorium on foreclosures because that kind of resistance threatens civil disorder."

But if millions of people, a couple million, refuse to go along with foreclosure proceedings, and refuse to pay off those mortgages that are under water, that will be enormous pressure on the banks. And if they do it in the form of a social movement, if they do it with pride and audacity, if they do it with a sense of self-righteousness, the political leaders of this country will not be able to round them up.[213]

ACORN euphemistically calls its illegal trespassing program, encouraging homeowners to stay in their foreclosed homes, "homesteading."

THE NATIONAL WELFARE RIGHTS ORGANIZATION

The activist group Cloward and Piven founded with Alinsky in 1966, the now-defunct National Welfare Rights Organization, was an urban terrorist organization that pioneered the in-your-face intimidation techniques ACORN later perfected. Funded in part with grants from the Teamsters, UAW, and AFSCME,[214] NWRO thrived and went on to become the parent organization of ACORN. After leaving the employment of Students for a Democratic Society as an organizer against the Vietnam War draft, Wade Rathke was hired as an NWRO organizer. Rathke used tactics advocated by Cloward, Piven, and Alinsky to expand welfare rolls by causing civil disturbances. NWRO sent Rathke to Arkansas in 1970 to try a new approach to community organizing and ACORN was born, ultimately outlasting its parent.

As they say in the corridors of power in Washington, personnel is policy. So it's no surprise that the founding head of the National Welfare Rights Organization, George Wiley, had a dim view of America. A renowned, Ivy League-educated chemistry professor who abandoned bow ties for dashikis and let his afro grow as he embraced radicalism, Wiley believed American society was infused with "fundamental racism."[215]

Wiley made a lasting impact on the left-wing organizing community, according to NWRO organizer Bert DeLeeuw. "There are hundreds of grass-roots activist-type organizations around the country," he said. "George's concepts have become the definition of what people in these groups say they are doing. They are doing the things locally that George Wiley talked about and dreamed about, building majority coalitions, trying to build bridges between the poor and the non-poor." DeLeeuw went on to marry and later divorce ACORN official Madeleine Adamson before he died in 1990.[216]

The FBI maintained a file on Wiley but when this writer tried to obtain it, the Obama administration would not produce it. The FBI indicated in April 2010 that Wiley's records had been destroyed in May 2009, just months after President Obama took office.[217] Is the Obama administration covering up something? We'll never know. When Wiley's biographers obtained his FBI file in 1977, it showed that "the FBI, through its agents and informers, maintained surveillance of Wiley's civil rights and welfare rights activities from 1961 until his death."[218]

Wiley laid out the struggle he felt needed to be waged against American capitalism in starkly racial terms. In a 1968 speech he told an audience:

> I am not at all convinced that white, comfortable, affluent, middle-class Americans are going to move over and share their wealth and resources with the people who have none. But I do have faith that if the poor people who have the problems can organize, can exert their political muscle, they can have a chance to have their voices and their weight felt in the political processes of this country—and there is hope.[219]

A master of manipulation, Wiley catered his words to suit his audience. As his biographers noted:

> In one speech he would say that NWRO was not a revolutionary movement but sought a gradual transition to a system of a more adequate income maintenance system for all; in the next breath he would quote Stokely Carmichael, the militant black separatist, and say, "If we don't get our rights, ain't nobody going to have peace in this country."[220]

Though this race-baiting careerist publicly professed a hatred of racism, Wiley took an interest in the racist poet Imamu Baraka because "Baraka was serious about grass roots organizing in New Jersey."[221] Indeed Baraka, who later changed his name to Amiri Baraka, was serious about grassroots organizing in New Jersey, but it's unclear if it was the kind Wiley may have been thinking of. As the state's poet laureate he used the opportunity of the 2001 Islamist terrorist attacks to incite hatred against Jews, writing, "Who knew the World Trade Center was gonna get bombed/Who told 4000 Israeli workers at the Twin Towers/To stay home that day." In the 1960s, when Wiley professed his admiration for Baraka, the self-described "Third World Marxist-Leninist" poet wrote that white women deserve to be raped and that "[m]ost American white men are trained to be fags." When a Caucasian woman approached Baraka to ask what sympathetic white people could do to advance the black cause, he answered, "You can help by dying. You are a cancer. You can help the world's people with your death."[222] Baraka was the kind of thinker Wiley, the man who sent Wade Rathke to Arkansas to start up ACORN, admired.

Like Rathke, Wiley believed violence was a useful tool to change society. He performed the same rhetorical tightrope walk that Rathke performed in the essay "Tactical Tension," simultaneously denouncing violence by name while endorsing specific violent tactics. While Wiley worked at the Congress of Racial Equality (CORE) in 1964, he could not bring himself to condemn the riots that followed after CORE activists Michael Schwerner, James Chaney, and Andrew Goodman were murdered in Mississippi.

> I'm not convinced that the riots didn't help though I remain committed to a nonviolent alternative. I think violence does play a role in bringing progress. The riots are a fairly natural response to ghetto conditions. If the conditions under which black people are forced to live existed for any substantial segment of the white community, there can be very little doubt, given our extremely violent American tradition, they would have produced a violent holocaust long before this.[223]

In another speech not long after Martin Luther King was assassinated and while NWRO was directing activists to use force against welfare caseworkers, Wiley weakly, perfunctorily disavowed violence. He suggested those who practiced it against the establishment occupied the moral high ground.

> I am not going to be throwing the bombs and shooting people, but I am here to tell you today that George Wiley is not going to be out there trying to cool people off so that you folks can be more comfortable in your apathy—that George Wiley is not going to be out there trying to sell out those black folks by making moves to help the power structure ameliorate the rage and anger that there is in this country. There are many of us—and I speak for our welfare rights leaders— who are not the least bit interested in protecting your security or your comfort or those in your family . . . It is a period of great ambivalence for people like myself, whose guts identify with those people who are going to be tearing down your cities, who are prepared to cheer secretly when people are planting bombs in Macy's and in Gimbel's and the department stores, who decry violence and don't want to see their families brutalized, but at the same time can't stand to see the kind of things that have gone on in this country tolerated any longer.

Sounding like a fossilized career politician who applauds himself for his years of supposedly selfless service to the public, Wiley gave himself a rhetorical pat on the back for having the self-restraint not to kill anyone. He congratulated himself for being "a dinosaur— because of my commitment to work within the channels, within the institutions, to use protest, to use direct action, to use the courts, to use the democratic process."[224]

NWRO BOSS PROFITS FROM MLK'S DEATH

Meanwhile, Wiley was incensed at the way King's funeral in Atlanta was used for political advantage by white politicians who sat in a place of honor in the front pews. This was "business as usual," he wrote in a newsletter, "the rich white folks up front and the poor black folks in the back." Yet Wiley wasted no time after King's murder trying to exploit the civil rights leader's death for his own political purposes. Wiley urged Congress to immediately enact legislation providing a national guaranteed income of $4,000 for a family of four. The NWRO newsletter for April 9, 1968, displayed a picture of King under which appeared "Don't Mourn for Me. Organize!" the last words of radical labor activist Joe Hill before he faced a firing squad for murder. "Martin Luther King is free at last, but when will poor people be free?" wrote Wiley. "How many deaths will it take before Congress will pass a welfare rights bill guaranteeing all people welfare and jobs now?"[225]

For all Wiley's stage-managed sanctimony, NWRO treated King with open contempt when he was alive. The leadership of Wiley's band of self-righteous welfare warriors ganged up on King when they met with them in early 1968. At the Chicago YMCA, King listened patiently to the welfare mothers while they harangued him for more than an hour, laying out what they considered to be their superior strategy for advancing the cause of poor people. An exasperated King agreed to incorporate NWRO's demands into his upcoming Poor People's Campaign and concluded the meeting by saying, "We have a date in Washington, April 22." King didn't make it; he was assassinated April 4. Years later King's chief aide, Andrew Young, who later became mayor of Atlanta, a congressman, and President Carter's ambassador to the United Nations, recounted the hostility the women showed to King:

> It was almost as though they were saying that we had no right to do anything for poor people—that poor folk were their property. And they jumped on Martin like no one ever had before. I don't think he had ever been that insulted in a meeting. But I think he understood. In a way, they were testing him. Just to deal with those kinds of women took a hell of a lot of energy and a particular kind of person, which George Wiley had to be. Not many black men could have done that. George had everything he could handle riding herd

on those strong black women. Martin King could not have done it, for instance.

But despite the shabby treatment afforded his boss by the NWRO leaders, Young still found a way to allow the women to escape responsibility for their actions. Divorced from common sense, Young blamed America for warping them and turning them into overbearing, domineering figures. The budding leftist politician marveled at how Wiley managed to work with them at all. "[A] system of oppression tends to produce weak men and strong women, and George somehow was a particularly strong man and really took on the task. I don't know how he did it, but he at least survived," said Young.[226]

Selling Wiley on the Cloward-Piven welfare strategy was easy, according to his wife Wretha, a radical who herself had organized an SDS chapter.[227] Wiley attended a conference in early 1966 called The Poor People's War Council on Poverty and came back "very excited about the Cloward-Piven theory. Nobody had ever described an idea to him that he accepted so quickly," she said. Although Cloward and Piven thought the best approach was to focus their welfare upheaval efforts on a few major cities and "literally . . . bring them to the brink of bankruptcy," Wiley argued they should opt for a national approach. He became national action coordinator for a new group called Citizens' Crusade Against Poverty and pitched his idea to the organization. At the Crusade's annual meeting the group's board rejected his plan, which he had expected it to do. However, Wiley wasn't prepared for what happened next. When OEO director Sargent Shriver delivered what was supposed to be an inspiring speech emphasizing the accomplishments of the War on Poverty, the crowd turned against him, interrupting and peppering him with angry questions and statements. "Tell us where the poor are being helped," they said, along with "He's lying!" and "Stop listening to him!" Shocked that people he considered to be his own constituents were giving him such a rough ride, Shriver left, saying, "I refuse to participate in a riot." Although Wiley was embarrassed because he had recruited some of those who rudely shut down the meeting, he recognized the noisy demonstrators' potential as agitators for the cause and made sure he collected their names and addresses.[228]

"We very consciously chose welfare rights as the battleground for our struggle," Wiley said. He regarded the welfare apparatus as "a very repressive nationwide system geared to disseminate economic benefits to large numbers of people" that if "forced to deliver any-thing like the amounts of cash benefits to which poor people were legally entitled . . . would collapse of its own weight." The beauty of the Cloward-Piven Strategy, in his view, was that it used the system to subsidize revolution. Packing the welfare rolls would give sup-porters "tangible benefits and rewards very early and very continu-ously." As welfare recipients waged war against their local welfare apparatus, that "could start them on the path of politicalization which led them first to the local welfare department, then to the state welfare agency, then to the state legislatures and governors, and eventually to HEW, the Congress, and the presidents of the United States."[229] Wiley promoted the strategy by using government resources in an attempt to turn Americans against capitalism. He used his college connections to finagle a $400,000 grant from the U.S. Department of Labor. Getting the money was especially sweet for Wiley because the money came out of a work-training program for welfare recipients that NWRO had fought in Congress.[230] Wiley recruited students from social work schools and begged taxpayer-supported antipoverty workers to help the cause on the taxpayers'· dime. "All these training programs and so forth are fine but people need to organize to get some power and money now. Help them get it!" he would tell them.[231]

Wiley delighted in using brute physical force and intimidation against welfare bureaucrats. The *New York Times* reported that NWRO's

> bands of organized clients descended on welfare centers demand-ing special grants for items provided under the law but in prac-tice rarely given out. The demonstrators have jammed the centers, sometimes camping out in them overnight, broken down adminis-trative procedure, playing havoc with the mountains of paperwork,

and have been increasingly successful . . . They have thrown the city's welfare program into a state of crisis and chaos.

Angry recipients stormed welfare offices, destroying case files and whatever stood in their way. NWRO activists had been convinced by Wiley that they were doing something public-spirited. In training sessions, welfare recipients were taught the ins and outs of welfare regulations and how to demand benefits they qualified for but were not receiving. "Wiley's constant repetition of the word *rights* got through to the women," the biographers note. "Most of them had been led to believe that they didn't have any rights under welfare, not even the right to look at the welfare manual to find the rules and regulations under which they received the dole." Wiley taught these welfare recipients that purposeful collective action could help them secure their welfare "rights."[232]

GEORGE WILEY'S WELFARE STORM TROOPERS

Wiley's supporters took over welfare offices, held sit-ins and harassed social workers across America. By 1968, NWRO had more than 8,000 dues-paying members in New York City. The group's benefit drives in that city precipitated a welfare crisis by bringing in $10 million to $12 million a month in grants for NWRO members, up from just $3 million the year before—and from 1966 to 1968 the city's welfare rolls had risen more than 100 percent to more than a million people. Nationwide, "[t]he flooding succeeded beyond [NWRO head George] Wiley's wildest dreams," according to Manhattan Institute scholar Sol Stern. "From 1965 to 1974, the number of single-parent households on welfare soared from 4.3 million to 10.8 million, despite mostly flush economic times." New York City felt Cloward and Piven's wrath. Their strategy was particularly successful in bringing the city to the brink of bankruptcy in 1975. Authorities there caved in to every demand from the group. "By the early 1970s, one person was on the welfare rolls in New York City for every two working in the city's private economy."[233]

During his push to overhaul the city's welfare system in the mid-1990s, Mayor Rudy Giuliani said New York had been a victim of economic sabotage. He blamed Cloward and Piven by name. "This wasn't an accident," Giuliani said. "It wasn't an atmospheric thing, it wasn't supernatural. This is the result of policies and programs designed to have the maximum number of people get on welfare." He condemned the "perverted social philosophy" advocated by Cloward and Piven and their ilk, which sapped the poor of their ambition and respect for work. "From 1960 to 1994, the work ethic was under attack in New York City," Giuliani said. "New York City viewed welfare as a good thing, as a wonderful thing. They romanticized it and embraced a philosophy of dependency, almost as if it's better to have somebody on welfare than to help somebody to work."[234]

Not long after NWRO launched its attacks, New York's liberal Republican governor, Nelson Rockefeller, demanded that the federal government take over state and city welfare burdens and provide level benefits throughout America. Rockefeller wasn't the only GOP governor to succumb to the Cloward-Piven juggernaut. Just as Massachusetts Gov. Mitt Romney surrendered to the Left in 2006 by enacting a type of universal healthcare plan in Massachusetts that was a precursor of Obamacare, in the 1960s, Mitt Romney's father, Republican George Romney, also gave in to pressure. NWRO extracted school clothing allowances and convinced the elder Romney to take a stand against welfare funding cutbacks. In Denver, NWRO demonstrated against the state welfare board and intimidated it into giving NWRO members seats on the boards. In Kentucky, NWRO petitioned for an emergency aid program. NWRO stormed the Delaware governor's office and the visitors' galleries of the Wisconsin legislature.[235]

NWRO also used thuggery against its supposed friends, an approach ACORN later copied. In 1969, about 40 NWRO members and the group's national leadership decided to shake down the National Conference on Social Welfare as it met at a New York hotel. The NWRO delegation, a group of angry, self-righteous, miscreants reeking of entitlement, grew enraged as they waited their turn to speak. "The ladies just got madder and madder as each successive group went up to the microphone to lay out their grievances," said one attendee. "They thought the others were stealing their thunder." When NWRO's turn came to address the 3,500 people in attendance, Beulah Sanders cried out "Block the doors," and as NWRO thugs blocked the exits Johnnie Tillmon said, "We demand $35,000 or you're not going to leave this room." The police came and freed the delegates. Meanwhile, Wiley completed the shakedown by negotiating with the conference chairman, Arthur S. Flemming, a former U.S. secretary of Health, Education, and Welfare. (HEW was the agency that preceded today's HHS—the Department of Health and Human Services.) The conference rewarded NWRO's audacious maneuver, giving the group the $35,000 it demanded.[236]

When he wasn't shaking down his friends, Wiley used litigation to break the welfare system. He worked with a group of lawyers headed by Edward Sparer who ran an OEO-funded legal clinic at Columbia University.[237] Not surprisingly, Sparer, who had also been involved with Cloward's Mobilization for Youth group, was a member of the Communist Party USA.[238] NWRO prevailed in seven important Supreme Court decisions involving welfare rights. Probably the most important of them was a case called *Goldberg v. Kelly*.

As David Frum writes in his history of the 1970s, "*Goldberg* was a decisive milestone en route to New York City's 1975 financial collapse." Notably, the legendary liberal Supreme Court Justice William Brennan considered *Goldberg v. Kelly* to be the most momentous decision of his career on the high court bench, according to Frum.

> It might seem strange that a case few non-lawyers have ever heard of should be rated by its author as outweighing his opinions outlawing school prayer, requiring states to provide indigent defendants with free lawyers, or smashing the ancient political power of farmers by mandating that all state senate districts contain roughly the same number of people. But Brennan was quite right.[239]

In the landmark 1970 Due Process Clause decision, the Supreme Court ruled 5 to 3 that the "brutal need" of a poor welfare recipient outweighed society's interest in trying to prevent welfare fraud.[240] The decision spat in the faces of the Framers of the Constitution by holding that welfare recipients were entitled to an evidentiary hearing before an impartial decision-maker at which they could call and confront witnesses and to receive a written, reasoned opinion before being deprived of benefits. The *Goldberg* decision wasn't just a full employment program for poverty lawyers, it was a radical assault on the Constitution that also gave a shot in the arm to the welfare rights movement by granting it some political legitimacy. Although the decision stopped just short of making the absurd declaration that welfare was a constitutional right, instead it made the equally absurd declaration that a welfare recipient had a "property" interest in welfare and that this interest deserves due process protections when the government wanted to take that so-called property away. In practice, this is a distinction with a difference. With Brennan's devious legal sleight-of-hand that perverted the meaning of the word *property*, welfare ceased to be a gratuity that could be granted and withdrawn at the discretion of the government and became an entitlement.

An early draft of the majority opinion prepared by Brennan's law clerk Taylor Reveley bought into Cloward and Piven's welfare-as-social-control argument, calling poverty "largely a product of impersonal forces." Welfare must be provided "both to help maintain the dignity and well-being of a large segment of the population and to guard against the societal malaise that may flow from a widespread sense of unwarranted frustration and insecurity," Reveley wrote. After Justice John Marshall Harlan indicated he considered the discussion "offensive" and Justice Byron White refused to accept the passage, it was removed. (Reveley is now John Stewart Bryan Professor of Jurisprudence and president of the College of William and Mary.) The version of the opinion Brennan ultimately settled on incorporated Cloward's opportunity theory: "Welfare, by meeting the basic demands of subsistence, can help bring within the reach of the poor the same opportunities that are available to others to participate meaningfully in the life of the community."[241]

Unlike Brennan, a one-man Constitution-wrecking crew worshipped by leftists, Justice Hugo Black actually cared about the

American values embedded in America's great national charter. Black denounced the atrocity known as *Goldberg v. Kelly* in unsparing terms. In his dissenting opinion, he wrote that the majority opinion would "paralyze the government's efforts to protect itself against making payments to people who are not entitled to them." Although "some recipients might be on the lists for payment wholly because of deliberate fraud on their part, the Court holds that the government is helpless, and must continue, until after an evidentiary hearing, to pay money that it does not owe, never has owed, and never could owe." Brennan's opinion in effect "says that failure of the government to pay a promised charitable installment to an individual deprives that individual of *his own property* in violation of the Due Process Clause of the Fourteenth Amendment." [italics in original] Black added, "The procedure required today as a matter of constitutional law finds no precedent in our legal system."

Goldberg v. Kelly was one of many key Supreme Court cases brought by NWRO. The organization also scored important policy victories such as raising benefits under the food stamp program and adding cost of living increases to it.[242]

After Wiley was forced out of NWRO in a dispute with its leadership, his radicalism burned as hot as ever. In 1973, he created a new group called the Movement for Economic Justice (MEJ). "[H]e believed that the poor and the blacks of America could not win further significant improvements in their status unless they became part of a new 'majority movement' to change the society," wrote his biographers. "Its purpose would be to achieve a redistribution of wealth and political power, helping both the poor and the average citizen at the expense of the rich." Wiley still believed that welfare was a good issue around which to organize the poor, but recognized a multi-issue organization such as ACORN would have a greater chance of long-term success. Wiley offered one final innovation to the world of left-wing community organizing. His new MEJ organization "sponsored more than a hundred tax clinics in 1973" for the poor.[243] ACORN probably got the idea to offer its own free tax return preparation clinics for the poor from Wiley.

WADE RATHKE JOINS NWRO

ACORN founder Wade Rathke got involved in left-wing organizing after dropping out of Williams College. He became a draft-resistance counselor and organized anti-war demonstrations for SDS. His father, Edmann, was angry with him. "You were an Eagle Scout. Now you're a traitor and a dropout!" His father's painfully accurate description didn't seem to bother Rathke, who has now been in the agitation business for more than four decades. But he tired of working for SDS. He was not, in his own words, "interested in setting up a service bureau for upper-middle-class college kids."

Rathke had been fascinated by Cloward and Piven's article in *The Nation*.[244] Some time later, Rathke was inspired by a speech Wiley gave in Boston. "I was young and had my eyes open and listened to everything I was hearing and couldn't resist being involved and doing something about it," Rathke said.[245] At NWRO, Rathke was trained by Bill Pastreich who had studied Saul Alinsky's techniques and was briefly employed by the United Farm Workers, which was headed by Alinsky acolyte Cesar Chavez.[246] Pastreich, NWRO's head organizer in Massachusetts, had been expelled from a Latin American country for radical agitation. He heard of Rathke's successful anti-war organizing and offered him a position organizing for NWRO in Springfield, Massachusetts.[247]

No long-haired hippie, Rathke turned down a ticket to attend the legendary Woodstock musical festival in August 1969 and instead checked out Springfield. "Looking back, Rathke would think of Woodstock as a symbolic moment that separated the political activists from the mostly tie-dyed and beaded cultural ones," John Atlas writes. Rathke liked what he saw in Springfield and accepted the job. He soon learned that NWRO had no intention of paying him for his work; he would have to bum money off friends working in the federally funded anti-poverty effort.[248] This merciless exploitation of workers was typical of NWRO, and later, of Rathke's ACORN. "Wiley would pay the telephone bill rather than the staff—even though the employees complained that they couldn't pay their rent," according to

Wiley's biographers. Wiley expected employees to "live off the land," like an invading army. They were encouraged to pool resources, get free meals and accommodation, or get onto another organization's payroll while still working at NWRO.[249]

A few months after arriving in Springfield, Rathke had built up a local empire of activism. He constructed an influential welfare rights organization consisting of 20 neighborhood groups with a combined membership of more than 2,000. The Springfield chapter of NWRO secured millions of dollars from the local welfare agency and encouraged hundreds of non-members to seek welfare benefits. Meanwhile, NWRO was doing its best to swamp welfare departments nationwide. Between December 1960 and February 1969 the Aid to Families with Dependent Children welfare program had grown 107 percent but in the 15-month period from February 1969 through October 1970 the program grew a staggering 55 percent as an extra 1.5 million families joined the rolls.[250]

Rathke was arrested after he led an invasion of the Springfield welfare office with 250 or more women and students armed with signs reading "More for the poor, less for the war." After the welfare director refused to give in to the crowd's demands for winter clothing benefits they were not entitled to, Rathke's members rioted. Millions of dollars' worth of property was destroyed over two days of unrest. The Soviet government used Rathke's riot as anti-American propaganda, publishing an article about it in *Pravda*. Rathke's experiences "reinforced his belief that one important resource for poor people was their ability to disrupt." He realized that despite the failure of the action to achieve its objective, his followers felt empowered by violence directed against the system. This empowerment by rioting became a staple of ACORN's playbook.[251] Not all members of MWRO, the Massachusetts branch of NWRO, were comfortable with such aggressive tactics. In 2001, Rathke recalled "crashing the doors into the Boston Statler Hilton as 250 welfare recipients in 1969 streamed in on a particular MWRO demonstration at a gubernatorial fundraiser." No one was arrested and the group felt it had made its point, but "some members were scared, because it was rough stuff."[252]

Over time Rathke came to agree with Alinsky that single-issue organizations were doomed to fail. A multifaceted approach was needed to radically transform the nation. Rathke offered this deal to Wiley:

> I'll go south, but you've got to let me organize a larger organization, beginning in Arkansas. We can't build a poor people's organization where the next-door neighbor to the welfare recipient was just as antagonistic to welfare as anyone else. We have to break out of the single-issue welfare campaigns to build a majority constituency where the next-door neighbors are in it together and not fighting each other.

Wiley accepted the offer and got a foundation to provide $5,500 to cover the first six months of Rathke's salary and expenses. In May 1970, Wade Rathke drove 1,500 miles from Boston to Little Rock and got down to work trying to turn the Natural State upside-down.[253]

[SIX]

Alinsky the Agitator: ACORN's Inspiration

A CORN's LEGACY OF destruction and lawlessness traces directly back to the fiendishly brilliant Saul Alinsky. Born in 1909, the group's spiritual sherpa into the abyss of planned anarchy was always fascinated by violence. His defenders present Alinsky as an advocate of civil disobedience who rejected violence as a political tool. This is rubbish. Alinsky adored violence.

Alinsky's enthusiasm for violence matters because his ideas and values permeate the Obama administration, ACORN, and the many ACORN-like organizations such as National People's Action and National Council of La Raza that have metastasized throughout the American body politic in recent decades. By the time he died, Alinsky had created an astounding 44 community organizations that aspire to pulverize the American system.[254] ACORN founder Wade Rathke worked with Alinsky, who trained activists from the Massachusetts chapter of ACORN's parent organization NWRO and other groups before he died in 1972. Alinsky "had done sessions with my staff at Massachusetts Welfare Rights in early 1970 and various other things," Rathke blogged.[255] According to one of Alinsky's senior organizers at the Industrial Areas Foundation (IAF), Nicholas von Hoffman,

Alinsky played no direct role in the creation of ACORN but believes the master, had he lived to see it develop, would have approved of ACORN's approach to agitation. The group's "cheekiness, truculence and imaginative tactical tropes have an Alinskyan touch," according to von Hoffman, a journalist who wrote a particularly nasty biography of Sen. Joseph McCarthy's counsel Roy Cohn.[256]

Von Hoffman soft-pedals the damage that Alinsky-style organizing does to the body politic, claiming Alinsky was sounding "the trumpet blast for democracy." If democracy includes "conking" picket line crossers on the head—something he admits Alinsky favored—then he's right. Alinsky shied away from praising violence in public because "[t]he subject was too touchy and to bring it up was to invite misquotation and distortion." But in private "he would say that violence has its uses."[257]

Alinsky developed a taste for violence early in life. When gangs of Polish boys invaded his Jewish neighborhood, he used force to repel them. "[W]e'd get up on the roofs with piles of bricks and pans of boiling water and slingshots, just like a medieval siege," Alinsky said. "I had an air rifle myself. There'd be a bloody battle for blocks around and some people on both sides had real guns, so sometimes there'd be fatalities." As a youngster, Alinsky embraced mob justice. When Polish kids beat up Alinsky's friend, the 12-year-old future agitator went with friends and gave the aggressors a good old-fashioned pounding. "They beat my friend up, so we beat them up. That's the American way. It's also in the Old Testament: an eye for an eye, a tooth for a tooth. Beat the hell out of them. That's what everybody does."[258]

As a University of Chicago sociology student in 1930, Alinsky took a criminology course called "The Study of Organized Crime." He decided the Al Capone gang would be an excellent case study. Alinsky tried to establish rapport with the organization but was rebuffed at first. He knew the mobsters hung out at Chicago's Lexington Hotel and eventually insinuated his way into the gang. Alinsky claimed he used charm to win over Capone's senior executioner, "Big Ed" Stash. The hit man was drinking with his criminal colleagues, getting ready to tell the same old story about picking up a redhead in Detroit that they'd heard a thousand times before. One of Stash's friends moaned, "Do we have to hear that one again?" Young Alinsky seized the moment, telling Stash he'd love to hear the story. Delighted, Stash invited him to sit down with the gang at the table.[259] Alinsky was on the inside with the community organizers he wanted to know better.

Later, Stash introduced Alinsky to Frank Nitti, the gang's top enforcer who took over the gang after Capone went to prison in 1931. They became so close Alinsky said Nitti "took me under his wing. I called him the Professor and I became his student." Alinsky was so comfortable around organized crime he took on the role of management consultant, trying to help the gang save money. As Alinsky told the story:

> Once, when I was looking over their records, I noticed an item listing a $7,500 payment for an out-of-town killer. I called Nitti over and I said, "Look, Mr. Nitti, I don't understand this. You've got at least twenty killers on your payroll. Why waste that much money to bring somebody in from St. Louis?" Frank was really shocked by my ignorance. "Look, kid," he said patiently, "sometimes our guys might know the guy they're hitting, they may have been to his house for dinner, taken his kids to the ball game, been the best man at his wedding, gotten drunk together. But you call in a guy from out of town, all you've got to do is tell him, 'Look, there's this guy in a dark coat on State and Randolph; our boy in the car will point him out; just go up and give him three in the belly and fade into the crowd.' So that's a job and he's a professional, he does it. But one of *our* boys goes up, the guy turns to face him and it's a friend, right away he knows that when he pulls the trigger there's gonna be a widow, kids without a father, funerals, weeping—Christ, it'd be a murder." . . . That was the reason they used out-of-town killers. This is what sociologists call a "primary relationship." They spend lecture after lecture and all kinds of assigned reading explaining it. Professor Nitti taught me the whole thing in five minutes.[260]

Alinsky's writing is awash in violent imagery. In his 1946 manifesto, *Reveille for Radicals,* he wrote that the radical "hits, he hurts, he is dangerous." Radicals, he proclaimed, "are most adept at breaking the necks of conservatives."[261] Alinsky acknowledges that violence is inevitable in the revolutionary struggle. "The radical may resort to the sword but when he does he is not filled with hatred against those individuals whom he attacks," he writes in *Reveille*. "He hates these individuals not as persons but as symbols representing ideas or interests which he believes to be inimical to the welfare of the people."[262] The radical is like a mobster who tells his prey, "It's nothing personal, it's strictly business," before shooting him in the heart.

Alinsky didn't reject violence—far from it—he simply believed it wasn't always the best course of action. When considering tactics, Alinsky's sole criterion was whether they advanced the cause: to him the ends justified whatever means it took to achieve them. This is the overriding theme of his anti-capitalist cookbook, *Rules for Radicals*. He wrote in the 1971 book that a pragmatic warrior for radicalism has to accept that "in action, one does not always enjoy the luxury of a decision that is consistent both with one's individual conscience and the good of mankind." The good of mankind must "always" come first. "Action is for mass salvation and not for the individual's personal salvation."[263]

The nonviolent civil disobedience practiced by the civil rights movement is one means to an end, but it's not always the best means, according to Alinsky. "The future does not argue for making a special religion of nonviolence," he writes. "It will be remembered for what it was, the best tactic for its time and place." Alinsky seems to argue, using cryptic wording, that blacks would be wise to embrace violence.

> As more effective means become available, the Negro civil rights movement will divest itself of these decorations and substitute a new moral philosophy in keeping with its new means and opportunities. The explanation will be, as it always has been, "Times have changed." This is happening today.[264]

What exactly was happening during the "today" Alinsky references, around 1971 when *Rules for Radicals* was published? Some black power groups were at war with America—and not in a metaphorical sense as with the War on Poverty. The newly formed Black Liberation Army was bombing targets and carrying out armed robberies which it described euphemistically as "expropriations." It was soon followed by the Symbionese Liberation Army which kidnapped Patty Hearst in 1974. The BLA was later assisted in these expropriation efforts by the Weather Underground Organization, which called for blacks to be liberated from oppressive, white-dominated "AmeriKKKa."

Could Alinsky have had something other than violence in mind when he wrote the earlier paragraph? Perhaps, though it seems unlikely that's what the author of *Rules for Radicals* was thinking, given that he embraced revolutionary violence and preferred confrontation over negotiation. There is an outside chance he may have been thinking of the Congressional Black Caucus, formally created in 1971 as a vehicle in Congress for radical left-wing black politicians. CBC may not be a terrorist group but it's still a radical organization. Fittingly, it's headed by longtime ACORN loyalist and small-c communist Rep. Barbara Lee (D-CA). CBC's agenda is more or less small-c communist and virtually indistinguishable from the agenda of the DSA-created Congressional Progressive Caucus, which Lee also once headed. David Horowitz describes Lee as "an anti-American communist who supports America's enemies and has actively collaborated with them in their war against America." Lee, according to Horowitz, passed sensitive U.S. military information to the Grenadian Communist dictatorship that Ronald Reagan overthrew by invading the Caribbean nation in 1983.[265]

PRISON IS GOOD TRAINING FOR AN ORGANIZER

Alinsky also taught that the Marxist revolutionary shouldn't be afraid of a little quality jail time. He embraced imprisonment as a stairway to personal growth. "It was through periodic imprisonment that the basis for my first publication and the first orderly philosophical arrangement of my ideas and goals occurred," Alinsky wrote.[266] But "revolutionary leaders" should keep jail terms "relatively brief, from one day to two months." Long jail sentences keep a revolutionary out of action so long that he loses touch and "everybody forgets about you."

> Life goes on, new issues arise, and new leaders appear; however, a periodic removal from circulation by being jailed is an essential element in the development of the revolutionary. The one problem that the revolutionary cannot cope with by himself is that he must now and then have an opportunity to reflect and synthesize his thoughts. To gain that privacy in which he can try to make sense out of what he is doing, why he is doing it, where he is going, what has been wrong with what he has done, what he should have done and above all to see the relationships of all the episodes and acts as they tie in to a general pattern, the most convenient and accessible solution is jail. It is here that he begins to develop a philosophy. It is here that he begins to shape long-term goals, intermediate goals, and a self-analysis of tactics as tied to his own personality. It is here that he is emancipated from the slavery of action wherein he was compelled to think from act to act. Now he can look at the totality of his actions and the reactions of the enemy from a fairly detached position.[267]

ACORN's Rathke agrees. In 2001 he complained about shrinking periods of incarceration. "Time in jail, much less jail time, which was once the standard fare for the fight, had become virtually non-existent," he wrote. It was "disturbing" that society was in "a post-Civil Rights period of 'pax protestiana' where arrests had in some cities devolved into a summons or a ticket, essentially a small speed bump on the swift ride home from the demonstration." In order "[f]or arrests to matter and have meaning, they have to transcend mere symbol and celebrity."[268]

Alinsky also taught that a radical should never let a good crisis go to waste: "The Chinese write the word 'crisis' with two characters. One means *danger* and the other means *opportunity*. Together they spell 'crisis.'"[269]

Obama's inner circle embraces this revolutionary wisdom. "Rule one: Never allow a crisis to go to waste," White House chief of staff Rahm Emanuel said after the 2008 election. "They are opportunities to do big things."[270] In a meeting with European Parliament leaders Hillary Clinton echoed Emanuel's remarks, making clear that the economic crisis was simply an excuse to transform America into a sclerotic European-style socialist state.

> I'm actually excited by this opportunity. I'm very well aware that we are not yet through this economic crisis but the chief of staff for President Obama is an old friend of mine and my husband's and was in the White House when Bill was there. And he said, you know, never waste a good crisis, and when it comes to the economic crisis don't waste it when it can have a very positive impact on climate change and energy security. And that's what we're trying to do.[271]

ALINSKY, THE HONORARY WEATHERMAN

Alinsky rarely missed an opportunity to taunt liberals. "A liberal is the kind of guy who walks out of a room when the argument turns into a fight," he said.[272] Alinsky considered liberals weak, timid, and ineffective because, like conservatives, they more or less accept the basic ground rules of the society he despised. To Alinsky, liberals were affective saps to be manipulated. They could sometimes be counted on for funding but constantly needed to be pushed to do whatever Alinsky considered to be the right thing. Radicals, on the other hand, were romantic, heroic figures crusading in a kind of Social Justice League. "Radicals precipitate the social crisis by action—by using power. Liberals may then timidly follow along or else, as in most cases, be swept forward along the course set by radicals, but all because of forces unloosed by radical action. They are forced to positive action only in spite of their desires." Liberals "have radical minds and conservative hearts," Alinsky wrote. "They really like people *only* with their heads. The radical genuinely likes people."[273]

Alinsky added, "The radical does what he does because of his love for his fellow men."[274]

Alinsky's declarations are distressingly similar to a quotation from bloodthirsty sociopath Ernesto "Che" Guevara. "At the risk of seeming ridiculous, let me say that the true revolutionary is guided by a great feeling of love," said the Communist guerrilla executed in 1967. "It is impossible to think of a genuine revolutionary lacking this quality." Alinsky and Che, in turn, echoed comments made the century before by Karl Marx. Although Marx argued that revolutionaries should make straightforward arguments in favor of Communist revolution, all was not lost if they didn't: an argument could still be made that socialism could be justified out of a "true love of humanity."[275] Weather Underground terrorists also thought of themselves as noble combatants in a war against an evil system. "We are neither terrorists nor criminals," said Weatherman David Gilbert, now serving a life term in prison for armed robbery and second-degree murder. "It is precisely because of our love of life, because we revel in the human spirit, that we became freedom fighters against this racist and deadly imperialist system."[276]

Alinsky rejected the violent methods of the Weather Underground Organization, not because they were violent but because he deemed them ineffective. The Weathermen "went berserk," Alinsky wrote. "When there are people who espouse the assassination of Senator Robert Kennedy or the Tate murders or the Marin County Courthouse kidnapping and killings [a 1970 radical attack that left four dead, including a judge] or the University of Wisconsin bombing and killing [a 1970 anti-war bombing that killed a physics researcher] as 'revolutionary acts,' then we are dealing with people who are merely hiding psychosis behind a political mask." This rather showy denunciation seems out of place for a man who preaches in *Rules for Radicals* that nearly any tactic was justifiable in the revolutionary struggle. It is as if Alinsky is pretentiously dangling this sudden attack of conscience like an amulet in front of his readers in order to be shielded from their bourgeois scorn.[277]

Don't be fooled. Alinsky and the Weather Underground were spiritual

foundation to Alinsky and leftist "consumer advocate" Ralph Nader. "I told Nader it was O.K. if he put us out of the muffler and exhaust business, so long as he put all of our competitors out of business too," Sherman said. Sherman's extra-curricular activities alienated customers and he was eventually forced out of the company.[284] Alinsky's IAF also received heavy funding from the radical Catholic Campaign for Human Development (CCHD) and its funding of IAF continues to the present day.

Alinsky's hostility to the U.S. military is difficult to distinguish from the rage expressed by Weather Underground bomber and ACORN ally Bill Ayers. Alinsky declares, "Of all the pollution around us, none compares to the political pollution of the Pentagon."[285] Compare Alinsky's anti-military sentiment to that of Ayers, who wrote that, upon hearing that his bombing of the Pentagon temporarily disrupted the U.S. air war in Vietnam, was transported "into deepening shades of delight."[286]

Holding these views was acceptable, in Alinsky's view, but expressing them in the terms the Weathermen used was not acceptable. Openly declaring a visceral contempt for the system, as the Weather Underground did, is a sure recipe for failure, according to Alinsky. "A mess of rhetorical garbage about 'Burn the system down!'" and cries of "murdering fascist pigs" will never work. "Militant mouthings" spouting quotes from Mao Zedong, Fidel Castro, and Che Guevara, are only going to turn people off. Such rants are harmful to the revolutionary cause because they "are as germane to our highly technological, computerized, cybernetic, nuclear-powered, mass media society as a stagecoach on a jet runway at Kennedy airport."[287]

ALINSKY'S SYMPATHY FOR COMMUNISM

Alinsky claimed he was not a communist yet his beliefs were clearly communistic. He frequently deflected questions about his worldview by saying he was not a "joiner." He claimed to reject ideology, arguing that it was merely a mechanism people used to adapt to the situations in which they found themselves. "Ideologies are not very significant in themselves," and people modify them to suit changing circumstances, he wrote.[288] This is a silly argument. It is a transparent evasion and it is difficult to believe someone as intelligent and politically astute as Alinsky actually believed it. Perhaps he was embracing his own twisted, inverted version of what Plato called the "noble lie"—a myth that promotes social harmony—in order to promote the social disharmony that is a prerequisite for radical change.

Communist sympathizers and activists typically claim to be non-ideological in order to escape the stigma of communism. "The slogan of the Communist Party when Stalin was around was 'peace, jobs, and democracy.' In fact, the Comintern paper was called 'For A Lasting Peace, For A People's Democracy,' and the reason is exactly what Alinsky says at the outset," David Horowitz said in an interview. The Marxist Left believes "that capitalist democracy's political democracy is a fraud and that it's really totally parallel to feudalism, slavery, and preexisting systems, so it intends revolution." The problem is that in a democratic society where everyone has a vote, "to be a revolutionary is to be an outlaw." Revolutionaries are "outlaws and traitors so obviously their first order of business is to conceal their agenda because if they reveal it at worst they'll be hung from the nearest lamppost and at best they won't get anywhere." The whole leftist agenda has to be disguised in America because it's out of sync with reality in a place where it's easy for workers to be upwardly economically mobile. The way radicals "operate, survive, and succeed is by concealing their true agendas and working to gain leverage and power within the system," he said.

Alinsky's friend, Herb March, who had been an organizer for the Young Communist League, admired his deceptiveness. March appreciated Alinsky's shunning of labels, which he felt could make an organizer less effective among certain people or groups. Alinsky associated with Communist Party USA members and Marxists who didn't belong to the party, yet, like Barack Obama in college, sought them out. Alinsky was "broadly sympathetic with March's politics," according to Alinsky's biographer.[289]

"I don't think he ever remotely thought of joining the Communist

Party [but] emotionally he aligned very strongly with it," said Chicago alderman and Alinsky college classmate Leon Despres. Despres joined the Trotskyist-influenced Socialist Party[290] and was later a member of the Communist Party USA splinter group known as the Committees of Correspondence for Democracy and Socialism.[291] Despres was also a mentor to young ACORN organizer Barack Obama.[292]

Alinsky favored class warfare, used an explicitly Marxist framework to view society, urged coercive government-directed redistribution of wealth, and worked with Communists. Yet Alinsky's biographer, Sanford D. Horwitt, buys into the fantasy that Alinsky was non-ideological. Horwitt writes that Alinsky disavowed Marxist-style "class analysis."[293] This is abject nonsense. Alinsky's Marxism is obvious to anyone who cares to look for it.

In *Rules for Radicals* Alinsky lays out his communistic catechism, which includes the precise Marxist-style class analysis Horwitt falsely claimed Alinsky rejected. Alinsky's Marxist trinity consists of the "Haves," as he calls them, who are the ruling class; the "Have-Nots," the working class; and the "Have-a-Little, Want Mores," are the bourgeoisie, or to use American parlance, the middle class. The Haves "want to keep things as they are" as they "suffocate in their surpluses while the Have-Nots starve." The Have-Nots abhor the system and "hate the establishment of the Haves with its arrogant opulence, its police, its courts, and its churches." The noble-sounding ideals of "[j]ustice, morality, law, and order, are mere words when used by the Haves, which justify and secure their status quo." In other words, the American system is not the carefully conceived product of thoughtful deliberations by the Founding Fathers and the Framers of the Constitution, a civil war, and various transcendent, transformative socio-political movements but a cynical game rigged by the powers that be. Alinsky views himself as a leveler, a man who equalizes the imbalances he sees in the American body politic.[294]

The Haves cling to their privileged position by creating and enforcing the rules that govern society. The Haves invent a self-serving morality that justifies their "their means of repression and all other means employed to maintain the status quo." The Haves usually write society's laws, including laws that make it illegal to change society.[295] He is openly hostile to capitalism and passionate about socialism. "Radicals want to advance from the jungle of laissez-faire capitalism to a world worthy of the name of human civilization," he writes. "They hope for a future where *the production will be owned by all of the people* instead of just a comparative handful."[296] [emphasis added] This is the textbook definition of socialism.

In *Rules for Radicals* he approvingly quotes an aphorism from Jean Jacques Rousseau—the intellectual godfather of communism who helped lay the groundwork for the murderous French Revolution— that "[l]aw is a very good thing for men with property and a very bad thing for men without property."[297] This sums up the Marxist conception of the legal system in a capitalist society. To them, law is an instrument of oppression and criminals are victims.

Capitalism twists and corrupts people, making them evil, according to Alinsky. When people "demonstrate a capacity for brutality, selfishness, hate, greed, avarice, and disloyalty," the radical understands that "these attitudes and actions are the result of evil conditions." The "circumstances that made them that way" should be judged, he writes. "[T]he people of today live in a system that places the highest premium on personal possessions and regards material poverty as failure," he continues. "It is a system within which, with few exceptions, the material ends justify the means."[298]

Alinsky's views roughly mirrored those of Richard Cloward, whose "opportunity theory" held that capitalism created criminals. "Prior to the transition of world society into capitalism, crime had been regarded as behavior inspired by the devil," Alinsky wrote. "During the feudal era the supernatural taboos and sanctions of the church wrapped the religious cloak of mysticism about human behavior," but as capitalism advanced, an individualistic view of criminality took hold and "[t]he social order generally was absolved from responsibility." This view was reinforced by psychiatrists such as Sigmund Freud whom Alinsky regarded not as a scientist but as a cog in the capitalist system. Economic factors were more responsible for criminal behavior than individual choices made by criminals. Delinquency was caused by "social disorganization, which, in turn, [is] largely the result of economic defects in our social order," Alinsky said.[299] It follows that such a supposedly sinister system should be fought with any and all means available.

Alinsky laughed off the grave existential threat Communism posed to the United States during the Cold War. Sounding much like radical pseudo-journalist Max Blumenthal, who today absurdly compares the American conservative movement to the Taliban, Alinsky claimed after World War II that "[C]ertain Fascist mentalities" were a greater threat to America than "the damn nuisance of Communism."[300]

CAMOUFLAGING COMMUNISM

Alinsky hailed one of his heroes, Lenin, as "a pragmatist" for concealing his game plan. He noted that when Lenin returned to Russia after years in exile following his Marxist and anti-Czarist activities, he said the Bolsheviks favored gaining power through the ballot box but would reevaluate their approach after they got their hands on firearms. Yet despite Alinsky's fawning over Lenin, the Bolshevik leader "was a pragmatist only with the revolutionary framework," David Horowitz notes. "As a revolutionary, he was a dogmatist in theory and a Machiavellian monster in practice."[301] Surely Lenin's Machiavellianism was one of the reasons Alinsky held him in such high esteem.

Alinsky was a pragmatic, businesslike gangster who realized that relying primarily on overtly violent campaigns against the system was not likely to bring about a lasting radical transformation of American society. Such an approach was too messy, too likely to generate a backlash. Alinsky's values, particularly the importance of using deceit to conceal one's true beliefs, guide ACORN, as they do President Barack Obama, a longtime Alinsky adherent, in everything he does. Alinsky taught his disciples to disguise their radical ideology. "Camouflage is key to Alinsky-style organizing," notes Richard Poe. For example, "[i]n organizing coalitions of black churches in Chicago, Obama caught flak for not attending church himself." How did

Obama the Alinskyite remedy this situation? "He became an instant churchgoer."[302]

Alinsky's most fundamental teaching, Horowitz writes, is that radicals have "to *lie* to their opponents and disarm them by pretending to be moderates and liberals." Deception is the most important arrow in the radical's quiver. "Racial arsonists such as Al Sharpton and Jeremiah Wright pose as civil rights activists; anti-American radicals such as Bill Ayers pose as patriotic progressives; socialists pose as liberals," Horowitz writes. "The mark of their success is reflected in the fact that conservatives collude in the deception and call them liberals as well."[303]

ACORN has always understood the importance of lying. Despite its radicalism, ACORN has long pretended to be just another activist group trying to make America a better place. When Fox News anchor Megyn Kelly asked Wade Rathke if he was a "socialist," at first Rathke played dumb and danced around the question.

> I don't know socialism, what that really means. We're not out advo-
> cating for an economic system; we're advocating for the rights that
> we have as a citizen to be fully respected. The very motto of ACORN,
> when I was there, was taken from the state motto of Arkansas which
> in Latin, I'll save you the Latin, but was "the people shall rule." We
> really believe in that and we may be some of the last people who
> really do.

Undeterred, Kelly pressed on. She read aloud the passage in ACORN's People's Platform in which the group vowed to continue fighting "until the American way is just one way, until we have shared the wealth." Rathke responded with mockery, as Alinskyites are trained to do when backed into a corner. "Ooooo, share the wealth," he said. "Well, yes we do believe in equitable distribution of any benefits and rights that people have. So yeah, we stand accused of that. We're guilty of believing that people should have a better life in this country. I don't think that's socialism."[304]

The Alinskyite organizing community has heaped praise on

Obama. Mike Kruglik, formerly one of Obama's fellow organizers, called Obama "a natural, the undisputed master of agitation."[305] After the exquisitely stage-managed 2008 national convention in Denver that nominated Obama, Alinsky's son David hailed the confab for having "had all the elements of the perfectly organized event, Saul Alinsky style." David Alinsky concluded from watching the extravagantly choreographed piece of political propaganda—complete with a façade of a Greek temple—that "Barack Obama's training in Chicago by the great community organizers is showing its effectiveness." He added he was "proud to see that my father's model for organizing is being applied successfully beyond local community organizing to affect the Democratic campaign in 2008."[306] One magazine suggested the Wagnerian spectacle in Denver was inspired by Industrial Areas Foundation-sponsored events. It quoted former New York City mayor Ed Koch on an IAF function he attended: "I had the feeling I was in some Nuremberg stadium. There was a military band. There were more than 1,000 people, chanting. They were thumping standards on the floor. It was like mass hysteria and very militant." Incidentally, the Koch quotation appears in Jim Rooney's book about the IAF, *Organizing the South Bronx*, which Obama's Hyde Park friend, unrepentant terrorist bomber Ayers, praised as an "important" book.[307]

Left-wing journalist John Judis notes that the Obama campaign itself painted "Obama the politician" as "a direct descendant of Obama the [IAF] organizer."[308] Obama has said his time as a community organizer was the "best education" he ever had. He's also never uttered an unkind word about IAF, which, in the Alinsky tradition, teaches would-be organizers the finer points of what has come to be known as the politics of personal destruction: inciting hatred, demonizing, and vilifying political opponents. IAF describes its mission as "build[ing] organizations whose primary purpose is power—*the ability to act*—and whose chief product is social change."[309]

As *World* magazine observes, "IAF organizers like Obama were thus trained to target individuals for hate and denunciation, to exploit the organizational benefits of having enemies, and to pursue 'justice' by creating conflict and confrontation. Personal targeting and scapegoating became a central organizing principle for IAF-trained community organizers, instigated by Alinsky's lieutenant and successor Ed Chambers." IAF is "brutally cynical about the constant need for fresh victims . . . political opponents were to be turned into personal enemies (or 'ripe targets')." One recent victim of this kind of orchestrated personal attack is former Alaska Gov. Sarah Palin, a popular conservative Republican who inspires fanatical hatred in the Left.

ALINSKYITES DOMINATE THE
MODERN DEMOCRATIC PARTY

It should come as no surprise that on the campaign trail, Obama refused to be interviewed about Alinsky. Presumably Obama, who taught courses on Alinsky's organizing techniques, declined to speak to reporters about the late guru because he knew such an interview would throw an unwanted spotlight on Alinsky's radicalism, and by extension, his own. Such counterproductive publicity would also have undermined the candidate's efforts to reinvent himself as a moderate.[310]

Alinsky's adherents now dominate the modern Democratic Party establishment. Apart from President Obama himself, they include Secretary of State Hillary Clinton, White House political director Patrick Gaspard, White House senior advisor Valerie Jarrett, Federal Communications Commission diversity chief Mark Lloyd, Obama's ex-green jobs czar Van Jones, former DNC trainer Heather Booth, Children's Defense Fund founder Marian Wright Edelman, former HUD Secretary Henry Cisneros, and Los Angeles Mayor Antonio Villaraigosa (who is so terribly, hopelessly, excruciatingly politically correct he fused his birth surname, Villar, with that of his then-wife, Raigosa, to make a political statement), to name just a few.

"Who the hell isn't [an Alinskyite] in this administration?" asks David Horowitz.[311]

Cisneros, who served as Bill Clinton's HUD secretary until scandal forced him out in 1997, has been particularly outspoken in his praise of Alinsky's Industrial Areas Foundation. He said IAF's mission was to "create a civic momentum on the left."[312] As San Antonio mayor, Cisneros lauded an IAF affiliate called COPS (Citizens Organized for Public Service) in his hometown for helping in "fundamentally altering the moral tone and the political and physical face of the city."[313] Later, as HUD secretary, he described himself as "a big fan" of IAF.[314]

Cisneros and Hillary Clinton worked with IAF during the Clinton administration. On the advice of HUD Secretary Cisneros, the then-first lady reached out to Washington Interfaith Network, a Washington, D.C.-based affiliate of IAF, helping the group raise money. Clinton pledged her strong support to WIN at a public rally. "It is time for all of us to ask ourselves and our neighbors, 'What can we do?' because there are solutions to every problem which faces us in Washington. The president and I will stand with you . . . We will work with you in WIN."[315]

Cisneros also stood by ACORN as its troubles came to a head in late 2009 and early 2010. Soon after ACORN Housing changed its name to Affordable Housing Centers of America, Cisneros appeared in a promotional video singing the group's praises: "The simple truth is that this is very important work, too important to let it slip away, to let it be destroyed, and that's why I am so pleased that the work will continue, the work of supporting families and helping them get into homes through Affordable Housing Centers of America."[316]

ALINSKY THE AGITATOR

Community organizing as taught by Alinsky is leftist, anti-capitalist agitation elevated to an ugly art form. It's about making people so frothing-at-the-mouth angry that they rise up and demand change, and the kind of change they seek while under the spell of Alinskyite insurrectionists isn't good. Community organizers in the Alinsky tradition are professional political activists who believe that something is terribly wrong with America and that they are the ones we've been waiting for to fix it. Change for the sake of change and action for the sake of action are their religion.

Working "within" the system is the only sensible way to overthrow the system, Alinsky believes. People need to be pushed to agitate for revolution. Because they are fearful of taking a new step, it is necessary to ratchet up the pressure so they can overcome their natural inhibitions. In order to usher in revolutionary change, the people must possess "a passive, affirmative, non-challenging attitude toward change." They have to "feel so frustrated, so defeated, so lost, so futureless in the prevailing system that they are willing to let go of the past and chance the future."[317]

Alinsky taught that the community organizer's first job is "community disorganization" by manufacturing crises in order to inflame the community. The organizer must "create the issues or problems." He must "rub raw the resentments of the people of the community" and "fan the latent hostilities of many of the people to the point of overt expression." The organizer must "agitate to the point of conflict" because without friction and controversy "people are not concerned enough to act." Having harangued the community out of its feelings of complacency, the organizer then directs its rage at specific targets and scapegoats, providing "a channel into which the people can angrily pour their frustrations."[318]

Former ACORN national board member Marcel Reid says ACORN is very good at dealing with adversaries "because they're organizers and because people don't understand what a really professional organizer does; they don't know how to stand up against an organizer." Reid adds:

I tell people that every great religion and every great war is the result of an organizer. If you don't understand how powerful they are and how they do what they do, then you have no way possible of understanding how to stop it. What organizers do is that they turn people's already [held] prejudices or opinions into something that they can galvanize and use.[319]

The organizer doesn't get all the glory. He is an omnipresent though nearly invisible force, manipulating events from behind a curtain and steering the people away from American values. "[T]he organizer serves as a protective shield: if anything goes wrong it is all his fault, he has the responsibility. If they are successful all credit goes to the local people." The organizer "acts as the septic tank in the early stages—he gets all the shit."

> From the moment the organizer enters a community he lives, dreams, eats, breathes, sleeps only one thing and that is to build the mass power base of what he calls the army. Until he has developed that mass power base, he confronts no major issues. He has nothing with which to confront anything. Until he has those means and power instruments, his "tactics" are very different from power tactics. Therefore, every move revolves around one central point: how many recruits will this bring into the organization, whether by means of local organizations, churches, service groups, labor unions, corner gangs, or as individuals. The only issue is, how will this increase the strength of the organization. If by losing in a certain action he can get more members than by winning, then victory lies in losing and he will lose.[320]

This Alinsky statement isn't much different from an observation President Obama had in 1995: "What if a politician were to see his job as that of an organizer, as part teacher and part advocate, one who does not sell voters short but who educates them about the real choices before them?"[321] It wasn't the first time Obama echoed Alinsky. In the 2008 campaign, Obama said, "We are the ones we've been waiting for. We are the change that we seek."[322] The Obama mantra varies only slightly from Alinsky's statement that "The people themselves are the future. The people themselves will solve each problem that will arise out of a changing world."[323]

According to Mike Miller, an Alinsky-trained organizer who worked for the Student Nonviolent Coordinating Committee, "An organizer doesn't like to do all the talking. He talks; he listens; he asks questions.

He operates on the principle that the people in the streets, in the neighborhoods, in the fields, in the plants, on the unemployed lines, on the welfare rolls know better than he what they want and need— but they don't know how to get it."[324] Miller's statement closely resembles a statement Obama made on the campaign trail in early 2008:

> I think that one of the most important things I learned as an organizer is, don't do all the talking, spend a little time listening and finding out what's on the mind of people, what they're concerned about, because the more you do that, the more you connect with them, and the more you can tie the act of voting or politics to their day-to-day lives.[325]

This is, of course, a standard technique for ACORN when it preys on the poor in recruiting drives. Organizers go door-to-door in a community asking residents what local issues are of concern to them. Regardless of what residents say, the solution is always more government spending. The charlatans at ACORN know that if they are trying to recruit desperate poor people, the idea of taking money from others and giving it to them sells itself.

ACORN organizers are taught to sell community residents on Big Government by stressing their short-term self-interest. They are sold, perversely, on statist collectivism by means of an appeal to individual well-being. As Alinsky taught, "The fact is that self-interest can be a most potent weapon in the development of co-operation and identification of the group welfare as being of greater importance than personal welfare."[326] This allows ACORN to wrap itself in the American flag as it campaigns to destroy America.

SEVEN

Rules for Radicals: ACORN's Action Plan

IN THE LIVELY organizing opus *Rules for Radicals*, published in 1971, Saul Alinsky describes tactics that can be used to subvert the American system. The principles he taught so thoroughly permeate ACORN to its core and are so taken to heart by ACORN organizers that they refer to the rules when planning attacks, sometimes by number.[327]

In a revealing gesture, Alinsky dedicates the book to Lucifer whom he hails as "the very first radical" who rebelled so effectively against the establishment of his time "that he at least won his own kingdom." Such tribute is not only an extended middle finger to America but is odd on several other levels. First, because Alinsky was a ferocious atheist. Second, because Lucifer was, to put it plainly, a loser. Lucifer *lost* his war against God; he was a fallen angel, cast out of Heaven by the victor. Third, because Lucifer, known as Satan after his forced emigration, is referred to in the New Testament as "the deceiver of the whole world" (Revelation 12:9). Maybe Alinsky admired Satan's public relations skills. Alinsky the nonbeliever even quipped that in the afterlife he would continue organizing in the underworld. "They'll send me to hell, and I'll organize it."[328]

According to David Horowitz, the salutation to Satan serves as a reminder that "the radical illusion is an ancient one and has not changed through the millennia." In Genesis 3:5 the serpent commonly thought by Christian scholars to be Satan tempts Adam and Eve to lay waste to their earthly paradise: revolt against God and "you shall be as gods."

> This is the radical hubris: *We can create a new world. Through our political power we can make a new race of men and women who will live in harmony and peace and according to the principles of social justice. We can be as gods.* And let us not forget that the kingdom the first radical "won," as Alinsky so thoughtlessly puts it, was *hell.* Typical of radicals not to notice the ruin they leave behind.[329]

It's no surprise that Alinsky views the organizer as a godlike being who is trying to build paradise on earth. To him, the organizer is a kind of superman, a leader of leaders. He is equipped with an ego that is "stronger and more monumental than the ego of the leader." The organizer must of necessity have a colossal ego, for

> How can an organizer respect the dignity of an individual if he does not respect his own dignity? How can he believe in people if he does not really believe in himself? How can he convince people that they have it within themselves, that they have the power to stand up to win, if he does not believe it of himself? Ego must be so all-pervading that the personality of the organizer is contagious, that it converts the people from despair to defiance, creating a mass ego.

The leader "is driven by the desire for power, while the organizer is driven by the desire to create." The organizer "is in a true sense reaching for the highest level for which man can reach—to create, to be a 'great creator,' to play God," Alinsky wrote.[330] According to Horowitz, the Alinskyite community organizer is the Marxist cadre, the vanguard of the proletariat. "And his institutes are cadre training institutes and they are the elite," he said in an interview.

The organizer is a crusader, the instrument of America's recovery from error whose initial task "is to build the mass power base of what he calls the army."[331] Speaking of God, Alinsky said that without aggressive organizers, the Christian church would never have gotten off the ground. The Apostle Paul, whose name was also Saul originally, was instrumental in defining and building the church, he said. "You don't have a tougher, harder more realistic operator than Paul in organizing Christianity. If Paul hadn't come around to organize the Christian church Christ would have been another guy hanging on a cross."[332] Incidentally, Alinsky put his godlike ego on display before a young Hillary Clinton. Alinsky told her that *he* was the second most important Jew in the history of Christianity.[333]

SEIZING POWER

Alinsky's ambition is to redeem America by creating "mass organizations to seize power and give it to the people," as if the people did not already rule America.[334] Power was best exercised in Alinsky's view through what he called "People's Organizations." He explained that "[a] People's Organization is dedicated to an eternal war. It is a war against poverty, misery, delinquency, disease, injustice, hopelessness, despair, and unhappiness." In the war such a group wages "against the social menaces of mankind there can be no compromise. It is life or death."[335]

It is certainly an odd choice of words for Alinsky, a self-professed champion of democracy, to say that these people's organizations must "*seize* power." Then again, Alinsky's book is not about democracy as most Americans understand the term. It is about power, pure and simple. The word *power* appears in the slender volume an astonishing 191 times.[336] Alinsky writes that his book shows "how to organize for power: how to get it and to use it." He intones ominously that failing to use "power for a more equitable distribution of the means of life for all people signals the end of the revolution and the start of the counterrevolution."[337]

The myth that Alinsky was a champion of American values persists on the Left. Alinsky created that myth, eagerly swallowed by generations of academics and activists, by positioning himself as a ferocious defender of democracy. In her college thesis, Hillary Clinton epitomizes this attitude, characterizing Alinsky as a courageous all-American trailblazer. Alinsky's ideas mesh easily into "the tradition of Western democratic theory," she writes. Although many regard him as "the proponent of a dangerous socio/political philosophy," he walks in the footsteps of great men such as Socialist leader Eugene Debs, poet Walt Whitman, and Martin Luther King. Alinsky is feared, like those three men, only because he "embraced the most radical of political faiths—democracy."[338]

To Alinsky the word *democracy* is a meaningless but powerful-sounding talisman he dangles when he needs to make his cause sound noble. Words such as *democracy* are "a common carrier of so many different meanings that they are meaningless." Words are vessels into which meanings calculated to advance the cause can be poured. "Morality is for words and not for work," he wrote, echoing philosopher Friedrich Nietzsche who cynically described morality as the "herd instinct in the individual."[339]

Despite Clinton's nonsense, it is more accurate to say that Saul Alinsky walks in the footsteps of Benedict Arnold or Julius Rosenberg, and not Tom Paine as some of his most fervent followers have claimed. This vicious charlatan was exactly the sort of institution-leveling rabble-rouser the Founding Fathers feared. Alinsky had not yet been born in the summer of 1787 when delegates gathered at the Constitutional Convention in Philadelphia, but the Framers of the Constitution foresaw his arrival. A hundred and twenty-two years before Alinsky's birth, they designed the U.S. Constitution precisely with demagogic troublemakers like Alinsky in mind. Remember that the essential point in *Rules for Radicals* is the ends justify the means. But as Thomas Sowell reminds us, "If you believe that the end justifies the means, then you don't believe in constitutional government."[340]

Alinsky gave lip service to venerable American institutions such as the Constitution but in reality had no use for them unless they could be used to advance his cause. In his earlier book *Reveille for Radicals* he essentially declares war on the Constitution, writing that "The radical places human rights far above property rights."[341] In *Rules for Radicals* he approvingly quoted his hero and mentor, John L. Lewis, the radical Depression-era Congress of Industrial Organizations leader. As some sit-down strikers at GM began to lose their nerve, Lewis thundered, "The right to a man's job transcends the right of private property!"[342]

The Founding Fathers would have answered that Lewis and Alinsky present a false dichotomy: property rights *are* human rights. The principal architect of the Constitution, James Madison, declared that: "Government is instituted to protect property of every sort; as well that which lies in the various rights of individuals, as that which the term particularly expresses. This being the end of government, that alone is a just government, which impartially secures to every man, whatever is his own."[343]

The mob actions Alinsky advocated and practiced have always been the antithesis of the American way of doing things. Abraham Lincoln denounced the "mobocratic spirit"[344] and in his farewell address in 1796 George Washington warned of the "frightful despotism" that could come from vicious interest group warfare.[345] Madison considered it the sacred duty of government to protect property from mobocracy: "That is not a just government, nor is property secure under it, where the property which a man has in his personal safety and personal liberty, is violated by arbitrary seizures of one class of citizens for the service of the rest."[346]

Alinsky describes *Rules for Radicals* this way: "*The Prince* was written by Machiavelli for the Haves on how to hold power. *Rules for Radicals* is written for the Have-Nots on how to take it away." The book was "a step toward a science of revolution."[347] Originally, Alinsky intended to call the book *Rules for Revolution*,[348] which would have been a more honest title. It is a cookbook for anarchy, a schematic diagram for reversing the American Revolution and imposing the aggressive alien cancer of revolutionary socialism on the American public.

Alinsky invents 24 individual rules in *Rules for Radicals*. Though a quirky writer, he was a brilliant man. It is important for anyone who aspires to understand modern American politics to have at least a passing familiarity with some of these rules because they have inspired and been practiced by countless influential ACORN imitator-groups, labor union activists, and by no less than the current president of the United States himself. They're worth examining up close.

This is not to say that President Obama looks into a mirror and sees Saul Alinsky. But Alinsky's ideas about how to change America make Obama get out of bed every morning. As First Lady Michelle Obama said on the presidential campaign trail after her husband was elected to the U.S. Senate, "Barack is not a politician first and foremost. He's a community activist exploring the viability of politics to make change." Notably, then-Senator Obama responded, "I take that observation as a compliment."[349]

Many of the rules in *Rules for Radicals* overlap or spring from other rules. Some are well thought out and explained; others seem hardly worth noting at all. Only 13 of the 24 rules are concerned with "power tactics"; the remaining 11 focus on "the ethics of means and ends." The 13 rules of "power tactics" are generally what commentators refer to when they speak of Alinsky's rules. Although Alinsky lists and explains the 11 "ethics" rules first, we'll start with the 13 "power tactics" rules. The rules are examined here because ACORN has used them all, often in combination with each other. (All 24 rules are listed in Appendix C at the back of this book.)

THE 13 RULES OF "POWER TACTICS"

The first rule of "power tactics" is, "*Power is not only what you have but what the enemy thinks you have.*" Organizing is war and war is deception. Power comes "from two main sources, money and people," Alinsky writes. Because the Have-Nots lack money, they "must build power from their own flesh and blood."[350]

If you build a "vast, mass-based people's organization, you can parade it visibly before the enemy and openly show your power." If your organization has few members, pretend to have a large membership. "[C]onceal the members in the dark but raise a din and clamor that will make the listener believe that your organization numbers many more than it does." If your organization is "too tiny even for noise, stink up the place."[351] Karl Marx himself counseled deception as an essential means of lulling society into a useful complacency about revolutionary socialism. "In order to relieve the bourgeoisie of the last trace of anxiety it must be clearly and convincingly proved to it that the Red bogey is really only a bogey, and does not exist," Marx wrote.[352]

Alinsky's second and third rules describe deadly serious strategic principles, yet he explains them in comedic fashion, as if he were directing a slapstick comedy. Perhaps this is an illustration of how Alinsky believes a sense of humor "is essential to a successful tactician." As he states in the fifth rule—to be discussed in a moment—"[r]*idicule is man's most potent weapon.*" Humor is so important to tacticians because "the most potent weapons known to mankind are satire and ridicule." A sense of humor allows a tactician "to maintain his perspective and see himself for what he really is: a bit of dust that burns for a fleeting second," and is "incompatible with the complete acceptance of any dogma, any religious, political, or economic prescription for salvation." A sense of humor "synthesizes with curiosity, irreverence, and imagination," he writes.[353] But in the end, the tactics he describes as examples of the two rules in action are less significant in this part of his book than the fact that Alinsky, like ACORN and Cloward and Piven, enjoys using black people as pawns on the chessboard of social justice.

Rules two and three relate to the familiarity of activists and targets with tactics. The second rule is "*Never go outside the experience of your people.*"[354] "People only understand things in terms of their experience, which means that you must get within their experience," he writes.[355] Actions or tactics outside their experience lead to "confusion, fear, and retreat."[356] In other words, keep it simple and fun.

The third rule is "*Wherever possible go outside of the experience of the enemy.*" In this case, "you want to cause confusion, fear, and retreat."[357] To explain the second and third rules, Alinsky recalls his proposal for "natural stink bombs," an idea that sounds more Marx Brothers than Karl Marx. To harass the local establishment in Rochester, New York, he proposed treating a hundred black members of the community to a baked bean feast three hours before a performance of the local symphony orchestra. By the middle of the concert, human digestive processes would create a competing musical performance of sorts. "Imagine the scene when the action began! The concert would be over before the first movement! (If this be a Freudian slip—so be it!)," writes Alinsky, delighting in the scatological.[358]

The disturbance at the concert would be a tactical masterstroke because it "would be utterly outside the experience of the establishment, which was expecting the usual stuff of mass meetings, street demonstrations, confrontations and parades." Moreover, it would "ridicule and make a farce of the law" because no law can ban natural bodily functions. Although "regular stink bombs are illegal and cause for immediate arrest," no one would be able to do anything about the action. "The law would be completely paralyzed" while the establishment was made to "look utterly ridiculous." The establishment would come to the bargaining table under pressure from the community. Wives would say to their husbands, "'John, we are not going to have our symphony season ruined by those people! I don't know what they want but whatever it is, something has got to be done and this kind of thing has to he stopped!"[359]

An added bonus of the symphony tactic was that it "connected" blacks "with their hatred of Whitey," Alinsky writes. "The one thing that all oppressed people want to do to their oppressors is shit on them. Here was an approximate way to do this."[360]

Continuing with his scatological train of thought, Alinsky envisioned "the nation's first shit-in" at Chicago's O'Hare Airport, one of the world's busiest air terminals. He proposed having activists occupy all the toilets and urinals all day long. "What are the police going to do? Break in and demand evidence of legitimate occupancy?" Airport users would be desperate to relieve themselves. "The whole scene would become unbelievable and the laughter and ridicule would be nationwide," he writes. "It would probably get a front page story in the London *Times*. It would be a source of great mortification and embarrassment to the city administration."[361]

It's unclear if Alinsky ever performed at Chicago's Second City comedy club on amateur night. He might have brought the house down.

Alinsky's fourth rule is *"Make the enemy live up to their own book of rules."* The ever-cynical organizing guru notes, "You can kill them with this, for they can no more obey their own rules than the Christian church can live up to Christianity."[362] Under this rule, radical organizers are encouraged to use their enemies' refusal to cross moral and ethical boundaries against them. As David Horowitz explains, "Because conservatives embrace the system they believe in its rules of fairness and inclusion. But these rules can also be used by its cynical enemies to destroy it. Remember that, as Alinsky's hero Lenin put it, 'The capitalists will sell us the rope to hang them.'"[363] NWRO senior official Tim Sampson said in 1970 that the Cloward-Piven Strategy was a fine example of this rule in action. It was "[a] very Alinsky thing," he said. "You beat the system by making it live by its own rules. Perhaps you could really develop a political constituency by putting bread on these people's tables like the old city machine."[364]

The fifth rule, *"Ridicule is man's most potent weapon,"* springs from the fourth rule, according to Alinsky. Ridicule is a rhetorical weapon of mass destruction. "It is almost impossible to counterattack ridicule," he notes. "Also it infuriates the opposition, who then react to your advantage."[365] It is easy to get away with threatening the enemy. "You can insult and annoy him, but the one thing that is unforgivable and that is certain to get him to react is to laugh at him. This causes irrational anger."[366]

The sixth and seventh rules pertain to the enjoyment of tactics by activists. The sixth rule is *"A good tactic is one that your people enjoy."* If activists aren't having fun "doing it, there is something very wrong with the tactic." The seventh rule is *"A tactic that drags on too long becomes a drag."* A high level of interest in a specific issue can be maintained only for a brief period of time. After that, "it becomes a ritualistic commitment, like going to church on Sunday mornings." There are always new issues and crises developing and activists can be overcome by compassion fatigue. The reaction becomes, "'Well, my heart bleeds for those people and I'm all for the boycott, but after all there are other important things in life'—and there it goes," Alinsky writes.[367]

Alinsky's eighth and tenth rules could easily have been counted as one. The tenth rule, which underlies the eighth, is actually more of a premise than a rule. Confused? So was Alinsky at times, it seems. This confusion may reflect the fact that Alinsky, then in his sixties, was attempting to come up with a retroactive rationale for a lifetime of community organizing in which he disregarded rules. In *Rules for Radicals* Alinsky is simply making up reasons for tactics, cloaking his behavior in what he called "moral garments." (See Alinsky's tenth rule of the ethics of means and ends.)

The eighth rule is "*Keep the pressure on, with different tactics and actions, and utilize all events of the period for your purpose.*"[368] The related tenth rule is "*The major premise for tactics is the development of operations that will maintain a constant pressure upon the opposition.*" Constant, unceasing pressure generates responses from the enemy, which, in turn, leads to new actions against the enemy, which generates a new response, and the process continues "ad infinitum."[369]

The ninth rule is that threatening works. "*The threat is usually more terrifying than the thing itself.*"[370] A well calculated threat can save a tactician a great deal of resources; it can even lead to an early victory, so threaten away!

The eleventh rule is "*If you push a negative hard and deep enough it will break through into its counterside.*" In other words, every bad thing can be turned into a good thing. Alinsky recounts how a corporate enemy broke into his office to steal files. It was obvious to everyone, including the police, that the corporation did it. Later an attempt was made on his life, which made people suspect the corporation was behind the effort. The corporation was forced to spend money on security in order to protect Alinsky's person. "This became another devil in the closet to haunt this corporation and to keep the pressure on," he writes.[371]

The twelfth rule is "*The price of a successful attack is a constructive alternative.*" No tactician can afford "being trapped by the enemy in his sudden agreement with your demand and saying 'You're right—

we don't know what to do about this issue. Now you tell us."[372] This is another way of saying, "be careful what you wish for." Don't target an enemy without having a specific objective in mind. This is not to say an organizer can't compromise during negotiations, but he should have a plan and know what he wants the other side to give him.

The thirteenth rule is the Alinsky "power tactics" rule that has come to epitomize the Age of Obama: *"Pick the target, freeze it, personalize it, and polarize it."*[373] As Alinsky explained, "In order to organize, you must first polarize. People think of controversy as negative; they think consensus is better. But to organize, you need a Bull Connor or a Jim Clark."[374]

Alinsky also relies on the Bible, asserting that "[t]he classic statement on polarization comes from Christ: 'He that is not with me is against me' (Luke 11:23)." Jesus "allowed no middle ground to the moneychangers in the Temple," he writes. The organizer must assume the complete moral correctness of his side and the utter moral degeneracy of the other side and then act decisively. "He can't toss forever in limbo, and avoid decision. He can't weigh arguments or reflect endlessly—he must decide and act."[375]

"[A]ll issues must be polarized if action is to follow," he writes. The organizer must relentlessly vilify his target, which should be an individual person rather than an institution. "It is not possible to develop the necessary hostility against, say, City Hall, which after all is a concrete, physical, inanimate structure, or against a corporation, which has no soul or identity, or a public school administration, which again is an inanimate system," he writes. Having a villain is good for an organizer's business. Alinsky cites approvingly the example of John L. Lewis, the legendary bushy eyebrowed radical labor leader from the Great Depression. Lewis never attacked General Motors by name, preferring instead to attack its president whom he referred to as Alfred "Icewater-In-His-Veins" Sloan. He called the Republic Steel Corporation's president "Bloodied Hands" Tom Girdler.[376]

The process is working as it should, Alinsky explains, when the target responds with similarly inflamed rhetoric, publicly attacking the organizer as a "dangerous enemy." Being so labeled puts the organizer "on the side of the people" and reveals the establishment's "fear of the organizer," a fear that "he represents a threat to its omnipotence."[377]

The Obama White House lives and breathes the thirteenth rule as it attempts to portray its opposition, particularly its conservative arch-nemesis Rush Limbaugh, as the embodiment of evil. Though government policy is obviously a major factor in the financial meltdown of 2008, only "greedy" bankers, corporations—and most of all George W. Bush—are to blame. Alinsky would be proud.

THE 11 RULES OF
"THE ETHICS OF MEANS AND ENDS"

Alinsky's 11 rules "of the ethics of means and ends," are interesting intellectual exercises, though they ring hollow (and overlap with each other to a maddening degree). They show the lengths to which Alinsky was willing to go to convince the reader—and perhaps to convince himself—that deep down he was a moral man who adhered to some ethical standards. This set of rules seems designed to help organizers justify things they already intend to do.

Alinsky didn't believe that ethics should figure much, if at all, in political tactics. Tactics have to be evaluated solely in terms of their effectiveness. It is a "myth" that "one approach is positive and another negative," he writes. "One man's positive is another man's negative. The description of any procedure as 'positive' or 'negative' is the mark of a political illiterate."[378]

His first rule "of the ethics of means and ends" is "*one's concern with the ethics of means and ends varies inversely with one's personal interest in the issue.*" In other words, if you have no personal stake in the issue, you can afford the luxury of worrying about the ethics of tactics. If the issue matters to you, ethical questions must take a back seat. A corollary to this first rule is that "*one's concern with the ethics of means and ends varies inversely with one's distance from the scene of conflict.*"[379]

The second rule is "*that the judgment of the ethics of means is dependent upon the political position of those sitting in judgment.*" This is a variation of Charles Maurice de Talleyrand's Machiavellian aphorism, "Treason is a matter of dates." Alinsky argues that to Americans the Declaration of Independence "is a glorious document and an affirmation of human rights," but to the British "it was a statement notorious for its deceit by omission." It is impossible in the heat of battle to remain objective. We always view means the opposition uses against us as "immoral" and regard the means we use against them as "ethical and rooted in the highest of human values."[380]

This second rule is barely distinguishable from the ninth rule "of the ethics of means and ends," wherein Alinsky attempts to dismiss his opposition. It is that *"any effective means is automatically judged by the opposition as being unethical."*[381] The remarkably similar seventh rule also echoes Talleyrand. It is that *"generally success or failure is a mighty determinant of ethics."* Translated into a bumper sticker: Everyone loves a winner. History tends to side with tactics that bring success. Victory is "the difference between the traitor and the patriotic hero," Alinsky writes. *"There can be no such thing as a successful traitor, for if one succeeds he becomes a founding father."* Perhaps Julius and Ethel Rosenberg, Soviet spies who in 1953 became the only American civilians ever executed for espionage, were merely misunderstood visionaries in Alinsky's eyes.

The third rule is that *"in war the end justifies almost any means."*[382] This is the rule that makes one wonder why Alinsky bothered with rules at all since tactical necessity in his view overrides nearly all rules. "In a fight almost anything goes," he writes. "It almost reaches the point where you stop to apologize if a chance blow lands above the belt."[383] The practical revolutionary, like a soldier on the battlefield, must recognize that "in action, one does not always enjoy the luxury of a decision that is consistent both with one's individual conscience and the good of mankind." Given that Alinsky feels he is doing his part to bring about a utopian paradise, "[t]he choice must always be for the latter. Action is for mass salvation and not for the individual's personal salvation."[384]

The fourth rule is a backward-looking rule that an organizer might use in a discussion of tactical efficacy with his comrades. It is that "*judgment must be made in the context of the times in which the action occurred and not from any other chronological vantage point.*"[385] In other words, don't beat yourself up now for not knowing then what you know now. Do the best you can with the knowledge you have and don't let the perfect become the enemy of the good.

The fifth rule "of the ethics of means and ends" is a slightly modified version of the second rule. It is that "*concern with ethics increases with the number of means available and vice versa.*" To explain the rule, here Alinsky pretends to have ethics. He describes how a corporate adversary tried to blackmail him by exposing his visit with a woman to a motel room. Alinsky brushes aside the threat telling his enemy, "Go ahead and give it to the press. I think she's beautiful and I have never claimed to be celibate. Go ahead!" The tactic works. But then an executive of the same company who is secretly sympathetic to Alinsky's cause suggests turnabout is fair play. He says he has proof that a leader on his side prefers boys to girls and suggests Alinsky use this fact to his advantage. As Alinsky tells the story, he rejects the offering saying, "Thanks, but forget it. I don't fight that way. I don't want to see it. Goodbye." The executive replies, "But they just tried to hang you on that girl." Alinsky then dons a false cloak of morality, replying, "The fact that they fight that way doesn't mean I have to do it. To me, dragging a person's private life into this muck is loathsome and nauseous." But it's a put-on. Alinsky admits the only reason he was able to turn down the executive was because he didn't believe he needed to use his enemy's homosexuality against him. "[I]f I had been convinced that the only way we could win was to use it, then without any reservations I would have used it." So much for Alinsky's morality tale.[386]

The sixth rule is that "*the less important the end to be desired, the more one can afford to engage in ethical evaluations of means.*"[387] In other words, don't lose sleep over ethics if your goal is modest. Save the Hamlet-style hand-wringing for something that matters.

The eighth rule is that "*the morality of a means depends upon whether the means is being employed at a time of imminent defeat or imminent victory.*" It means that tactics that would be unthinkable if one were coasting along to an easy victory become absolutely essential when defeat is in the process of being snatched from the jaws of victory. "[E]thics are determined by whether one is losing or winning," Alinsky writes.[388]

In an effort to explain his rationale for the eighth rule, Alinsky then goes off on a strange tangent in which he uses rhetorical questions to condemn the U.S. bombing of Hiroshima in 1945 through implication. It is an argument that many college undergraduates toiling under Marxist history professors have had to endure—though, in their defense at least they have had the moral courage to make their case explicitly instead of hiding like a coward behind Socratic dialogue. Alinsky never comes out and declares definitively that the American government's bombing of Hiroshima was evil, but he comes as close to it as he feels he can without the average reader tossing his manual for mayhem in the garbage.

After noting correctly that "From the beginning of time killing has always been regarded as justifiable if committed in self-defense," he then writes, "Let us confront this principle with the most awful ethical question of modern times: did the United States have the right to use the atomic bomb at Hiroshima?" When the U.S. military bombed Hiroshima, "[d]efeat for Japan was an absolute certainty and the only question was how and when the coup de grace would be administered."[389]

If the atomic bomb had been invented soon after December 1941 when America was "defenseless" after Japan's surprise bombing of Pearl Harbor, afraid the Pacific coast was going to be invaded, and committed to the war in the European theater, dropping the bomb known as Little Boy on Hiroshima at that time "would have been universally heralded as a just retribution of hail, fire, and brimstone." Bombing Hiroshima "would have been hailed as proof that good inevitably triumphs over evil" and "[t]he question of the ethics of the use of the bomb would never have arisen at that time."[390]

Alinsky stops short of suggesting the bombing of Hiroshima was motivated by a racial animus against Asians, something some of his Marxist counterparts today routinely claim. However, after characterizing his own country as a mass-murdering pariah state, Alinsky steers clear of the question of how many lives of American military personnel, of Japanese civilians, of civilians and military personnel in lands under Imperial Japanese occupation, were actually *saved* by the bombings of Hiroshima and then Nagasaki three days later.

It's quite a cop-out, to use one of Alinsky's favorite expressions.

In any event, as applied to community organizing, the eighth rule "of the ethics of means and ends" seems to mean you can (and ought to be able to) get away with tactics of maximum viciousness and devastation if your situation is desperate.

The tenth rule "of the ethics of means and ends" is that "*you do what you can with what you have and clothe it with moral garments.*"

According to Alinsky, all great leaders lie and use moralistic propaganda in order to accomplish their goals. "All great leaders, including Churchill, Gandhi, Lincoln, and Jefferson, always invoked 'moral principles' to cover naked self-interest in the clothing of 'freedom,' 'equality of mankind,' 'a law higher than man-made law,' and so on," he writes. "This even held under circumstances of national crises when it was universally assumed that the end justified any means. *All effective actions require the passport of morality.*"[391] [emphasis in original]

Alinsky pontificates that Mohandas Gandhi, the legendary apostle of nonviolent civil disobedience who laid the foundation for India's independence, was a fraud and a hypocrite who would have embraced violent tactics if necessary. In other words, Gandhi was an Alinskyite, he argues. Gandhi's embrace of nonviolent tactics was "the only intelligent, realistic, expedient program which Gandhi had at his disposal." The morality in which he cloaked his program was public relations window-dressing. "If he had had guns he might well have used them in an armed revolution against the British," but Gandhi didn't have the guns and worse, didn't have people to use the guns. Gandhi was disgusted that his own countrymen lacked the ability "to give organized, effective, violent resistance against injustice and tyranny." Gandhi's approach against the British Empire was the only one that could have succeeded, Alinsky writes. The empire had a chink in its armor because its traditions "granted a good deal of freedom to its colonials." Although Gandhi took advantage of the empire's weaknesses by using passive resistance, it "would never have had a chance against a totalitarian state such as that of the Nazis," and in such a situation he would probably have embraced revolutionary violence, Alinsky implies.[392]

Like Gandhi, the American civil rights movement embraced a non-violence strategy in the 1950s only because it had to, Alinsky contends. Violence in the South at that time "would have been suicidal." Passive resistance was "a good defensive tactic" because it gave the establishment few opportunities "for forcible repression." As in the case of Gandhi, a halo then began floating over the civil rights movement but, also as with Gandhi, it was undeserved, Alinsky suggests. There is no reason to make "a special religion of nonviolence." It was simply "the best tactic for its time and place." Writing at a time when the sometimes violent black power movement was gaining steam, Alinsky leaves open the possibility that in the future, violent confrontation may be the best means for blacks to advance. "As more effective means become available" the black civil rights movement will abandon nonviolence "and substitute a new moral philosophy in keeping with its new means and opportunities."[393]

The eleventh and final rule "of the ethics of means and ends" is that *"goals must be phrased in general terms like 'Liberty, Equality, Fraternity,' 'Of the Common Welfare,' 'Pursuit of Happiness,' or 'Bread and Peace.'"*

In this rule, Alinsky embraces sloganeering and the techniques of Madison Avenue. Practice good salesmanship. Emphasize only the positives of your program and don't get bogged down by being specific. Use cheery phrases.[394]

All of the rules from *Rules for Radicals* are practiced in varying degrees by ACORN and the Obama administration. When it comes to getting things done, Alinsky is their guiding light.

EIGHT

Funding the Revolution:
ACORN's Stealth Accounting

G UIDED BY THE tactical ruthlessness of Saul Alinsky, the Association of Community Organizations for Reform Now lies at the intersection of community organizing and organized crime. It is a vast, well-funded, multi-national criminal enterprise whose ringleaders routinely evade justice and brag about their exploits behind closed doors. Its nebulous legal status and opaque corporate structure allow it to keep its activities largely hidden from public view.

The structure of the ACORN network is incomprehensibly labyrinthine. There is nothing even remotely like it in the world of activism—on the Left or the Right. Organizational flow charts drawn up to explain how the parent nonprofit interacts with its affiliates never quite do it justice.

Some critics of ACORN don't give its mazelike organizational structure the credit it deserves, said former ACORN national board member Marcel Reid. "They don't appreciate the prowess that ACORN operates with, that it's mean and lean, that they keep their operating costs down, and they can strike a number of targets simultaneously with military precision."

ACORN "really is just a paper corporation," Reid said. "So ACORN invites fire and invites lawsuits because once you start to probe, there's nothing you can get your hands on. It's just paper. So it's structured brilliantly. The next thing you need to know . . . is that the people who structured ACORN are geniuses when it comes to corporate law. They know exactly how to get around it and they've done so successfully through so many years." Before "there can be a really good prosecution of ACORN for what they've done and the people that they've hurt, there has to be someone who will do the research to find out what ACORN actually is because without that, this will continue to go on," she said.[395]

Experts can't even agree on the legal status of ACORN. Reid, who now heads the ACORN 8 whistleblower group, insists ACORN is a nonprofit social welfare/advocacy organization under section 501(c)(4) of the tax code. Congressional investigators disagree. Investigators on the House Oversight and Government Reform Committee found that "ACORN, the parent company, is not a 501(c)(4), but rather a taxable nonprofit corporation."

Committee staffers asked the Congressional Research Service (CRS) why a nonprofit organization would choose to pay corporate income taxes. "The CRS stated they were aware of only one corporation in the United States structured that way: ACORN. But CRS could not explain why ACORN would structure itself this way." Investigators contacted "a preeminent nonprofit tax lawyer," named Bruce Hopkins, who is director of the Nonprofit Law Center. "This attorney explained that the ONLY reason a nonprofit would want a nonexempt status would be *to conduct political activities without reporting them to the Internal Revenue Service*," committee staffers wrote. [italics added; block capitals original][396]

Sometimes it's partisan and sometimes it's not. It has specialized subsidiaries that perform partisan political work and it runs candidates for office under the banner of its minor party, the Working Families Party. It trains organizers and activists who rage against capitalism and the American system and work on behalf of the Democratic Party. Yet the relationship between affiliates and parent is so confusing to lawmakers and investigators that the racketeering probes that need to be initiated rarely get off the ground.

Founder Wade Rathke designed ACORN's corporate family tree to confound ACORN's enemies. Only Rathke and a few other people truly understand how it all works, ACORN insiders say.

ACORN ally John Atlas has a different take. He suggests Rathke's brother, Dale, who stole close to a million dollars from the group around 2000, was deeply involved in designing ACORN's corporate structure. "Since [Wade's] talent and attention focused on building relationships, tactics, and campaign strategies, he delegated administration to others, especially his younger brother, Dale," who presided over ACORN's financial affairs. Dale, "a Princeton graduate, had created a Rube Goldberg machine to manage ACORN's two hundred affiliated corporations," writes Atlas. "Only Dale, Wade, and, to some extent ACORN's attorney [Steve Bachmann], really understood how the interconnected complex web of entities worked."[397]

Whether Atlas or ACORN insiders are correct, it is clear that both Rathke brothers were brilliant and talented in their respective spheres of expertise. Wade, in particular, is "an organic genius," according to Reid. "He sprung forth to the earth five I.Q. points brighter than everyone else and he's been doubling it every decade since."[398] ACORN was designed by Rathke to thwart investigations and allow the group to pursue its illegitimate program with a minimum of outside interference.

PLAYING CORPORATE MUSICAL CHAIRS

ACORN plays a game of corporate musical chairs. When an ACORN affiliate's behavior reflects well on the group, ACORN emphasizes its ties to that affiliate. When an affiliate does something infamous, ACORN plays dumb and its byzantine organizational structure affords it plausible deniability. It's always a rogue employee or a subsidiary acting without permission from the top, ACORN claims. Trying to get the goods on ACORN and affiliates turns into a game of whack-a-mole. Titles change constantly, people move around, money is transferred, and outsiders often give up investigating ACORN out of sheer frustration.

Craig Becker, one of President Obama's nominees to the National Labor Relations Board (NLRB), took advantage of the confusion that surrounds ACORN's structure. The radical union-backed nominee lied to a Senate confirmation panel about his ties to ACORN. Becker was longtime associate general counsel to ACORN's sister union SEIU. Becker is considered radical in part because he believes that "employers should have no role in the unionization process," according to Brian Johnson, executive director of the Alliance for Worker Freedom. Becker also believes that all Americans should be forced to join unions whether they want to or not. The only choice a worker should have is which union to join, he has said.

President Obama gave a recess appointment to Becker in March 2010 after his nomination was decisively rejected by the Senate the month before. At a hearing of the Senate Health, Education, Labor, and Pensions Committee, Sen. John McCain (R-AZ) asked Becker this question: "Do you perform work for and provide advice to ACORN or ACORN-affiliated groups while employed by your current employers or on a volunteer basis?"

Becker responded, "Senator McCain, I have never done so." But that answer—that Becker "never" provided advice "to ACORN or ACORN-affiliated groups"—is demonstrably false. Becker gave advice to SEIU Local 880, which was part and parcel of ACORN, before it merged with another SEIU bargaining unit. As the *Wall Street Journal* noted, Becker acknowledged previously that he had "worked with and provided advice" to Local 880.[399] And in a blog post, ACORN founder Wade Rathke couldn't help bragging about Becker's NLRB nomination, calling it "a big win no matter how you shake and bake it."

Rathke, who is also founder and chief organizer of SEIU Local 100 in New Orleans, reminisced about the good old days. "I can still remember Keith Kelleher negotiating the subsidy for SEIU Local 880 in Chicago and always making sure that there was the money for the organizers, but that SEIU was also still willing to allow access to Craig."[400]

Local 880 no longer exists. Local 880 official and ACORN leader Keith Kelleher filed documentation with the Department of Labor disclosing that the local wound up its affairs on March 31, 2009. It merged with SEIU Healthcare Illinois and Indiana (also known as SEIU HCII). On the form, Local 880 gave its address as 209 W. Jackson Ave., Suite 200, Chicago, Ill., which just so happens to be in the same building as the national headquarters of ACORN Housing. Back in the day, SEIU Local 880 was such an important member of the ACORN family of affiliated groups that ACORN listed the local on the "allied organizations" page of its website. The local was included in a list with a select group of major ACORN affiliates such as ACORN Housing and President Obama's former employer, Project Vote.

Ever since the hidden camera videos surfaced in fall 2009 showing ACORN employees acting badly, SEIU has been trying to publicly distance itself from ACORN. But it is far from clear if SEIU really has severed its ties to what's left of the ACORN network.

An SEIU spokeswoman explained in October 2009 that even though Local 880 and Local 100 affiliated with SEIU in the mid-1980s, the union's international executive board moved in September to revoke Local 100's charter because the bargaining unit was "not financially viable" and "simply couldn't meet requirements to be a stand alone union." The local had until September 30, 2009, to appeal the disaffiliation decision but didn't do so, she said.

Who knows if we should believe Anna Burger, who was SEIU's international secretary-treasurer, when she told a congressional hearing in fall 2009 that her union "cut all ties to ACORN" after paying the group a total of $1,835,000 in 2008 and 2009.

SEIU's then-boss Andrew Stern, who sits on ACORN's Independent Advisory Council, was less than forthright when asked in January 2010 if SEIU was planning to renew its relationship with ACORN. "From what I understand ACORN is reconstituting itself differently so it would be hard to know, and many of their local affiliates are reforming themselves as independent entities separate from the national organization," said Stern. "I think it's unclear."[401]

This sort of headache-inducing lawyerly complexity scares away journalists. Very few investigative reporters have the patience and endurance to wade through layers of obfuscation in order to properly study ACORN. It's no surprise that few have bothered to do so. No one—except maybe for Wade Rathke—knows for sure how many ACORN affiliates exist. Congressman Darrell Issa (R-CA), chairman of the House Oversight and Government Reform Committee in the new Congress, says the figure is 361. Stephanie Strom of the *New York Times* reports that ACORN has 174 affiliates. Pablo Eisenberg, a left-wing scholar, says ACORN has 103 affiliates.

Even members of ACORN's national board apparently had no idea how vast ACORN's network was because Rathke hid most operations from view. "I always thought that there were 12 or 15 ACORN iterations," said Reid. She said she only found out at the national board meeting in Detroit in 2008 at which Rathke was fired "that they had 100 and I was in a state of shock and I was on the board and I knew nothing about that." Later she received "a list of 204 corporations and I knew then there was something desperately wrong." When a congressional report came out the next year she learned that there were 361. "I did not know," Reid said.[402] In fact, ACORN has at least 370 affiliates. (See Table "The 370 Faces of ACORN" near the end of this book on 353.)

In 2008 blogger Larry Johnson of "No Quarter" did a Nexis corporate filings search for ACORN's southern headquarters at 1024 Elysian Fields Avenue, New Orleans, Louisiana 70117. He found that there were an incredible 294 ACORN-related entities and nonprofits and businesses using that address. Let's hope there was more than one bathroom in the building.

According to Robert Huberty, executive vice president of Capital Research Center, ACORN's tax-exempt affiliates "have no reason for existence other than to get grants from the government and foundations."[403]

ACORN, the parent organization, never obtained tax-exempt status because if it did, it would have to abide by a dizzying array of legal constraints. One unattractive obligation is making basic information about its internal operations public. Such transparency would hinder ACORN's radical activities. ACORN community organizers prefer to operate behind closed doors. Avoiding tax exempt status is the same approach employed by billionaire leftist George Soros's Democracy Alliance, a piggybank for left-wing political infrastructure that is registered as a taxable nonprofit (in the District of Columbia) in order to prevent public scrutiny of its finances and internal affairs.

HOW TO CONFUSE INVESTIGATORS

Understanding how ACORN officials hold key positions in the ACORN network is crucial to understanding how ACORN operates. The term "interlocking directorates" describes the practice of individuals serving as directors on multiple corporate boards. This practice is common in the ACORN family; it is widespread and lawful in the business world too. Even so, in both the nonprofit and business worlds it raises questions about the quality and independence of board decision-making. Board members are supposed to look after the interests of the corporations they serve, but if they serve on the boards of multiple corporations, allegations of conflicts of interest and corruption often follow. "The potential for abuse in an interlocking arrangement governed top-down from New Orleans is as obvious as a thicket of 'Change' signs at an Obama rally," observes Charlotte Allen.[404]

At first glance, the ACORN network appears organic and decentralized, a bastion of locally constituted grassroots community activists united in common cause and perhaps to take advantage of economies of scale. The ACORN network attempts to reinforce this image by claiming to be a "family" of organizations, embodying the ethos of community organizing, which stresses local action and decentralized authority.

However, the existence of ACORN's flagrantly abusive interlocking directorates indicates that even though each ACORN affiliate may be legally separate, it is subject to centralized control. Members of the boards of the various ACORN affiliates coordinate their activities and take orders from above.

"One of my huge issues with ACORN has always been that its decisions don't flow from the bottom up," said Reid. "Decisions flow from the top down. And it doesn't show that way but ACORN is very stratified and there seems to be the bulk of this information in the hands of maybe 100 people and then everyone else below that really doesn't know what's going on. So it is corrupt and I would say it's entrenched in corruption but it's at the top. The people at the bottom really do not know."[405]

Rathke used interlocking directorates as one means of maintaining control over his empire of agitation. Rathke "sought to put the national organization in control of operations of the group's affiliates," according to Pablo Eisenberg, a senior fellow at the Georgetown University Public Policy Institute. ACORN bylaws gave Rathke "the power to appoint the head organizers of both local and state affiliates." Although local boards "technically had the authority to overrule his appointments, they rarely did, according to senior staff members," Eisenberg wrote.

> The decision to keep so much control over the affiliates seems at odds with ACORN's mission—its goal is to empower local people to fight their own battles—but some organizers agree with Mr. Rathke that it is important to centralize operations. They say only a unified network led by headquarters has the power and speed needed to wage successful national advocacy efforts.[406]

Ironically, Rathke condemned interlocking directorates in the corporate world. In 1980, he endorsed the proposed "Corporate Democracy Act" which would have fined directors up to $10,000 per day for "serving more than two corporations" simultaneously.[407]

The particulars of the interlocking directorates that follow help to demonstrate the elite command structure to which the ACORN family of organizations has been subject. It is by no means an exhaustive account.

As of late 2008, ACORN founder Wade Rathke was chief organizer of SEIU Local 100, president of ACORN International Inc. (later renamed Community Organizations International), and president and a director of Affiliated Media Foundation Movement Inc. (AM/FM), which produces left-wing programs for public radio stations. ACORN national president Maude Hurd, a champion of the Community Reinvestment Act, was secretary-treasurer of ACORN International Inc. and director of AM/FM. ACORN's national secretary Maxine Nelson was president and a director of Project Vote and secretary of Arkansas Broadcasting Foundation Inc. Vernon Bolden was vice president of ACORN International Inc. and president and a director of SEIU Local 100.

ACORN operative Donna Pharr is incredibly busy, a search of the tax returns of ACORN affiliates suggests. She was listed as assistant treasurer and director of 385 Palmetto Street Housing Development Fund Corp. and ACORN Community Land Association of Illinois. Pharr was also assistant treasurer of ACORN 2004 Housing Development Fund Corp., ACORN Community Land Association of Pennsylvania Inc., ACORN Dumont-Snediker Housing Development Fund Corp., ACORN Law for Education Representation & Training, ACORN Housing Corp. Inc., ACORN Housing Corp. of Pennsylvania Inc., ACORN Housing Corp. of Missouri Inc., ACORN Institute Inc., ACORN International Inc., ACORN Tenant Union Training & Organizing Project Inc., AM/FM, American Institute for Social Justice Inc., Arizona ACORN Housing Corp. Inc., Arkansas Community Housing Corp. Inc., Association for Rights of Citizens Inc., California Community Network, MHANY 2003 HDFC, Mott Haven ACORN Housing Development Fund Corp., New York Agency for Community Affairs Inc., and Project Vote.[408]

Pharr was also deputy treasurer of Minnesota ACORN Political Action Committee and is an official of Communities Voting Together, which is an ACORN political action committee or PAC.[409]

The use of interlocking directorates is just one arrow in ACORN's quiver. It also structures some of its affiliated nonprofits so that they do not have to make public reports on their finances. ACORN's tangled family tree includes a host of subsidiaries and affiliated nonprofits, and key entities that do not have to honor public disclosure laws. The six most important affiliates in the ACORN empire are: Citizens

Consulting Inc. (CCI), ACORN's financial command post; Citizens Services Inc. (CSI), which conducts political projects such as get-out-the-vote efforts; ACORN Housing Corp., which arranges mortgages; ACORN Institute, which provides leadership training for activists; American Institute for Social Justice which trains budding community organizers and conducts research; and Project Vote, which leads voter registration and mobilization campaigns. ACORN saw to it that CCI and CSI were not tax-exempt so prying eyes would be kept away from those affiliates' finances.

FOLLOWING THE MONEY: MISSION IMPOSSIBLE

Citizens Consulting Inc. is especially important to the ACORN network because it handles all of its financial affairs. ACORN member dues, government money, and foundation grants, are all sucked into the CCI vortex never to be seen again. Although CCI registered as a nonprofit corporation in Louisiana, it did not obtain tax-exempt status from the IRS. "CCI was a clearinghouse where all of the money came in and then the money was partitioned out anyway it wanted to be," said former ACORN national board member Marcel Reid. "The reason why checks are written to everyone except ACORN is that ACORN is not tax exempt."[410]

According to former ACORN official Michael McCray, CCI "is basically the financial nerve center for ACORN and all its entities. So, if you really want to try to follow the money, that's why we requested a forensic examination and financial audit of CCI."[411]

CCI "is where the shell game begins," said former ACORN official Charles Turner. "ACORN has over 200 different entities that the money gets moved around to—for this purpose to that purpose, this organization to that organization," said Turner. "We believe the way the money has been moved around, they've been laundering money."[412]

The suspicions of McCray and Turner are well-founded. The Employment Policies Institute discovered that SEIU Local 100 gave

$58,654 of union members' money to another labor group, the Hospitality, Hotel & Restaurant Organizing Council (HOTROC), which was founded by Wade Rathke. The research organization also found that CCI took in $520,000 from ACORN between 1998 and 2004 for lobbying, and that CCI and ACORN took in more than $1.7 million from Project Vote from 2000 through 2003. Since 1997, ACORN Housing Corp. shelled out more than $5.1 million in fees or grants to other entities in the ACORN network.[413]

ACORN's Enron-style accounting raises red flags. The group participates in a "shell-game of corporate financing that enables ACORN to commingle funds and potentially divert federal monies into partisan activities in violation of federal law," according to a congressional report. ACORN has also "attempted to evade federal law governing lobbyist disclosures." Federal law requires that ACORN register with Congress as a lobby but it has not done so. Failing to comply with the Lobbying Disclosure Act can lead to a fine of $200,000 or five years imprisonment or both. Why wouldn't ACORN bother to register? It's a relatively simple process. "[T]he negligible cost of disclosing its affairs to the government is too high a price to pay for an organization that has covered-up illegal activities. If ACORN was to register under the Lobbying Disclosure Act, ACORN's ability to access public funds would be limited, or meet higher scrutiny, and more public disclosure of their activities would be required."[414]

The intra-network transactions of ACORN Housing are the most troubling because out of all of ACORN's affiliates, it is the most dependent on taxpayers for support and has a long history of abusing taxpayer funds. In 2008 alone, over 67 percent of gift and grants to ACORN Housing came from the federal government and Bank of America.[415] According to its tax returns, ACORN Housing gave the following grants to ACORN's American Institute for Social Justice: $253,226 (2007); $67,112 (2006); $846,617 (2005); $947,609 (2004); $476,702 (2003); $566,535 (2002); $606,873 (2001); and $292,500 (2000).[416]

ACORN Housing grew out of crime: squatting. It emerged from a 1982 squatting campaign in which ACORN built a squatters' tent city behind the White House, and is viewed by ACORN as a reliable source of funds for the ACORN network.[417] Mike Shea of ACORN Housing characterizes squatting as "a very old American tradition" that stretches back to the days of the California Gold Rush and the settlement of the West. "People would squat on the land and claim it," Shea said.[418]

Shea's version of history isn't exactly true. After President Lincoln signed the Homestead Act of 1862, squatters occupied unowned land as "homesteaders." By satisfying certain specific legal conditions they eventually gained title to it. The squatters sponsored by ACORN use force to break in and illegally occupy property already owned by others. In some cases, ACORN helps former owners break into their own foreclosed property.

Squatting helped ACORN gets its foot in the door of the real estate industry, a move that helped the group gain access to serious capital. Its housing subsidiary, ACORN Housing, has "raise[d] significant funds for ACORN, help[ed] enforce and monitor its housing victories, and become a vehicle for ACORN's role in the redevelopment of the cities of New Orleans and New York." ACORN Housing has constructed hundreds of low-income housing units in Chicago, Dallas, Little Rock, and Phoenix. In New York City, New York ACORN Housing Co. owns and runs 700 low-income units.[419] (ACORN Housing has at least three subsidiaries: ACORN Housing Corp. of Missouri, ACORN Housing Corp. of Pennsylvania Inc., Texas ACORN Housing Corp. Inc., and Arizona ACORN Housing Corp. The Arizona entity has its own subsidiaries, Desert Rose Homes LLC, and ACORN Beverly LLC.[420])

According to academic Heidi Swarts, ACORN had to find "creative methods of fund-raising" because foundations were reluctant to fund confrontational groups. ACORN pushed mortgage lenders to give below-market home loans to low-income home buyers. Those banks paid ACORN

to screen and counsel loan applicants from ACORN neighborhoods. These campaigns fulfill multiple goals. First, they extract resources for poor and working-class people—over $4.6 billion in home loans from 1995 to 2004. They also increase ACORN's visibility and value to constituents, use selective incentives to recruit new potential members, and fund the ACORN Housing Corporation. Some of the ACORN Housing budget supports ACORN's issue organizing. Corporate campaigns mobilize resources while also winning gains for low-income people, making new potential members aware of ACORN, and building support for investment in inner-city communities.[421]

Project Vote, also known as Voting for America Inc., disclosed in its tax returns that it paid ACORN $10,861,825 from 2000 through 2006. Project Vote also paid CSI $1,206,942 in 2005 and 2006, and paid $1,266,967 to CCI from 2000 through 2004. Since 2000, ACORN Housing Corp. paid CCI and ACORN affiliate Peoples Equipment Resource Center $1,566,228 and (at least) $58,003, respectively.

Since 2002, ACORN Institute paid ACORN $861,783, CCI $61,443, ACORN Services $117,261, ACORN Associates Inc. $61,451, and ACORN International $83,966.

Since 2000, AISJ paid ACORN $1,926,831, CCI $362,464, and ACORN Associates $258,593.

On its 2002 tax return, AISJ disclosed a $1,684,184 "community reinvestment" grant to ACORN, along with a $9,637 loan to SEIU Local 100. On the same document, AISJ also reported receiving a $50,000 interest-free loan from the notoriously radical Tides Foundation for "purchase of equipment," and a $4,000 interest-free loan from the George Soros-endowed Open Society Institute's Progressive America Fund Inc. In an LM-2 (labor union disclosure) form, SEIU Local 880 revealed that it gave $60,118 to ACORN for "membership services." On its 2006 tax form, AISJ disclosed that it provided a $4,952,288 "community reinvestment" grant to ACORN.

Was any of this money that bounced around between taxpayer-supported ACORN affiliates and ACORN government money? Were taxpayer dollars laundered and spent on partisan political activities? No one with firsthand knowledge seems to be talking. A criminal investigation could uncover the answer.

ACORN'S SHELL GAME

Wade Rathke laid out the rationale for having a complex corporate structure for ACORN in a 1993 memo. Stanley Kurtz describes the document as "a masterpiece in the art of hiding money trails— penned by the master himself." Rathke wrote:

> I think pragmatically the politics are such that we would be wise to resist grants and/or contracts directly to ACORN, Inc. but try and either set up separate corporations . . . or use existing corporations . . . that are less overtly moving the money directly into ACORN, Inc., though in truth it would be going there in other ways.[422]

Federal lawmakers have known about ACORN's unorthodox finances for years. There is "a pattern of loose financial accounting and no firewalls" within ACORN's network of hundreds of affiliated groups, said Congressman Darrell Issa. "It's very clear that that's for a reason." It is impossible to hand over government money "to ACORN and its affiliates without knowingly delivering it to partisan operatives who in fact engage in campaigning," Issa said.[423]

Issa's investigators concluded that ACORN illegally spends taxpayer dollars on partisan activities, commits "systemic fraud," and violates racketeering and election laws. They also found that by "intentionally blurring the legal distinctions between 361 tax-exempt and non-exempt entities, ACORN diverts taxpayer and tax-exempt monies into partisan political activities."

The investigators' findings were included in "Is ACORN Intentionally Structured As a Criminal Enterprise?" a report issued in summer 2009. The report declares that "[t]he weight of evidence against ACORN and its affiliates is astounding."[424]

"Operationally, ACORN is a shell game played in 120 cities, 43 states and the District of Columbia through a complex structure designed to conceal illegal activities, to use taxpayer and tax-exempt dollars for partisan political purposes, and to distract investigators," the report says. Structurally, it is "a chess game in which senior management is shielded from accountability by multiple layers of volunteers and compensated employees who serve as pawns to take the fall for every bad act."

The report examines the ACORN network's abusive interlocking directorates, and claims that the group deliberately organized itself to escape legal and public scrutiny. "ACORN hides behind a paper wall of nonprofit corporate protections to conceal a criminal conspiracy on the part of its directors, to launder federal money in order to pursue a partisan political agenda and to manipulate the American electorate."

ACORN should be subject to criminal investigation in order "to bring to justice the responsible parties who have heretofore been shielded from prosecution by ACORN's obscure organizational structure; to protect the American system of democratic self-government from manipulation and disruption; and to free our political climate from the choke of corruption that threatens to strangle free and fair elections."

The report accuses ACORN of carrying out "a nation-wide strategy of tax fraud, racketeering, money-laundering and manipulating the American electorate." Specifically, the report accuses ACORN of racketeering, evading taxes, sloppy accounting, defrauding donors, defrauding the U.S. government, filing false statements, obstructing justice, and plundering employee pension funds.

The report singles out for special criticism the group's handling of a nearly $1 million embezzlement around 2000 by Dale Rathke. The misappropriation was covered up by management, including Wade Rathke, for eight years until it was revealed to the group's national board in 2008. The report notes that failing to report the misappropriation to the IRS in itself constitutes fraud, and that ACORN apparently raided pension funds to help cover the financial shortfall.

ACORN has used government resources to promote legislation and has long commingled funds within its network of affiliates. A congressional report from 1997 noted that there was "apparent cross-over funding between ACORN, a political advocacy group and ACORN Housing Corp. (AHC), a non profit, AmeriCorp [sic] grantee." The government-funded AmeriCorps, which promotes public service, suspended AHC's funding "after it was learned that AHC and ACORN shared office space and equipment and failed to assure that activities and funds were wholly separate."[425]

AmeriCorps Inspector General Luise Jordan told a congressional subcommittee that ACORN Housing deliberately misrepresented its relationship with ACORN, the parent company, when it sought the grant from AmeriCorps. Jordan said she found information showing ACORN created ACORN Housing "to serve purposes common to both organizations" and that there were "numerous transactions and activities involving AHC and other 'fraternal' ACORN-related corporations." ACORN Housing also used the AmeriCorps grant as a recruiting tool for ACORN. According to Jordan, one Dallas ACORN member said "the only reason for having the AmeriCorps program was to gain new ACORN members, and that if AmeriCorps loan counseling clients did not start becoming ACORN members, she could and would halt the AmeriCorps project."

ACORN Housing also used its taxpayer-supported mortgage counseling program to pressure people into joining ACORN, she said. AmeriCorps members working for ACORN Housing were threatened with immediate termination if they refused to pressure counseling clients to become dues-paying ACORN members. Even though they had been subpoenaed ACORN and ACORN Housing both refused to supply documents that "were critical in supporting the conclusions of our investigation," Jordan said.[426]

The report noted that, "AmeriCorps members of AHC raised funds for ACORN, performed voter registration activities, and gave partisan speeches. In one instance, an AmeriCorps member was directed by ACORN staff to assist the [Clinton] White House in preparing a press conference in support of legislation."[427]

THE SMOKING GUN LEGAL MEMO

ACORN lawyer Elizabeth Kingsley of the Washington, D.C.-based law firm Harmon, Curran, Spielberg & Eisenberg has admitted that such chicanery is standard operating procedure at ACORN. In a hush-hush internal legal memo in 2008, Kingsley described the hoops that ACORN jumps through to create the façade that its affiliates are independent of each other. The beauty of the memo, which this writer was the first to publish in 2009, was that it confirmed in black and white nearly every bad thing that has ever been said about ACORN while providing a window into the everyday workings of America's most notorious activist group.

The memo was aimed at shoring up ACORN's organizational structure, which supports the group's unending campaign of disinformation, half-truths, legalisms, and outright deception. In other words, the memo was calculated to protect the organization while it advanced the cause of radicalism in America. It was drawn up after Dale Rathke's embezzlement had been exposed and was aimed at insulating ACORN from the attacks that were certain to follow the news that ACORN's founder covered up his brother's massive misappropriation for eight years.

ACORN insiders say that even though in the memo Kingsley appears to be alarmed, it was an Oscar-worthy performance. In meetings with ACORN donors, Kingsley arrogantly bragged about the mind-boggling complexity of ACORN. "They thought they had a formula that could not be penetrated and the person that was most proud of it was Beth Kingsley in telling all of the funders at the meeting that this was the only organization in the country that was structured the way it was," an ACORN insider said. "She took great glee in it." Insiders call the memo a lawyerly exercise in "CYA"—"covering your ass."

Kingsley wrote the memo because it was her duty to keep ACORN on track and out of harm's way. It just so happens ACORN's mission is putting America in harm's way, but that's her law firm's mission too. Harmon, Curran, Spielberg & Eisenberg has a long history of representing radical groups. Founded around the same time as ACORN, it has "served the legal needs of individuals and organizations to help them advance social, economic and environmental justice." The law firm helps "[p]olitical committees and others working for the election of progressive candidates" and supports

ACORN's antisocial policy agenda. "As individuals and as a firm, we are knowledgeable—and passionate—about strengthening citizen advocacy, electing progressive candidates, achieving social and economic justice, expanding civil rights, and promoting environmental stewardship."[428]

Harmon Curran's clients constitute a rogue's gallery of organizations committed to destroying America as we know it. They include: the SDS veteran-run Campaign for America's Future and its sister group Institute for America's Future; the Hugo Chavez-funded illegal immigrants' group Casa de Maryland; the ACORN-like Center for Community Change, which is run by ACORN alumnus Deepak Bhargava whose ties to small-c communists might take a whole book chapter or more to document[429]; the Center on Budget and Policy Priorities, a think tank that reflexively cheers for tax increases and more government spending; the ecoterrorist-friendly Friends of the Earth; George Soros's Media Matters for America and its advocacy arm, the Media Matters Action Network; and ACORN's election-disruption arm, Project Vote.[430]

In the memo, Kingsley wrote that key ACORN affiliates argue they are not "'affiliated,' 'related,' or 'controlled' by or with each other, for various legal purposes, while allowing actual control to be exercised in a highly coordinated manner." ACORN suffers from "an organizational culture that resembles a family business more than an accountable organization." It is time to stop "trying to pretend that these groups are not connected to one another and create control mechanisms behind the scenes."[431]

The group's problems are "systemic," Kingsley wrote. She broke her concerns into four categories: "respect for corporate integrity, the necessary separation between different types of political work, the niceties of 501(c)(3) tax compliance and accounting for those funds, and a big-picture question about organizational capacity." Echoing Congressman Issa's conclusion, she observed that "[t]he political world of ACORN lacks the protective 'walls' needed to ensure that various types of activity are kept sufficiently separate."

Kingsley wrote that there are no discernible institutional firewalls that separate ACORN from its many tax-exempt nonprofit affiliates:

There is no point in having these different corporations in place if they are not respected. If not properly operated, they create difficulties (e.g., potential conflicts of interest for lawyers, non-trivial administrative burden of state filings, and the appearance that someone is trying to hide something under a byzantine corporate structure) without generating the desired benefits, whatever those may be.

This is "the natural result of thinking of all these different corporations as part of the family, or 'us.'" Kingsley also noted that affiliates failed to maintain proper documentation showing that they had been following IRS rules on nonprofit behavior. There was no way to demonstrate that no charitable money was being spent on political activities or about which ACORN entities held sway over the decision making process.

After reviewing the Kingsley memo and interviewing ACORN sources, Stephanie Strom of the *New York Times* reported that the close ties between Project Vote and ACORN "made it impossible to document that Project Vote's money had been used in a strictly nonpartisan manner." Until news spread of the Dale Rathke embezzlement scandal in summer 2008, "Project Vote's board was made up entirely" of ACORN staffers and members.

"The same people appeared to be deciding which regions to focus on for increased voter engagement for ACORN and Project Vote," Strom wrote. "Zach Pollett [sic], for instance, was Project Vote's executive director and ACORN's political director, until July, when he relinquished the former title. Mr. Pollett [sic] continues to work as a consultant for Project Vote through another ACORN affiliate."[432]

"As a result, we may not be able to prove that 501(c)(3) resources are not being directed to specific regions based on impermissible partisan considerations," Kingsley wrote in her memo, referring to the section of the federal tax code that governs charities.

Strom noted that "Project Vote, for example, had only one independent director since it received a federal tax exemption in 1994, and he was on the board for less than two years, its tax forms show.

Since then, the board has consisted of ACORN staff members and two ACORN members who pay monthly dues."

Strom also interviewed George Hampton and Cleo Mata, two former Project Vote board members. Both denied serving on the board and Hampton, who acknowledged he had been an ACORN member, said he had never heard of Project Vote.[433]

[NINE]

Financial Affirmative Action: ACORN's Mortgage Madness

WHEN THE HISTORY of the Great Economic Meltdown of 2008 is written, in-your-face shakedown groups like ACORN will be held to account. With wanton disregard for the economic well being of America, the social justice entrepreneurs of ACORN let Americans know more than a decade ago of their strategy for bringing equality to the housing market—at all costs.

ACORN bragged about its success in redistributing wealth and creating market chaos. A 1999 pamphlet from ACORN Housing called the American Dream a sham and boasted about bringing the Russian roulette approach to mortgage underwriting. There may be isolated "stories of hope and success" in some communities, but "they also belie the supposition that if you simply work hard, sacrifice and save, you can easily buy a home of your own," said the brochure written by ACORN's Madeleine Adamson.

The ACORN affiliate also took credit for crafting "several innovative strategies" to avoid traditional lending guidelines, which it called unfair because they "were geared to middle class borrowers." Instead of using passé measures of creditworthiness such as, say, credit history and having an adequate income, ACORN talked banks into using "more flexible underwriting criteria that take into account the realities of lower-income communities." It even managed to get some inner-city lenders to use "less traditional income sources such as food stamps."[434] In his recent book ACORN admirer John Atlas confirmed that ACORN "helped negotiate for alternative borrowing eligibility requirements that would count welfare, Social Security, and food-stamp benefits as income and substitute records of regular rent and utility payments for a credit record for people who had none."[435]

Steven Malanga of the Manhattan Institute traces ACORN's campaign to destroy underwriting standards to 1986 when it black-mailed Louisiana Bancshares. ACORN threatened to oppose a bank acquisition "until it agreed to new 'flexible credit and underwriting standards' for minority borrowers—for example, counting public assistance and food stamps as income." In 1987 ACORN launched a coalition of activist groups demanding the watering down of lending requirements. The coalition leaned on Fannie Mae, demanding that it buy unconventional mortgages. This pressure eventually led Congress to pass legislation forcing Fannie and Freddie Mac "to devote 30 percent of their loan purchases to mortgages for low- and moderate-income borrowers."[436]

Encouraging homeownership among people dependent on government relief programs for their survival makes sense only to radical leftists pathologically preoccupied with economic egalitarianism and to nihilistic anarchists who want to destroy the financial system.

This sort of financial tomfoolery was encouraged by the Community Reinvestment Act of 1977 (CRA), which helped to change the way U.S. financial institutions operate. The law was enacted because liberals were unwilling to recognize that the impoverishment of America's inner cities was caused largely by their own social engineering schemes and policies. They made the banking industry a scapegoat for their own failures and argued that lending practices that favored people who could actually pay the money back were somehow unfair. Poor neighborhoods, which tend to be minority-dominated, were hardest hit by the alleged "discrimination" committed by lenders, which came to be known as "urban disinvestment" or by the dysphemism "redlining." Before it became a politically charged epithet, the term *redlining* referred to the way lenders draw lines with red markers around high-risk sections of cities on maps.

Illinois, the heart of Saul Alinsky's community organizing efforts, was the first to enact anti-redlining legislation in 1975, just three years after Alinsky died. Gov. Dan Walker, a Democrat, signed two anti-redlining bills that year.[437] Walker's top adviser was Squire Lance, a protégé of Alinsky who succeeded Nicholas von Hoffman as executive director of The Woodlawn Organization, an Alinsky group active in Chicago's slums. Lance led the Walker administration's push against redlining.[438]

Years later ACORN launched a public relations campaign aimed at convincing the public that banks were rife with racism. In the early 1990s, ACORN convinced House Banking Committee chairman Henry Gonzalez (D-TX) and Senate Banking Committee chairman Donald Riegle Jr. (D-MI) to demand that the Fed hold public hearings on supposed race-based discrimination by mortgage lenders.[439]

OLD BUDDIES FROM ARKANSAS:
BILL CLINTON AND ACORN

Soon after, Bill Clinton arrived at the White House in 1993. The president and ACORN were old friends. Clinton got comfortable with ACORN when he was Arkansas attorney general (1977–79) and governor (1979–81 and 1983–92). ACORN endorsed him in 1978 when he ran for governor.[440]

As president, Clinton did ACORN's bidding. "ACORN used its considerable influence within the Clinton administration to spread the practice of subprime lending well beyond those sections of the banking system controlled by" the Community Reinvestment Act.[441] During his administration ACORN developed a close working relationship with HUD Secretary Henry Cisneros. "HUD, under Clinton, gave ACORN and other grassroots community groups funds to 'test' banks and landlords to uncover redlining and racial discrimination."[442] The testing consisted of sending in activists of different races undercover to pretend to be housing applicants. If applicants of color were rejected this was interpreted as proof of discrimination.

Such testing was necessary, according to Marxist sociologist Joe R. Feagin. "Americans still live in a country where White racism remains the core reality," Feagin wrote in an official HUD journal called Cityscape. "Housing segregation is only one of the critical manifestations of that reality." He spews a litany of extremist grievances about the supposedly pervasive racism of Americans:

> Systemic racism in the United States is a four-centuries-old system that denies African-Americans and other people of color many of the privileges, opportunities, freedoms, and rewards that this Nation offers to White Americans. The unjust enrichment of Whites and unjust impoverishment of Blacks, created by the first generations of White Americans, have been maintained now for about 15 generations.

Whites suffer from a "tooth-fairy delusion" because they believe "institutional racism is no longer a fundamental problem in this society and Black Americans have only themselves to blame for persisting inequalities," he writes. ACORN, however, is built on Feagin's delusion. When low-income blacks are turned down by banks it's not because they lack financial resources: it's the fault of the racism that is a fundamental feature of American society.

"Many Whites work hard to keep city residential areas and schools as White as possible," Feagin writes. As proof he cites "Secret Apartheid," a 1996 report by ACORN that claimed that there was widespread racial discrimination in New York City schools. Trained white parent-testers posing as parents were welcomed with open arms at schools but "Black and Latino parent-testers" were given the bum's rush, the study alleged.[443]

Feagin's article was published after Cisneros left HUD in 1997 and Andrew Cuomo took his place. Cuomo's counsel at HUD was Kirsten Gillibrand, now the junior Democratic senator representing

New York. Cuomo also worked closely with ACORN. At the end of his tenure as HUD secretary Cuomo had the agency publish "Exposing Injustice: A Chronicle of HUD's Mission in the Forgotten America 1997–2001," an expensively produced glossy 104-page booklet that depicted HUD as the savior of America and painted Cuomo as a heroic crusader for justice. This piece of publicly funded leftist propaganda also hailed ACORN for its activism. It featured a page-length photo of Los Angeles ACORN members holding signs reading "ACORN SAYS STOP THE SHARKS. STOP PREDATORY LENDERS." The 10,000 copies of "Exposing Injustice" cost taxpayers $162,509 and featured at least 11 pictures of Cuomo. "There have been former cabinet secretaries who have had political ambitions but they have not been as blatant about it as Secretary Cuomo," Tom Schatz, president of Citizens Against Government Waste, said at the time.[444]

EXTORTING THE BANKS

The Clinton administration also issued regulations under the CRA that compelled banks to find low-income minority home mortgage borrowers. "Without saying so, the revised law established quotas for loans to specific neighborhoods, specific income classes, and specific races," according to economic historian John Steele Gordon. "It also encouraged community groups to monitor compliance and allowed them to receive fees for marketing loans to target groups." In effect, ACORN had secured a federal subsidy to strong-arm lending institutions to lend money to people with dubious credit histories.[445]

Clinton's changes helped to give groups such as ACORN a golden opportunity to shake down banks that received CRA compliance report cards from regulators. ACORN and similar groups were given a role in the evaluation process and they used this new power to threaten to block bank mergers and acquisitions. This is akin to handing a submachine gun to a bank robber, and turned the CRA into a cash cow that left-wing groups would fight to the death to protect. The CRA legitimized mob rule. It is economic sabotage.

The Clinton administration "turned the Community Reinvestment Act, a once-obscure and lightly enforced banking regulation law, into one of the most powerful mandates shaping American cities—and, as Senate Banking Committee chairman Phil Gramm memorably put it, a vast extortion scheme against the nation's banks," wrote Howard Husock in 2000. "Under its provisions, U.S. banks have committed nearly $1 trillion for inner-city and low-income mortgages and real estate development projects, most of it funneled through a nation-wide network of left-wing community groups, intent, in some cases, on teaching their low-income clients that the financial system is their enemy and, implicitly, that government, rather than their own striving, is the key to their well-being," wrote Husock, director of the Manhattan Institute's Social Entrepreneurship Initiative.[446]

Other observers likened the CRA to gangsterism. "You see really weird things when you look at the Code of Federal Regulations . . . like federal regulators are encouraged to leave the room and allowing community groups to negotiate ex parte with bankers in a community reinvestment context," said Yale law professor Jonathan Macey. "Giving jobs to the top five officials of these communities or shakedown groups is generally high up on the list of demands. So, what we really have is a bit of Old World Sicily brought into the U.S., but legitimized and given the patina of government support." Former First Union Corp. CEO Edward Crutchfield was more succinct, calling the CRA process "pure blackmail."[447]

CRA evaluations for banks sometimes take months to complete and waste banks' resources, according to Michelle Minton of the Competitive Enterprise Institute.

This has become a major point of leverage—and source of funding—for "community" activist groups. Lending institutions, rather than face the increased expense of a slowed deposit facility application due to a CRA challenge, have committed over $7 billion to such groups and $23 billion to community development lending projects since 1977. Some companies seek to mitigate the threat by funding activist groups' projects, instead of reforming their overall approach to community reinvestment, according to Jonathan Macey of Yale Law School. Groups like the Association of Community Organizations for Reform Now (ACORN), aware that even small delays in approval can result in substantial losses of money for financial institutions, have been exploiting such a strategy for years. For example, Chase Manhattan and J.P. Morgan donated hundred [sic] of thousands of dollars to ACORN around the time that they applied for permission to merge.[448]

Although it didn't cover all mortgages, CRA opened the door for community organizers to weaken lending standards. Political activism drove the banks to make irresponsible decisions, and it has put taxpayers on the hook for bank and housing bailout packages potentially costing trillions of dollars. The current mortgage market debacle is "a direct result of an intentional loosening of underwriting standards—done in the name of ending discrimination, despite warnings that it could lead to wide-scale defaults," said economist Stan Liebowitz of the University of Texas.[449] Economists disagree on the precise impact CRA had on the mortgage market, but anyone can see that pressing banks to lower underwriting standards, as ACORN did, must have contributed to the real estate bubble that began bursting in the twilight years of George W. Bush's administration.

ACORN has never hesitated to use the CRA to raise quick cash. ACORN freely admits it uses the CRA to shake down banks for $25,000 grants in the midst of acquisitions even when it has no interest in blocking the deal. "It takes a merger for (banks') upper management to listen to their CRA folk about neighborhoods where they don't have penetration," said ACORN Housing's Mike Shea.[450] ACORN acknowledges it used the CRA to hold up major banks including Chase, PNC, Mellon, First Union, Fleet, CalFed, and NationsBank.[451] ACORN has also conducted housing-related actions against Salomon Smith Barney, Norwest Financial, and Advanta Corp.[452] Since 1985, ACORN Housing has consummated at least 24 memorandums of understanding (MOUs) and partnerships with the corporate world.[453]

After ACORN mastered the art of the CRA shakedown, competing community groups began to copy it. ACORN was angry that its imitators were cashing in on its shakedown success. "These groups were reaping the fruits of ACORN's organizing victories," writes John Atlas. "ACORN wanted a piece of the action."

> To get more than crumbs from the banks' CRA table and earn the same benefits as the less feisty [community development corporations], ACORN had to overcome two barriers. It would have to enter into partnerships with its targets, the banks, and it would have to find members within its ranks willing to lead its campaigns. For some of ACORN's left-leaning organizers, who viewed the banks as part of the capitalistic system responsible for racism, poverty, and inequality, the idea of partnering with banks was hard to swallow.[454]

Meanwhile, as banks felt the heat from community organizers and CRA commissars, instead of fighting they made loans they shouldn't have and, as Minton notes above, they paid out tens of billions of dollars in protection money to ACORN and related groups.

Some suggest the actions of ACORN and other Alinsky-inspired organizations adhere to the Cloward-Piven Strategy of orchestrated crisis and helped cause the meltdown on Wall Street. It is not difficult to imagine Cloward and Piven embracing the CRA as a means of redistributing wealth, generating market chaos, and smashing the system.

Leftist academic Gregory D. Squires acknowledges that CRA is a federal law that emerged from "Alinsky-style radicalism."[455] The angry speeches and Alinskyite confrontation tactics of Gale Cincotta, co-founder of National People's Action, were instrumental in getting the CRA enacted in 1977.[456]

Radicals did help to design the CRA, but the problem with the theory that Cloward and Piven were behind it is that they had very little to say about housing as an issue. Although "breaking the bank" is what they were all about, evidence they were personally responsible for this particular legislation is elusive.

However, the CRA could be considered an honorary plank of the Cloward-Piven Strategy because ACORN and similar groups that

followed their subversive model were behind the law and have stead-
fastly defended it for decades. Those groups understood the power
of overwhelming the system in order to generate crises that provide opportunities for radical change. Anyone who, like ACORN,
thinks people on food stamps—a type of welfare benefit—should
be buying houses is clearly hell-bent on destroying America as we
know it. Stanley Kurtz takes it a step further, writing that ACORN's
"mortgage activism was part of an overall strategy that did seek to
contribute to, and certainly to take advantage of, periodic crises in
capitalism." ACORN advisor Peter Dreier argued for provoking "an
entitlement crisis that would undermine America's fiscal health,
thus opening the way to socialism as a solution. A federally sponsored subprime lending policy would fit nicely into this scheme."[457]

Leftists bristle at the suggestion that the CRA had anything to do
with the nation's financial problems. Responding to GOP attacks on the
CRA, longtime ACORN ally House Financial Services Committee chairman Barney Frank (D-MA) chose to respond with racial demagoguery.
Frank said criticism of the law was tantamount to attacking poor people
and minorities. "They get to take things out on poor people," Frank said
of Republicans. "Let's be honest: The fact that some of the poor people
are black doesn't hurt them either, from their standpoint. This is an
effort, I believe, to appeal to a kind of anger in people."[458]

There is no doubt in the mind of Edward Pinto that the CRA has
been a catastrophe. Pinto was a consultant to the mortgage finance
industry and the chief credit officer at Fannie Mae in the 1980s. "The
pain and hardship that CRA has likely spawned are immeasurable," he
writes. From 1992 to 2008 banks committed to lend $6 trillion under
the act. About half of the CRA loans for single-family homes went to
high-risk borrowers who had low credit scores and made down payments of five percent or less. Amazingly, the federal government hasn't
tracked the performance of these loans but "the chances are good that
many of them have defaulted or remain at high risk for doing so."[459]

Cheered on by ACORN, the Obama administration has proposed
expanding the CRA. It was an easy sell to President Obama, who has
long been a strong supporter of the law. As an ACORN benefactor,

organizer and trainer, Obama helped turn up the heat on lenders when he represented plaintiffs in the 1995 class action lawsuit *Buycks-Roberson v. Citibank*. The suit demanded the bank's mortgage lending be apportioned equally among minority and non-minority applicants. Citibank settled and reportedly took on riskier borrowers.

The advent of Mortgage-Backed Securities (MBSs) by Fannie Mae and Freddie Mac gave banks an added incentive to write risky loans. Banks knew they could dump their dubious mortgages onto investors in these public-private "government sponsored enterprises" who counted on a government bailout if things got rough. The two companies bundled the high-risk subprime mortgages and sold them as MBSs—which should have been called Mortgage Junk Bonds. This helped to spread the financial contagion across America and the world. MBSs received strong bond ratings from credit agencies in part because Fannie and Freddie, which had been ordered to place politics over profit making, had long enjoyed an implied guarantee from the U.S. government, so investors bought them with confidence.

ACORN Housing got in on the action. It negotiated what it called "a groundbreaking program with Fannie Mae to buy" loans on which the ACORN affiliate had provided counseling. In other words, ACORN Housing brought in the uncreditworthy borrowers and then dumped their mortgages on Fannie Mae.[460] ACORN Housing also turned its corporate victims into customers: banks pay the nonprofit a commission for successful loan candidates it refers.[461]

"[T]here is no question that as the government pursued affordable-housing goals—with the CRA providing approximately half of Fannie's and Freddie's affordable-housing purchases—trillions of dollars in high-risk lending flooded the real-estate market, with disastrous consequences," according to Pinto.[462]

ACORN'S RENT-A-MOB SERVICE

For all its supposed championing of underdogs and the disadvantaged, ACORN isn't always on the side of the little guy. ACORN is perfectly happy to crush the dreams of poor people if the price is right. Although ACORN is not officially opposed to charter schools in principle, it does not want them spreading over the country unless it gets a piece of the action. ACORN operates charter schools of its own and indoctrinates students in these taxpayer-supported institutions. In New York City it runs at least three schools.

Public education offers a telling example of ACORN's apparently lucrative protest-for-profit program. In 2009, ACORN agreed to provide instant protesters to its allies in the labor movement in exchange for cash. In Manhattan ACORN provided rent-a-mob services to a teachers' union in order to block the expansion of Harlem Success Academy, a charter school that is part of Success Charter Network. The episode, which took place in 2009, was captured by filmmaker Madeleine Sackler in a powerful 2010 documentary called "The Lottery."[463]

The teachers' unions, which are dominated largely by white leadership, "don't want to be the face of the opposition to charters," said Eva Moskowitz, CEO of Success Charter Network. The unions will often "hire an outside group, like an ACORN . . . and they'll bus in hired guns—protesters—who will protest charter schools in general or a particular school." Moskowitz told a New York City Council meeting that there is "a union-political-educational complex that is trying to halt the progress and put the interests of adults above the interests of children."

The battle was fought over PS194, a public school that was being shut down for poor academic performance. At the invitation of the city's education department, charter school Harlem Success Academy applied to move into the school. ACORN showed up in force at a public hearing on the proposed move after being paid about $500,000 by United Federation of Teachers, the New York City affiliate of the American Federation of Teachers. UFT paid ACORN "to protest this charter school in particular but also the expansion of charter schools in New York in general," according to Sackler.[464]

From 2006 to 2008 the National Education Association gave $396,452 to ACORN for "nonpartisan voter registration" and "community education." The goal was for "ACORN to rally the kind of low-income parents and traditional defenders of public education who can oppose the voter initiatives and school reform-minded candidates that would adversely impact the NEA's agenda," which includes opposition to charter schools.[465]

At the hearing, bussed in ACORN members chanted ominously, "We are ACORN, mighty, mighty ACORN. Fighting for justice. Saving schools," and "The people united, will never be defeated." Longtime ACORN ally New York Assembly member Keith L.T. Wright, a Democrat who represents a Harlem district, joined in the attack on local residents who wanted a better future for their children.

"It was very clear that most of the people who were there were paid to be there," said Sackler. "They didn't know much about the school. They didn't know much about the community."[466] In the end, the hired guns of ACORN prevailed. Harlem Success Academy didn't get the space at PS194.

ACORN's alliance with teachers' unions is cynical on both sides. "ACORN isn't going to be anyone's go-to guy on anything related to improving education and the teachers' union leaders have no interest in anything other than preserving their slipping stranglehold on education," RiShawn Biddle, editor of education magazine *Dropout Nation*, said in an interview. "ACORN got paid and the unions got a sliver of political support for their agenda. Only the kids lost out."

Attorney Heather S. Heidelbaugh, who serves on the executive committee of the Republican National Lawyers Association, told a congressional subcommittee that ACORN routinely provides protest-for-hire services and extracts donations from the targets of demonstrations by shaking them down mafia-style. ACORN calls it the "Muscle for the Money," program, she said. Heidelbaugh's statement was based on court testimony provided by former ACORN employee Anita MonCrief. MonCrief testified against ACORN at an injunction hearing during the 2008 election cycle about the group's shakedown tactics and unlawful voter registration practices. Heidelbaugh, who represented a Republican candidate in the legal proceeding, succeeded in gaining a partial injunction against ACORN's fraudulent voter registration activities in Pennsylvania.[467]

Although Reid acknowledges ACORN offered protest-for-hire services, she disputes parts of MonCrief's story. "There was never a 'Muscle for Money' program," Reid said in an interview. "It was never named that. I never heard that term until Anita MonCrief said it and it was repeated" in the media.

"With the people who were in the room [at ACORN national board meetings], it never came up. It never existed," Reid said. And there is no paper trail proving its existence, she added. "They were very good at not putting a lot of stuff in writing . . . long ago Wade [Rathke] issued an edict that nothing was to be written, very little was to be written."

At the court hearing MonCrief had testified that ACORN would harass a company by protesting it. The company would then pay money to ACORN to make the protests stop. ACORN didn't mind being accused of voter registration fraud because that was familiar terrain and because such accusations diverted media attention away from ACORN's shakedown campaigns, MonCrief told the court.[468]

MonCrief said an ACORN office accepted payments from SEIU to harass the Carlyle Group, an international private equity firm, and its co-founder, David Rubenstein. "Even though D.C. ACORN had no interest in the Carlyle Group, they were paid by SEIU to go break up a banquet and protest at his house," according to MonCrief.[469] SEIU was agitating against the Carlyle Group because it wanted to organize workers at Manor Care, a nursing home company Carlyle was in the process of acquiring. The union ran radio ads giving out Rubenstein's telephone number and urging the public to call him to ask that he not reduce Manor Care's workforce.[470] Chanting, "It's Not Fair, Pay Your Share," ACORN stormed an investors' conference in New York City in 2007. The target was Rubenstein, who was scheduled to give a speech to more than 1,000 analysts and investors. Demonstrators hung a banner reading "Why does David Rubenstein pay taxes at a lower rate than an NYPD officer?" Members of ACORN's minor political party, the Working Families Party, and another radical group called Make the Road New York participated in the action.[471] Unlike most of ACORN's corporate targets, Carlyle refused to give in to extortion.

[TEN]

Follow the Money: ACORN's Shakedown Special

WHY IS ACORN's chief organizer friendly with the Marxist anti-American governments of two South American countries?

Within ACORN CEO Bertha Lewis's Rolodex may be found contact information for then-Bolivian ambassador Gustavo Guzman and for Sabine Kienzl, a professional propagandist employed by the Venezuelan embassy. The listing for Guzman contains what appears to have been a direct office telephone number.

An ACORN insider confirmed the authenticity of the Rolodex, first unveiled by Erick Erickson of the website RedState. In September 2009, after President Obama claimed not to have knowledge of ACORN's troubles, Erickson concluded it was "implausible to think, based on Bertha Lewis's White House contacts, that Barack Obama is not paying attention to ACORN."[472]

Both Bolivia and Venezuela are now headed by radical, anti-American leftists friendly to Communist Cuba—and officials of those hostile nations somehow ended up as business associates of Bertha Lewis. Before the Rolodex surfaced in September 2009, Bolivian President Evo Morales denounced economic freedom as a concept. "I would like to say that the origin of this crisis is the unbridled consumption and accumulation of capital in a few hands, the looting of natural resources, the commercialization of Mother Earth, and above all, I believe its origin lies in an economic model—capitalism," he told the United Nations. In a diplomatic row with Bolivia, the U.S. government expelled Guzman in September 2009. However, Kienzl apparently remains a "political economist" with Venezuela's embassy. A true-believing *chavista*, she describes herself as "an Austrian by passport but a Venezuelan in my heart."

Venezuelan President Hugo Chavez's hatred of America and its freedoms is better publicized. Chavez calls capitalism "savagery" and has allowed Hezbollah and the Palestinian Hamas terrorists to open offices in Venezuela's capital, Caracas.

Add to this a listing in the Rolodex for CITGO executive Andres Rangel and the whole picture begins to come into clearer focus. CITGO operates a chain of gas stations in the U.S. and is a wholly owned subsidiary of Petroleos de Venezuela SA (PDVSA). PDVSA is owned by the government of Venezuela and has been described as a "black box" because it is believed to also fund Chavez's overseas political ambitions. Oil export revenues fuel Chavez's petro-diplomacy.

DID VENEZUELA'S COMMUNIST STRONGMAN HUGO CHAVEZ FUND ACORN?

Chavez may have funneled money to ACORN. The Marxist leader has been attempting to export chaos to America for years. While he was still a leftist, community organizer Brandon Darby took a trip to Venezuela that helped to kill off his remaining radical impulses. The visit came as the U.S. government was taking a beating in the media for its post-Katrina relief efforts. At the time, Chavez was trying to embarrass the Bush administration by providing aid to the Katrina-hit Gulf Coast.

Chavez had already been running what political scientists call a "public diplomacy" campaign in the U.S. to help bolster American support for his regime. The propaganda effort consisted of funneling discounted home heating oil to the nonprofit group Citizens Energy

Corp., which is run by longtime ACORN ally former Congressman Joe Kennedy II (D-MA). The nonprofit then distributed the oil to poor people, and Kennedy went on TV to berate the Bush administration, which he said "cut fuel assistance." Kennedy boosted his benefactor, boasting about how Venezuela's socialism had helped to ease suffering in America. In a commercial he said that "CITGO, owned by the Venezuelan people," had helped poor Americans while their own government stood idly by.

Darby traveled to Caracas in 2006 as part of a delegation from his own nonprofit, Common Ground, to the Chavez government to seek funding to keep the organization afloat. "I had this idea of having 'Chavez trailers' for displaced residents to live in. This would embarrass FEMA into supplying trailers," he said. Darby said he didn't realize when he came up with the concept that using money from abroad to influence the U.S. government might be illegal, but Chavez government officials he met with insisted it would violate U.S. law. "They told me I would get in trouble, and they wanted to work out a way to make the project happen," he said.

During the month he was there, Venezuelan officials introduced him to PDVSA executives. They pressured Darby to journey to neighboring Colombia to meet with a group aligned with the communist narco-terror organization FARC and to visit another revolutionary group in Maracaibo, Venezuela.

According to Darby, Chavez wanted to create a terrorist network in Louisiana after Hurricane Katrina. This is the same Chavez who blamed an earthquake in Haiti on the United States and who called President George W. Bush "the Devil" during a United Nations speech, so some might find his efforts at subversive activities in the United States hard to take seriously. However, it's important to remember that Chavez has close ties to the terrorism-sponsoring states of Iran and Cuba and allows terrorist groups to operate in Venezuela.

To Darby's astonishment, during his stay in Caracas, senior officials in the Chavez government and in PDVSA told him they wanted him to create a revolutionary army of guerrillas in the swamps of Louisiana. Darby refused, returned to America, and abandoned radicalism.[473]

Instead of using the Red Cross in his post-Katrina relief efforts, Chavez called on radical left-wing charities including the Vanguard Public Foundation and the Peoples Hurricane Relief Fund. Apparently an informal charity, Peoples Hurricane Relief Fund maintains a MySpace page filled with rabidly anti-American propaganda. "Katrina put a spotlight on the horrors of racism, sexism, national oppression, poverty and environmental destruction in the U.S.," the page lectures. It also demands that "the American Government [be put] on trial for its Katrina related crimes against humanity."

As part of his propaganda campaign, Chavez has given $1.5 million to Casa de Maryland, a Washington, D.C.-area charity that advocates for illegal aliens. The grant is being paid by CITGO.[474] The donation came as the tyrant issued new decrees increasing government control over agriculture and creating the National Bolivarian Militia. Under one of the decrees, food retailers or distributors who violate government-imposed price controls or hoard products will face six years imprisonment.[475]

Other radicals with ties to the Chavez regime, particularly the strongman's Hollywood friends, are listed in Lewis's Rolodex.

There's *chavista* Danny Glover, the renowned *Lethal Weapon* actor. Glover, an outspoken radical, is so tight with Chavez that the Venezuelan government has given him money to make movies. On a trip to Venezuela in 2006 Glover said he was "excited to get back to the United States to talk about what is happening [in Venezuela], knowing that you are in a transformative stage and that you are the architects of your own destiny."

Co-chairman of far-left Vanguard Public Foundation in San Francisco, Glover also serves on the advisory council for La Nueva Televisora del Sur ("The New Television Station of the South"), also known as teleSUR. The station has been broadcasting from Caracas since 2005. Rep. Connie Mack (R-FL) observes that teleSUR, "the Chavez-funded network . . . has teamed up with Al-Jazeera to spread anti-democratic messages across Latin America."

Glover travels frequently to Venezuela. In 2003, he visited that country with a delegation that included SEIU International Vice

President Patricia Ford. Also in the delegation was Marxist economist Julianne Malveaux who is listed in Lewis's Rolodex. Now president of Bennett College for Women in North Carolina, Malveaux has called Supreme Court Justice Clarence Thomas a traitor to fellow blacks. Of Thomas, Malveaux said: "I hope his wife feeds him lots of eggs and butter and he dies early like many black men do, of heart disease . . . He is an absolutely reprehensible person."

Radical singer Harry Belafonte appears in the Rolodex. After making a pilgrimage to Venezuela in 2006, Belafonte observed: "No matter what the greatest tyrant in the world, the greatest terrorist in the world, George W. Bush says, we're here to tell you: Not hundreds, not thousands, but millions of the American people...support your revolution."

Fenton Communications senior account executive Eliza Brinkmeyer also has a Rolodex listing. She works for left-wing image maker David Fenton, whose firm manufactured the Alar scare in 1989. Fenton portrayed Alar, a preservative used in apples, as carcinogenic, and caused a public panic. The firm also handled media relations for the Communist regimes in Angola, Nicaragua, and Grenada in the 1980s. Fenton was reportedly the only journalist trusted enough by Bill Ayers's Weathermen group to be allowed to take terrorist cell members' photographs.

Democratic Party strategist David Sirota, who frequently uses Marxist terminology, is in the Rolodex. In a blog post about Americans' resistance to Obama's socialist policies titled "This Is What the Class War Looks Like," he characterized Obama's opponents as hate mongers. Sirota also went to the mat defending Obama's former green jobs czar Van Jones, a 9/11 "truther" and self-described "communist" who resigned under fire during the Labor Day weekend in 2009. Sirota called commentator Glenn Beck a "right-wing political terrorist" and said Jones was "originally targeted because he's an African-American man."

Sex in the City actress Cynthia Nixon has a Rolodex entry. She's worked with ACORN's political party, the Working Families Party, which she described in an ad as "the progressive New York political party that fights for people like you and me."[476] Nixon was also on the host committee for a March 2010 fundraiser for New York Communities for Change, ACORN's rebranded New York organization.[477]

The Rolodex also contains contact information for a constellation of Democratic politicians. It is heavily skewed towards New York, which makes sense because Lewis's home base is in New York and because she only took over as ACORN CEO in mid-2008.

The list includes New York Gov. Andrew Cuomo, who worked closely with ACORN when he was Bill Clinton's HUD secretary, and former New York City mayor David Dinkins. Rep. Edolphus (Ed) Towns, (D-NY), who was chairman of the House Oversight and Government Committee and who could have launched an investigation into ACORN but refused to do, is listed. Then-Sen. Hillary Clinton (D-NY) and then-New York Gov. Eliot Spitzer are in the Rolodex. So are Sen. Charles Schumer (D-NY), Reps. Nydia Velazquez (D-NY), Jose Serrano (D-NY), Gregory Meeks (D-NY), Charles Rangel (D-NY), and Democratic strategist Donna Brazile, whose claim to fame is that she ran Al Gore's presidential campaign in 2000.

ACORN'S FAVORITE LOAN SHARKS

Radical South American regimes and Hollywood actors have some fascinating company when it comes to supporting ACORN. In 2007, toxic mortgage tycoons Herb and Marion Sandler gave $600,000 through their foundation to the Pew Charitable Trusts to protect sharks from their human predators.

It was an act of professional courtesy.

The Sandlers, leftist loan sharks whom *Time* magazine included in its "25 People to Blame for the Financial Crisis" list,[478] preyed on the poor for years and paid ACORN, which also preys on the poor, to help them. It was a perfect fit. It was the Sandlers' World Savings Bank that was the first to offer an exotic mortgage product called the option ARM (adjustable rate mortgage). "And they pushed the mortgage, which offered several ways to back-load your loan and thereby reduce your early payments, with increasing zeal and misleading advertisements over the next two decades."

Their bank flogged an exotic species of mortgage known as an option adjustable rate mortgage, or option ARM. Borrowers could make payments so low that they experienced "negative amortization," which meant that the total debt grew over time because payments didn't cover the interest accumulating on the loan. In the expanding housing bubble, many borrowers chose that option expecting housing prices would keep rising. Soon the bank's portfolio was bursting with toxic loans as ARM borrowers kept burying themselves deeper and deeper in debt. "This product is the most destructive financial weapon ever deployed against the American middle class," said housing lawyer William Purdy. When World Savings was sold to Wachovia in 2006 its portfolio included an astounding $122 billion in ARMs.[479]

The Sandlers' rise from humble origins reads like a great American rags-to-riches success story. Herb was born into a poor family on the Lower East Side of Manhattan while his wife came from a family in Maine that owned a hardware store. They started their financial institution in 1963 in Oakland, California, with two branches, transforming it over time into the second-largest savings and loan in America.

The Sandlers know how to lay it on thick. "I am deeply opposed to wealthy people who exploit the poor, powerful people who prey on the weak, and government representatives who betray the trust of the people they supposedly represent," said Herb.[480]

In a *New York Times Magazine* puff piece of a profile, the Sandlers explained their approach to charitable giving. "It starts with outrage," said Herb. "You go a little crazy when power takes advantage of those without power. It could be political corruption . . ."

"Or subprime lending," interrupted his wife. Shaking his head, Herb continued, "The story of subprime is worse than anyone has written so far." Marion nodded saying, "It is."[481] They should know.

The Sandlers paid ACORN and several other organizations millions of dollars to protect their interests. ACORN members told reporters that the Sandlers paid ACORN "to go out and attack their primary competition, Wells Fargo." Marcel Reid added that protesters were paid to march in the streets to demand an end to Wells Fargo's supposed predatory lending practices.[482]

"Wells Fargo was the Sandlers' biggest competition in California for subprime mortgages," an ACORN insider said in an interview. "ACORN was deployed to put so much pressure on Wells Fargo that they would not be able to do the subprime loans." Many ACORN members participated in the actions against Wells Fargo believing that they were part of a legitimate campaign against predatory lending. In reality it was just another protest-for-hire operation, the source said.

Although the Sandlers have a low public profile, their activist grantmaking is often more generous than that of George Soros, the preeminent funder of left-wing activism in America. In 2004, they gave $13 million to political committees such as MoveOn. Those donations made them the third most generous donors to liberal political groups in that election cycle, below Soros ($27 million) and insurance billionaire Peter B. Lewis ($23 million). The Sandlers gave around $1 million to Democratic political campaigns nationwide. Through their charity they have given tens of millions of dollars to groups that seek to hobble America's fight against Islamic fundamentalism such as Human Rights Watch ($23 million) and the ACLU ($4.6 million in 2007). The Sandlers also helped underwrite the creation of the Center for American Progress (CAP), the liberal think tank—"on steroids," according to its president, John Podesta. Podesta was Bill Clinton's White House chief of staff and was a leader in President Obama's transition team. CAP employs Obama's disgraced "green jobs" czar Van Jones as a senior fellow and also serves as a troubleshooting response team for the national Democratic Party. The foundation has given CAP close to $16 million since 2004.[483]

The Sandlers have carefully cultivated an image of themselves as people deeply concerned about helping the poor. They gave close to $11 million to ACORN affiliates from 1999 through 2008 through their charity. The Sandler Foundation paid $7.7 million to the American Institute for Social Justice in that period and $3.2 million to Project Vote in 2007.

ACORN apparently used the Sandlers' money to wage a campaign against Wells Fargo that lasted for years. In 2003, ACORN published a report accusing the company's two units, Wells Fargo Financial and Wells Fargo Funding, of predatory lending and other unethical business practices.[484] In New Mexico, ACORN filed 14 complaints against the bank, alleging unfair business practices.[485]

In 2004, ACORN initiated a nationwide class action lawsuit against the bank accusing it of "a broad range of unfair and deceptive lending practices, including misleading borrowers about the real terms and conditions of their loans, 'bait and switch' sales tactics, and routinely failing to inform borrowers with good credit that they can qualify for credit at significantly better rates and fees than those charged them by Wells." On the date the suit was filed, ACORN held a march and rally in Los Angeles involving 2,000 ACORN members. "ACORN will not allow Wells Fargo to continue to swindle and steal from our communities," said ACORN national president Maude Hurd. "We will fight until they stop their abusive loan practices, and the Wells stagecoach is no longer delivering misery to homeowners." Two weeks before, ACORN filed a separate class action lawsuit in Illinois accusing the bank of "collecting fees on high rate loans in excess of what is permitted by state law."[486]

In 2005, ACORN unveiled a study of the bank's loans in 42 metropolitan areas that the group claimed showed "a huge racial and economic disparity between the company's prime (less costly) mortgage lending and its higher-cost subprime lending." ACORN also demanded that the Federal Reserve Board remove the bank's CEO, Richard Kovacevich, from its advisory council, "because of Wells Fargo's discriminatory and predatory financial practices."[487]

Reid thought it was ironic that people who worked at the Center for Responsible Lending (CRL) gave ACORN demonstrators their marching orders during the Wells Fargo campaign.[488]

The Sandlers founded the taxpayer-supported CRL, a longtime ACORN ally that champions the Community Reinvestment Act and rages against lending practices. Their foundation has given the Center at least $19.1 million since 2005. According to journalist Sean Higgins, their giving has transformed the North Carolina-based nonprofit into "a major player in financial services and banking policy-making." In its corner of the policy world, CRL has become "what the ACLU is to civil rights or AARP is to seniors' entitlements: It is the dominant left-wing advocacy/lobbying group—the one political and media elites in Washington, D.C. listen to regarding low income lending policies." CRL also enjoys the fat-cat trappings of success in the nation's capital. CRL is a player in Washington's infamous "K Street" corridor of lobbying firms a few blocks away from the White House. In 2004, it bought an 11-story building in the corridor for $23 million.[489]

While ACORN's campaign against Wells Fargo was in progress, CRL began pointing its propaganda artillery at Wells Fargo while ignoring the predations of the Sandlers. A 2004 report from CRL condemned Wells Fargo. "Lulled by favorable analyst reports, Wells Fargo investors may not realize they are subsidizing a predatory lender . . . Sadly, the people who see these problems most clearly are the unit's customers, who too often face the loss of their home or financial ruin as a result."[490]

After the stock market collapsed in September 2008, the Sandlers were buried in an avalanche of adverse publicity. They found themselves mocked and parodied by the late night TV show *Saturday Night Live* for their contribution to the economic meltdown. In a comedy skit an actress portraying then-House Speaker Nancy Pelosi (D-CA) introduces "Herb" and "Marion Sandler." "Herb" says, "My wife and I had a company which aggressively marketed subprime mortgages, and then bundled them into securities to sell to banks such as Wachovia." He laments that their portfolio is now valued near zero, though it had been worth much more.

"Pelosi" asks if the Sandlers were able to get anything for their portfolio. Yes, $24 billion, "Herb" responds. "You're not, so to speak, actual victims?" says Pelosi. "Oh no, that would be Wachovia bank," "Herb" chuckles. "Actually we've done quite well," says "Marion." "We're very happy."

"We were sort of wondering why you asked us to come today," "Herb" adds. While he speaks a fake C-SPAN caption appears at the bottom of the screen showing the couple with the words: "People who should be shot." As "Herb" and "Marion" walk away they thank an actor playing then-House Financial Services Committee Chairman Barney Frank (D-MA) and "Pelosi" for "helping block congressional oversight of our corrupt activities." "Marion" and "Pelosi" even exchange cheek kisses.

The real Sandlers were not happy. After the skit aired Paul Steiger, editor-in-chief of ProPublica, a journalism nonprofit that churns out left-leaning investigative reports, contacted NBC to complain. Herb Sandler is chairman of ProPublica, and the Sandlers have reportedly donated $10 million to it. Soon the show's producer, Lorne Michaels, apologized and the "People who should be shot" caption was cut from the program's video clip, which NBC has since deleted from its website.[491]

The Sandlers, who are key members of George Soros's Democracy Alliance, a group of super-rich leftists that aspires to build a permanent political infrastructure of think tanks, media outlets, and activist groups to keep pushing America ever leftward, decided to cash in their chips in late 2006. They sold Golden West Financial Corp., the parent of World Savings Bank, to Wachovia for $25 billion, pocketing $2.4 billion for themselves. In the end, the shaky loan portfolio built up by the Sandlers drove Wachovia to the brink of bankruptcy as the housing bubble began to burst. Wachovia was sold to Wells Fargo in late 2008.

The $2.4 billion from the sale of Golden West turned the Sandlers into kingmakers in the left-wing activist community. They donated roughly half of their profits to their foundation. "Thanks to the Sandlers, Wachovia's loss is the American Left's gain," noted John J. Miller.[492]

SELLING OUT BROOKLYN'S POOR FOR COLD, HARD CASH

Ever mindful of its public face as a defender of the poor, ACORN has long depicted itself as an opponent of "gentrification"—or what the rest of America calls "market forces." As rising property values drive the poor out of neighborhoods, ACORN has fought this natural pro-cess in an effort to keep low-income people from having to relocate.

And yet the group became the most prominent cheerleader for a controversial real estate development that is relying on eminent domain to remove the same poor people ACORN claims to repre-sent. It has taken money from the project's developer and signed a binding agreement forcing it to stand behind the project no matter what. In the world of corporate shakedowns, it is commonplace for liberal activist groups to use the money they coerce from a "donor" to fund operations. But it is unusual for a group to take money in exchange for betraying those it claims to represent.

In 2005, ACORN signed an agreement with Forest City Ratner Companies LLC, a megabucks real estate development firm, pledging its support for the ambitious Atlantic Yards development in Brooklyn. This taxpayer-subsidized 22-acre mixed-use project has been priced at $4.9 billion. The sprawling complex will be built in the neighborhood of Prospect Heights and include the Barclays Center, the new home of the New Jersey Nets basketball team. In exchange for ACORN's support, the developer agreed to set aside 50% of the expected 4,500 rental housing units for what the agreement's income tables define as "affordable housing." At a staged media event, ACORN's Bertha Lewis publicly sealed the deal by planting kisses on the mouths of New York City mayor Michael Bloomberg and Bruce Ratner, CEO of the devel-opment company and principal owner of the money-losing Nets.[493]

A few years before ACORN was paid off by Ratner, it was waging war in the streets against him. In 2000, then-New York ACORN head Bertha Lewis sent 70 demonstrators to Ratner's office lobby to pres-sure him to force those renting retail space from him to pay their employees "living wages" of at least $10 an hour plus full health ben-efits. The activists were met by an equal number of police in riot gear. ACORN said it believed Ratner could "force retailers to implement changes." ACORN also demanded that Ratner encourage employees to unionize and that ACORN have influence in hiring practices.[494]

But that was then. ACORN wasted no time after the U.S. Supreme Court threw the door wide open for expropriation for private profit in the infamous *Kelo v. New London* eminent domain case, which held that the government can take land from one private owner and award it to another. The *Kelo* decision was handed down June 23, 2005. The formal "community benefits agreement" between ACORN and other local groups and the developer was signed on June 27. Without ACORN's horse-traded support for the project, "it was unlikely the Atlantic Yards deal would prevail," ACORN hagiographer John Atlas wrote a few months later in *Shelterforce* magazine. "And if Atlantic Yards gets built, ACORN will need all of its muscle to ensure that promises are fulfilled and the poor are protected."

ACORN, supplier of instant supporters for public hearings on the project, and the government subsidy-seeking developer are a perfect fit. "We like working with ACORN," an unnamed Forest City Ratner executive told the *Brooklyn Paper* in 2005. "They have that radical feeling, they really fight for what they believe in. We just love their history, how they started, and feel it really represents what we're working to do here."

That executive wasn't kidding. Left-of-center political activism runs in the Ratner family. Bruce, who used to teach law, ran the Consumer Protection Division in New York City Mayor John Lindsay's administration. He was also Consumer Affairs commissioner under Mayor Ed Koch. "Bruce is an old lefty, he's an old hippie," one friend told *New York* magazine. He also worked for the Model Cities Program, an artifact of President Johnson's ill-fated anti-poverty crusade. His brother is Michael Ratner, a Che Guevara admirer who has long campaigned for the closure of the U.S. military's Guantanamo Bay detention center in Cuba. Michael heads up the Greenwich Village-based Center for Constitutional Rights (CCR), which has scored legal victories that undermined the Global War on Terror. (CCR was later to represent ACORN in a lawsuit challenging a ban on federal funding to the group.) Their sister Ellen is a left-wing journalist who said in 2002 it was "my hope" that President George W. Bush "messes up the war" in Iraq so he wouldn't be reelected in 2004.

Although in 2005, Ratner, struggling to move forward with Atlantic Yards, might have needed ACORN more than ACORN needed it, by

2008 roles were reversed. Stung by internal scandal, election fraud allegations galore, unprecedented nonstop negative media coverage, and cash flow problems, ACORN agreed to accept a cash infusion from the developer.

With millions of dollars in back taxes owing to the IRS, states, and localities across the nation, ACORN sold its continued backing for Atlantic Yards fairly cheaply at $1.5 million in 2008. This bailout consisted of a $1 million loan and $500,000 in donations. The loan agreement spread out the payments over time to make sure ACORN couldn't renege on backing the project.[495] Ratner's company pledged to disburse $500,000 in grants but the money wouldn't go to ACORN directly. The grants were to be made to the ACORN Institute. Whether the money stayed there is anyone's guess.

ACORN held up its end of the bargain with Ratner, using the usual thug tactics against its opposition. ACORN activists wearing blue "Atlantic Yards NOW!" buttons disrupted an oversight hearing held by the New York legislature. In mid-2009 supporters of the project shouted down speakers at a New York Senate Committee on Corporations, Authorities, and Commissions oversight hearing on the project. Demonstrators shouted, demanding that the hearings end and the project move forward. They loudly booed state Sen. Velmanette Montgomery, a Democrat representing Brooklyn. "Despite holding a microphone to her mouth, the union workers, on hand to show support for the controversial project that eventually might promise work for them booed, yelled and blew loud whistles until the senator stopped talking."[496]

"Some of the people were members of construction unions," said Brooklyn blogger Norman Oder. "There were also people dressed up in very new hard hats and very new reflector vests who were probably not construction workers, probably from one of the groups that's supported financially by Forest City Ratner, the developer."[497]

As doubts have surfaced about whether Forest City Ratner will honor the promise it made to build 2,250 units of affordable housing—the promise that helped it win the support of ACORN and the Prospect Heights community—ACORN has remained silent. Local politicians are becoming increasingly nervous about the afford-able housing component of the project. "The sweeping promises of affordable housing made by the developer at the onset of this project have now evaporated to a mere whisper," said Assemblyman Hakeem Jeffries, a Brooklyn Democrat who backed the original plan. "At this point, it is not clear that the developer plans to build anything other than an arena and a few affordable apartment units, and that is sim-ply unacceptable."[498]

Although the officially approved plan called for the affordable housing to be built over 10 years, the developer is trying to back out of some commitments. "Before the economic downturn, September 2007, the city and state signed funding agreements that require For-est City Ratner to build much, much less," said Oder, keeper of the encyclopedic Atlantic Yards Report blog. "They can get away with building much less without penalty, maybe three towers, only 300 units of affordable housing in 12 years."

The idea that the developer would construct only three residential buildings was floated by Bruce Ratner himself. In a rare *New York Times* report on the difficulties the project was facing, Ratner said in 2008 that the bad economy and credit crunch were delivering a double-whammy to his plans. "It may hold up the office building," he said. "And the bond market may slow the pace of the residential buildings." Inciden-tally, the Old Gray Lady barely covered the Atlantic Yards story at all. The newspaper of record's virtual news blackout might stem from the fact that the New York Times Company and Forest City Ratner were development partners in the Times Company's new headquarters on Eighth Avenue in Manhattan. Eminent domain was used in the project.

Although ACORN takes credit for saving residents of places such as Hurricane Katrina-ravaged New Orleans from having their homes seized, the displacement of Brooklyn residents doesn't seem to bother Bertha Lewis. Lewis patted herself on the back for her group's work on the Brooklyn project, which she described as "sexy, sexy, sexy Atlantic Yards." For an Alinskyite, she was uncharacteristically straightforward, acknowledging ACORN had provided the developer "political cover—let's face it—and political might."

When entering into talks with a developer, "You really have to know your shit," boasted the bard of ACORN. "You need to be big enough and have the strength and have enough expertise and be able to bring the political capital to the table."[499]

Lewis may not be bothered by her conscience, but the displacement of property owners and poor people to make way for private developments should bother prominent ACORN supporters. Three months after the *Kelo* ruling that allowed revenue-hungry state and local governments to take private property and give it to private developers, lawmakers of every political stripe, including the radical leftist Rep. Maxine Waters (D-CA), were incensed. Waters, who frequently speaks at ACORN events, said "the taking of private property for private use, in my estimation, is unconstitutional. It's un-American, and it's not to be tolerated."

WHO FUNDS ACORN? *You* FUND ACORN.

Taxpayers have long helped to fund ACORN through grants at the federal, state, and local level. Consumers fund ACORN indirectly through a kind of invisible tax. Every time a consumer patronizes a business that gives to ACORN, that person is donating to ACORN. Every dollar that goes to ACORN could have gone to shareholder dividends or to reducing the prices of goods and services.

Governments don't make it easy to find out how much tax money flows to ACORN and similar groups. Forensic accountants and a large team of Freedom of Information Act requesters would be needed to determine exactly how many taxpayer dollars have gone to the ACORN network. The quality of public disclosure about government spending varies widely in states, localities, and throughout the various arms of the mammoth U.S. government.

Based on an extensive search, it appears the federal government has directed at least $79 million in grants to ACORN and affiliates since 1994. Undoubtedly the real total is much higher. (See Table of Federal Grants on page 211.)

TABLE OF FEDERAL GRANTS

Recipient	State	Amount	Grantor	Date Announced, or if not available, date of grant
ACORN INSTITUTE	LA	$997,402	FEMA	9/4/2009
ACORN INSTITUTE	AZ	$8,539	DOJ	fiscal 2009
ACORN HOUSING	NI*	$16,000,000	NEIGHBORWORKS	December 2008
ARKANSAS BROADCASTING FOUNDATION INC. (KABF FM)	AR	$81,250	CPB	fiscal 2009
AGAPE BROADCASTING FOUNDATION INC. (KNON FM)	TX	$97,249	CPB	fiscal 2009
ACORN HOUSING	NI*	$1,200,000	NEIGHBORWORKS	December 2008
ACORN INSTITUTE	DC	$124,324	HUD	11/10/2008
ACORN INSTITUTE	OH	$189,171	HUD	11/10/2008
ACORN TENANT UNION TENANT ORGANIZING PROJECT	NV	$124,965	HUD	11/10/2008
ACORN INSTITUTE	LA	$450,484	FEMA	8/29/2008
ACORN HOUSING AND SUBSIDIARIES	IL	$729,218	unknown sub-grantor (CDBG funds from HUD)	6/30/2008
ACORN HOUSING AND SUBSIDIARIES	IL	$206,651	unknown sub-grantor (CDBG funds from HUD)	6/30/2008
ACORN HOUSING	PA	$1,628,829	HUD	3/26/2008
ACORN HOUSING	PA	$1,821,596	HUD	3/6/2008
ACORN HOUSING	NI*	$7,850,939	NEIGHBORWORKS	2/24/2008
ACORN INSTITUTE	DC	$362,378	HUD	1/28/2008
NEW YORK AGENCY FOR COMMUNITY AFFAIRS	NY	$99,427	HUD	fiscal 2008
ACORN ASSOCIATES	NM	$99,974	HUD	fiscal 2008
ACORN	NY	$20,000	CCNYC(I)	fiscal 2008
ACORN HOUSING	PA	$1,623,570	HUD	2008
ARKANSAS BROADCASTING FOUNDATION INC. (KABF FM)	AR	$77,475	CPB	fiscal 2008
AGAPE BROADCASTING FOUNDATION INC. (KNON FM)	TX	$103,839	CPB	fiscal 2008
ACORN INSTITUTE	TX	$179,916	HUD	12/31/2007
ACORN INSTITUTE	TX	$124,915	HUD	12/31/2007
ACORN INSTITUTE	TX	$124,693	HUD	12/31/2007
AMERICAN INSTITUTE FOR SOCIAL JUSTICE	CO	$99,887	HUD	11/20/2007
ACORN HOUSING	MN	$100,000	HUD	11/20/2007
NEW MEXICO ACORN FAIR HOUSING	NM	$99,757	HUD	11/20/2007

ARKANSAS COMMUNITY HOUSING CORP.	AR	$99,948	HUD	11/20/2007
ACORN HOUSING AND SUBSIDIARIES	IL	$372,950	unknown sub-grantor (CDBG funds from HUD)	6/30/2007
AMERICAN ENVIRONMENTAL JUSTICE PROJECT	MD	$99,716	HUD	1/17/2007
AMERICAN INSTITUTE FOR SOCIAL JUSTICE	DC	$99,080	HUD	1/17/2007
NEW MEXICO ACORN FAIR HOUSING	NM	$99,724	HUD	1/17/2007
ACORN ASSOCIATES	NM	$49,997	HUD	1/17/2007
ACORN COMMUNITY LAND ASSOCIATION OF LOUISIANA	LA	$100,000	HUD	1/17/2007
ACORN HOUSING	PA	$4,666,258	NEIGHBORWORKS	tax year 2007
ACORN HOUSING	IL	$60,500	NEIGHBORWORKS	tax year 2007
ACORN HOUSING	IL	$3,184,681	NEIGHBORWORKS	tax year 2007
ACORN INSTITUTE	MO	$13,000	DOJ	fiscal 2007
ARKANSAS BROADCASTING FOUNDATION INC. (KABF FM)	AR	$87,388	CPB	fiscal 2007
AGAPE BROADCASTING FOUNDATION INC. (KNON FM)	TX	$110,162	CPB	fiscal 2007
ACORN TENANT UNION TRAINING AND ORGA-NIZING PROJECT	DC	$278,636	HUD	10/10/2006
ACORN TENANT UNION TRAINING AND ORGA-NIZING PROJECT	DC	$230,500	HUD	10/10/2006
ACORN HOUSING	IL	$351,000	HUD	8/29/2006
ACORN HOUSING	IL	$527,000	HUD	8/29/2006
ACORN FAIR HOUSING	DC	$79,988	HUD	9/8/2006
ACORN FAIR HOUSING (A PROJECT OF AMERI-CAN INSTITUTE)	DC	$80,000	HUD	9/8/2006
AMERICAN ENVIRONMENTAL JUSTICE PROJECT	MD	$80,000	HUD	9/8/2006
ACORN HOUSING CORP. OF TEXAS	TX	$49,865	HUD	9/8/2006
ACORN INSTITUTE	LA	$79,897	HUD	9/8/2006
ACORN INSTITUTE	LA	$80,000	HUD	9/8/2006
ACORN HOUSING	MN	$80,000	HUD	9/8/2006
ACORN COMMUNITY LAND ASSOCIATION	NM	$99,775	HUD	9/8/2006
ACORN COMMUNITY LAND ASSOCIATION OF LOUISIANA	MD	$200,000	HUD	9/8/2006
ACORN COMMUNITY LAND ASSOCIATION OF LOUISIANA	LA	$80,000	HUD	9/8/2006
ACORN HOUSING OF ARIZONA	AZ	$95,000	HUD	9/8/2006
ACORN HOUSING OF ARIZONA	AZ	$99,840	HUD	9/8/2006
ARKANSAS COMMUNITY HOUSING CORP.	AR	$100,000	HUD	9/8/2006
ARKANSAS COMMUNITY HOUSING CORP.	AR	$50,000	HUD	9/8/2006
ACORN FAIR HOUSING	DC	$100,000	HUD	9/6/2006

ACORN HOUSING	MN	$100,000	HUD	9/6/2006
ACORN COMMUNITY LAND ASSOCIATION OF LOUISIANA	LA	$100,000	HUD	9/6/2006
ACORN HOUSING	MN	$100,000	HUD	9/6/2006
ARKANSAS COMMUNITY HOUSING CORP.	AR	$100,000	HUD	9/6/2006
ACORN HOUSING AND SUBSIDIARIES	LA	$238,809	unknown sub-grantor (CDBG funds from HUD)	6/30/2006
ACORN ASSOCIATES	LA	$1,999,920	HUD	6/14/2006
ACORN HOUSING	PA	$1,197,255	HUD	3/21/2006
ACORN HOUSING	PA	$78,354	HUD	3/21/2006
ACORN HOUSING	PA	$323,439	HUD	3/21/2006
ACORN HOUSING	PA	$275,000	HUD	3/21/2006
ACORN HOUSING	NI*	$572,000	HUD	2/23/2006
PROJECT VOTE	DE	$16,875	EAC	fiscal 2006
PROJECT VOTE	MI	$16,875	EAC	fiscal 2006
ARKANSAS BROADCASTING FOUNDATION INC. (KABF FM)	AR	$84,801	CPB	fiscal 2006
AGAPE BROADCASTING FOUNDATION INC. (KNON FM)	TX	$115,484	CPB	fiscal 2006
AGAPE BROADCASTING FOUNDATION INC. (KNON FM)	TX	$80,000	CPB	fiscal 2006
PROJECT VOTE	DC	$912,378	HUD	2006
AMERICAN INSTITUTE FOR SOCIAL JUSTICE	DC	$100,000	HUD	12/13/2005
ARKANSAS COMMUNITY HOUSING CORP.	AR	$100,000	HUD	12/13/2005
MISSOURI TAX JUSTICE RESEARCH PROJECT	MO	$100,000	HUD	12/13/2005
ACORN HOUSING	MN	$100,000	HUD	12/13/2005
ACORN INSTITUTE	TX	$96,953	HUD	12/13/2005
NEW YORK AGENCY FOR COMMUNITY AFFAIRS	NY	$99,975	HUD	12/13/2005
ACORN HOUSING AND SUBSIDIARIES	LA	$367,560	unknown sub-grantor (CDBG funds from HUD)	6/30/2005
ACORN HOUSING	PA	$1,812,471	HUD	5/2/2005
ACORN HOUSING	PA	$325,000	HUD	5/2/2005
ACORN HOUSING	PA	$275,000	HUD	5/2/2005
ACORN ASSOCIATES	LA	$2,000,000	HUD	4/22/2005
NEW YORK AGENCY FOR COMMUNITY AFFAIRS	NY	$138,130	DOJ	fiscal 2005
NEW YORK ACORN	NY	$140,000	DOJ	fiscal 2005
ARKANSAS BROADCASTING FOUNDATION INC. (KABF FM)	AR	$37,694	CPB	fiscal 2005
AGAPE BROADCASTING FOUNDATION INC. (KNON FM)	TX	$19,508	CPB	fiscal 2005

ARKANSAS BROADCASTING FOUNDATION INC. (KABF FM)	AR	$15,000	CPB	fiscal 2005
AGAPE BROADCASTING FOUNDATION INC. (KNON FM)	TX	$15,000	CPB	fiscal 2005
ACORN HOUSING	NI*	$2,700,000	HUD	7/28/2004
ACORN HOUSING AND SUBSIDIARIES	LA	$221,007	unknown sub-grantor (CDBG funds from HUD)	6/30/2004
ACORN HOUSING	PA	$2,024,511	HUD	2/23/2004
ACORN HOUSING	PA	$380,282	HUD	2/23/2004
ACORN HOUSING	PA	$250,962	HUD	2/23/2004
ACORN (LOUISIANA JUSTICE PROJECT)	LA	$100,000	EPA	2004
ACORN ASSOCIATES	LA	$999,974	HUD	11/25/2003
ACORN FAIR HOUSING	DC	$100,000	HUD	11/19/2003
ACORN COMMUNITY LAND ASSOCIATION	LA	$100,000	HUD	11/19/2003
ACORN HOUSING	MN	$100,000	HUD	11/19/2003
ACORN HOUSING AND SUBSIDIARIES	LA	$388,273	unknown sub-grantor (CDBG funds from HUD)	6/30/2003
ACORN HOUSING	PA	$1,167,044	HUD	1/13/2003
ACORN HOUSING	PA	$1,032,192	HUD	1/16/2002
ACORN HOUSING	NI*	$351,000	HUD	10/24/2002
AMERICAN INSTITUTE FOR SOCIAL JUSTICE	DC	$20,000	DOJ	fiscal 2002
ACORN FAIR HOUSING (A PROJECT OF AISJ)	NI*	$300,000	HUD	11/9/2001
ACORN HOUSING	IL	$300,000	HUD	4/11/2001
ACORN HOUSING	PA	$597,474	HUD	4/11/2001
ACORN TENANT UNION TRAINING AND ORGANIZING PROJECT	DC	$150,000	HUD	12/20/2000
ACORN HOUSING	PA	$1,000,000	HUD	6/23/1999
ACORN TENANT UNION TRAINING AND ORGANIZING PROJECT	DC	$99,900	HUD	4/13/1999
ACORN HOUSING	IL	$751,500	HUD	2/12/1999
ACORN HOUSING	PA	$839,865	HUD	1999
ACORN HOUSING	PA	$1,000,000	HUD	8/27/1998
ACORN TENANT UNION TRAINING PROJECT	NY	$250,000	HUD	4/8/1998
ARKANSAS ACORN FAIR HOUSING	AR	$100,000	HUD	2/19/1998
LOUISIANA FAIR HOUSING ORGANIZATION	LA	$350,000	HUD	2/19/1998
ACORN HOUSING	PA	$900,000	HUD	10/29/1996
ACORN TENANT UNION	DC	$100,000	HUD	5/24/1996
SOUTH-CENTRAL ACORN TENANT UNION	TX	$100,000	HUD	5/24/1996
ACORN TENANT UNION	NY	$100,000	HUD	2/6/1996

ACORN HOUSING	PA	$850,500	HUD	10/27/1995
ACORN HOUSING	TX	$120,000	HUD	12/8/1994
ACORN HOUSING	AZ	$100,000	HUD	12/8/1994
LOUISIANA FAIR HOUSING ORGANIZATION	LA	$250,000	HUD	12/8/1994
ACORN HOUSING	NI*	$944,961	AmeriCorps	8/22/1994
ACORN NEW ENGLAND FAIR HOUSING PROJECT	LA	$95,000	HUD	7/14/1994
ACORN PEACHTREE COALITION FOR FAIRNESS IN HOUSING	LA	$95,000	HUD	7/14/1994
ACORN MIDWEST FAIR HOUSING CONSORTIUM	LA	$95,000	HUD	7/14/1994
ACORN SOUTHERN FAIRNESS IN HOUSING COALITION	LA	$95,000	HUD	7/14/1994
ACORN MISSOURI CONSORTIUM FOR FAIR HOUSING	LA	$95,000	HUD	7/14/1994
ACORN FAIR HOUSING FOR WASHINGTON COALITION	LA	$95,000	HUD	7/14/1994
ACORN HOUSING CORP. OF ILLINOIS	IL	$893,750	HUD	3/22/1994
MISSOURI ACORN	MO	$6,665	EPA	fiscal 1994
		$79,074,694		

(1) Citizens Committee for New York City, Inc. gave a sub-award to ACORN from the Department of Justice's Office of Justice Programs (OJP).

NI* The state of the grant recipient was not indicated.

Abbreviations:
CCNYC Citizens Committee for New York City, Inc.
CDBG Community Development Block Grants
CPB Corporation for Public Broadcasting
DOJ Department of Justice
EAC Election Assistance Commission
EPA Environmental Protection Agency
FEMA Federal Emergency Management Agency
HUD Department of Housing and Urban Development

Sources: The Federal Register, Department of Housing and Urban Development, Environmental Protection Agency, Department of Justice, Government Accountability Office, Census Bureau, Judicial Watch, Neighbor Works, FireGrantSupport.com, House Oversight and Government Reform Committee, and various databases.

Some of the funding came from the Community Development Block Grants (CDBG) program, a congressional slush fund administered by HUD. The CDBG funding ACORN has received is extremely difficult to track because ACORN receives the money indirectly, that is, as a "subgrantee" of state and local governments that take in CDBG funding directly from HUD. Often the CDBG grant will be matched by other sources, giving ACORN even more money.

CDBG is good old-fashioned graft. Local politicians of both parties adore CDBG because it is flexible. The program gives them wide latitude when spending grant money and allows local leaders to use federal dollars on local projects that they wouldn't dream of asking local taxpayers to fund. ACORN loves the program because it is adept at extracting CDBG funds from local governments. In recent years, Congress has gotten into the habit of appropriating between $4 billion and $5 billion annually for CDBG.

Of the $79 million in federal grants, most of the money came from the Department of Housing and Urban Development. The runner-up in taxpayer giveaways to ACORN is NeighborWorks, which has handed over $33 million to the group. NeighborWorks is a congressionally chartered community development nonprofit that leftist housing groups use as a piggybank. The other federal funders of ACORN are the Federal Emergency Management Agency ($1.4 million), AmeriCorps ($945,000), Department of Justice ($339,000), Environmental Protection Agency ($107,000), and Election Assistance Commission ($17,000). The EAC provides grants aimed at improving the administration of federal elections. Why EAC gave a grant in 2006 to ACORN's election fraud factory, Project Vote, is unclear. It is also unclear why HUD gave Project Vote nearly a million dollars the same year.

ACORN has long had friends on the inside at HUD. ACORN worked with the Clinton administration to quietly provide money to the group. Two weeks before the 1992 election, Dreier and Atlas met with Marc Weiss, presidential candidate Bill Clinton's senior housing policy advisor. Together they plotted to funnel tax dollars to ACORN by "'hiding' financial support for ACORN inside nondescript government programs," according to Stanley Kurtz. "ACORN agreed with this tactic of stealth." Clinton's first HUD secretary, Henry Cisneros, looked for ways to raid the public fisc on ACORN's behalf.[500]

Although legal authority for HUD appears nowhere in the Constitution, the department is ACORN's best friend in the federal government and a critical component of the modern welfare state. Today it is the most visible arm of the federal government involved in social engineering. HUD is all about meddling in people's lives. It has long defended the Community Reinvestment Act and other misguided policies. HUD works closely with the financially troubled Fannie Mae and Freddie Mac. In fact, HUD set goals for lower-income and "underserved" housing areas for Fannie and Freddie and was part of the disastrous push to expand home ownership that caused the now-deflating housing bubble. HUD runs the FHA (Federal Housing Administration) which insures mortgages, a practice that exposes taxpayers to massive financial risks.

HUD:
ACORN'S PARTNER IN TRANSFORMING AMERICA

HUD's bureaucracy tells people how to live and where to live. It tells cities they are racially out of balance and pressures them to change their zoning to allow more "affordable housing" so the community has the politically correct mixture of economic development and racial diversity. HUD has, for the most part, hurt cities. It has helped to make city dwellers increasingly dependent on government for handouts. HUD is wasteful and its grants are frequently abused by recipients. HUD funds not only ACORN, but also National Council of La Raza and other left-wing organizations through its mortgage counseling grants and through CDBG. HUD pushes "smart growth," which is an effort to force Americans to live in high-density cities whether they want to or not. HUD also distorts markets by funding Section 8 vouchers which low-income people use to help pay their rent.

There are some alarming patterns in the grant-making of HUD, which gave $42.2 million to ACORN and its affiliates. It ought to concern taxpayers that $1.7 million of their money went to ACORN's Alinskyite training arms, ACORN Institute ($1.4 million) and American Institute for Social Justice ($300,000). They should also be concerned that $1.4 million in HUD grants went to "ACORN Tenant Union," "ACORN Tenant Union Training Project," "ACORN Tenant Union Training and Organizing Project" and "South-Central ACORN Tenant Union."

It is important to note that the figures shown for ACORN Housing are well below the actual level of government housing-related grants to the ACORN network. ACORN has many state- and local-level housing affiliates that have also accepted government money.

ACORN Housing bragged on its website in 2007 that from 1986 through 2006 it has "counseled" 250,226 clients and "educated" 284,758 more, "created" 79,539 mortgages in the amount of $10,080,912,633. At that time it claimed to have 37 offices nationwide.[501] "Our staff has counseled more than 250,000 low- and moderate-income people and helped more than 100,539 families acquire homes totaling more than $14.9 billion."[502] In early 2008, ACORN Housing unveiled its non-profit mortgage brokerage in 34 U.S. cities. The brokerage, called Acorn Housing Affordable Loans LLC, partners with CitiMortgage, Bank of America, First American Title Insurance Co., and Fannie Mae. "The new mortgage brokerage will also help homeowners faced with resetting adjustable rates that may make their current home mortgage payments unaffordable," the nonprofit said in a statement.

Even though the ACORN organization itself has declared bankruptcy, a network of ACORN successor groups may take in more taxpayer dollars in the future—if the financially troubled Fannie Mae and Freddie Mac survive. That's because the housing bailout bill enacted in mid-2008 contains language creating a $5 billion so-called affordable housing trust fund that conservatives quite properly label a slush fund. This unusual off-budget funding mechanism siphons off funds from Fannie and Freddie but provides virtually no safeguards ensuring that the money will actually be spent on affordable housing. It would fund housing subsidies, financial counseling, and mortgage restructuring programs.

The funding would go to left-wing housing advocacy groups in the ACORN mold, including the National Council of La Raza, and the Greenlining Institute and "[t]here are no explicit requirements for recipients of the grants to fill out timesheets for housing activity, or restrictions on groups using grant money to pay employees who also happen to do other things—such as lobbying and political campaigning," writes John Berlau of the Competitive Enterprise Institute. "And there are really no penalties other than being forced to give the money back and being disqualified for a new grant."[503]

Much of the taxpayer money ACORN Housing has taken in from HUD has been for mortgage counseling. HUD-funded mortgage counseling didn't prevent the housing market meltdown, observes Michelle Malkin. Mortgage counseling "is a thriving racket that benefits far Left groups ranging from the AARP to ACORN to La Raza and Legal Aid," she wrote. Why should one more cent "be thrown at the problem—money that will go to heavy-hitting left-wing groups who will turn around and undermine principles of economic conservatism at every turn?"[504]

It is supremely ironic that ACORN and its affiliates, all reliable cheerleaders for higher taxes, are perpetual tax deadbeats.

As of November 2009, a mountain of tax liens was pending against the activist network. At that time ACORN and its affiliates owed more than $2.3 million in long overdue back taxes to all levels of government. The ACORN network owed money to the Internal Revenue Service, Arkansas, California, Delaware, District of Columbia, Indiana, Iowa, Kentucky, Louisiana, Maryland, Michigan, Mississippi, New Mexico, New York, New Jersey, Ohio, Oklahoma, Pennsylvania, South Carolina, Texas, Washington, Wisconsin, and to the cities of New York and Philadelphia. A government tax agency reluctantly issues a tax lien only after other attempts to collect the tax debt have been made and the tax debt is seriously delinquent.[505] A year later, on November 2, 2010, ACORN filed Chapter 7 bankruptcy and reportedly closed its doors.

It is unclear what kinds of taxes ACORN and its affiliates failed to pay. We may never know because tax agencies are tight-lipped about tax debts, but because almost all ACORN affiliates are exempted from paying most or all taxes, it seems likely that the liens were issued for non-payment of employees' payroll taxes—the same payroll taxes that fund the social and wealth-distribution programs that ACORN so staunchly supports.

ACORN's financial paperwork is notoriously fishy. Its amended tax return for Tax Year 2003—the only tax return for the parent company that this writer was able to find—listed $246,796 for "payroll taxes payable." ACORN declares on the form that it took in $1,329,765 in "membership dues and assessments." This is hard to believe. In 2010, ACORN membership cost $120 annually, but in 2003 when ACORN claimed to have 200,000 members, it appears to have charged members $60 for annual dues. If only half the members paid full dues the total would be $6 million, which is more than four times the sum disclosed. ACORN tries to steer people toward full memberships but if it's in danger of losing the sale it offers associate memberships at half the price of full memberships. Associate member status is less than desirable because associates aren't allowed to run for office within the group. ACORN also offers provisional membership for the very poor who are allowed to pay what they can afford or nothing at all. It seems the only way the $1,329,765 figure for member dues could be correct is if most of those involved in the group have second-class status. This would further undermine ACORN's claim to be a democratically run organization.

FOUNDATIONS AND CORPORATE CHARITIES

Although ACORN affiliates ACORN Housing, ACORN Institute, AISJ, and Project Vote took in least $106.9 million in donations from 1993 through 2007, detailed grant data on the ACORN network goes back only to 1998 in philanthropy databases. The total figure is certainly higher than $107 million, which, according to Wade Rathke, is roughly equivalent to ACORN's budget for a single year.

Evidence of ACORN's shakedowns can be difficult to find. The company that has been blackmailed or otherwise terrorized isn't always eager to publicize its ordeal. It views any payments it has agreed to make to ACORN as protection money that is supposed to make the pain ACORN generates go away. Of course buckling in to ACORN only encourages more attacks because, money-hungry bully that it is, ACORN views such payments as weakness.

At an ACORN "banking summit" in New York City in 1992, keynote speaker Jesse Jackson explained why activists should go after banks. "Get the money from where the money went," said the maestro of shakedowns. "Don't make things complicated. Why did Jesse James rob banks? Because that's where the money was."[506] ACORN listened.

"ACORN knows that corporate America has no starch in their shorts and, therefore, what they try to do is buy peace from groups that agitate against them," said Robert L. Woodson. "The same corporations that pay ransom to Jesse Jackson and Al Sharpton pay ransom to ACORN." Woodson is president of the Center for Neighborhood Enterprise, a pro-market community group that emphasizes individual responsibility.[507]

Banks are especially easy marks. They tend to have a very conservative approach to public relations, which makes them ideal targets for money-hungry activists. Banks will sometimes cave in almost immediately when threatened by ACORN. The fact that a corporate foundation has given money to ACORN is telling. Evidence of such funding should in most cases create a presumption that the corporation doing the giving has been victimized by ACORN. The larger the payment, the more likely the corporation was responding to a severed horse's head in the bed instead of a direct-mail solicitation.

Donors to ACORN from the charitable world include the far-left Marguerite Casey Foundation ($3 million), the appropriately named Robin Hood Foundation ($821,000—a board member is NBC newsman Tom Brokaw), Beldon Fund ($750,000), Edna McConnell Clark Foundation ($595,000), the radical Annie E. Casey Foundation ($65,000), George Soros's Open Society Institute ($25,000), Barbra Streisand Foundation ($22,500), Haymarket People's Fund ($15,000), Union Bank of California Foundation

($15,000), Provident Bank Foundation Inc. ($5,000), and Deutsche Bank Americas Foundation ($5,000).

Institutional donors have given $23,732,987 to ACORN Housing Corp. since 1998. Donors include JPMorgan Chase Foundation ($5,307,500), Bank of America Charitable Foundation Inc. ($5,054,000), US Bancorp Foundation ($755,000), Annie E. Casey Foundation ($685,500), PNC Foundation ($95,000), Wachovia Wells Fargo Foundation ($30,000), Home Depot Foundation ($25,000), and Capital One Foundation ($10,000).

At least one other housing-related affiliate has also received donations from foundations. Brooklyn-based Mutual Housing Association of New York Inc. (MHANY) has accepted funding from the New York Community Trust ($150,000), Ben & Jerry's Foundation ($7,500), and M&T Charitable Foundation ($5,000). MHANY is a nonprofit housing developer.

Corporate and family foundation donors have given at least $2,933,526 to the ACORN Institute. Donors include Citigroup Foundation ($500,000), Tides Foundation ($268,668), Evelyn & Walter Haas Jr. Fund ($175,000), Stephen M. Silberstein Foundation ($100,000), Annie E. Casey Foundation ($100,000), HKH Foundation ($100,000), Needmor Fund ($62,500), Wachovia Wells Fargo Foundation ($52,500), Roseanne Foundation, as in actress-comedienne Roseanne Barr ($50,000), Carnegie Corp. of New York ($50,000), Wallace Global Fund ($50,000), Starbucks Foundation ($44,313), JPMorgan Chase Foundation ($40,000), Gill Foundation ($20,000), Lear Family Foundation, as in TV producer Norman Lear ($15,000), and the hard-left Arca Foundation ($10,000).

ACORN's election destruction arm, Project Vote (Voting for America Inc.), has taken in more than $27 million in foundation grants since 1999. Project Vote donors include Rockefeller Family Fund Inc. ($4,047,500), Tides Foundation ($3,708,575), Vanguard Charitable Endowment Program ($3,004,800), Bauman Family Foundation ($1,600,000), HKH Foundation ($950,000), Sandler Foundation ($700,000), Eli & Edythe L. Broad Foundation ($700,000), Wallace Global Fund ($675,000), Carnegie Corp. of New York ($600,000), Omidyar Network Fund Inc.

($400,000), Picower Foundation ($400,000), Beldon Fund ($383,000), Open Society Institute ($350,000), Arkay Foundation ($250,000), Arca Foundation ($180,000), Stephen M. Silberstein Foundation ($100,000), Barbra Streisand Foundation ($70,000), and Ben & Jerry's Foundation ($15,000).

ACORN's American Institute for Social Justice has received at least $42.6 million in foundation grants since 2000. The Institute's donors include the Sandler Foundation ($7,122,722), Marguerite Casey Foundation ($6,625,000), Rockefeller Family Fund Inc. ($4,130,000), Charles Stewart Mott Foundation ($4,047,500), Vanguard Charitable Endowment Program ($3,300,000), Ford Foundation ($1,550,000), Bill & Melinda Gates Foundation ($1,100,000), Annie E. Casey Foundation ($925,000), Tides Foundation ($874,429), W.K. Kellogg Foundation ($829,285), Nathan Cummings Foundation ($610,000), Citigroup Foundation ($500,000), Bauman Family Foundation ($450,000), William Penn Foundation ($438,925), Wallace Global Fund ($425,000), Open Society Institute ($350,000), Rockefeller Brothers Fund Inc. ($315,000), Edward W. Hazen Foundation Inc. ($290,000), Discount Foundation ($285,000), Needmor Fund ($265,000), Z. Smith Reynolds Foundation ($210,000), Woods Fund of Chicago ($145,000), JPMorgan Chase Foundation ($100,000), and Wachovia Wells Fargo Foundation ($5,000).[508]

Other notable ACORN benefactors include the shadowy Tides Foundation, the "800-pound gorilla of radical activist funding." Tides is a donor-directed fund that wealthy leftists use to hide their donations from public scrutiny. "By using Tides to funnel its capital, a large public charity can indirectly fund a project with which it would prefer not to be directly identified in public."[509] Wade Rathke is a longtime member of the foundation's board of directors. So is Maya Wiley, daughter of the late NWRO leader George Wiley. Since 2002, Tides has directed at least $1,186,668 to ACORN and its affiliates.

Organized labor is both a client and ally of ACORN. ACORN and its affiliates took in almost $3 million in 2007 alone from unions to assist unions with anti-corporate campaigns, provide strike support, and help with research and staffing, among other things.[510]

BERNARD MADOFF, DE-FUNDER OF THE LEFT

Hedge fund manager Bernard L. Madoff's $50 billion swindle put two left-wing charities that supported ACORN out of business. Through his Social Security-like Ponzi scheme that paid older investors with incoming funds from newer investors, Madoff, a heavy donor to Democratic candidates, also did irreparable harm to the liberal and far-left causes he loves.

The giant Picower Foundation had the misfortune to choose Madoff to manage its $1 billion-plus in assets. The charity gave away more than $235 million since 1999. The foundation gave $200,000 to ACORN's Project Vote. A sizeable chunk of its funding has gone to abortion groups, including the National Abortion Rights Action League NARAL ($3.2 million), Center for Reproductive Rights ($2.5 million), Planned Parenthood ($2.4 million), and Center for Reproductive Law and Policy ($625,000). The foundation gave $2.9 million to the Southern Poverty Law Center, a public interest law firm founded by leftist fundraising empresario Morris Dees that uses politically skewed definitions of racism to indoctrinate children while smearing conservatives who question racial preference programs.

Madoff's crimes also shut down the JEHT Foundation, whose benefactors invested in his hedge fund. JEHT, whose acronym stands for Justice, Equality, Human (dignity) and Tolerance, was a reliable funder of far left causes and gave away more than $95 million since heiress and Democratic donor Jeanne Levy-Church founded it in 2000.

JEHT gave $250,000 to ACORN's American Institute for Social Justice. The foundation also gave $1.7 million to the ACLU and its foundation, along with $839,500 to the ultra-leftist public interest law firm, the Center for Constitutional Rights. CCR helped to convince the Supreme Court in *Boumediene v. Bush* (2008) to confer habeas corpus rights for the first time in history on alien enemies detained abroad by the U.S. military in wartime. The decision gives terrorists a green light to manipulate our justice system and flout the well-established laws of civilized warfare.

JEHT gave $55,000 to Nan Aron's Alliance for Justice, a group that systematically distorts conservative judges' records in an effort to block their elevation to higher courts. The group helped to torpedo the Supreme Court nomination of Robert Bork in 1987 and nearly succeeded in "borking" Clarence Thomas in 1991. More recently, the group fought President George W. Bush's nominations of Charles Pickering and Priscilla Owen to federal courts. JEHT also gave more than $4.2 million to the Tides Foundation and its affiliates. Tides funds abortion rights advocacy, environmental extremism, anti-war activism, gun control, and opposes free trade.[511]

CORPORATE SHAKEDOWNS

John Hewitt, CEO of Liberty Tax Service, felt ACORN's wrath when it staged a violent protest against his company in 2005. More than 100 angry ACORN members showed up at Liberty's Virginia Beach headquarters. ACORN accused the company of charging excessive interest rates on the refund anticipation loans it offers to income tax filers.

"All of sudden, four bus loads of homeless people pull up in front of our headquarters here in Virginia Beach," Hewitt said. "They came pouring into the building like a Mongolian horde. There was screaming and fighting. One employee was bitten and another was scratched. They both had to go to the emergency room."

The demonstrators were arrested and the company filed a legal complaint but withdrew it later because it would have been too expensive to pursue, Hewitt explained. The company agreed to pay an ACORN affiliate $50,000 a year and to explain the terms of the loans more carefully to borrowers.[512] "To me, it's just to stop them from harassing us," said Hewitt. "Even though I felt dirty by paying them money, I said, you know, it's a business decision."[513]

Unless they see a public relations advantage in going public with the fact they've been victimized by ACORN, corporations don't necessarily relish the prospect of letting the public know they've been pushed around. In such cases, detecting the group's corporate shakedown campaigns can be hard work. Regulatory filings with the Securities and Exchange Commission (SEC) sometimes reveal financial agreements between ACORN and corporations. Sometimes the documents disclose lawsuit settlements. ACORN usually sues its targets not because a wrong needs to be made right but because the group wants to extract money from a deep-pocketed business. ACORN's lawyers might as well be members of its development department.

What follows below is a small sample from ACORN's corporate blackmail portfolio disclosed to the SEC.

- In 2008, as Countrywide Financial was acquired by longtime ACORN funder Bank of America, it reached "an agreement with the Association of Community Organizations for Reform Now (ACORN) to serve as a blueprint for home retention and foreclosure prevention initiatives in the mortgage industry, with a particular focus on subprime borrowers." ACORN wannabe group Neighborhood Assistance Corporation of America (NACA) had muscled Countrywide the year before by forcing it to pour money into "a groundbreaking partnership" that would "leverage Countrywide's market leading home retention programs and NACA's unique model for counseling borrowers."[514]
- In 2006, HSBC Finance settled a class action lawsuit by agreeing to change its mortgage lending practices. The company agreed to provide "funding over a three-year period for ACORN financial counseling and literacy programs."[515]
- Exelon Corp. agreed in 2006 to hand over undisclosed sums to ACORN after the group withdrew its objection to a merger between Exelon and New Jersey-based Public Service Enterprise Group Inc. Exelon agreed to make "an annual contribution" to "community-based organizations."[516] Orkin Exterminating Co. acknowledged it "partnered" with ACORN to treat hurricane-damaged homes in New Orleans for mold and mildew.[517]
- TCF Financial Corp. disclosed in 1993 it was "[w]orking with community development agencies and such neighborhood groups as the Association of Community Organizations for

Reform Now (ACORN)" to offer "special loan programs and funding for loan counseling."[518] The same year Roosevelt Financial Group Inc. said "in cooperation" with ACORN it "arranged to make a special pool of more than $8 million available for loans to low- and moderate-income borrowers in St. Louis and Kansas City."[519]

But occasionally details of shakedowns, concealed by carefully crafted euphemisms, emerge from deep in corporate reports. Sometimes the corporate victims publicly tout the settlements they reach with ACORN in the hope of generating public goodwill. Ironically, this is an application of Alinsky's eleventh rule of "power tactics" (turning a negative into a positive).

- In a major score, ACORN victimized Bank of New York to the tune of at least $750 million. ACORN had objected to the bank's plan to acquire 64 branches of Barclay's Bank of New York. ACORN withdrew its objection after the bank agreed to lend $750 million in low- and moderate-income areas, weaken its underwriting standards for low-income homebuyers, and fund the creation of alternative schools in low-income communities.[520]
- After it was accused of violating consumer protection laws, Capital One was encouraged to give a sizeable donation to ACORN as part of a legal settlement. Minnesota Attorney General Lori Swanson and her predecessor, Mike Hatch, both Democrats, played a role in making the credit card company give $249,999 to Minnesota ACORN as part of a $749,999 settlement agreed to by Capital One. Why was the settlement $749,999? Because Minnesota requires that settlements of $750,000 and up be paid to the state. Minnesota ACORN's political action committee endorsed Hatch's candidacy three weeks later.[521]
- In 2002, ACORN enlisted its ally, New York's Democratic comptroller Carl McCall, to join in its attack on Household Finance.

He threatened to dump $100 million of the stock from the state's pension fund if the company failed to change its ways.[522]

- Household Finance Corp. agreed to pay ACORN in order to settle several class action lawsuits that accused it of predatory lending practices. ACORN said it valued the agreement at between $100 million and $125 million.[523] The company agreed to make changes to its mortgage lending practices and the practices of "certain of its lending subsidiaries, including Beneficial Corporation."[524] The company also pays ACORN to run programs that "educate" mortgage borrowers.[525]

- Citigroup agreed to pay off ACORN in 2004 but refused to say how large the payment was. The bank also agreed to make fixed rate 30-year mortgages available to ACORN members with minimal documentation and with a waiver of the requirement to purchase private mortgage insurance.[526] Citigroup's charity made large payments to ACORN affiliates.

ACORN conducted shakedown campaigns against several financial services firms: H&R Block, Jackson Hewitt, and Money Mart. ACORN first targeted H&R Block in 2004 by threatening to have its members protest "overpriced tax refund loans" outside the company's offices in 30 cities. After pressure was applied, H&R Block agreed to pay to create tax centers for ACORN members, according to MonCrief.

ACORN held more than 400 protests at H&R Block offices. It used the money it extracted from the company to build what, by 2008, was the third-largest nonprofit tax preparation service in the nation. ACORN's Tax Benefit Centers provided free tax preparation in 62 locations after participating in a joint project with H&R Block to promote the Earned Income Tax Credit (EITC).[527] The problem is that the EITC, which is a tax credit, functions as a form of welfare.

Two former members of ACORN's national board grew tired of the group's heavy-handed tactics. "I don't mind being up on a soapbox to get someone's attention but I would much rather talk and negotiate," said Karen Inman. "But I just refuse to go [to] someone's home, that's a privacy issue."

In 2005, about 400 red-shirted ACORN members crashed a meeting of the National Paint & Coatings Association at a Cleveland hotel. After that they protested at a Sherwin-Williams office. "We went there with busloads of people and those people went into a room and really frightened the people at the hotel who were having this convention," said Marcel Reid.

"These tactics were really heavy, many of us became disillusioned," said Reid. The idea is to isolate the target so they don't have time to build up sentiment with neighbors and co-workers. We would intrude into a person's social life."[528] ACORN and two other groups asked the National Paint & Coatings Association for an astounding $38 billion payoff, according to ACORN insiders who asked not to be identified. "We asked them for a significant amount of money," said Reid. "I couldn't carry the meeting on because I just thought this was just an outrageous amount of money."

Wade Rathke acknowledged that the attack on the trade association failed. "We certainly did everything, threw the sink at them, but never could get them to negotiate."[529] After Sherwin-Williams refused to play ball, ACORN participated in a class action lawsuit against the company over the lead content of the company's paint and won a court order that required the company to clean up contaminated homes in Rhode Island. The estimated cost of the cleanup was $1 billion.[530]

ELEVEN

Organizing Chaos:
ACORN's Shock Troops

"**W**E DO WHATEVER it takes to get our goals met," said ACORN's Jeff Ordower.[531]

Even in its early days, ACORN was known for corruption, in-your-face tactics, and subversive activities. Little Rock Mayor George E. Wimberly criticized the group in the 1970s. "I have never seen a group so secretive," he said. "They refuse to tell where their money comes from." One particularly prescient VISTA volunteer denounced ACORN, claiming, "ACORN is really interested in power, not helping people. They may even be a threat to the government." By 1976, Arkansas state representative Boyce Alford had labeled ACORN a "possible threat to capitalism and democracy."[532]

By 1979, ACORN members were describing ACORN as a cult. "Wade Rathke is a silver-tongued pied piper with the ability to look you in the face and change everything and make it look right," said one member in Little Rock. "We took Wade Rathke on faith just like someone would accept Jesus Christ, no questions asked. We accepted everything he proposed as gospel," said another.[533] Dorothy Perkins of North Little Rock, a former Arkansas ACORN chairman, complained that ACORN was "run like a Jim Jones cult." Rev. Daniel Perkins said funds raised by ACORN were "never seen" by the low- to moderate-income people the organization was supposed to help.[534]

In 2009, former national board member Marcel Reid partly echoed early complaints about Rathke. "There's definitely a difference between Wade-ism and Alinskyism," she said in an interview. "Alinsky respected poor people, but I think Rathke does not."

"Alinsky was trying to empower poor people to leverage the only thing they had, which was their sheer numbers," Reid said. "Alinsky wanted poor people to lift themselves out of poverty; Wade needs poor people to stay in poverty because that allows him to stay paternalistic and it allows him to maintain his power over people. Wade wants to help poor people just enough so that they are beholden to him but never capable of breaking away from him and never completely independent."

Right from the start, Arkansas Community Organizations for Reform Now set about organizing welfare recipients around Little Rock and trying to broaden the base. The new group led a campaign in the state to tax "intangible" property such as stocks and bonds. ACORN helped push through changes to the property tax law that amount to naked redistribution through burden-shifting. The wealthy, whose taxes went up, were forced to subsidize the poor, whose taxes went down.[535] From its earliest days, ACORN viewed government as a thing to be manipulated. By 1971, ACORN officials in Arkansas had registered as lobbyists in order to promote a public defender system, an expansion of collective bargaining, and universal healthcare. In its first non-welfare campaign ACORN forced the North Little Rock School District to "provide free or reduced-price school lunches to the non-welfare poor." It also aimed to expand state welfare programs in order to get more people addicted to welfare. This was, as ACORN's first staff organizer Gary Delgado acknowledges, consistent with the "breaking the bank" strategy advocated by Cloward and Piven. At the 1979 ACORN national convention in St. Louis, 2,000 delegates from 19 states showed up and paid the ultimate tribute to Cloward and Piven. Delegates considered a guaranteed income plank equal to "a minimum annual family income at a figure equivalent to the current Bureau of Labor Statistics' medium living standard.'" It passed.[536]

Though single parenthood is one of the most reliable predictors of low household income, ACORN has never been concerned about the prevalence of single-parent households in inner-city neighborhoods. Sol Stern of the Manhattan Institute asked ACORN executive director Steve Kest about his group's failure to address illegitimacy as a cause of social problems. "We are more focused on irresponsible behavior in the corporate sector," Kest replied. "I don't think [illegitimacy] comes anywhere close to the irresponsible behavior of people running the largest businesses in this country."[537]

ACORN initially organized farmers but quickly lost interest in them as a constituency because they were too middle class. This Trotskyist disdain for the middle class was on display when Cloward and Piven wrote the foreword for Delgado's book on ACORN, *Organizing the Movement*. ACORN has "consistently and self-consciously targeted the poor and minority neighborhoods, carefully avoiding cutting too wide a geographic swath in their organizing work because experience has taught them that if they do, middle class residents will come to dominate their organization."[538]

ACORN also organized property owners to take on plans for a freeway, pushed Vietnam veterans to obtain state benefits, and helped unemployed workers combat supposedly unethical employment agencies. It wasn't long before ACORN was pushing into Texas and North Dakota after putting 40 local groups in Arkansas under the ACORN umbrella.[539] By the end of 1975, ACORN signaled its intention to spread from coast to coast by changing the "A" in ACORN from "Arkansas" to "Association."[540]

RED-SHIRTED SHOCK TROOPS

ACORN activists "are best understood as shock troops" for organized labor and the Democratic Party, writes *Wall Street Journal* columnist John Fund. The group's leaders excel at creating a sense of urgency.

"This is why they never call people for actions [i.e., protests, campaigns] more than 48 hours in advance so that there's always some breathlessness on the other end of the phone," Marcel Reid said in an interview. "Sometimes you have people showing up for actions not knowing exactly why they're there," she explained. "They know they're fighting some power, but they don't know which power, because ACORN keeps information on a need-to-know basis right before the action."

"In that aspect they are not different from a military operation, because many soldiers are deployed not knowing where they're going or why until the last minute," she said.

Most grassroots members of the group really do want to improve America, Reid said, but ACORN's leadership is dedicated to an extremist agenda that seldom mirrors the beliefs of members, who are usually not terribly ideological. "These people are not radical leftists, but the people at the top of ACORN are."

Reid explained how ACORN targets businesses. Before ACORN hits a corporation, it finds out who on its board of directors is the weakest. "It's amazingly easy to find. Go for the person with the least power and the most access to knowledge because generally corporations treat the lowest-level employees the worst. You call the receptionist in the corporation and you start a conversation," she said.

"In all corporations the receptionist tends to know the most about the corporation and is the least respected, which means that you can establish a rapport with them and that will eventually give you the information you need," she said.

After identifying the weakest board member, ACORN follows Saul Alinsky's thirteenth rule of "power tactics": "Pick the target, freeze it, personalize it, and polarize it." Reid added, "Go to their homes and picket and do actions, use direct action to ostracize the person, which softens up the corporation for negotiations."

"The idea is to go to private homes where wives and children are present and stand outside so the family members of a company official could be harassed and subjected to intimidation," said former ACORN staffer Anita MonCrief. "Protestors would also go to company functions like banquets where they would be as disruptive as possible."[541]

ACORN also finds front groups useful. Ever notice a typical poster or pamphlet for a leftist event, whether in a big city or on a university campus? It contains a list of endorsing groups and supporters. The bigger the list, the greater support the event or cause appears to have. The problem is that the groups, whether they're West Side Vegan Grannies for Nuclear Disarmament or Differently Abled Transgendered Pet Owners' Collective for a Living Wage, often have overlapping membership. This political recycling program can make a few dozen activists appear as hundreds or even thousands of supporters.

Another advantage of front groups, as noted earlier, is if they get into trouble, it's easy to disassociate the main group from them. If ACORN Housing happens to get caught on hidden video facilitating child prostitution, for example, ACORN can point out *ad nauseam* how ACORN Housing is a legally separate organization. (This is exactly what happened in 2009.) But if through inadvertence ACORN Housing helps people, ACORN can blast out press releases to the far corners of the earth heralding the accomplishments of its housing subsidiary without explaining that the two entities are legally distinct.

A 1973 ACORN campaign that utilized front groups is a case study in killing the goose that lays the golden egg. ACORN created two front groups—Protect Our Land Association (POLA) and Save Health and Property (SHAP)—in order to sabotage Arkansas Power and Light's plan to construct a 2,800-megawatt coal-burning power plant. The $1 billion plant would have been the all-time largest private investment in that state. ACORN blackmailed the utility, demanding a $50 million "deposit in reverse" against any damage local farmers might have suffered. After AP&L refused to pay, ACORN discovered the company was a subsidiary of Middle South Utilities and that Harvard University was MSU's largest stockholder. POLA and SHAP pressured Harvard to conduct an environmental impact study and, aided by Steve Kest, at the time a Harvard student and former ACORN intern, the front groups manufactured outrage on campus. The university urged AP&L to install sulfur controls and paid $5,000 for an adverse "fact-finding" report to the Investor Responsibility Research Center, which is part of the "corporate social responsibility" movement. ACORN used the report to force the company to scale back its plans by half and the AP&L eventually dropped the project altogether. A loss for poor, job-hungry Arkansas was a "win" for ACORN.[542]

HOW ACORN ACTS IN PUBLIC

For ACORN, anything goes, from rude protests to crude intimidation and violence. The bigger, the louder, the more obnoxious, the more destructive, the better. Wade Rathke summed up ACORN's approach to doing business in a single sentence: "One can almost taste the adrenaline when people take a crowbar to a door and pop it open to begin squatting."[543] ACORN leadership doesn't care if people get hurt or property is damaged: as long as the action advances the cause, it's fair game.

"ACORN protests have turned violent, at times as soon as the rallies began," writes Sol Stern of the Manhattan Institute. "Some protests disrupted Federal Reserve hearings and busted into closed city council meetings."[544]

In Stern's opinion ACORN embraces "undisguised authoritarian socialism" when it demands that large companies that desire to leave the community be coerced into getting "an exit visa from the community board signifying that the company has adequately compensated all its employees and the community at large for losses due to relocation." To combat pressure from ACORN seven states have enacted laws blocking local governments from enacting their own minimum wage laws.[545]

- Members of ACORN assaulted New York state Sen. James Alesi, a Republican, and his chief of staff, during a raucous 2009 protest. Alesi said an angry mob nearly knocked him to the floor of the chamber and spat in the face of his chief of staff. ACORN was protesting after two Democratic state senators switched parties giving Republicans control of the New

York Senate.[546] ACORN's political party, the Working Families Party, had invested considerable resources in state senate elections in the Empire State. WFP took credit for ending "30 years of right-wing Republican rule" in 2008.[547]

- ACORN operatives were labeled extortionists in Washington, D.C., in 1992 "after demanding cash contributions from shop owners and threatening them unless they bankrolled an ACORN project."[548] Two years before, the local ACORN organization there wasn't interested in negotiating with the federal government to buy HUD properties. HUD official Lorraine Richardson said the group hadn't bothered to qualify for the customary 10 percent discount HUD offered nonprofit groups. "ACORN is not interested in that," said Richardson. "They virtually want us to give the houses to them."[549]

- In 1989, about 50 ACORN members stormed a Chicago liquidation office of the Federal Savings and Loan Insurance Corp. demanding vacant properties be handed over and that no-interest housing renovation loans be made.[550]

- Inspired by homeless "squeegee" people, ACORN harassed motorists as part of the group's "toll roads" program. ACORN risked the safety of its employees and motorists by pushing them into the streets to solicit donations from trapped motorists at intersections.[551] When proselytizing in communities, ACORN won't take no for an answer, even around hospital emergency rooms. Activists created a furor when they distributed leaflets in a busy hospital.[552]

- In 2001, ACORN protests outside the San Diego Gas & Electric chairman's home were so disruptive (demonstrators handed out fliers with a picture of the chairman below the word "WANTED") that the company won a court order requiring demonstrators to stay 1,000 yards away from SDG&E employees' homes. The company said protesters shouted derogatory comments outside the chairman's home, banged on his windows, and pounded on his front door.[553]

- Senior ACORN organizer Mitch Klein put ACORN's Baltimore operation on the map in 2002 when his members dumped garbage in front of Baltimore's City Hall to protest a lack of services in low-income neighborhoods. They also demonstrated outside the home of then-mayor Martin O'Malley, who dismissed the group as "professional protesters." O'Malley said, "They unloaded a busload of people shouting pretty ugly things and scared the daylights out of my wife and kids. I thought it was a pretty cruddy thing to do." Baltimore ACORN, which in the 1990s took in $50,000 annually in grants from the city of Baltimore, also brought gigantic inflated rubber sharks to disrupt a dinner for banking executives. In addition, ACORN succeeded in getting Baltimore's city charter changed "rejiggering city council districts in ways that ACORN activists believe will make it easier for them to gain more control over the body." A busload of members from Baltimore and Philadelphia also jumped the queue and muscled out lobbyists who had reserved seats at a congressional committee hearing.[554]
- In Sacramento, ACORN sided with low-income tenants facing eviction because a Japanese company planned to sell their apartment buildings. The campaign brought in donations that allowed the group to expand. ACORN got legislation enacted in California making it more difficult for tenants to be evicted.[555]
- In Chicago, ACORN beat the legendarily tough Mayor Richard Daley, winning a new law that boosted the pay of employees at companies that do work for the city. During its three-year campaign ACORN picketed Daley as he greeted delegates to the 1996 Democratic national convention. The group also stormed a closed city council meeting as a publicity stunt. The Chicago chapter became one of ACORN's most effective. In 2002, it prevailed in another fight, strengthening the wage law.[556]
- Sol Stern notes that "in cities where the political culture already tilts way to the left, ACORN has scored its biggest

victories." In Los Angeles, ACORN pushed through legislation similar to the Chicago wage law. It also weakened welfare reform. In New York, when term limits brought in a freshman city council, "ACORN was ready with a host of bills—from its trademark wage legislation to an anti-predatory-lending measure—that willing council members rushed into law." It replicated the strategy in other cities.[557]

- ACORN sometimes uses religious leaders to advance its strictly secular agenda. In Los Angeles it helped to create Clergy and Laity United for Economic Justice (CLUE), a coalition of local churches to push for a living wage law. CLUE used sanctimonious claptrap to advance ACORN's objectives. The coalition portrayed opponents as Egyptians enslaving the chosen people. Bringing churches into a fight gives a radical agenda an air of sanctity, according to an ACORN manual. "Religious involvement highlighted the moral and theological reasons for a Living Wage."[558]

- ACORN has tried to undermine "workfare" programs by unionizing the welfare recipients who participate in them in exchange for welfare benefits. The purpose of workfare is to instill discipline and good work habits in people who often lack them. ACORN "successfully agitated for the creation of workfare grievance processes in Los Angeles and New York, and it seeks to expand rights and entitlements on all workfare jobs." This activism is "subversive of reform," according to Stern, because it teaches recipients of government charity to fight those trying to help them and to think of themselves as victims. "But with workfare, as with all aspects of welfare dependency, ACORN has never learned the most important lesson from the failures of 1960s radicalism—that there is a tight connection between irresponsible personal behavior and poverty," he writes.

- In 1992, 80 ACORN members occupied a Crossland Savings Bank branch in Brooklyn "to demand a vacant apartment building be turned into housing for low and moderate income families."[559] In 1991, ACORN threatened to carry out a "citizen arrest" of HUD official Harry I. Sharrott at a federal building in Detroit to protest HUD policies regarding the sale of properties the department held. ACORN said members didn't follow through only because half of those who gathered for the action were denied access to the building. An ACORN organizer snarled that it was "ridiculous" and "outrageous" that the protesters who planned to mete out mob justice were denied entrance to the office. The same week ACORN dropped off two tires at the office of the director of Detroit's public works department to press its demand that a local tire dump be cleaned up.[560]

- In 1992, about 60 bullhorn-bearing ACORN members took over the Manhattan offices of the Federal Deposit Insurance Corp. in an attempt to intimidate the banking regulator into giving it an unoccupied apartment building in Queens. ACORN submitted a bid of $1.2 million for the building it planned to convert into low-income housing but claimed FDIC treated it unfairly. In fact, FDIC, which gained possession of the property after the bank that owned it collapsed, was waiting for the bidding process to close when ACORN launched its protest. ACORN couldn't be bothered to wait another two weeks for bidding to close.[561]

- In 1993, after 30 chanting ACORN members descended on the lobby of United Missouri Bancshares and gave bank officials ACORN's "Bad Corporate Citizen of the Year" award, UMB Vice Chairman Peter Genovese lost his cool. "We're not going to be blackmailed." ACORN demanded UMB lend $50 million in low-income neighborhoods in Missouri and accused it of race-based discrimination in lending. The bank was outraged that "ACORN also wants $15,000 for itself plus $500 for every loan made with help from ACORN's loan counseling office."[562] ACORN paid Genovese back by sending 50 protesters to his home to terrorize him. Genovese won a court order barring ACORN from harassing his family.[563]

- In 2001, ACORN protested a fare hike by picketing the home of Robert T. Wooten, a Southeastern Pennsylvania Transportation Authority (SEPTA) board member. ACORN's Jeff Ordower said the group went after Wooten personally after two protests at SEPTA headquarters failed to change policy. Board members "really don't want to talk turkey about the things that matter to poor people."[564]

- In 1991, ACORN members picketed St. Louis mayor Vincent C. Schoemehl Jr.'s home to complain about budget reductions for demolition projects. They left rubbish on his front steps.[565]

- ACORN was outraged in 1996 when a local business owner in Clayton, Mo., publicly took a stand against an ACORN-backed state ballot question to raise the minimum wage. Chanting angrily, ACORN stormed Bob Candice's Italian restaurant and gave him a mock award for "Keeping People in Poverty." ACORN acknowledged in-your-face tactics were part of the group's standard operating procedure. "Intimidate the guy with the money bags," said member Gus Stroud. "Try to make them understand."[566]

- ACORN tactics include irritating a target's customers. To protest utility rates, ACORN members overwhelmed a Philadelphia Gas Works payment office, forcing its closure. One ACORN member presented her $172 utility bill by tendering $100 in pennies as part payment. Although it is part of ACORN's strategy to disrupt in order to force change, ACORN organizer Jeff Ordower insisted the group's "purpose was not to prevent other customers from paying their bills."[567]

ACORN'S HOME INVASIONS

In a made-for-TV moment ACORN member Louis Beverly used bolt cutters to cut a padlock off the front door of the Baltimore home of Donna Hanks in early 2009. "This is our house now," he said. According to ACORN, the sinister lenders had been vanquished by

ACORN's heroic "home defenders." ACORN's illegal actions have been repeated all across America.

Homeowner Hanks seemed sympathetic on TV. The poor lady lost her house because she couldn't keep up with her monthly $1,995 mortgage payments. What Hanks didn't tell the media was that her house had been sold seven months before ACORN's home invasion after two years of legal proceedings that gave her multiple opportunities to save the property—chances she squandered.

Michelle Malkin tracked down Hanks's legal documents. She found that Hanks bought the two-story property in 2001 for $87,000 and later refinanced it for $270,000. It is unclear where the extra $183,000 went. The house went into foreclosure proceedings in spring 2006. Hanks filed for bankruptcy and agreed to pay $10,500 in arrears, which halted the foreclosure process. In September 2006, the bankruptcy court ordered Hanks's employer to set aside $340 a month from her total net monthly take home pay of $1,228. The money was for various creditors including America's Servicing Co. and Bank of America. Hanks also reported having $1,625 in additional monthly income from a second and third job, along with a tax refund.

Hanks did not keep up with the mortgage payments and in late 2007, the mortgage servicing company sent her a default notice for nearly $7,000 in arrears. In February 2008, a second foreclosure action was initiated. When Hanks told a TV station "that her evil bank raised her mortgage by $300 ("The mortgage went up $300 in one month") she's talking about the amount in arrears that *she* agreed to pay back," writes Malkin. Meanwhile, Hanks "managed to collect rent on her basement (for which she was taken to court) and rack up a criminal record on charges of theft and second degree assault."[568] The Hanks saga is a perfect illustration of ACORN's illegal squatting program: Criminals helping criminals.

ACORN has been involved in the squatting scam for decades. It advertised for squatters by distributing flyers reading: "Need a house? Call ACORN." During one squatting campaign in New York City, an ACORN leader said through a bullhorn: "We're entitled to decent housing and we're going to have decent housing, even if we have to take it."[569]

ACORN claims that using force to break and enter a house is a legitimate form of nonviolent protest. ACORN, as usual, is lying. Former New York Mayor Ed Koch denounced squatting: "It is not nonviolent. It is violent. They break down doors. What is now to stop other people in Brooklyn from simply saying, 'There is no law, the D.A. has said you can take law into your own hands.'" Charles Perkins of New York City's Department of Housing Preservation and Development protested squatting. "Why should we allow the person with the greatest muscle, who breaks down the door first, to have the unit rather than other people who may be on a waiting list?"[570]

Tolerating squatting of government-owned properties not only rewards lawbreakers for their antisocial behavior but wastes taxpayer resources. It deprives governments of the ability to rent out the properties to poor people on government-assisted housing waiting lists or to sell the properties to new owners or to redevelopers. It is confiscation by mob action—unrestrained participatory "democracy" in the Marxist sense of the term.

Eventually Koch tired of the squatting fight. His administration handed over 58 city-owned properties to ACORN squatters. ACORN created a new spinoff entity, the Mutual Housing Association of New York (MHANY). The city also gave rehabilitation grants and $2.7 million in loans to cover renovations that would generate housing for 180 families.[571] ACORN learned once again that might makes right.

While Koch was slugging it out with ACORN, several Democratic politicians in New York flocked to endorse ACORN's illegal so-called homesteading campaign. In 1985, Brooklyn Borough President Howard Golden pressed Koch on the group's behalf. At a rally outside a squatter-occupied house, state Sen. Thomas Bartosiewicz told the assembled mob, "Sometimes in order to remake the law you have to break the law." Rep. Major Owens (D-NY), bemoaned President Reagan's stubborn insistence on defending America from the Soviet threat. "This country is too broke to spend $500 million more on housing for the poor," said Owens. "At the same time, they're spending $75 million every time they purchase an MX missile."[572]

In 1987, Ronald Shiffman of the Pratt Institute Center for Community and Environmental Development bragged to a newspaper reporter that his liberal group had talked some sense into ACORN at the behest of the borough of Brooklyn. Shiffman, then the institute's naïve director, said he convinced ACORN to drop squatting from its repertoire, a move "which calmed down the city." New York housing official Felice Michetti also gave herself a pat on the back for what she thought she accomplished. "Once ACORN was willing to recognize that squatting is illegal and not an answer, it paved the way for a mutual sharing of ideas and financing by the city," Michetti said.[573]

In the 1980s, Sen. James Inhofe (R-OK) dared to stand up to the ACORN mob as mayor of Tulsa. In May 1982, ACORN members avoided jail by vacating about 20 houses they occupied that were owned by the Tulsa Urban Renewal Authority. The squatters demanded that they be allowed to buy the homes for a dollar each and be awarded taxpayers' money to rehabilitate the structures. Inhofe said no. ACORN members chanted slogans as the windows of the houses were boarded up. The experience helped to turn Inhofe into an ACORN critic. He remains an adversary of ACORN today as the senior U.S. senator for Oklahoma.[574]

A month later, ACORN set up a squatters' tent city near the White House to protest the policies of the Reagan administration. The action led to the creation of ACORN's housing affiliate.

That same month, 30 ACORN squatters broke past security at HUD headquarters and stormed the office of HUD Undersecretary for Housing Philip Abrams. ACORN protesters frequently exude a sense of entitlement and that day was no exception. "We were in the hall, and they told us we could not walk peacefully in a government building," said St. Louis ACORN member Clarene Royston. "We may be poor people, but we paid for this building."[575]

By 2009, ACORN decided to try a new public relations approach, putting a happy face on its illegal squatting projects and changing the name of the program to match the public's sour mood about the economy. With foreclosure rates skyrocketing, ACORN rechristened its squatting program the ACORN "Home Defenders" campaign. Writer Stuart Whatley helped push ACORN propaganda by describing the violent campaign as legitimate civil disobedience aimed at helping "*victims* of foreclosure."[576] [emphasis added]

JACKBOOT TACTICS AGAINST CONGRESS SAVE THE CRA

ACORN holds out an intimidation action it conducted against Congress as a shining example of its commitment to social justice. The storming of a House Financial Services subcommittee hearing by thugs in 1995 has become a legend within ACORN circles.

ACORN mobilized when a congressional panel began considering reforms to the Community Reinvestment Act (CRA). Led by ACORN national president Maude Hurd, the activists disrupted a March 8, 1995, hearing by chanting, "CRA has got to stay!" and "Banks for greed, not for need!" When they tried to commandeer the microphone, five demonstrators, including Hurd, were arrested. Efforts to free them by ACORN allies Sen. Ted Kennedy (D-MA) and Rep. Joe Kennedy II (D-MA) failed. The U.S. Capitol Police let them go only when Rep. Maxine Waters (D-CA) showed up at the detention facility and threatened to stay put until the demonstrators were released. Congressman Kennedy refused to condemn ACORN. Instead, he criticized the hearing's presiding officer for having one of his constituents arrested. Kennedy said Republicans were readying "an all-out attack on CRA" and vowed new legislation to expand the law's reach to mortgage bankers and major credit unions.[577]

ACORN's court historian, John Atlas, tells the story differently. He distorts events to make ACORN look good. As he tells it, Hurd had a "chilling experience" before the subcommittee. "Bank lobbyists convinced hard-line Republicans to eliminate some of the law's key provisions, which would weaken the government's ability to monitor and punish redlining in big cities," he writes. "Confident Republicans on the committee, working behind closed doors, offered a series of innocuous-sounding reforms that, in effect, would have repealed the CRA."

According to Atlas, ACORN showed up in force for the hearings, but its members were denied the right to speak and victimized by the Republican lawmakers, who at that time were in the majority.

> Dozens of ACORN members stood in line the night before the hearings (displaying the persistence important in ACORN's successes) to squeeze out paid banking lobbyists for seats in the hearing room. At the hearing, Hurd insisted on speaking. When she tried to testify, police grabbed her, slapped handcuffs on her, and locked her up. 'It was the most frightening thing,' she recalls. To cope, she and the other four others who were arrested sang freedom songs. After a call from Massachusetts representative Joe Kennedy and a rainy day visit to the jailhouse by California representative Maxine Waters, the protestors were finally released. As they left, a guard told Hurd, "I don't know who you are, but you must know somebody important." Hurt's later comment: "We are up there rubbing elbows with some very powerful people. We are a force to be reckoned with. We're ordinary people doing some extraordinary things."[578]

Alas, it is a fairy tale. There was nothing unusual about the ACORN action. It was a run-of-the-mill disruption.

The official congressional transcript shows ACORN deliberately disrupted the hearing, interrupting its leftist ally, Rep. Kennedy, in mid-sentence. Kennedy may even have agreed in advance to participate in ACORN's political theater. Just after the hearing began at 9:45 a.m. a female demonstrator interrupted Kennedy to say, "Madam Chair, we are from ACORN Association." The head of the subcommittee, Rep. Marge Roukema (R-NJ), told the woman she was out of order. The woman persisted, saying, "We want to save the CRAs." Again Roukema tried to gain control of the hearing.[579]

Roukema then recessed the hearing and the ACORN demonstrators were arrested and removed from the hearing room. She explained to the subcommittee what had happened and why the protesters were arrested.

The people who were representing that community group had been informed by staff as well as by the Capitol Police about what the rules were of the subcommittee and of the House. And the rules were explicitly stated to them that they would jeopardize themselves to the point of being arrested if they did not comply with the requirement that they must come to order and after three notifications that they would be subject to arrest. I believe that they—well, obviously, they chose not to understand the warning or not to comply with the warning. And whether or not their intention was to cause the confrontation and action on behalf of the police, you can make your own judgment. But in my opinion, I had no alternative but to comply with the rules, and after a repeated fourth and fifth time of informing their leadership what would happen, they still directly opposed my order to come to order. And I felt, in the confrontation here at the Chairman's platform, that they were purposely provoking that confrontation and insisting on an arrest order. I want you also to know that they were informed, and they knew this before they arrived, but they were informed again that there would be other opportunities for them to testify, but they refused. They wanted to testify now on the spot and submit their testimony, and I had no alternative but to deny them that action. If we were to permit that of this group or any other group there would be continuous chaos at any subcommittee hearing. So there was no alternative.[580]

It's classic ACORN. A belligerent herd of activists wanted something and they wanted it *right now*. Even ACORN stalwart Rep. Barney Frank (D-MA) condemned ACORN's behavior, saying Roukema acted appropriately in having the demonstrators arrested. The transcript shows Frank commending Roukema:

I just want to say that I think you behaved appropriately. I think the people who orchestrated that made a very grave error on a number of grounds. And as someone who will fight very strongly to protect CRA, I hope that people will not continue to make the mistake of thinking that this helps their cause. I think it, in fact—although it should not it—may detract from it. And I hope both sides will be able to forget about that and deal with this on the merits.[581]

As the hearing continued the next day, another ACORN ally on the subcommittee, Rep. Bruce Vento (D-MN), also condemned ACORN's unlawful demonstration. "[W]hen people intend to disrupt a hearing . . . I don't think [they] should be rewarded."[582]

Just before Vento spoke, Roukema explained that ACORN did not file a request to appear before the subcommittee "until very late in the process, and . . . rather than resubmit a written request rather than just a telephone inquiry, they chose to be disruptive at the hearing yesterday, demanding priority in terms of giving testimony now, as they put it."[583]

Hurd's temper tantrum was a tactic. She was arrested because she disrupted a congressional hearing. It happens all the time and there is no evidence to suggest Hurd was treated any differently than any other troublemaker. There was no Republican attempt to silence ACORN.

Despite Hurd's outburst, Roukema graciously allowed ACORN to file written testimony in the official record. Former ACORN national president Elena Hanggi filed a statement about the "successes" of the CRA.[584] Other left-wing pro-CRA groups had no difficulty finding the time to follow the proper procedure to present in-person testimony. Gale Cincotta, a Chicago-based activist who played a significant role in enacting the original CRA legislation in the 1970s, testified on behalf of National People's Action, a group she co-founded.

In the end, ACORN's thuggery paid off. It helped "to protect the CRA from GOP reforms" and expanded "the reach of quota-based lending to Fannie, Freddie and beyond," according to Stanley Kurtz. "By steamrolling the GOP that March, it had crushed the last potential barrier to 'change.'" Three months later, the Clinton administration unveiled a new plan to artificially bolster the ranks of homeowners, regardless of how much credit standards would need to be weakened. Onerous subprime lending quotas were then imposed on Fannie and

Freddie. By the end of the 1990s, the quotas rose to roughly half of their total business.

"Urged on by ACORN, congressional Democrats and the Clinton administration helped push tolerance for high-risk loans through every sector of the banking system—far beyond the sort of banks originally subject to the CRA," Kurtz writes. "Soon, Democratic politicians and regulators actually began to take pride in lowered credit standards as a sign of 'fairness'—and the contagion spread." Banks figured out they could profit from dealing in what had previously been deemed junk mortgages, and the financial system began to destroy itself.[585]

As far as ACORN members were concerned, their tactics had worked—and the incident helped ACORN activists portray themselves as saintly martyrs for the poor who helped defend the CRA.

ACORN DEMANDS BLACKMAIL DETAILS BE KEPT SECRET

In 1999, Senate Banking Committee chairman Phil Gramm (R-TX) proposed to bring a tiny little bit of public disclosure—good government groups call it "sunshine"—to the CRA shakedown process, which he correctly noted facilitated "extortion." ACORN panicked because it knew its revenue stream was threatened. Gramm proposed amending the law so banks would have to disclose grants of more than $10,000 made to any group that offered an opinion of the bank's CRA record.[586] For the first time in history, community organizers became enemies of increased governmental burdens on corporations.

Robert Gnaizda, general counsel of the Greenlining Institute, an ACORN wannabe group, said Gramm's proposal would discourage shakedown organizations from putting banks in a vise grip. "It's a mischievous action," he said, perhaps with his fingers crossed behind his back. "Many banks feel they benefit from the private conversations they have with community groups."[587]

ACORN ginned up a dubious study to "prove" mortgage lenders were discriminating on the basis of race. "The report makes it clear that Congress should be looking at strengthening CRA, not weakening it," Hurd said. Visions of dollar signs dancing in his head, ACORN competitor Jesse Jackson attacked Gramm. "The Community Reinvestment Act is to economic justice what *Brown v. Board of Education* is to public accommodations," he said. "I will fight with every last ounce of energy I have to preserve the CRA." Jackson played the race card too, likening Gramm's position to George Wallace preventing black students from going to Alabama public schools.[588]

To ACORN, extortion is a constitutional right. The group made the outrageous argument that the proposed rule change violated its *free speech rights*. ACORN's legislative director Christopher Saffert said the change "subjects one set of bank contracts to government intervention and surveillance."[589] "Gramm is trying to both discourage banks from entering into those [shakedown] agreements and hinder the efforts of community groups who have limited resources," Saffert said. "It's part of a larger attack on CRA. He's tried to create scandals, but when you find the real details of a situation, there's nothing scandalous there."[590]

"The courts will recognize sunshine for what it is," added Hurd, "[A]n unconstitutional attempt to restrict groups from speaking out about how banks serve our neighborhoods—and the first step in Gramm's plan to repeal the CRA."[591]

But the CRA wasn't ACORN's only means of undermining the mortgage industry. In 1993, the group strong-armed several banks into providing $55 million in mortgages to welfare recipients—with a mere $1,000 down payment. Instead of presenting actual credit histories, borrowers were allowed to use rent receipts or utility payment receipts. Participating lenders included PNC Financial, Bank of New York, Chemical Bank, and Magna Bank. GE Capital Mortgage Insurance Corp., whose parent company, General Electric, has long been a facilitator of the Left, agreed to insure the loans. Banks didn't have to worry whether borrowers could actually pay off the mortgages because Fannie Mae agreed to purchase the loans after the banks made them.[592]

ACORN waged a campaign against Ameriquest. In March 2000, the group filed a complaint against the company with the Federal

Trade Commission, alleging unfair business practices.[593] It put the heat on Ameriquest's business partners. The same month ACORN picketed the Washington, D.C., offices of Salomon Smith Barney, because, as an ACORN official explained, the firm was one of the biggest buyers of loans from Ameriquest which "we believe is one of the most egregious of the subprime lenders we have studied." The year before, Salomon Smith Barney bought more than 6,200 mortgages from Ameriquest for almost $800 million.[594] In the Ameriquest deal ACORN even worked in a provision to allow foreclosed properties to be donated to community groups such as itself.[595]

As ACORN's Jeff Ordower said, ACORN does whatever it takes to spread its agenda—of chaos.

TWELVE

Leveraging the Liberals: ACORN's Partners

THE LEFT HAD wanted to force big government healthcare on America for decades. In 2007, radicals saw their chance to put the nation on a path to a single-payer system.

ACORN and its labor movement doppelganger SEIU, both long-time supporters of socialized medicine, played a key role in foisting Obamacare on the American public. ACORN and SEIU were part of an effort before the 2008 election aimed at generating irresistible political momentum for government-run healthcare, the crown jewel of the welfare state.

Although in March 2007, the punditry was betting on Hillary Clinton, it was still unclear who would be the Democrats' nominee for president. Former SEIU president Andy Stern and his comrades were determined that the candidate ultimately selected would be totally committed to statist medicine. SEIU sponsored a healthcare conference with the George Soros-funded Center for American Progress Action Fund, the lobbying arm of the think tank run by former Clinton White House aide John Podesta. Stern took care that purple-shirted SEIU members were always visible at healthcare rallies waving signs reading, "I'm a healthcare voter." Although in 2004, contenders for the Democratic nomination shied away from the healthcare issue, in 2008, all the major candidates signed on. Barack Obama and Hillary Clinton had similar proposals. Clinton was in favor of forcing Americans to buy health insurance while Obama *said* he wasn't. The strategy to put healthcare on the front burner had succeeded.

Stern had his 2.2 million-member union go all out for Obama in February 2008 during the primary fight with Clinton. The union's support gave Obama's campaign a significant lift. SEIU, which is now in serious financial trouble, spent a reported $60 million to get Obama elected and generated 100,000 so-called volunteers.

After Obama's path to the nomination was clear, SEIU and ACORN took the lead in creating a left-wing advocacy coalition called Health Care for America Now (HCAN), Other groups on HCAN's 13-organization steering committee included the American Federation of State, County and Municipal Employees, Campaign for America's Future, Center for American Progress Action Fund, the ACORN wannabe group Center for Community Change, MoveOn, National Council of La Raza, National Education Association, and Planned Parenthood Federation of America. HCAN vowed to plow $40 million into an organizing and public relations push but raised $51 million in all.[596]

Each committee member had to kick in $500,000 in startup costs. The Atlantic Philanthropies, a huge Bermuda-based foundation run by Soros protégé Gara LaMarche, contributed $10 million early. As a 501(c)(4) advocacy organization, HCAN wasn't obliged to disclose its funders. The group's affiliate, the Health Care for America Education Fund, is a project of the shadowy Tides Center. The far left Tides Center, which is related to the Tides Foundation, is a so-called fiscal sponsor which means donors take a charitable tax deduction when they give their money to the Center. The Center, in turn, is then able to hand out the money to specific recipients without disclosing its source.

Before the election, Obama endorsed HCAN's list of what should be in the new healthcare legislation. When he won, HCAN kept up the pressure by running TV ads that included outtakes from speeches in which he said creating a national healthcare system was a priority.

Stern and Obama became constant companions. On January 20,

2009, Stern viewed the inaugural parade from the presidential box in front of the White House. He was also the top White House visitor, logging 22 appointments in the first six months of the administration.[597]

LABOR MOVEMENT

ACORN and the labor movement go way back.

In ACORN's first decade, Rathke urged that it create "independent unions" to help, in Gary Delgado's words, "penetrate other spheres of people's lives." Having such union locals operating would help bring new members to ACORN and allow it to use economies of scale in its various assaults on governments and corporate America.[598]

In the 1980s, ACORN created the United Labor Unions (ULU), which it used to organize low-wage, fast-food, and home healthcare workers.[599] Ties to the labor movement gave ACORN a steady of source of funding and members and allowed it to leverage its power.

ACORN and union interests are tightly intertwined. Rathke continues to serve as chief organizer of the New Orleans local of SEIU. SEIU and ACORN had shared office space, personnel, and email servers. Until 2009, SEIU 880 in Illinois was an ACORN affiliate. On many of ACORN's campaigns, telling SEIU apart from ACORN is an exercise in futility.

ACORN supports raising the minimum wage and enacting so-called living wage policies, eliminating "predatory" financial practices by subprime lenders, increasing funding for urban public schools, and wants federal and state laws enacted that guarantee paid sick leave for all full-time workers. ACORN claims it organized community and labor coalitions that succeeded in enacting "living wage" laws in 41 cities by the end of the 1990s. A "living wage" is usually several dollars higher than the minimum wage prescribed by law. ACORN often refuses to pay its employees either.

ACORN puts minimum wage propositions on the ballot in order to drive up turnout among poor voters. "We would like it to become a fact of political life where every year the other side has to contend with a minimum wage law in some state," said Jen Kern, director of ACORN's Living Wage Resource Center. "This is what moves people to the polls now. This is our gay marriage," she said.[600] For example, Florida ACORN gathered almost a million signatures to put its wage increase measure on that state's November 2004 ballot, "partly as a strategy to boost low-income voter turnout for the presidential vote."[601]

ACORN supports the proposed "Employee Free Choice Act" (EFCA), which would take away the right of workers to cast secret ballots on whether to form a union. The proposed law, also known as "card check," would open the door to harassing and intimidating workers that union organizers target for signatures indicating that they agree to be represented by a labor union. "Card check" is tantamount to having union officials follow you into the voting booth and stay with you until you vote the way they want.

ACORN president Maude Hurd joined Senate Labor Committee chairman Ted Kennedy (D-MA) and House Labor Committee chairman George Miller (D-CA) at a pro-EFCA rally outside the U.S. Senate in December 2006. She said, "ACORN members are low- and moderate-income workers and their families. We see with our own eyes how their lives improve when they are members of unions. When labor is weakened, we all are weakened and when labor is strong we all are strong."

Unions say EFCA will make it easier for employees to join a union without corporate harassment, but former Sen. George McGovern (D-SD) says the measure would allow labor organizers to intimidate workers. "It's hard to believe that any politician would agree to a law denying millions of employees the right to a private vote," said McGovern, the Democrats' presidential nominee in 1972.[602]

ACORN was planning a major expansion into the labor movement. Don Loos, a former Labor Department employee, obtained a memo in early 2010 showing that ACORN and SEIU were so close that they were considering sharing member dues. ACORN viewed the move as a way of increasing its organizing power and opening up new frontiers in the world of shakedowns. In Loos's words, ACORN also intended "to create union organizing partnerships with other labor unions and Big Labor funded auxiliary organizations."

The ambitious project was described in emails between ACORN operatives. An email detailed ACORN's plan to use "dirty money hungry lawyers" to compel "employers to open up negotiations." ACORN also planned to create "a model for [union] organizing" that "building trades [unions] do not have," according to the email.

This would make ACORN a labor organization under federal law, according to Loos. The law defines a labor organization as "any organization of any kind so engaged in which employees participate and which exists for the purpose, in whole or in part, of dealing with employers concerning grievances, labor disputes, wages, rates of pay, hours, or other terms or conditions of employment." If so, ACORN may have violated labor union disclosure laws.

An email from Ross Fitzgerald, national field director for the ACORN Community Labor Organizing Center (ACLOC), seems to suggest a dues-sharing arrangement might already have been in place somewhere. Fitzgerald wrote: "Houston, Dallas—SEIU Local 1 has asked if we can specifically target janitorial contractors for litigation in the Dallas and Houston markets. This will be a contract that can hopefully lead to a recognition, affiliation and shared dues arrangement."

"ACORN's legal agitation approach is designed to create fear and anxiety between the employer and the employee," said Loos, who is senior advisor to Mark Mix, president of National Right To Work.[603] An ACORN insider said in an interview that the dues-sharing arrangement had been in the works since at least 2007.

ACORN'S "MINI ME":
THE WORKING FAMILIES PARTY

After ACORN abandoned bipartisanship in the 1980s it embraced partisanship with a vengeance in the 1990s.

In 1998, ACORN's partisan appendage, the Working Families Party, was officially recognized in New York State. WFP's headquarters is at the same address as ACORN's on Nevins Street in Brooklyn. One of the SEIU-funded party's co-founders is ACORN chief organizer Bertha Lewis. Obama White House political director Patrick Gaspard, a former SEIU executive, also contributed to the creation of the party and sat on its board. WFP's executive director is longtime ACORN operative Dan Cantor, as noted earlier, a reader of obscure Marxist philosophers. WFP takes credit for raising taxes both in the city and state of New York and for pressuring the state's congressional delegation to oppose desperately needed Social Security reforms. The party has sister WFP-branded parties in Connecticut, Delaware, Massachusetts, Oregon, South Carolina, and Vermont.

"The great strength of the Working Families Party," writes reporter Edward-Isaac Dovere, "is its field operation, an unmatched collection of voter files, experienced operatives and organized per-hour canvassers which even its detractors admit is unmatched in New York City, and increasingly, the whole state."[604]

Taking a page from Saul Alinsky's playbook (the part that encourages mob actions outside the homes of targets), in 2009 Connecticut's WFP sent busloads of thugs to confront American International Group Inc. (AIG) executives at their homes. The protests were calculated to intimidate executives who had been receiving death threats after the company reportedly paid out bonuses using taxpayer bailout funds. "There is a human cost to the economic meltdown that we're experiencing," said Connecticut Working Families director Jon Green. "It's scary," one executive told reporters. "People are very, very nervous for their security."[605] To the strains of Vivaldi's "Four Seasons" violin concertos, a video on the party's website shows WFP members delivering letters of protest to suburban mansions and harassing the families of AIG executives. Any unsightly confrontations have been edited out.

Like ACORN, WFP is part of the radical Left. Working with its radical friends at SEIU, it advocates more government spending, higher taxes, universal government-run healthcare, campaign finance restrictions, free universal higher education, oppressive rent control, same-sex marriage, an immigration amnesty for illegal aliens, "greening" the economy by creating heavily subsidized union jobs in the energy sector, and mandatory paid sick leave for all workers.

WFP does virtually everything that ACORN does. It is an ACORN within ACORN. It leads anti-landlord protests and supports an open borders immigration policy. It pushes for increased government spending. It does the bidding of its allies in the labor movement by pushing legislation to expand unions' organizing reach. It fights privatization of government services and organizes thuggish protests that intimidate corporations and elected officials. It takes credit for passing "living wage" laws and minimum wage increases throughout New York State.

Apparently it also shares ACORN's contempt for the electoral process. WFP was accused of vote fraud in local elections in upstate New York. Authorities tossed a total of 38 forged or fraudulent ballots— enough votes to determine the outcome in city and county elections in Rensselaer County.[606]

The crucial distinction is that, unlike ACORN, it runs candidates for office. New York State allows "fusion voting." This means a candidate can be nominated by both a major party and a minor party. Voters who vote for the candidate on the minor party line of the ballot have their votes pooled with those who voted for the same candidate on the major party line. This arrangement allows the WFP to influence the candidate's platform. "Votes on the WFP ballot line count the same, but they send a powerful message about the world we want to see," the party declares on its website.

WFP claims to have secured 150,000 votes for Barack Obama (2008) on its ballot line, 169,000 for Sen. Chuck Schumer (D-NY) (2004), and 120,000 for Hillary Clinton's Senate campaign (2000). The party claims to have provided the margin of victory for Rep. Tim Bishop (D-NY), who defeated Rep. Felix Grucci (R-NY) in 2002 by 2,700 votes. Bishop received 2,900 votes on the WFP line. The party claims its efforts in 2006 against Republicans in New York and Connecticut helped to elect Reps. Mike Arcuri (D-NY), Chris Murphy (D-CT), and Kirsten Gillibrand (D-NY), who was later appointed to fill Clinton's Senate seat when she became President Obama's secretary of state.

In 2010, WFP endorsed lawmakers and candidates all over New York State. In New York, its congressional endorsements included the irretrievably corrupt Rep. Charles Rangel (D-NY) and one of ACORN's best friends in Congress, Rep. Jerrold Nadler (D-NY).

In 2003, its first WFP-only officials (i.e., not also running on the Democratic Party's ballot line), Letitia James and Lucille McKnight, were elected to New York City Council and the Albany County legislature, respectively.[607]

Five Staten Island voters sued WFP in 2009, claiming that in ACORN-like fashion, it created a political consulting firm in order to help its candidates evade campaign spending limits. According to the lawsuit, WFP created Data and Field Services (DFS), which the party uses to "circumvent state election and local campaign finance laws." WFP's candidates hire DFS for campaign services but pay it only "a nominal sum, well below fair market value," which provides a significant, unfair advantage over other candidates who have to abide by spending limits.

"This is a case about an audacious scheme to violate the law by using corporate subterfuge to hijack our local election process," the lawsuit claims. "It goes to the very heart of our local democracy and undermines the fairness and integrity of our local elections."[608] The same year, four New York City Council candidates made suspicious payments totaling $38,000 to a mysterious company called NY Citizens Services Inc., which shares the same address as DFS, WFP, and ACORN. "The candidates' public disclosures listing the company's name are the only listing in public records for the company available," *City Hall News* reported.[609]

Edward-Isaac Dovere of *City Hall News* found that WFP's confusing organizational structure is amazingly ACORN-like. Through the party's multiple arms it enjoys "the benefits of a political party (legitimacy in voters' minds, ballot line), a non-profit (tax-exemptions, uncapped donation limits and tax deductions) and a for-profit (no disclosure requirements, ability to collect fees backed by taxpayer-supported matching funds from candidates)."

WFP's structure—like ACORN's—baffles legal experts. "I've never seen this kind of a set-up before," said lawyer Allen Bromberger, a specialist in "hybrid" legal structures that weave together nonprofits with other entities. The structure is "problematic," he said. "[T]hey may have designed it carefully and put enough safeguards in place— but the primary purpose of the 501(c)(4) [advocacy organization] cannot be to engage in political activities. So if they're not able to show some substantial non-political activity by the 501(c)(4), I think they've got a pretty significant problem."[610]

The 2009 lobbying records of a WFP-related entity, the Working Families Organization, show it has a relationship to the Progressive America Fund. Within the fund is a think tank called the Center for Working Families. A co-director is Lisa Donner, formerly a staffer for ACORN and SEIU. "Currently, the Center's interim director is listed as David Palmer who has been identified in news articles as also being the legislative campaigns director for the Party," writes Dovere. "This makes him an employee of a 501(c)(4) [advocacy organization], a 501(c)(3) [educational organization] and a political party, all at once."[611]

Confused? Don't feel so bad. You're not the only one.

ABUSING WORKERS

For a group that is entangled in the labor movement and claims to be an advocate for workers, ACORN doesn't treat its workers well.

"ACORN campaigns for seven sick days a year but only gives its staff five," according to former ACORN organizer Gregory Hall. "ACORN has founded unions but busts unions when its own employees try to organize. And every time the organization's machine creates voter fraud allegations, the group throws its poorly trained temporary workers under the bus." Most of ACORN's full time staff "complain of the group's 'crony' management system," Hall said. "And many say they've been coerced into lying to ACORN's low- and moderate-income membership about how their 'dues' will be spent."[612]

Complaints like Hall's about ACORN have been exhaustively documented across America.

ACORN doesn't like paying its employees overtime. In 1996, the federal Department of Labor sued ACORN affiliate Citizens Consulting Inc. The next year, a federal court ordered CCI to cough up $10,000 in back wages.[613]

In 2006, $250-a-week Baltimore ACORN intern Sandra Stewart complained to a local newspaper that the Baltimore chapter hadn't bothered to pay her for her work. "I find it completely ironic that an organization that fights for social justice" can't be bothered to pay its workers, Stewart said. Three other former ACORN workers told the paper that the group failed to pay them back wages. The paper also found that the local chapter had a $7,000 civil judgment entered against it for unpaid office rent. Another Baltimore area ACORN affiliate failed to pay its real estate taxes and water bills.[614]

While ACORN pressured jurisdictions across America to adopt "living wage" statutes, it actually sued the state of California seeking an exemption from the law that requires it to pay its own employees a *minimum* wage. ACORN argued in a legal brief that paying its employees more would reduce their activist zeal for the poor:

> As acknowledged both by the trial court and California, the more that ACORN must pay each individual outreach worker—either because of minimum or overtime requirements—the fewer outreach workers it will be able to hire.[615]

ACORN argued it was necessary to impose an involuntary vow of poverty on its employees. Sounding much like a cult, the group argued it was

> devoted not only to articulating and expressing the concerns of low and moderate income people. It is an organization devoted to recreating them as people, reforming them according to a certain conception of what low and moderate income people can be and achieve. When California attempts to enforce its wage and hours provisions on ACORN employees, it affects the identities which

ACORN members might prove able to develop, in violation of the federal and California constitutions.

Not surprisingly, ACORN lost. In dismissing the case, a California appeals court described the claim as an "absurdity."[616]

Even though it supports the continued imposition of equal employment opportunity laws on the rest of America, it argued it shouldn't have to comply with those same laws. The Equal Employment Opportunity Commission had to sue ACORN to force it comply with Title VII of the Civil Rights Act of 1964, the crowning achievement of the civil rights movement's legislative accomplishments.[617]

A 2003 study of ACORN by the Employment Policies Institute found the group paid a wage of $5.67 per hour, which was "less than half the level demanded by many proposed 'living wage' ordinances that ACORN supports."

Although it demands all workers be allowed to organize unions, ACORN doesn't like it when its own workers try to organize. It has tried to block its own employees from signing up with unions, and in 2003, the National Labor Relations Board determined it had unlawfully blocked its workers from organizing. The Industrial Workers of the World (IWW, also known as "Wobblies") complained that Rathke's SEIU Local 100 sabotaged a union drive by employing union-busting techniques. In 2003, the National Labor Relations Board determined ACORN had unlawfully blocked its workers from organizing.

In 2002, IWW supported ACORN workers trying to organize unions at ACORN offices in San Jose, California, and St. Petersburg, Florida. The local NAACP and IWW backed the San Jose employees against ACORN. The workers filed a successful claim against ACORN for intimidating workers from organizing. "Now I understand 100 percent why we needed a union," said Lyn Rose, who was San Jose ACORN's housing chief.[618]

Fed up with long hours and paltry pay, four ACORN organizers were canned by ACORN two days after they started a union certification drive against the group in Portland, Oregon. "We felt there was a lot of deceit in the organization," organizer Sarah Manowitz told *Williamette Week.* Employees reportedly worked 54 hours per week, including Saturdays, for annual pay of just $20,200. Two organizers said they were often paid late.

Miami ACORN got a taste of its own medicine after it stiffed dozens of its 2004 election workers. The canvassers had helped pass Amendment 5, a ballot initiative to raise the state minimum wage, with an impressive 71 percent of the vote. During a sit-in, the disgruntled unpaid employees set fire to the office kitchenette and stole computers.[619]

ACORN does not treat its voter registration canvassers well either. Seattle area resident Claire Hanson said she was approached by a woman from ACORN who walked into her driveway. Over time she was "highly pressured to join ACORN so that they could get their money." Over several months she watched as other people got involved with ACORN. "And every single one of them outside of one person, they were used and abused. They had to walk the streets in the rain. I picked them up off the street. I took them to restaurants. I dried them off. I listened to them complain about the forced work, hours that they were not paid overtime for, that they had to get quota signatures not for anything related to Boulevard Park. It was being used to benefit national issues for ACORN."[620]

LOBBYING SHENANIGANS

Citizens Consulting Inc., the shadowy financial nerve center of ACORN, filed false lobbying disclosure reports with Congress, according to former ACORN employee Ron Sykes.

When Sykes learned that CCI registered him as a lobbyist, he was angry. "It's like identity theft," Sykes said in an interview. "I have no idea why they registered me. I didn't register myself and was not aware that they were doing it." Whether this reflects ACORN's institutional carelessness or a calculated effort to deceive, the discovery throws some light on how ACORN treats its employees, moves money around the ACORN network, and deals with the federal government.

Sykes came to the nation's capital as an intern for ACORN's national legislative program, working there from April 2006 to February 2007. He was never a lobbyist although he did help to prepare lobbyists to meet with lawmakers on issues of interest to ACORN such as voting rights, housing programs, minimum wage laws, and predatory lending. Occasionally he went along on Capitol Hill visits, but arguing for or against specific legislation was not his job, he said.

According to forms CCI filed under the federal Lobbying Disclosure Act, Sykes lobbied for ACORN as a CCI employee between January 1, 2006, and June 30, 2007. Three disclosure forms call him a "fellow." When a person ceases lobbying, the registering organization (CCI) is supposed to declare this fact, but there was no indication in the online lobbying disclosure database maintained by the Office of the Clerk of the House of Representatives that CCI did so.

Sykes said he received a scholarship from ACORN to help him cover living expenses but that it was abruptly cut off months ahead of schedule in February 2007. After he became curious about ACORN's financial affairs and began to ask a lot of questions about where the money was going, he was let go. "I guess they got a little irritated and the scholarship money from the ACORN executive board was cut off," he said. The legendarily smooth Wade Rathke, who was then chief organizer of ACORN, offered him thanks and told him that he did a great job. "I asked him if there were any positions open and said I'd like to stay but he said there was no funding at this time for a salary for me," Sykes said.

Former ACORN official Marcel Reid said in an interview that she and other board members were unaware CCI even did lobbying. Legal reform advocate and lawyer Zena Crenshaw said in an interview that CCI's behavior raises several red flags. "They certainly should be segregating 501(c)(3) funds from their lobbying activities," said Crenshaw, executive director of the National Judicial Conduct and Disability Law Project Inc. "I'm not sure how you can segregate them if the lobbyist is handling the money. I don't know how CCI can be both a lobbyist and a financial manager handling ACORN's 501(c)(3) funds."

"This just confirms the need for an examination of the organization's affiliates," said Crenshaw, who also chairs the legal affairs committee of ACORN 8, a group of former ACORN members co-founded by Reid that is calling for a forensic audit of ACORN.

POISONING THE MINDS OF THE YOUNG: ACORN AND SCHOOLS

ACORN claims to support education reform, but it doesn't. ACORN is content to let poor children suffer in inferior public schools in the inner city, instead of letting them have a real chance to succeed.

ACORN has close ties to the teachers' unions and, as described elsewhere in this book, provides protest-for-hire services to them. Teachers' unions are staunch opponents of tuition vouchers and all true reforms because they threaten their members' jobs and the unions' power. So it was hardly surprising when ACORN fought New York mayor Rudy Giuliani's 2001 plan to let for-profit Edison Schools Inc. operate five of the city's worst schools. In those schools, more than four-fifths of students were unable to do math or read at grade level.

Yet ACORN used every tactic in its comprehensive playbook to scuttle the Edison plan. It intimidated schools chancellor Harold Levy into letting it print leaflets at city expense, filled with false information about Edison's record, including the charge that the firm expelled children for poor grades. ACORN obtained from school officials lists of the addresses and phone numbers of parents, whom it then barraged with calls and letters. When Edison reps tried to make their case at public forums in Harlem, ACORN activists shouted them down. For good measure, ACORN staged a noisy demonstration outside Edison's headquarters, complete with the 12-foot-high inflated rat that is an ugly staple of all union demonstrations in New York against non-unionized companies.[621]

Unfortunately, "ACORN's bullying tactics won the day, and the parents at all five schools voted against the plan," writes Sol Stern. The anti-Edison campaign was run by Bertha Lewis, at the time head of New York ACORN and co-chairman of ACORN's political party, the Working Families Party. Throughout the Edison saga, ACORN sent hundreds of demonstrators to protest at Edison's offices but it never criticized the teachers' unions that are the primary reason for the city's educational problems. Polls show that inner-city parents overwhelmingly favor real reforms such as vouchers, but ACORN doesn't care what the community thinks.

Lewis said vouchers were just "a hoax to destroy the public schools." The voucher movement isn't about improving education but is about "race and class." "This is capitalism at its worst," she yelled. "You always do it on the backs of the poor. It's all bullshit, and you know it. I grew up in the ghetto. These vouchers are just a life raft for a few people to get out. It's another education urban renewal plan. It's gentrification."[622]

ACORN also runs taxpayer-supported schools and indoctrinates the students who attend them. In New York City, it runs the ACORN High School for Social Justice (Brooklyn), ACORN Community High School (Brooklyn), and Bread and Roses High School (Harlem). It had an ACORN-branded school in Oakland, California, but former ACORN leader Fannie Brown, who joined the reform group ACORN 8, said in an interview that school intends to disaffiliate from ACORN. ACORN is also involved in "collaborative efforts" with schools in Boston, Chicago, St. Paul, and Seattle.[623]

But Stern describes ACORN schools as "political-indoctrination centers with mediocre academic records." They teach courses with "'social justice' themes that wouldn't be out of place at an ACORN community organizers' training school." Bread and Roses conducts an annual "Why Unions Matter" art program to "teach students how labor unions work and what they do to support social change, economic growth and democratic principles." ACORN schools have transported students to the nation's capital to protest "tax cuts for the rich."[624] Not surprisingly, Bill Ayers was a consultant to Chicago

ACORN. Three hundred ACORN members attended an Ayers presentation on radical education in 1993.[625]

One ACORN Community High School student wrote on the ACORN website about a 2001 field trip to Washington, D.C. Students went to Washington "to protest against tax cuts for the rich, low wages for low income employees, and single premium insurance." Jesse Jackson Jr. compared ACORN's "fight for change to the Civil War, and the Emancipation Proclamation," she wrote. According to Jackson, "12 million adults and 24 million children will not benefit from President Bush's tax cuts" which will lead to "massive budget cuts for schools and after school programs." She added, after "Bill Clinton left office, there has not been any health care for 150 million people of the working class. It has been 100 days since Bush has been in office and he has never spoke [sic] about health reform."[626]

Ironically, being steeped in left-wing thinking may serve this student well if she attends an American university, so this may be one of those rare cases in which ACORN has helped someone. If she graduated at all. Just 27 percent of ninth-grade students at ACORN Community High School made it to 12th grade in four years, according to an analysis of U.S. Department of Education data by *Dropout Nation* editor RiShawn Biddle, while only 33 percent of ninth-graders at ACORN High School for Social Justice and 24 percent of ninth-graders at Bread and Roses made it to senior year. "ACORN created three new dropout factories where we once had none," Biddle said in an interview. "Their students won't be able to do anything that matters like read or do algebra. But they will be able to spout off looniness."

OBAMA'S PLAN TO DESECRATE 9/11

By June 2009, ACORN realized how much money was to be made by jumping on the "green economy" bandwagon. Brian Kettenring, deputy director of national operations, said ACORN decided to get more involved in environmental issues after seeing how vulnerable cities such as New Orleans, its home base at the time, was to hurricanes and rising ocean levels. "ACORN families understand that building a green economy that's sustainable and builds jobs for working families is good for them, good for the environment, and good for communities." ACORN expected to lobby Congress for federal funding to weatherize urban buildings, he said.[627]

A "green economy" is utopian fantasy. The kind of economy radical environmentalists want to force on America is heavily subsidized by the government and bans oil and coal, forcing people to rely on inferior "sustainable" energy sources. "For all the hype over wind and solar, the reality is that they contribute very little to our energy supply," said Kerry Lynch, senior fellow at the American Institute for Economic Research. Wind generates under one percent of all U.S. energy and solar power accounts for a mere tenth of one percent. "Together, they could power the country for all of three days a year," she said.[628] Going "green" would turn the U.S. into a Third-World country.

So it only made sense when ACORN joined the Obama administration in a cynical, coldly calculated political effort to erase the meaning of the September 11, 2001 terrorist attacks from the American psyche and convert September 11 into an unseemly celebration of radical environmentalism and Big Government.

To do the deed President Obama counted on two Marxists who blame America for the 9/11 attacks. The two men charged with this politically correct exercise in desecration and icon-smashing are the boorish Rev. Lennox Yearwood and the comparatively suave, articulate Van Jones. Yearwood chants "power to the people" with a fist in the air to get his message out. Jones, the more urbane and media-savvy of the two, was the president's green jobs czar at the White House Council on Environmental Quality (CEQ). Jones uses Web 2.0 and the language of capitalism—non-threatening words like *investment*—to sell socialism.

This effort to reshape the American psyche was about easing the nation along in its ongoing radical transformation. In April 2009, President Obama signed the Edward M. Kennedy Serve America Act into law. The law calls for a "National Day of Service and Remembrance," but the White House dropped the "and Remembrance" and started calling the observance the "National Day of Service." It's not likely many lawmakers thought this meant that day was going to be turned into a celebration of radical community organizing, bicycle paths, ethanol, carbon emission controls, and solar panels.

The administration's plans were outlined in an August 11, 2009 White House-sponsored teleconference call run by Yearwood, president of the far-left Hip Hop Caucus. When Yearwood is in the news it's usually for getting arrested. He was handcuffed outside a congressional hearing in 2007 when Gen. David Petraeus was to testify. Yearwood told the "Democracy Now" radio program he wanted to attend the hearing because, "I knew that when officers lie, soldiers die."

COMMUNIST VAN JONES ORGANIZES
SECRET WHITE HOUSE CALL

The call was organized by former community organizer Jones, the self-described "communist" and "rowdy black nationalist" who was forced out of the White House in September 2009. Jones was fired after it was revealed he signed a 9/11 "truther" petition blaming the terrorist attacks on the Bush administration. On the call, Yearwood and other leaders kept saying they wanted 9/11 to be used for something "positive," "forward-leaning," and "productive," said a source on the call. The plan was to turn what the call participants referred to as a "day of fear" that helps Republicans into a day of activism that helps the Left. In other words, leftists were trying to drain 9/11 of all meaning.

"They think it needs to be taken back from the right," said the source. "They're taking that day and they're breaking it because it gives Republicans an advantage. To them, that day is a fearful day." The people behind the effort thought it best to launch their public relations campaign under the radar of the mainstream media because 9/11 is a sensitive subject. "The organizing term is to 'go dark,'" said the source. "You don't tell the press, don't tell people you think will tell the press."

The coalition of about 60 groups on the call included ACORN, the racial grievance mongers of Color of Change, AFL-CIO, Apollo Alliance, Friends of the Earth, Mobilize.org, Jesse Jackson's RainbowPUSH Coalition, National Urban League, and Young Democrats of America. Color of Change was co-founded by Jones and James Rucker, who is its executive director. Rucker was grassroots mobilization director for MoveOn Political Action and its sister group MoveOn Civic Action. He is also co-founder of George Soros's Secretary of State Project which aims to install left-wing Democrats, who are notoriously indifferent to election fraud, as chief electoral officers in as many states as possible.

Although the annual commemoration of the 2001 terrorist attacks belongs to the entire nation, the activist Left doesn't see it that way. Radicals view the nationwide remembrance of the murder of nearly 3,000 Americans by Islamic totalitarians as an obstacle to winning over the hearts and minds of the American people. "When you criticize them, they are prepared to say, 'Did you want 9/11 to be another day of selling mattresses, like Presidents Day?'" the source on the call said. "They are truly trying to change the American mindset."

The leftists at ACORN view September 11 as a "Republican" day because it focuses the public on supposedly "Republican" issues like patriotism, national security, and terrorism. They complain that 9/11 was long ago hijacked by Republicans and their enablers and unfairly used to bludgeon helpless Democrats every election. MSNBC host Keith Olbermann, summed up this ugly perspective, calling 9/11 "a brand name. A Republican campaign slogan. Propaganda of the lowest form."

On August 4, 2009, the White House offered a glimpse into its plans to desecrate 9/11 for political advantage. Van Jones appeared in a 33-minute video on the White House official blog to discuss the administration's plan to flush 9/11 down the memory hole just as it has tried to do by rechristening the Global War on Terror the "Overseas Contingency Operations." Jones said the new rebranded 9/11 will be a great opportunity "for people to connect, to find other people in your peer group who are also passionate about repowering America but also greening up America and cleaning up America."

Jones is now a senior fellow at the Center for American Progress. After initially agreeing to be interviewed for this book, he later backed out.

The same day the White House video was posted, HUD Secretary Shaun Donovan, EPA Administrator Lisa Jackson, Department of Energy Under Secretary Kristina Johnson and activists held a press conference. Yearwood said the new 9/11 would be "the first milestone" of a larger effort called Green the Block aimed at convincing Americans to embrace a "green economy." "From policy creation to community implementation, the Green the Block campaign wants to see access and opportunity created for all Americans, to build prosperity and a healthier planet for future generations." Yearwood never explains why this National Day of Service has to be held—of all the 365 days in a year—on September 11.

This wasn't the first time the Obama administration tried to use taxpayer resources to push its left-wing agenda. The day before the 9/11 teleconference, the Obama administration used government resources in an attempt to get artists to create art that furthered its political agenda.

In a conference call sponsored by the White House, National Endowment for the Arts, and Corporation for National and Community Service, Buffy Wicks, deputy director of the White House Office of Public Engagement, told artists the administration had "specific asks" in mind. Yosi Sergant, then the communications director of the NEA, said, "I would encourage you to pick something, whether it's health care, education, the environment, you know, there's four key areas that the corporation has identified as the areas of service." He added, "You're going to see a lot more of us in the next four and hopefully eight years."[629]

APOLLO ALLIANCE:
HOME OF TERRORISTS AND COMMUNISTS

One of the major groups on the 9/11 call, Apollo Alliance, also has ties to ACORN. The San Francisco-based Apollo Alliance is a hard-left environmentalist group that wields tremendous clout in Congress and with the Obama administration. The group acknowledged dictating parts of the $787 billion stimulus bill that passed Congress in February 2009. Thanks to Apollo Alliance, the bill designates $50 billion for heavily taxpayer-subsidized so-called green jobs. ACORN expected to get its cut of the money.

Like the Health Care for America Education Fund, Apollo Alliance is a project of the Tides Center, so its financial affairs are not public knowledge. The Apollo Alliance has been described as combining "bottom-up activism by social justice-oriented community organizers with top-down, command-and-control supervision by corporate financiers, union bosses and government bureaucrats." It calls itself a "coalition of labor, business, environmental, and community leaders working to catalyze a clean energy revolution." It is endorsed by ACORN, Greenpeace, Sierra Club, SEIU, AFL-CIO, AFSCME, United Steelworkers, and other unions.

Van Jones was a member of its board. An even more notorious Jones is involved with Apollo Alliance. Jeff Jones, a co-founder of the Weatherman faction of SDS that became the Weather Underground, is director of Apollo Alliance's New York state affiliate and a consultant to the national Apollo Alliance. Jones was a fugitive for more than decade, and like Bill Ayers, doesn't regret what he did. "To this day, we still, lots of us, including me, still think it was the right thing to try to do," he said in 2004.

Jones's consultancy counts as clients the Natural Resources Defense Council and the Workforce Development Institute (WDI) a labor-dominated nonprofit. WDI receives government funding and Jones's grant proposals help it win federal stimulus funding under the legislation Apollo helped to draft. The government funding "could promote even bigger changes in public policy, creating a permanent cycle of grantmaking that will benefit union bosses, environmental bureaucrats, social justice community activists, and corporations that profit from government favors," observes commentator Phil Kerpen.[630]

[THIRTEEN]

Election Follies:
ACORN's Voter Fraud

IN THE MONTHS after President Obama was inaugurated, the new administration tried to move oversight of the Census into the White House in order to exercise more control over the once-in-a-decade headcount that determines how many seats each state gets in the House of Representatives. It would have been an unprecedented power grab. The plan failed after it was exposed in the media but the administration still had a Plan B.

The Obama administration was so eager to let ACORN work its mischief on the U.S. Census that it bent over backwards to accommodate its favorite community organizing group. But when questioned by the media, the Census Bureau downplayed ACORN's participation, labeling the notion that ACORN would be involved in the count as "baseless."

Judicial Watch obtained government documents proving that ACORN wasn't just an ordinary participant in the 2010 Census: it was involved in planning the operation. Under Obama, the Census Bureau offered ACORN the opportunity to "recruit Census workers" who would participate in the count. As an "executive level" partner, ACORN was allowed to "organize and/or serve as a member on a

Complete Count Committee." The committee helps "develop and implement locally based outreach and recruitment campaigns." Under Obama, the Census Bureau even retroactively extended an already expired deadline so ACORN could apply to be part of the decennial count.[631]

Former ACORN organizer Gregory Hall warned about the dangers of letting ACORN participate in the Census. "There is no reason to believe the problems of staff mistreatment or systematic fraud will be any different if and when the federal government asks ACORN to take its show on the road to households across the country."[632]

With its track record ACORN shouldn't be allowed anywhere near the Census, election fraud expert Hans von Spakovsky said in an interview. "Of all the organizations in the country that do voter registration drives there's only one organization that has consistently in election after election after election been accused of and had dozens of employees convicted of voter registration fraud," said von Spakovsky, a senior legal fellow at the Heritage Foundation and a former member of the Federal Election Commission. "That to me is an indication that they cannot be trusted to have anything to do with the Census because we could not trust that any forms which they help or persuade people to fill out don't have incorrect information in them or that they are engaged in fraudulent behavior to build up the population in poor urban areas because they know that the higher the population numbers in those areas the more money comes in."

TO ACORN VOTER FRAUD EQUALS SOCIAL JUSTICE

What do "Mickey Mouse," "Mary Poppins," and "Jive Turkey" all have in common? ACORN has registered them to vote—and sometimes more than once.

Two thousand and eight was a banner year for ACORN's egregious election fraud campaigns. That year ACORN field workers gave 19-year-old Freddie Johnson cash and cigarettes for registering to vote 72 times. "Sometimes, they come up and bribe me with a cigarette, or they'll give me a dollar to sign up," he said. "The ACORN people are everywhere, looking to sign people up. I tell them I already registered. The girl said, 'You are?' I say, 'Yup,' and then they say, 'Can you just sign up again?'" Johnson said.[633] Seven-year-old O'jahnae Smith was registered to vote by ACORN 11 years too early. Roberta Casteel found out ACORN filed two registrations in her name, showing her on one as a Democrat, and on the other as an Independent. Her signature was apparently forged on both documents.[634]

More so than all its other misdeeds, ACORN is best known for its adventures in election fraud. David Horowitz sums up the group's attitude. ACORN has

> contempt for the election process because they don't believe in the electoral system as it is constituted in a capitalist democracy. To them, elections are already a fraud—an instrument of the rich, or as Alinsky prefers to call them, the Haves. If the electoral system doesn't serve "the people," but is only an instrument of the Haves, then election fraud is justified as the path to a future that will serve the Have-Nots.[635]

ACORN's greatest legislative accomplishment is the National Voter Registration Act of 1993, commonly known as Motor Voter, which makes fraud relatively easy to accomplish. Its enactment gave ACORN new incentives to subvert the electoral system. ACORN is well aware that every fraudulent vote cancels out the legitimate vote of a law-abiding American. That doesn't bother the group. ACORN employees say the group doesn't make much of an effort to remove bogus voter registrations. "There's no quality control on purpose, no checks and balances," said Nate Toler, who worked on an ACORN voter effort in Missouri. "The internal motto is 'We don't care if it's a lie, just so long as it stirs up the conversation.'"[636]

Sometimes ACORN is complicit in the fraud committed in its name and sometimes it's a victim of the criminals it hires to conduct voter registration drives. But ACORN is always guilty, at best, of a wanton disregard for electoral integrity, and at worst, of a desire to destroy the electoral system. That's why ACORN opposes voter ID laws using the specious argument that requiring any kind of identification whatsoever will somehow disenfranchise low-income voters. You need ID to get a library card, board an airplane, or buy a beer, so why not to exercise the sacred civic duty of electing the nation's leaders? Polls show that most Americans—including blacks and Hispanics—back voter ID laws. And so does the U.S. Supreme Court, which ruled 6–3 in April 2008 that states can require voters to show identity cards. Voting to uphold an Indiana law, liberal Justice John Paul Stevens wrote that the state has a "valid interest in protecting 'the integrity and reliability of the electoral process.'" Stevens also noted there was a lack of evidence that Indiana voters would suffer inconvenience by the requirement to produce ID at the polls.[637]

Kansas City's experience with ACORN is typical. In 2006, the city's election director Ray James said more than 15,000 of the 35,000 registrations submitted by ACORN were problematic. There were problems "such as duplicates, questionable or unreadable information, or names, addresses and Social Security numbers that don't match existing records." Authorities said one person completed seven different applications. "ACORN member Todd Elkins, who was at the election office on Tuesday checking the voting rolls, said it's possible the applicant was just friendly. 'And maybe he kept coming up to our voting canvassers and kept signing up,' Elkins said." In another case 11 applications had been filed in the name of a 19-year-old woman. The election board returned a form with incomplete information to a voter. The man's wife called in reporting the man died 27 years before.[638]

Election fraud isn't Project Vote's only misdeed. Project Vote was involved in a Teamsters scandal that brought down the union's president, Ron Carey. Fundraiser Charles Blitz was charged "with lying to investigators about his role in a money-laundering scheme in which he agreed to solicit money for two socially progressive groups—Citizen Action and Project Vote—with the understanding that a percentage of the money raised would be passed on to the Carey reelection campaign." In 1996, the Teamsters gave $175,000 to Project Vote and $475,000 to Citizen Action, a group co-founded by Alinskyite organizer Heather Booth. Blitz also raised $185,000 for an ironically named Carey group, Teamsters for a Corruption Free Union. An internal memo from the Teamsters stated that the voter mobilizations efforts funded "will benefit the [1996] Clinton campaign but also, and more specifically, congressional and Senate races that we are tracking." Blitz pleaded guilty to making false statements to federal election officials.[639]

ACORN's vote manufacturing affiliate was also involved in a corruption scandal in Ohio. Thaddeus J. Jackson, chairman of the Cuyahoga County Board of Elections, took a $2,400 payment from Project Vote. He claimed he worked as a consultant for Project Vote, which a judge said was probably an ethical breach. Jackson was convicted of improperly using his influence to obtain the payment.[640] The workers of Project Vote, which until a few years ago was headed by former Ohio Democratic Party chairman David J. Leland, are available as hired guns. Project Vote took $20,000 from a pro-gambling group in Missouri to register voters. On the ballot was a proposed constitutional amendment to permit slot machines on riverboat casinos.[641]

ACORN has worked diligently to disrupt the democratic process. Jefferson County, La., voter registrar Dennis DiMarco complained in May 2008 that Louisiana parishes were being inundated with bad voter registration forms. "Registrars have begun to see a disturbing pattern of misinformation on the forms, including duplicates, cards filled out with different colors of ink, or using the names of pets and dead people." DiMarco said he had already used the bulk of his mailing budget because so many error-ridden cards had to be sent back. In Louisiana the cards were generated by Voting Is Power, a national Democratic Party voter drive in which ACORN participated. Shreveport registrar Ernie Roberson said of the 6,000 registrations his office had received, a mere 2,200 were valid.[642]

ACORN fights against election list integrity. Project Vote and SEIU challenged a Pennsylvania law that allowed officials to remove nonvoters from voter registration. They argued doing so discriminated against minorities. They lost. Judge Leonard I. Garth of the Third Circuit Court of Appeals ridiculed the lawsuit. "It is not the state which prevents citizens from exercising their right to vote," he wrote in the opinion. "Rather, we are faced with the fact that, for a variety of historical reasons, minority citizens have turned out to vote at a statistically lower rate than white voters." Garth added, "purge statutes are a legitimate means by which the state can attempt to prevent voter fraud."[643]

ACORN regards any effort to take voters off polluted, fraud-ridden rolls as an affront to democracy. Its position is that efforts to make sure voter rolls contain only living, eligible, voters who reside in the district are sinister acts of vote suppression morally equivalent to KKK attacks on black voters in the Old South.

ACORN's Project Vote affiliate issued a report condemning such list integrity measures as "voter caging." Caging is a term borrowed from the direct mail industry. It refers to the practice of sending non-forwardable mail to registered voters in order to determine if they exist, are known by the name listed, and reside at the address specified. It's not rocket science: If the mailing is returned to the sender, a presumption is created that the voter listing is invalid.

Republicans, of course, are the villains in the report: "During the last half century, the focus of Republican organizations on voter caging operations has had less to do with voter fraud and more to do with a desire to use state voter challenge statutes to suppress minority and urban votes." It's all an evil plot to prevent poor people from voting, according to ACORN.[644]

Even after the dissolution of ACORN's national structure in April 2010, Project Vote remains a threat to clean elections. Earlier that year an inside source confirmed that Project Vote was on track to take in at least as much money in 2010 as it received in 2008. Project Vote had gross receipts of $14,635,032 in 2008, according to its tax return. It acknowledged in spent $11,226,965 that year on its fraud-heavy voter registration program.

DOES PROJECT VOTE HAVE RACIST GOALS?

Zach Polett, who was executive director of Project Vote, seems to confirm the worst about ACORN's voter drives. ACORN and Project Vote, incidentally, are interchangeable. Their staffs overlap, they share office space, and they share money. Employees migrate between the two legally separate organizations constantly. "Real change will only happen when people demand it, and right now the people who need and want change the most—low-income Americans, minorities, immigrants and youth—are being left out of the discussion," according to Polett. "The electorate going to the polls is disproportionately old, wealthy and white, and our national public policy agenda is skewed accordingly."[645]

Is Polett's statement racist? It's an arguable point but imagine the outcry if a conservative or Republican voter mobilization group made this statement: "The electorate going to the polls is disproportionately young, poor and black, and our national public policy agenda is skewed accordingly."

Like all senior ACORN personnel, Polett dismisses public concern about voter fraud and is contemptuous of the rule of the law:

> Progressives should speak out clearly against efforts to maintain the status quo by excluding voters through illegal restrictions, intimidation, manipulation or misinformation. We have to take a stand for fair and accessible elections, and recognize that efforts to curb so-called 'voter fraud' are in reality attempts to disenfranchise and silence our least powerful citizens.

Polett is channeling Richard Cloward and Frances Fox Piven here. His statement translates as: All efforts to ensure electoral integrity and the rule of law are illegitimate and aimed at bolstering the oppressive capitalist system. We could care less about voter fraud because poor people and their radical agitator friends have every right to game the electoral system in order to bring about change. Cloward didn't worry about fraud either. "It's better to have a little bit of fraud than to leave people off the rolls who belong there," he said.[646]

Even though it is America's foremost enabler of election fraud, Project Vote tries to get rid of the fraud problem by moving the semantic goalposts and defining it out of existence. In a Project Vote report called "The Politics of Voter Fraud," the group says voter fraud is a myth. "The claim that voter fraud threatens the integrity of American elections is itself a fraud," writes Lorraine C. Minnite, assistant professor of political science at Columbia University's Barnard College. "It is being used to persuade the public that deceitful and criminal voters are manipulating the electoral system."

"The exaggerated fear of voter fraud has a long history of scuttling efforts to make voting easier and more inclusive, especially for marginalized groups in American society," she writes. "With renewed partisan vigor fantasies of fraud are being spun again to undo some of the progress America has made lowering barriers to the vote."[647]

According to ACORN and Piven, trying to guarantee the integrity of voter lists is a terrible thing called "vote suppression." Piven smears advocates of voter list integrity as no better than Ku Klux Klansmen or lynch mobs. "Like vote suppression since the days of Reconstruction, vote suppression today masquerades under the cover of party-run 'ballot-security' campaigns to fight fraud, and is also embedded in the rigmarole of 'prudent' election administration," she wrote in a 2009 book co-authored with Minnite and another leftist academic, Margaret Groarke. To the radical left, those who insist that the law is followed, those who insist that only real, live, eligible voters are on the voter rolls, are part of a vast, right-wing, racist conspiracy.[648]

USING THE BALLOT BOX TO
PROMOTE DEPENDENCY ON GOVERNMENT

Of course it is not illegal or immoral to register poor people to vote, but ACORN is not trying to involve them in the electoral process out of nobility. ACORN's focus on registering those dependent on government programs is leftist constituency-building consistent with the Cloward-Piven Strategy. ACORN is using the poor in a bid to overthrow the American system.

Bad economic times are likely to encourage more people to register to vote at welfare offices. Under the Motor Voter law, more than 2.6 million registered at such offices in 1995–1996, or 6.3 percent of all applicants. With good economic times the figure fell below 1 million by 2007–2008. Jason Torchinsky, who was a lawyer in President Bush's Justice Department, says liberal groups want welfare offices to do the voter registration work ACORN did. "With the demise of ACORN, the left needs somebody to pick up that function."[649] In a 2005 report ACORN, Project Vote, and a left-wing group called Demos, complained that states weren't doing enough to register welfare recipients to vote for increases in government spending.[650]

ACORN's first staff organizer warned long ago of the dangers of entering the voter registration business. In his 1986 history of the group, Gary Delgado argued the "minuses" of the field far outweighed the "pluses." "Since the voters registered are seldom recruited into the community organization, the action becomes a benefit for the Democrats at little or no cost to the party. A great deal of organizational time and energy is expended on registration efforts with very little tied to ongoing organizational activities. The effort also opens up a new flank to attack from conservative forces."[651]

The Left claimed the fact that the Bush administration fired several U.S. attorneys including the outspoken David Iglesias—reportedly for a lack of zeal in pursuing voter fraud allegations—was proof that voter fraud is a myth.[652] This is nonsense, according to election lawyer J. Christian Adams, a veteran of the Voting Rights Section at the Department of Justice.

Although some claim voter fraud is a myth "as common as unicorns and Sasquatch" and others insist fraud routinely affects election outcomes, "[t]he truth lies somewhere in between," writes Adams. "The truth is that voter fraud occurs frequently, and it determines who wins elections infrequently." He argues the "integrity of the electoral process is perhaps more important than who wins and loses an election. Lawlessness in elections corrodes the entire democratic process."[653]

According to Adams, the ACORN attitude to election fraud now infects the Obama Justice Department, which, apart from studying how much money it has given to ACORN, refuses to investigate the group. Attorney General Eric Holder also refuses to enforce the voter list integrity provisions of the Motor Voter law (Section 8), which require states to remove the names of ineligible felons, the dead, and non-residents. Political appointee Julie Fernandes told lawyers in the DOJ's Voting Section that the Obama administration would not enforce the law. Section 8 "doesn't have anything to do with increasing minority turnout," said Fernandes. "We don't have any interest in enforcing that part of the law." But, as if taking orders from ACORN, Holder vigorously enforces the provisions of Section 7 requiring states to register voters at welfare offices. In contrast, the Bush administration enforced both Section 7 and Section 8.[654]

ACORN has long argued that fraudulent registrations cannot become fraudulent votes. "How would you know if people using fake names had cast votes in states without strict ID laws?" said GOP Indiana Secretary of State Todd Rokita, who in 2008 won an important Supreme Court case sustaining Indiana's photo identification law. "It's almost impossible to detect and once the fraudulent voter leaves the precinct or casts an absentee ballot, that vote is thrown in with other secret ballots there's no way to trace it." Anita MonCrief agreed. "It's ludicrous to say that fake registrations can't become fraudulent votes," she said. "I assure you that if you can get them on the rolls you can get them to vote, especially using absentee ballots."[655]

VOTER FRAUD IS A FIGMENT OF YOUR IMAGINATION, YOU RACIST REPUBLICAN

ACORN's allies don't care about voter fraud. Its hairsplitting defenders are quick to point out that whatever the group has done it's not "voter fraud" that ACORN's employees have committed but "voter registration fraud." (In fact, at least two people registered by ACORN, Claudel Gilbert and Darnell Nash, have been convicted of actual fraudulent voting.) Those trying to justify the group's actions define voter fraud very narrowly. Voter fraud (also called electoral fraud or election fraud) is a blanket term encompassing a host of election-related improprieties including forgery, impersonation, identity theft, bribery, manipulating a voting machine, ballot box stuffing, false swearing, absentee ballot fraud, and many, many other crimes.

To justify the lawbreaking of ACORN and its employees, the group's allies also "define deviancy down," arguing that taking steps to commit fraud by filing a false voter registration is not worrisome as long as the perpetrator doesn't succeed in casting a ballot. By the same logic conspiring to commit a crime isn't a crime in itself if the person gets caught before committing it.

After the names of several Dallas Cowboys showed up on voter rolls in Nevada in 2008, Rep. Jesse Jackson Jr. (D-IL) wrote, "Obviously it's not right for a fake 'Tony Romo' to be registered in Las Vegas . . . but remember the basic point—it's not voter fraud unless someone shows up at the voting booth on Election Day and tries to pass himself off as 'Tony Romo.'"

Jackson called ACORN "one of the strongest, hardest-working, most dedicated community organizations in both Chicago and in 40 states across the U.S." Opposition to ACORN in 2008 was based on the fact that "ACORN, along with Project Vote, just announced that they had successfully registered 1.3 million poor people this year."[656]

Jackson had egg on his face two weeks later. The *New York Times* reported that Project Vote was forced to admit that 850,000 of the 1.3 million registrations from allegedly new voters were not from new voters at all. About 400,000 of the registrations "were rejected by election officials for a variety of reasons, including duplicate registrations, incomplete forms and fraudulent submissions from low-paid field workers." ACORN acknowledged it fired "829 of the 10,000 canvassers it hired during the election for job-related problems, including falsifying registration forms."[657]

Former ACORN national board member Marcel Reid has her own theory about ACORN and election fraud. Those on the Left, and particularly those on the Right, don't really understand the true nature of ACORN or how it does business, according to Reid. "ACORN prospers from chaos because chaos presents an opportunity for change."

She believes ACORN's ambitious record of electoral fraud is part of a deliberate strategy of misdirection by the group's leadership. "What everyone calls voter registration fraud is really funder fraud, because these foundations pay for people to be registered to vote and for every one of these people registered who is not a real person the funders are being defrauded," she said in an interview.

"It's not that ACORN actually believes it can influence elections by fraud," said Reid. "It just doesn't care." In fact, "ACORN doesn't mind being accused of election fraud because it has never attempted to commit election fraud. Fraud allegations are useful because they distract from ACORN's other, more profitable operations," she said.

Former ACORN/Project Vote employee Anita MonCrief said employees were well briefed on what to say when accusations of election fraud popped up. "We have prepared responses that everyone was given to say that voter registration fraud doesn't really happen, voter IDs affect people," MonCrief testified. "It was certain spiels that we were all given to say."[658]

A document dump from the FBI in 2010 threw some light on how ACORN and Project Vote do business. In St. Louis, Missouri ACORN employees told the FBI the point of ACORN filing "[f]raudulent cards" was "[t]o cause confusion on election day to keep polls open longer," "[t]o allow people who can't vote to vote," and "[t]o allow [people] to vote multiple times." An investigator wrote in a report that another said "Project Vote will pay them whether cards [were] fake or not—whatever they had to do to get the cards was [their] attitude." Project Vote pays based on the quantity of cards and "that's why they were so reckless." One report quotes an employee saying, "I don't like our system. I don't think we should do voter registration." It notes that employees were "[c]onstantly threatened" and that staff were "instructed on what to say to [the] FBI." Another report said an employee told the investigator that ACORN "[t]old employees not to talk to the FBI." The FBI is "'trying to intimidate you.'"

An FBI synopsis dated October 19, 2006, said "it is alleged by

ACORN workers they were instructed by ACORN management to campaign for U.S. Senate Democratic candidate, Claire McCaskill, in further violation of election laws." It continued, "Investigation to date has determined Project Vote, a 501(c)(3) organization head-quartered in Washington, D.C., funded 100 percent of ACORN's voter registration drive. It is also alleged Project Vote is an arm of George Soros and the National Democratic Party." The statements were included in FBI reports obtained by Judicial Watch from an investigation of eight Project Vote workers. All eight employees, including Tyaira L. "Tootsie Roll" Williams, later pleaded guilty to voter registration fraud.[659]

During the St. Louis saga election officials mailed out 5,000 letters to people registered by ACORN asking them to reply. Fewer than 40 did. Officials' attempt to protect the voter rolls brought a scathing rebuke from Wade Rathke. He called them "slop buckets" and said they had "broken the law in trying to discourage new voters illegally." Democrat Matt Potter, the St. Louis deputy elections director, told John Fund his employees were already working 13 hours a day and "dumping this on them isn't fair."[660]

FRAUD INVESTIGATIONS AND CONVICTIONS

There were at least 14 open election fraud investigations of ACORN in progress in early 2009. The figure was mentioned in a confiden-tial attorney-client memo, provided by a source within ACORN. In the legal memo dated March 9, 2009, Brian Mellor, senior counsel at Project Vote, provided ACORN officials Zach Polett, Brian Ketten-ring, and Michael Slater an update on the "Status of Law Enforce-ment Investigations of ex-ACORN canvassers."

In Las Vegas, Nevada, there were "approximately 44 ex-canvassers that ACORN had terminated for suspicion of turning in voter regis-tration applications that had not been completed or signed by the applicant named on the application," the memo said. Canvassers turned in 140 "problematic" voter registration card packages. A Clark

County grand jury subpoenaed employment information and voter registration applications collected by canvassers.

In October 2008, Nevada executed a warrant on ACORN's Las Vegas office, seizing computers and documentation. In mid-January 2009, the grand jury sent over a second subpoena "seeking policy information on training, discipline, and payments to canvassers."

Nevada Attorney General Catherine Cortez Masto and Secretary of State Ross Miller, both Democrats, unveiled voter registration fraud charges against two senior ACORN employees in May 2009. It was bad enough that ACORN's deputy regional director Amy Adele Busefink and Las Vegas field director Christopher Howell Edwards were implicated in a massive conspiracy, but for the first time in its history ACORN was charged with election fraud. Edwards pleaded guilty months after being charged and has turned state's evidence.

ACORN and Busefink were scheduled to be tried jointly in late November 2010, but Busefink cut a deal with prosecutors in hopes of avoiding prison time for her role in the conspiracy. Busefink entered an "Alford plea" which is similar to a "no contest" plea. In January 2011, she received a two-year suspended sentence.

Soon after news of Busefink's plea bargain was reported, Michael McDunnah, communications director for Project Vote, sent this writer an email to protest a brief blog post about the plea deal. As part of Project Vote's push to distance itself from ACORN, McDunnah wrote that "Amy Busefink worked for Project Vote, not ACORN." The facts suggest otherwise.

The criminal complaint filed against Busefink by the Nevada attorney general stated that as "ACORN Regional Director for Voter Registration" Busefink "did aid, abet, counsel, encourage, hire, command, induce or procure ACORN to commit the crime of Compensation for Registration of Voters by approving ACORN Las Vegas Field Director Christopher Howell Edwards' blackjack or '21' bonus program . . ." The *New York Times* reported that Busefink had been a "deputy regional director" at ACORN.

Busefink ran the 2010 national voter drive for Project Vote. She also ran ACORN's fraud-ridden 2008 voter registration drive. As noted earlier, in that drive, officials chucked about 400,000 bogus registrations.

At time of writing, multiple counts of election fraud remained pending against ACORN. Prosecutor Conrad Hafen, who until he was elected justice of the peace in 2010 was Nevada's chief deputy state attorney general, previously said neither bankruptcy nor dissolution would "necessarily protect (ACORN) from prosecution" in Nevada.

If ACORN is convicted it would cause an earthquake in leftist organizing circles across the U.S. More prosecutors might be emboldened to take on ACORN and similar groups. Until it was charged by Nevada, ACORN had frequently boasted about how it—as opposed to its employees—had been able to duck prosecution for voter fraud-related offenses.

In the Nevada case, ACORN rolled out the usual propaganda to distract from its misdeeds. After its office was searched, ACORN complained the raid was a "stunt" calculated to frustrate its minority voter registration drive. Las Vegas chief elections officer Larry Lomax called ACORN's boasts that it had strict quality assurance procedures in place to weed out fraudulent registrations "pathetic." Lomax pointed out that ACORN gave voter registration jobs to 59 inmates from a work-release program and that several of them who had gone to the hoosegow for identity theft were made supervisors. "That led some local wags to joke that at least ACORN was hiring specialists to do their work," the *Wall Street Journal*'s John Fund reported.[661]

The complaint listed 26 counts of voter fraud and 13 counts of providing unlawful extra compensation to those registering voters, which is forbidden under Nevada law on the theory that it incentivizes fraud. The complaint said voter registration canvassers were paid between $8 and $9 an hour but that continued employment was conditioned on a quota of 20 voters per shift. "From July 27 through Oct. 2 ACORN also provided additional compensation under a bonus program called 'Blackjack' or '21+' that was based on the total number of voters a person registered." Canvassers bringing in 21 or more completed forms per day would receive a $5 bonus. The complaint said that Edwards created the illegal bonus scheme and that "ACORN timesheets indicate that corporate officers of ACORN were aware of the Blackjack bonus program and failed to take immediate action to stop it."[662]

The Mellor memo also said "approximately 350" problem voter registration packages were under investigation in Orlando, Florida. ACORN handed over documentation to FBI agent Denise Day. The FBI was involved in an investigation of 94 problem packages by the state attorney's office in Miami-Dade County.

The other "problematic" packages mentioned in the memo were: Durham, NC (184); Allegheny County (Pittsburgh), PA (140); Cleveland, OH (83); Gary, IN (63); Jackson County (Kansas City), MO, (37); Bridgeport and Stamford, CT (5); and Brevard County, FL (not specified). The memo also indicated that in El Paso County, Colorado, authorities asked for information on two canvassers. Michigan asked for information "on the canvasser they indicted last fall." In Milwaukee there were "39 canvassers ACORN (32) and Voters Project (7) organizations were caught up in the investigations near the end of the election."

To date, at least 54 individuals connected to ACORN have been convicted of election fraud and related offenses. The Executive Office for United States Attorneys (EOUSA) and FBI opened six investigations of ACORN from 2005 through 2009. Four of the probes were closed for lack of evidence. One case in 2008 was referred to U.S. attorneys who closed the investigation because there were criminal charges pending in a state. One case in 2009 was referred to U.S. attorneys who in turn referred the case to a local district attorney. (See Table of ACORN Election Fraud Convictions below.)

TABLE OF ACORN ELECTION FRAUD CONVICTIONS

Individual (surname first)	state	connection to ACORN	case description	status of case
Baird, Valensia Kaye	AR	Project Vote contractor	VRF	convicted 1998
Cason, Kym Michelle	CO	See Note 1	VRF	convicted 2005
Herrera, Lloyd "Frosty"	CO	See Note 2	VRF	convicted 2004
Mora, Monique	CO	ACORN employee	VRF	convicted 2005
Page, Pelonne	CO	ACORN employee	VRF	convicted 2005
Childress, Maurice	FL	ACORN employee	VRF	convicted 2010
John, Kashawn	FL	ACORN employee	VRF	convicted 2010
Rhodes, Liltovia	FL	ACORN employee	VRF	convicted 2010
Torres, Carlos	FL	ACORN employee	VRF	convicted 2010

Williams, Evangeline	FL	ACORN employee	VRF	convicted 2010
Williams, Lilkevia	FL	ACORN employee	VRF	convicted 2010
Williams, Richard	FL	ACORN employee	VRF	convicted 2010
Johnson, Antonio	MI	ACORN employee	VRF	convicted 2008
Reed, Joshua	MN	ACORN employee	VRF	convicted 2004
Bland, Brian	MO	ACORN employee	VRF	convicted 2008
Cheeks, Bobbie Jean	MO	ACORN employee	VRF	convicted 2008
Cowan, Cortez	MO	ACORN employee	VRF	convicted 2008
Davis, Carmen R. a.k.a. Latisha Reed	MO	ACORN employee	VRF	convicted 2007
Franklin, Dale D.	MO	ACORN employee	VRF	convicted 2007
Gardner, Brian	MO	ACORN employee	VRF	convicted 2007
Gibson, Golden	MO	ACORN employee	VRF	convicted 2008
Humphrey, Deidra	MO	ACORN employee	VRF	convicted 2009
Reliford, Anthony M.	MO	ACORN employee	VRF	convicted 2008
Smith, Radonna Marie	MO	ACORN employee	VRF	convicted 2008
Stenson, Kwaim A.	MO	ACORN employee	VRF	convicted 2007
Williams, Kenneth Demond	MO	ACORN employee	VRF	convicted 2008
Williams, Tyaira L. a.k.a. "Tootsie Roll"	MO	ACORN employee	VRF	convicted 2008
Busefink, Amy	NV	ACORN employee	VRF	convicted 2010
Edwards, Christopher	NV	ACORN employee	VRF	convicted 2009
Dooley, Kevin Eugene	OH	ACORN employee	VRF	convicted 2004
Gilbert, Claudel	OH	See Note 3	VF	convicted 2007
Nash, Darnell	OH	See Note 4	VF	convicted 2009
Barksdale, Jemar	PA	ACORN employee	VRF	convicted 2008
Brown, Richard W.	PA	ACORN employee	VRF	convicted 2008
Givner, Alexis M.	PA	ACORN employee	VRF	convicted 2010
Godfrey, Wendy	PA	ACORN employee	VRF	convicted 2008
Grisom, Mario	PA	ACORN employee	VRF	convicted 2010
Jones, Eric L.	PA	ACORN employee	VRF	convicted 2010
Kinney, Latasha Leann	PA	ACORN employee	VRF	convicted 2010
Torres-Serrano, Luis	PA	ACORN employee	VRF	convicted 2009
Greene, Robert Edward	WA	ACORN employee	VRF	convicted 2007
Johnson, Tina	WA	ACORN employee	VRF	convicted 2007
Mitchell, Clifton	WA	ACORN employee	VRF	convicted 2007
Olson, Ryan	WA	ACORN employee	VRF	convicted 2007
Thill, Kendra Lynn	WA	ACORN employee	VRF	convicted 2010
Woods, Jayson	WA	ACORN employee	VRF	convicted 2007
Adams, Endalyn	WI	ACORN employee	VRF	convicted 2009

Blakely, Robert M.	WI	Project Vote employee	VRF	convicted 2005
Clancy, Kevin L.	WI	ACORN employee	VRF	convicted 2010
Lewis, Latoya	WI	ACORN employee	VRF	convicted 2009
Lewis, Marcus L.	WI	Project Vote employee	VRF	convicted 2005
Lilly, Urelene	WI	Project Vote employee	VRF	convicted 2006
Miles, Maria L.	WI	ACORN employee	VRF	convicted 2010
Walton, Frank Edmund	WI	See Note 5	VRF	convicted 2010

Sources: FBI; media reports; news releases on prosecutors' websites; interviews with officials in the offices of the Michigan and Wisconsin attorneys general and with officials in prosecutors' offices in Cleveland, Denver, Miami, and Seattle.

The crime of voter registration fraud is a blanket term covering various frauds committed in the voter registration process. It includes but is not limited to falsification, forgery, uttering a forged document, perjury, misconduct in public office, identity theft, multiple registrations, mail fraud, and inducing others to commit fraud.

VRF = voter registration fraud
VF = voter fraud (balloting)

(1) girlfriend of ACORN employee
(2) filled out forms for ACORN employees Pelonne Page and Monique Mora
(3) registered to vote in 2 counties by ACORN
(4) registered to vote 9 times by ACORN
(5) claims to have become ACORN employee shortly after fraud occurred

- Sen. Amy Klobuchar (D-MN) successfully prosecuted Joshua Reed for voter registration fraud in 2004 when she was the prosecutor in Hennepin County, Minn. "It was very important for the public integrity of our electoral system that somebody, if they do something like this, gets charged, gets convicted and gets consequences," she said. Reed was found with 323 completed cards that he failed to file with the Minnesota secretary of state's office. State law requires that the cards, which were weeks or months old, be filed within 10 days. "I just got lazy and kept them in the back of my car," Reed said.[663]

- In Berks County, PA, Wendy Godfrey helped ACORN voter registrar Richard W. Brown create fraudulent voter registration forms. Godfrey was convicted of tampering with public records. Brown was convicted of making 29 fake forms. Her sentence was 23 days to one year in the county jail; his sentence was 146 days to 23 months.[664]

- Clifton Mitchell played a role in registering close to 2,000 nonexistent voters for ACORN. He was convicted of voter registration fraud in 2007 and served almost three months in prison. "I needed money; I had to support my family and I was new to the area," he said. ACORN threatened to shut down the local office if Mitchell's team failed to register 13 to 20 voters every day. "We came up with the idea: Let's make fraudulent cards. I tell my crew, 'I don't care how you get 'em, just get 'em,'" he said. Washington Secretary of State Sam Reed called it "the worst case of voter registration fraud in the history of the state of Washington.[665] Prosecutor Dan Satterberg got ACORN to agree to reimburse authorities $25,000 for the cost of the investigation and improve employee oversight, which he described as "lax." Of the 1,805 names filed by ACORN in the 2006 election cycle, more than 97 percent were thrown out.[666]

- ACORN's Pittsburgh operation was especially fraud-ridden. Employees said they faced termination if they failed to meet voter registration quotas. "We did it the way they trained us," said Mario Wyatt Grisom. "Know what I'm saying? So why are we getting picked up, when it should be the people that's above us getting picked up? We only did what they asked us to do." In court, a voter testified he received a voter registration card for his wife even though she died almost two years earlier. A county elections official said she filled out a card but didn't sign it or provide her Social Security number on it because she'd heard ACORN employees sometimes illegally insert missing information. "I just wanted to see if they'd put a forgery on it," Denise Halliburton testified. After ACORN filed the card it bore a fake signature and made-up Social Security number.[667]

- Washington state ACORN voter registration canvassers Ryan Olson, Tina Johnson, and Jayson Woods were convicted in 2007 of two counts, eight counts, and eight counts of voter registration fraud, respectively.[668] King County, WA., removed 1,762 names from voter rolls.[669]

HIRING CRIMINALS FOR VOTER REGISTRATION

Just got out of prison? Need a job? Call ACORN. No background checks required. ACORN and Project Vote don't care if you're honest or a criminal. If you can fill out a form, honestly or dishonestly, you've got the job registering voters.

TV station KRQE in Albuquerque, NM, reported in 2008 that ACORN hired a slew of criminals for its voter drives. They included: Jeffrey Mahaffey, a habitual offender who was convicted of two counts of raping a minor and one count of stealing a car; Yvonne Chacon, convicted of two counts of forgery; Michelle Rael, while under supervision of probation and parole authorities for three counts of possession of a controlled substance and one count of identity theft; and Vernon Saltwater, who was convicted of two counts of attempting to commit a fourth-degree felony. Other ACORN canvassers had serious criminal charges pending against them while they worked for ACORN. They included: Rudolph Serrano, who was charged with car theft, burglary, and two counts of credit card fraud; and Desiree Gabaldon, who was charged with nine counts of credit card fraud, burglary, and shoplifting.[670]

In Pittsburgh, ACORN hired a man in 2008 even after he filed fraudulent registrations in a previous election.[671] In Detroit, Antonio Johnson, who was hired by ACORN just after getting out of prison for drunk driving, was convicted on three counts of submitting fraudulent registrations. Johnson said he received two hours of training from ACORN. In 2009, he was sentenced to three years probation.[672]

Deidra Humphrey of East St. Louis, Ill., who registered voters for ACORN and the Missouri Progressive Vote Coalition (ProVote), submitted fraudulent cards. She was convicted of mail fraud. Humphrey was sentenced in 2009, to three years probation and fined $100, the FBI confirmed. "There's never been any voter impersonation fraud," said ACORN's Jeff Ordower. "The system works. People do not end up voting fraudulently."[673]

In Arizona, Project Vote illegally hired a convict on work release to do voter registration work. The felon signed up as many as 12 convicts, some of whom registered repeatedly. One registered up to 15 times.[674]

In Florida, consultant Joe Johnson stopped working with ACORN because he was concerned the group was not submitting complete voter registration cards to election officials.[675] In that state, ACORN hired convicted armed robber Mac Stuart in 2003 as a petition signature gatherer, apparently without checking his background. Stuart rose up the ranks quickly and was put in charge of the Miami voter registration drive.[676]

DID ACORN GIVE US *SENATOR* AL FRANKEN?

Joseph Stalin once remarked, "The people who cast the votes decide nothing. The people who count the votes decide everything."

In the months following the November 2008 election, an outspoken ACORN ally presided over the tallying of votes in the Minnesota

Senate race. The fact that ACORN-backed Mark Ritchie, a Democrat and former community organizer, largely controlled the electoral process in the Land of 10,000 Lakes may have been decisive.

Was it coincidence that incumbent Republican Norm Coleman's lead over ACORN-endorsed Democrat Al Franken kept dwindling as the votes were counted over and over and over again? The morning after the election, Coleman led Franken by 725 votes. As the ACORN-endorsed secretary of state Mark Ritchie presided over the process, over the next five days, Coleman's lead had dwindled to just 221. Election officials claimed they had to correct typos on vote tally sheets and that these corrections gave Franken 435 votes and took 69 away from Coleman. In the end, somehow Franken was declared the winner by 312 votes.

To list every single known irregularity might require a separate book, but suffice it to say, there were plenty of them. To provide an overview, let's recount what went on early in the counting process, while a national audience was still paying somewhat close attention to the election. Ballots were discovered in an election judge's car and other votes appeared as if by magic across the state. One county discovered 100 new votes for Franken and blamed a clerical error. Another had vote tallies 177 higher than the total recorded on Election Day. Another county reported 133 fewer votes than its voting machines recorded. Almost every time new ballots materialized, or tallies were updated or corrected, Franken benefited.

Research performed by John Lott, senior research scientist at the University of Maryland, who exhaustively documented the countless logic-defying decisions used by officials during the original count and the recount process, threw light on many of the irregularities. Lott said this massive vote-switch was if not statistically impossible, highly improbable. He wrote that in Minnesota, "corrections were posted in other races, but they were only a fraction of those for the Senate." Franken's Senate vote gains were "2.5 times the gain for Obama in the presidential race count, 2.9 times the total gain that Democrats got across all Minnesota congressional races, and 5 times the net loss that Democrats suffered for all state House races."

Lott noted a few days after the election that almost all of Franken's new votes came from three out of the state's 4,130 precincts, and nearly half of the new 246 Franken votes came from one heavily Democratic precinct in Two Harbors. This is suspicious because "[n]one of the other races had any changes in their vote totals in that precinct."[677]

Most media reports at the time left out Ritchie's extensive ties to ACORN. In 2006, the Minnesota ACORN Political Action Committee endorsed Ritchie and donated to his campaign. According to the Minnesota Campaign Finance and Public Disclosure Board, contributors to Ritchie's campaign included liberal philanthropists George Soros, Drummond Pike, and Deborah Rappaport, along with veteran community organizer Heather Booth, who co-founded the Midwest Academy, a school for radical community organizers. One article on Ritchie's 2006 campaign website bragged about the fine work ACORN did in Florida to pass a constitutional amendment to raise that state's minimum wage.

Ritchie, who defeated two-term incumbent Republican Mary Kiffmeyer in 2006, received an endorsement and financial assistance for his run from the Secretary of State Project, a below-the-radar nonfederal "527" pressure group.

The founders of the Secretary of State Project, which claims to advance "election protection" but only backs Democrats, religiously believe that right-leaning secretaries of state helped the GOP steal the presidential elections in Florida in 2000 (Katherine Harris) and in Ohio in 2004 (Ken Blackwell). The secretary of state candidates the group endorses sing the same familiar song about electoral integrity issues: Voter fraud is largely a myth, "vote suppression" is used widely by Republicans, cleansing the dead and fictional characters from voter rolls should be avoided until embarrassing media reports emerge, and anyone who demands that a voter produce photo identification before pulling the lever is a racist, democracy-hating Fascist.

The group was co-founded in July 2006 by MoveOn veteran James Rucker. "Any serious commitment to wrestling control of the country from the Republican Party must include removing their political operatives from deciding who can vote and whose votes will count," said another co-founder, Becky Bond, to the *San Francisco Chronicle* in 2006. Its website claims, "A modest political investment in electing clean candidates to critical Secretary of State offices is an efficient way to protect the election." Political observers know that a relatively small amount of money can help swing a little-watched race for a state office few people understand or care about.

The strategic targeting of the SoS Project yielded impressive results in 2008 and 2006. In 2008, SoS Project-backed Democrats Linda McCulloch (Montana), Natalie Tennant (West Virginia), Robin Carnahan (Missouri), and Kate Brown (Oregon) won their races. Only Carnahan was an incumbent. The Center for Public Integrity reported in September 2008 that the group had raised a mere $280,000 for the 2008 election cycle. Talk about return on investment!

In 2006, along with Minnesota's Ritchie, SoS Project-endorsed Jennifer Brunner (Ohio), who in 2008 defied federal law by refusing to take steps to verify 200,000 questionable voter registrations, trounced her opponent, 55 percent to 41 percent. Democrats supported by the group also won that year in New Mexico, Nevada, and Iowa. The group claims it spent about $500,000 in that election cycle.

It was revealed during a panel discussion at the Democratic Party's 2008 convention in Denver that the Democracy Alliance, a financial clearinghouse created by Soros and insurance magnate Peter B. Lewis, approved the Secretary of State Project as a grantee. The Democracy Alliance aspires to create a permanent political infrastructure of nonprofits, think tanks, media outlets, leadership schools, and activist groups—a kind of "vast left-wing conspiracy" to compete with the conservative movement. It has brokered well over $100 million in grants to left-wing groups including ACORN. Pike and Rappaport, who gave money to Ritchie's campaign, are members of the Democracy Alliance. According to IRS 8872 disclosure forms, the Secretary of State Project received donations from Democracy Alliance members including Soros, Rob Stein, Gail Furman, and Susie Tompkins Buell.[678]

A conservative watchdog group, Minnesota Majority, claims felons' illegally cast votes may have put Franken over the top in the Senate race. Over 18 months, the group analyzed state data and found "evidence that hundreds of ineligible felons may have voted [in] the 2008 General Election."[679] Minnesota Majority believes at least 341 felons voted in Minnesota in the 2008 election, which is 29 more votes than Franken's final margin of victory. Even if the group is correct about the felons voting, there is no way to know how the felons actually voted. Nonetheless, the fact that they did raises questions about the legitimacy of Franken's victory.

"ACORN-endorsed Franken no doubt benefited from the 43,000 new voters that ACORN and its affiliates claimed to have registered in Minnesota before the election," said Peter Flaherty, president of the National Legal and Policy Center. "Even assuming only half of these people voted, and the level of fraud was only 2 percent, it is likely Franken would have lost. Of course, ACORN voter registration fraud rates have been shown to be exponentially higher." Minnesota Gov. Tim Pawlenty, a Republican who may run for president in 2012, said the fraud allegations were credible. "There's a serious allegation to that effect and if it turns out to be true, it's quite possible," he told Fox News.[680]

It's unclear if ACORN had anything to do with any felons voting in Minnesota, but ACORN strongly favors felons voting. You might even say that because ACORN aspires to smash the American system felons are the group's natural constituency.

In 2009, left-wing lawmakers Sen. Russ Feingold (D-WI) and ACORN ally Rep. John Conyers (D-MI) introduced the proposed "Democracy Restoration Act," which would have overruled states and given the right to vote in federal elections to felons who have completed their sentences. The proposal was previously a pet project of ACORN, long a supporter of felon voting rights, according to Aaron Klein of World Net Daily.[681]

Weather Underground member Linda Evans is an avid supporter of giving felons voting rights in national elections. Evans was arrested with 740 pounds of explosives she admitted were to be used to bomb

U.S. government buildings. She served 15 years of a 40-year sentence but was pardoned by President Clinton in his final days in office, reportedly on the recommendation of President Obama's attorney general, Eric Holder.

Evans, co-director of a San-Francisco-based nonprofit called All of Us or None that seeks to organize prisoners, ex-prisoners, and felons, promoted the plan to give felons national voting rights alongside ACORN. All of Us or None and ACORN worked together on many voter registration efforts including one in August 2008 in which voter information was distributed in visitor lines at San Diego Central Jail. Evans received a Soros Justice Fellowship.[682]

[FOURTEEN]

Scandal Upon Scandal: ACORN's Self-Destruction

DALE RATHKE, YOUNGER brother of ACORN founder Wade Rathke, is a Princeton graduate "brilliant with electronics and numbers."[683] That must be why he was chosen to run ACORN's mafia-like financial affairs.

Rathke used his penetrating intellect to steal a bit over $948,000 from ACORN in 1999 and 2000. It appears he had a lot of fun with the money, some of which came from pension funds. He ran up $157,000 in American Express charges that he couldn't repay when his embezzlement was first discovered. The credit card company sued Rathke in 2003 in Louisiana. Court documents show he was a big spender who enjoyed shopping at luxury stores, riding in limousines, and visiting five-star hotels and restaurants. He used various credit cards to shop at Gucci and Neiman Marcus. He visited New York and shelled out $700 for a fancy meal at La Cote Basque and $2,000 to stay at the Waldorf-Astoria.[684]

A regular in New Orleans social circles, Rathke's name appears in the society pages of the New Orleans *Times-Picayune* on no fewer than 67 occasions from 1996 through 2008 according to a Nexis search.

Not long after Rathke stole from his employer, his big brother discovered the shortfall in ACORN's bank accounts. It is unclear what Wade said to Dale about his behavior. Wade was less interested in the embezzlement than in the damage news of it could do to the organization he'd built up from nothing over three decades. He did what so many political animals do when faced with similar situations: he covered up. And he couldn't even bring himself to fire his thieving spendthrift of a sibling.

Dale remained on the ACORN payroll until spring of 2008. The missing money was disguised as a loan to an officer on the books of the mysterious CCI. The Rathke family signed a restitution agreement with ACORN, promising to repay the amount stolen at the rate of $30,000 per year. They reportedly repaid $210,000 as of 2008 when the embezzlement was made public. When the *New York Times* reported the embezzlement, Wade's close friend Drummond Pike, founder and CEO of the radical Tides Foundation, stepped in and secretly bought up the remaining debt of $738,000. Pike bought the promissory note to protect the identities of his wealthy donors who would prefer to keep their extreme political views hidden from the public. Even though senior ACORN officials signed confidentiality agreements forbidding them from disclosing the identity of the buyer, someone in the group leaked the information to the media.

"Decisions were made to protect the organization," Wade Rathke told Megyn Kelly of Fox News in 2009. "It's not like the organization doesn't have a phalanx of enemies out there, and had so 10 years ago as well." Rathke said he didn't turn Dale in to authorities because "management made a decision that between restitution and retribution, that restitution was more in the interest of the organization, and that decision was unanimous."[685] The upper echelons of ACORN management held their tongues for years.

In 2008, ACORN's national board finally learned about the missing money for the first time. Board members were furious that they had been kept in the dark for eight years. They grilled the senior leaders in the ACORN Staff Management Council who served in 2000 and were presumably aware of the embezzlement for years.

Minutes identify the members of the council as executive director Steve Kest, field director Helene O'Brien, and Project Vote head Zach Polett. There is no indication in the minutes of what the three said. Inside ACORN sources suspect that the media was alerted to the embezzlement by the Needmor Fund, an ACORN donor organization that was justifiably concerned about its social justice investment.

At that time, many ACORN members, including board members, began to realize many of the terrible things the group's critics were saying about ACORN were actually true. They were dejected.

At the June 20, 2008, board meeting in Detroit, the board officially fired Wade Rathke as ACORN's chief organizer, or CEO. On a vote of 29 to 14 the board approved a motion that Rathke "shall immediately and permanently be terminated from all employment with ACORN and its affiliated organizations or corporations. Further more [sic], Mr. Rathke should be removed from all boards & any leadership roles within ACORN or its affiliated organizations or corporations."[686]

The board's minutes suggest it was a grueling, painful meeting filled with in-depth discussions of ACORN's arcane organizational structure, accounting system, and newly wary donors. It got underway at 6:25 p.m. The discussion about what to do about Rathke didn't start until 11:00 p.m. The minutes say Rathke gave a PowerPoint presentation on the "attacks this organization has endured." He said "he never misused funds," and "that this wasn't a coverup."

Rathke, who claims he resigned voluntarily, said he only decided "to step aside after someone went to the funders." He added "that one can always look back in hindsight and see where things could have been handled differently, but that he and the Staff Management Council thought that was a reasonable decision at that time."

The board elected new members to its Interim Staff Management (ISM) committee. Marcel Reid of Washington, D.C., was selected to examine ACORN's organizational structure. Karen Inman of Minnesota, a lawyer by training, was supposed to look into legal matters. Carol Hemingway of Pennsylvania was responsible for financial issues.

DON'T MESS WITH BOSS BERTHA

Reid and Inman thought they were supposed to investigate ACORN's shortcomings, and asked to see various documents related to the embezzlement. They ran into a steel girder-reinforced brick wall in the person of Bertha Lewis, the head of the New York chapter who replaced Rathke as national chief organizer. Lewis, a scrappy, profane former actress who used to be a squatter, gave them nothing. Reid and Inman filed suit in ACORN's name in order to find out all the details of the financial scandal. This infuriated Lewis who said the two board members lacked legal standing to sue on the board's behalf. Lewis also said the civil suit had distracted the group from answering "Republican right-wing attacks" on ACORN voter registration, which became especially intense in 2008. She branded Reid and Inman traitors and threw them off the national board in the fall. That's how ACORN's elite deal with dissent.

The whistleblowers co-founded a reform group called ACORN 8. They said they still believed in the mission of ACORN but thought the group had become corrupt, even criminal. Talk show host Glenn Beck became intensely interested in ACORN and had Reid on his Fox News TV show repeatedly in 2009. He likened her to civil rights activist Rosa Parks, a comparison that makes the soft-spoken Reid blush.

ACORN tried to intimidate Reid's group into silence. In June 2009, ACORN legal thug Arthur Z. Schwartz sent a "cease and desist" letter to Inman and Reid. Schwartz accused the group of violating ACORN's intellectual property by using the word "ACORN" in its name. It was very lame and in the end it was a bluff; ACORN didn't follow through.[687] Around the same time, ACORN affiliate Project Vote sued former employee Anita MonCrief to shut her up. MonCrief previously admitted she made unauthorized purchases on an ACORN credit card but said that fact didn't mean her public statements about ACORN's corruption were false. How do we know it was an intimidation suit? In part because it took Project Vote 17 months after firing MonCrief to file suit against her. ACORN was also upset that she testified against ACORN and Project Vote in a Pennsylvania election fraud case in October 2008.[688] MonCrief countersued Project Vote for abuse of process and added ACORN as a party. Project Vote and ACORN dropped the case in March 2010 and settled out of court. No money changed hands.

News of the embezzlement couldn't have come at a worse time for ACORN. Unlike in past election cycles, suddenly the public was interested in this strange profession known as community organizing. The fact that Barack Obama, a former community organizer who had worked for ACORN's Project Vote affiliate, was the Democrats' presidential candidate, threw a spotlight on ACORN like never before. Thanks to a constellation of conservative talk radio hosts such as Glenn Beck, Rush Limbaugh, Mark Levin, Sean Hannity, Laura Ingraham, G. Gordon Liddy, and Michael Savage, the 2008 campaign cycle served as a massive consciousness-raising exercise for Americans. They learned about the criminal corruption and extortion rackets run by ACORN, the harsh tactics of Saul Alinsky, and the subversive plots of Richard Cloward and Frances Fox Piven.

ACORN'S CATHOLIC GUARDIAN

After the embezzlement became public in summer 2008, a steady stream of donors skedaddled. One of the biggest donors to dump ACORN was the Alinsky-inspired Catholic Campaign for Human Development (CCHD), a radical charity that shares ACORN's small-c communist beliefs.

Every Thanksgiving, American Catholics donate to CCHD. A lot of money is at stake—some $7 million annually—and so it only made sense when CCHD announced in November 2008 it would stop giving money to the controversial community organizer group ACORN. There was a real likelihood that some of the $7.3 million that CCHD had given to ACORN over the previous decade had been badly misspent. Bishop Roger Morin of Biloxi, Mississippi, announced that ACORN would no longer receive grants "because of serious concerns about financial accountability, organizational performance and political partisanship."

In damage control mode, Morin said at the time that CCHD and the Bishops' Conference had hired forensic accountants "to help determine if any CCHD money was taken or misused." It's unclear if that audit was ever completed. This writer has asked for it repeatedly but CCHD has never handed it over.

It must have been excruciating for CCHD to excommunicate ACORN, its own flesh and blood in the class struggle. It must have been especially painful for Morin, an old social justice stalwart who had been an auxiliary bishop in ACORN's hometown of New Orleans. Morin was at one time a member of the two relevant committees of the United States Conference of Catholic Bishops (on "Domestic Justice and Human Development" and "National Collections") and chairman of the subcommittee that oversaw CCHD and, at a distance, ACORN.

President Obama's association with CCHD began years before he ran a voter drive for ACORN's Project Vote that helped get then-Sen. Carol Moseley Braun (D-IL) elected. From 1985 to 1988 he ran the Developing Communities Project from an office in Chicago's Holy Rosary Church. "I got my start as a community organizer working with mostly Catholic parishes on the South Side of Chicago that were struggling because the steel plants had closed," Obama told *Catholic Digest*. CCHD "helped fund the project, and so very early on, my career was intertwined with the belief in social justice that is so strong in the Church." Obama has said he "tried to apply the precepts of compassion and care for the vulnerable that are so central to Catholic teachings to my work [such as in] making health care a right for all Americans."

CCHD has problems of its own going back all the way to its inception. Created in 1969—a year before ACORN launched—CCHD is not a charity the way people ordinarily use the term. It doesn't help the poor. It seems to take Jesus's admonition in the Book of Matthew, "The poor you will always have with you," as a command to ignore the poor. Most Catholics are unaware that CCHD was created to feed and foster radical groups like ACORN even though CCHD isn't exactly keeping its goals secret. Its website declares CCHD's purpose is to support "organized groups of white and minority poor to develop economic strength and political power."

CCHD claims to have given more than $290 million not to help the poor, though some observers say the grand total not given to help the poor is closer to $450 million. Its website brags that the money went to fund more than 8,000 "low-income-led, community-based projects that strengthen families, create jobs, build affordable housing, fight crime, and improve schools and neighborhoods."

CCHD director Ralph McCloud admitted some of the funds CCHD "contributed to ACORN in the past undoubtedly were used for voter registration drives." Even worse, most, perhaps all, of the voter drives ACORN conducted were "in support of politicians who support abortion-on-demand and other policies that most Catholics oppose," notes conservative Catholic activist Richard Viguerie. CCHD somehow failed to notice until 2008 that ACORN had been in the election fraud business for decades.

As Helene Slessarev, professor of urban ministries at the Claremont School of Theology has written, marginalized, angry, alienated people susceptible to social justice indoctrination aren't exactly hard to find in the nation's pews. Once identified, they can be recruited. Alinsky the calculating atheist understood this. In his Chicago organizing days, he was always eager to forge alliances with religious leaders—including Catholic priests.

The point has not been lost on CCHD (and ACORN) that churches hold vast untapped reservoirs of disgruntled people. Nor has it been lost on ACORN's Catholic-friendly brethren in the world of left-wing community organizing. There are so many of them and regardless of what happens to ACORN, they're not going away anytime soon.

CCHD continues to fund a long list of ACORN-like organizations filling the space that ACORN once occupied. Among them are the Industrial Areas Foundation (IAF), which was founded by Alinsky himself. Like Alinsky, IAF is relentless in its determination to create villains to serve as straw men it can then attack. IAF is the mother of all community organizing networks with dozens of affiliates nationwide and overseas. Alinsky referred to IAF's training institute as a "school for professional radicals." Its model for organizing church congregations into powerful advocacy groups is widely imitated.

Another CCHD grantee is the Midwest Academy, founded by Heather and Paul Booth. IAF trained Alinskyite organizer and SDSer Heather Booth is the founder of a number of activist training academies, including the Midwest Academy, Citizen Action and USAction. Her husband is Paul Booth, a founder and former national secretary of SDS, now an aide to Gerald McEntee, president of the powerful public sector union AFSCME.

CCHD funds People Improving Communities Through Organizing (PICO), which was founded in 1972 by Father John Baumann, a Jesuit priest trained in Alinsky's techniques. The training school and activist group claims to have 53 affiliates in 17 states. The group's mission as trying to "increase access to health care, improve public schools, make neighborhoods safer, build affordable housing, redevelop communities, and revitalize democracy."

Direct Action and Research Training Institute (DART), created in 1982, receives money from CCHD. It boasts 20 locally affiliated organizations in six states and claims to have trained more than 10,000 community leaders and 150 professional community organizers. It focuses on congregation-based community organizing.

CCHD also funds Gamaliel Foundation, founded in 1968 in Chicago. Gamaliel says its mission is "to be a powerful network of grassroots, interfaith, interracial, multi-issue organizations working together to create a more just and more democratic society." Its executive director is Gregory Galluzzo, a former Jesuit priest. Gamaliel claims 60 affiliates in 21 states, as well as affiliates in the United Kingdom and South Africa. The group claims to represent more than one million people and brags on its website about its connection to President Obama.

Former Gamaliel organizer Rey Lopez-Calderon said the group had "a strange and warped culture." Lopez-Calderon said Gamaliel "actually used the word *ruthless*." Gamaliel leaders said "if people are getting in the way of what you want to achieve as an organizer, you should be willing to push those people out of the way."[689]

PARTING WASN'T SWEET SORROW
FOR REP. DONNA EDWARDS

"Some day, and that day may never come, I will call upon you to do a service for me," said the Don Corleone character in "The Godfather," a movie released in 1972, two years after ACORN was formed. That day came for Congresswoman Donna Edwards (D-MD) in 2008.

The leaders of ACORN thought they owned Edwards. ACORN's political action committee endorsed Edwards enthusiastically in 2006 and 2008. ACORN's CSI affiliate handled her get-out-the-vote effort in 2006. The campaign paid CSI $204,746.[690]

"They felt like they had won the [2008] election for her and they wanted to collect," a highly placed ACORN source said in an interview. Edwards is a veteran community organizer. When she worked as executive director of the Arca Foundation, it gave ACORN $400,000.[691] Funders tend to be more business-like than the activists they finance. They shrink away from financial scandals.

So it shouldn't have been a surprise when Edwards tried to distance herself from ACORN after news of the embezzlement broke. But ACORN wouldn't take no for an answer.

ACORN executive director Steve Kest and Project Vote head Zach Polett cornered Edwards at a summertime fundraiser for her campaign. They were so aggressive and so persistent that Edwards told friends the two were "stalking" her. Edwards threatened to obtain a restraining order to keep the ACORN vultures at bay, the source said.

When asked about the incident, a shocked expression came over Polett's face. He played dumb, claiming he knew nothing about it.[692] Initially Edwards seemed receptive to an interview, smiling and showing courtesy, but when asked about the incident at a left-wing conference, she abruptly turned away without saying a word. She ignored the question when it was repeated and continued walking away.[693]

ACORN felt so invested in Edwards because it went all out to get her elected, the source said. During the 2008 campaign, Mitch Klein, former head organizer for Maryland ACORN, was "throwing money up in the air like a one-armed piano player."

Edwards's Democratic opponent, incumbent congressman Albert Wynn, a decreasingly liberal congressman who had grown increasingly cozy with business interests and Republicans in his final years in the House, grew enraged at the aggressive insurgent campaign ACORN was waging against him. "There seems to be a vast, dare I say, left-wing conspiracy designed to circumvent campaign finance laws," Wynn said. "I think the main thing is, the public needs to know this is a not a person with a halo over her head, as she has tried to portray."[694]

Wynn's campaign manager, Lori Sherwood, retaliated against the Edwards campaign by filing a complaint against it with the Federal Election Commission. Tellingly, Sherwood also named ACORN and four of its affiliates in the complaint—CCI, CSI, Communities Voting Together, and SEIU Local 100. Obama White House political director Patrick Gaspard in his capacity as treasurer of the 1199 SEIU Federal Political Action Fund, was also included as a respondent. The complaint was eventually dismissed.[695]

Then-SEIU 1199 executive Patrick Gaspard hailed Edwards. "Donna Edwards is, for us, the prototype of what a new Democrat in the new Democratic majority in Congress ought to look and sound like." Hard-left journalist Katrina vanden Heuvel sounded a similar note, praising Edwards as a progressive champion who would help push the Democratic Party even farther to port. Her contest against Wynn was viewed by some as "a bellwhether contest in the fight for the soul of the Democratic Party," she wrote.[696]

Until the embezzlement news arrived, the love affair between ACORN and Edwards was mutual. Edwards had been attending ACORN events since at least 2006. Her stump speech was that after her divorce, she was poor and started to understand the plight of the poor and wanted to work to help them. She saw ACORN as the Rolls Royce of these poor people's organizations.

A few months before breaking with ACORN, Edwards appeared in an ACORN promotional video singing the group's praises. "ACORN organizes low-income workers and there are just so few avenues for people who are some of the most vulnerable people in our communities to have a real voice in policy and a real voice in organizing and I think that's what makes ACORN really special."[697]

JOHN CONYERS GETS LEANED ON

For a few weeks in early 2009 it seemed like longtime ACORN ally House Judiciary Committee chairman John Conyers (D-MI) was preparing to throw ACORN under the bus.

During a congressional hearing, Conyers heard testimony from Heather Heidelbaugh, a member of the Republican National Lawyers Association, who accused ACORN of mafia-style behavior. The allegations against ACORN were "a pretty serious matter," said Conyers. "I think that it would be something that would be worth our time," he said. "I think in all fairness we ought to really examine it." Conyers's newfound determination immediately put him at odds with the chairman of the subcommittee holding the hearing that day, Rep. Jerrold Nadler (D-NY), another longtime ACORN ally. Nadler, who has run on the Working Families Party line, was dismissive, saying not enough "credible evidence" existed to justify holding a hearing on ACORN alone.[698]

It was startling that someone like Conyers, who is very sympathetic to ACORN's policy goals and who has defended the group in the past, was now suddenly considering examining the many wrongdoings of ACORN. Conyers received a 100% rating from ACORN in its 2006 legislative scorecard. Just five months before, Conyers called ACORN "a longstanding and well regarded organization that fights for the poor and working class."[699]

While Conyers was mulling over whether to probe ACORN, John Podesta's Center for American Progress Action Fund invited several left-wing groups to a meeting May 28, 2009, to discuss how to use rhetorical misdirection to take the focus off ACORN's increasingly well-publicized corruption. The crisis management session was titled "Reframing the Attack on Voter Registration."

Two weeks after the hearing, Conyers confirmed that he would "probably" convene his own hearing on ACORN. "That's our jurisdiction, the Justice Department. That's what we handle—voter fraud. Unless that's been taken out of my jurisdiction and I didn't know it."

But by May, Conyers caved in to behind-the-scenes pressure. After teasing good government advocates for a month and a half, Conyers reversed himself saying an ACORN hearing wasn't justified. When asked to explain his decision the next month, the congressman said simply, "The powers that be decided against it." He refused to elaborate. His spokesman Jonathan Godfrey later said Conyers was referring to *himself* as "the powers that be."[700]

Unless you believe "the powers that be" is a newfangled variation of the editorial "we," it's clear Conyers wasn't referring to himself and that somebody "got" to him.

VIDEO SAGA

ACORN had no idea it would sign its own death warrant in 2009.

For all the group's hyperventilating about *eeevil* corporations, ACORN was taken down by two young, self-funded conservative activists, not by one of the group's many corporate victims. Never in its wildest dreams could ACORN's leadership have imagined that hidden camera videos—an approach more often used against badly behaving businesses—would be the group's undoing. ACORN thought it was untouchable.

In fall of 2009, those undercover videos surfaced in which ACORN's employees counseled conservative activists posing as a pimp and a prostitute on how to set up a house of ill repute using tax dollars. Videos showed ACORN officials advising the pretend prostitute and her procurer about how to obtain taxpayer funds under false pretenses, launder money, commit tax fraud, smuggle illegal aliens into the country, and facilitate child prostitution.

In the videos, James O'Keefe III played the pimp; Hannah Giles portrayed the prostitute. O'Keefe met Giles in 2009, some time before the sting operation began. Giles approached him through Facebook, the online social networking website, and pitched the proposal.

Giles liked a Planned Parenthood sting O'Keefe carried out and wrote a column about on Townhall.com in fall 2008. O'Keefe had called the abortion rights group on the telephone, posing as a racist who wanted to donate money specifically to abort black babies. Planned Parenthood development officials responded warmly to O'Keefe's offer of funds. When the recordings were made public the group received an avalanche of bad publicity. The project "only confirmed the evidence [that] Planned Parenthood's eugenic ideology is consistent with the agenda of their founder, Margaret Sanger," Giles quoted O'Keefe saying. Giles expressed her admiration for O'Keefe, whose status quo-challenging investigative videos have been periodically banned by YouTube. Describing him as "full of prospects and dreams," she wrote, "O'Keefe takes no prisoners and calls things as they are."[701]

"I didn't go into it as an experiment to see if ACORN would go for it," O'Keefe said in an interview. "I got into it because Hannah had a really creative idea and I had the ability and the know-how to make it happen. The motives, I don't think, matter because what we found is so outlandish, so shocking."

"No one gave us any money," O'Keefe said. "It cost $1,500 to do and Hannah paid for her own plane ticket to California. I couldn't find someone to fund it. We paid for it independently. That's what made it such a big story."

The first video aired Sept. 10, 2009. It showed ACORN Housing employees in the group's Baltimore office giving the activists advice on setting up a brothel. The pair told ACORN employees that underage girls from El Salvador were ready to enter the U.S. and start working as child prostitutes. For the most part, ACORN workers didn't raise an eyebrow. All in a day's work.

The remaining videos, shot in six other cities from coast-to-coast, were more or less the same with slight variations. The two claimed to want to get a mortgage and government aid to buy a house that would become their base of operations. O'Keefe claimed to want to run for Congress someday and wanted to keep this illegal business secret so it wouldn't ruin his chances. In one California ACORN office, the pair asked for help in smuggling the underage hookers across the border.

Only one employee showed reluctance to help. Another ACORN worker seemed to grasp that something was awry and teased the activists, concocting a wild story in which she confessed to a murder. All the rest were happy to help facilitate crime.

One helpful staffer offered to help the couple claim the child tax credit for the underage prostitutes from El Salvador. One worker offered the couple a discount on tax preparation fees for the prostitution business. One told them how to hide undeclared income by burying it in a tin can. Another counseled lying in the mortgage application process. "Honesty is not going to get you the house," she said. ACORN's abysmally paid employees are trained not to let prospects walk out that door without trying to get them to purchase memberships. They push and push and push. The only reason the employees didn't participate in the schemes they devised was that O'Keefe and Giles never followed through after their initial visits.

Predictably, ACORN and its defenders in the media griped about the undercover video sting, claiming Giles and O'Keefe had acted unethically, but ACORN routinely used similar techniques against its own targets. ACORN used undercover testers in an effort to uncover racial bias in schools, lending, and other areas. For example, ACORN might send a white person posing as a mortgage applicant to a bank. It would then follow up by sending a black person who claimed to have a similar income and credit history to apply for a mortgage of roughly the same size at the same bank. If the white's application was approved but the black's was rejected, racial bias was inferred.

When the Office of the Comptroller of the Currency unveiled a plan to use undercover testers to monitor possible racial bias in banks' mortgage lending, Obama mentor and bank shakedown artist Madeline Talbott of Chicago ACORN was ecstatic. ACORN "has been fighting for testing on lending discrimination in the banks for years, and we are very pleased that the (comptroller) is coming around," she said.[702]

ACORN even worked with NBC News on a sting operation against

Jackson Hewitt Tax Service. According to ACORN's 2005 annual report, member Christina Talarczyk of San Antonio, Texas, pretended "to be a naive tax preparation customer." She "walked into a Jackson Hewitt office with a Dateline producer who had a camera hidden in his sunglasses. The tax preparation employees were caught on camera as they tried to convince Christina to take out a high-interest [Refund Anticipation Loan]."[703]

The first O'Keefe-Giles video was shown on Andrew Breitbart's website Big Government, and was then featured the same day on Glenn Beck's TV program. Giles, daughter of Christian preacher Doug Giles, told Beck she got involved in the project "to expose ACORN." "I saw them as a thug organization that was getting my tax dollars," Giles said.

Soon after the videos surfaced, Citigroup senior executive Eric Eve quit ACORN's advisory council. Citigroup announced it had cut off funding for the group and that it was "deeply concerned about the recent media reports regarding ACORN." The advisory council's other members were then-SEIU boss Andy Stern, John Podesta, former Maryland lieutenant governor Kathleen Kennedy Townsend, Clinton-era HUD Secretary Henry Cisneros, Con Edison lobbyist John Banks, Lawcash president Harvey Hirschfield, and Dave Beckwith, executive director of the Needmor Fund.

The left was paralyzed by shock—for about five minutes. Then it leapt into action to protect an organization it treasured. Obama supporter Patricia Jessamy, Maryland State's Attorney for Baltimore, claimed the video might violate the state's anti-wiretapping law that was used against Linda Tripp after she recorded telephone conversations with President Clinton's Oval Office paramour Monica Lewinsky. The law requires consent to recording by both parties in a conversation.

Always ready to smear conservatives, left-wing journalist Joe Conason said on the Sept. 10 "Lou Dobbs Tonight" show that O'Keefe was dodging the media because he feared prosecution for unlawful recording, as if the First Amendment's press protections didn't apply in the state of Maryland.

The attacks steamed O'Keefe. He was scathingly critical of Associated Press reporter Justin Pritchard who wrote a detailed, 1,800-word behind-the-scenes feature article on the ACORN video operation.[704]

O'Keefe said he was upset that Pritchard's article questioned their motives. "I mean, who gives a shit?" he said in an interview. "Where were these Associated Press reporters with the telescopic lenses and note pads? Why weren't they investigating the ACORN employees? Why are they doing investigative journalism into the investigative journalists? Isn't that absurd?"

ACORN backers said—as they have always said without fail whenever ACORN faces an employee-related scandal—that the prostitution-facilitating workers were just a few bad apples and that ACORN is focused, as Democratic strategist Paul Begala says, on improving "the real lives of real people."

In the days following the first video, as new ones surfaced, Conason appeared on CNN, reflexively dismissing the videos, which he called "propaganda." He wrote a whiny column on Salon.com and bemoaned the fact that the Right had finally learned the power of political theater. The longtime Bill Clinton apologist blamed ACORN's troubles on the Right: "Like so many conservative attacks, the crusade against ACORN has been highly exaggerated and even falsified to create a demonic image that bears little resemblance to the real organization."

Conason kept digging a hole for himself, arguing that "ACORN's troubles should be considered in the context of a history of honorable service to the dispossessed and impoverished." Although the undercover operatives may have had fun duping "a few morons into providing tax advice to a 'pimp and ho,'" what ACORN actually does is help poor families file for the Earned Income Tax Credit and fight foreclosure so they can stay in their homes, he wrote.

Actress Whoopi Goldberg weighed in on "The View." "There are boneheads in all organizations . . . but do you kill the whole thing?" The *American Prospect*'s Adam Serwer wrote that the Right takes "the ACORN scandal as a kind of vindication of all their paranoid fantasies of what ACORN was responsible for." Later, other leftists argued the video saga was a "hoax" because O'Keefe wasn't dressed like a stereotypical pimp when he visited ACORN offices. They brought this up because O'Keefe appeared in B-roll footage in the videos wearing his grandmother's fur stole and a pimpalicious fedora. The fact that O'Keefe is a good showman didn't undercut the videos, but extremist defenders of ACORN were running out of arguments.

Meanwhile, ACORN went into damage control overdrive. When ACORN learned of the first video, it fired the Baltimore workers, called Fox News racist for airing the footage, and threatened a lawsuit. ACORN claimed to be the victim of a smear campaign. Stuart Katzenberg, lead organizer for ACORN's Maryland branch and a key figure in the Donna Edwards campaign, said that the employees were canned because they "did not meet ACORN's standards of professionalism." Sonja Merchant-Jones, head of Baltimore ACORN, said that the workers were low-level part-time workers unsupervised by senior staff at the time. Strangely, ACORN and the two employees sued O'Keefe, Giles, and Breitbart but allowed the case to be dismissed for want of prosecution.

The reaction in Washington's corridors of power was swift. Congress voted to cut off federal funding for ACORN. The Census Bureau banned ACORN from participating in the 2010 head count. The IRS booted ACORN out of a tax return-preparation program for the poor. There were a few threshold investigations that barely skimmed the surface of ACORN's long history of lawbreaking, but no in-depth investigation of ACORN's gangster-like behavior was ordered.

The bad ink hurt ACORN's cash flow. How did ACORN deal with the problem? It asked its workers to defraud the government. Former ACORN official Michael McCray, spokesman for ACORN 8, said ACORN organizers and staff complained that "senior management has ordered them to continue to work for ACORN as 'volunteers' but for them to apply for unemployment insurance." Initially ACORN 8 thought "no one in their right mind would ever agree to do this. But we kept hearing these same allegations, over and over again, from different people in different parts of the country."[705] It was yet more evidence that ACORN is like that guy at the racetrack who bums cigarettes off other people because he wants to spend what's left of his welfare check on the sure thing in the 7th race.

DEMOCRATS PROTECT THEIR OWN

Democrats circled the wagons to protect ACORN in the wake of the undercover illegal alien sex slave videos. There were a handful of cursory probes of ACORN but they didn't get far. In late 2009, there was never any reason to believe that then-California Attorney General Jerry Brown was going to conduct an even-handed investigation into the California ACORN offices caught on video cooperating with O'Keefe and Giles. He was far more interested in helping ACORN by prosecuting the duo under a state law that forbids secret electronic recordings of "confidential communication."

The radical, perpetual office holder who handed out acorns during mayoral inauguration festivities in 1999—describing them as "seeds of change"—goes way back with ACORN. The New Left crusader known as Governor Moonbeam when he was the state's chief executive from 1975 to 1983 has had close ties to the group for years, according to former California ACORN leader Fannie Brown (no relation).

ACORN endorsed Brown and performed voter registration and get-out-the-vote work for his campaigns for Oakland mayor and state attorney general, she said in an interview. The *Oakland Post* reported in 2001 that Mayor Brown worked with ACORN and ACORN Housing on an anti-predatory lending campaign called "Don't Borrow Trouble." ACORN gave Attorney General Brown an "A" grade on its "Real Leadership in Fighting Foreclosures" scorecard in 2008.

When he was California governor, he singled out ACORN as a group he trusted: "[I]n this job I spend my time calling on that same network of community organizers that has been there right along," he said. "When I talk to people about community programs, I want to talk to the people from ACORN and Fair Share and Mass Advocacy— all the community groups that I've known over a period of years."

Around the same time, Brown praised the aggressive tactics of the taxpayer-funded community service organization VISTA, which became part of AmeriCorps during the Clinton era. When asked whether "[t]he rich, the corporations, Republicans in general, may still regard a highly publicized VISTA program and your volunteers as a threat," he replied, "I assume they will, and they ought to; if they don't, then I'm not doing my job." Brown said VISTA "ought not to be just a bunch of low-paid social workers. It ought to be people helping to get themselves together to build new institutions." Brown must believe that the War on Poverty was a success.

ACORN's lead organizer in San Diego, David Lagstein, was caught on tape suggesting Brown's investigation was a sham. "The attorney general is a political animal as well," Lagstein told a Democratic gathering. "Every bit of communication we've had with [Brown's office] has suggested that fault will be found with the people that did the video and not with ACORN."

In the end Brown copped out. His report concluded ACORN's interaction with O'Keefe and Giles broke no criminal laws. He gave the pair legal immunity in exchange for the raw footage they shot at ACORN offices. But he chastised ACORN's San Diego office for a separate incident in which workers threw 500 pages of data regarding employees and others in a dumpster as a possible violation of the law.[706]

ACORN itself commissioned an allegedly independent report to exonerate itself. The review of the ACORN undercover prostitution video saga unveiled by former Massachusetts Attorney General Scott Harshbarger in December 2009 was a breathtaking work of fiction. The report faulted ACORN only for poor management practices. Harshbarger, a former president of the left-wing group Common Cause, was selected by ACORN to aid in damage control.

ACORN ally Harshbarger let the crooks at ACORN off the hook. "While some of the advice and counsel given by ACORN employees and volunteers was clearly inappropriate and unprofessional, we did not find a pattern of intentional, illegal conduct by ACORN staff," he wrote. ACORN chief organizer Bertha Lewis gloated. "ACORN's leadership is pleased that this evaluation shows that even the low level employees did not engage in any illegal activity or seek to encourage it." Reporters, including this writer, participated in listen-only mode in Lewis's teleconference so the sounds of robust laughter did not disrupt the event.

OUT OF HER DEPTH

In the wake of the undercover video scandal, national ACORN officials such as chief organizer Bertha Lewis got involved in spinning the corruption crisis. If she had been following ACORN's past practices, she wouldn't have defended the employees captured on video, according to Marcel Reid. (No doubt the wily Wade Rathke would not have made that mistake had he been in charge of ACORN at the time.)

That's because Giles and O'Keefe actually conducted their sting operations in the offices of ACORN Housing, which "on paper is not ACORN," Reid said. In theory at least, ACORN Housing "is a separate free-standing corporation." During an October 2009 appearance at the National Press Club, Lewis appears to have forgotten ACORN's oft-repeated claim that ACORN Housing is not controlled by ACORN. As noted in an earlier chapter, when an ACORN affiliate's behavior reflects well on the group, ACORN emphasizes its ties to that affiliate. When an affiliate does something disreputable, ACORN downplays its connection with the affiliate. As Reid explained:

> If you understand this fine point of ACORN, then you'll under-stand why ACORN has been so very effective at never, ever being caught because technically [Giles and O'Keefe] never went into the ACORN offices. Those employees, some of whom I knew, they didn't work for ACORN. They worked for ACORN Housing which is a separate corporation. So when Bertha Lewis got up and started to defend ACORN Housing, she shouldn't have done. ACORN Housing should have been defended by the chair of ACORN Housing, who is Alton Bennett, or defended by the executive director of ACORN, who is Michael Shea.[707]

During her presentation at the National Press Club, Lewis deserved an Academy Award nomination for depicting ACORN as an innocent victim. Even the *Washington Post*'s Dana Milbank, a wellspring of conventional liberal wisdom, couldn't resist beating Lewis up.

> In creativity, the ACORN boss's denials were matched only by her assignments of blame. She blamed her predecessor: "I don't think it's fair to judge me, as I'm cleaning up a previous administration." She blamed the powerful: "We've seen this play before, whether it was the civil rights movement or whatever, when you organize poor people to have real power, what you do is often turned against you." And most of all, she blamed Republicans: "The RNC . . . because we've been inflated as the boogeyman, raises almost $2 million a day, every day, and this form of modern-day ACORN McCarthyism has got to stop."

Lewis's statement about the Republican National Committee was immediately undermined by the frequently tone-deaf RNC chairman Michael Steele who, incredibly enough, *defended* ACORN. A video of Steele from a September 21 speech surfaced on a left-wing website the day of Lewis's press club appearance. Steele praises Lewis. "The current head of the organization, she's done a phenomenal job getting out in front of it," Steele said. "I applaud her. I take her at her word that she wants to work to make sure that the bad apples are thrown out." Steele said he respected ACORN's history of "working in the community and helping the poor." So much for the Republican boogeyman.

Lewis's speech was a rambling defense of ACORN. Ignoring mountains of evidence to the contrary, she said allegations of election fraud against the group have "proved to be an utter fabrication and a work of fiction that was created by the people who wrote it." She claimed ACORN had "500,000 member families," even though ACORN's own website said the group had "over 400,000 member families." Of course, 500,000 is more than 400,000, but you can't just round *up* from 400,000. Lewis wanted to make ACORN sound even larger than it was.

Lewis understated her group's influence in creating the mortgage bubble and argued that ACORN was a voice in the wilderness demanding that banks adhere to sensible underwriting guidelines. "We had to negotiate with banks, force them—*force them*—to adhere to the Community Reinvestment Act which said, you needed to make sound loans in these low income neighborhoods, sound loans. I dare say, if some of our biggest financial institution [sic] had followed the underwriting guidelines that ACORN put out for sound loans, we would not be in this foreclosure crisis right now." Whatever half-hearted calls ACORN put out for banks to be financially responsible are outweighed by ACORN's decades of demands through in-your-face direct-action techniques that banks lend money to homebuyers who had no business trying to buy homes.

Lewis pooh-poohed Sen. Charles Grassley's (R-IA) statement that ACORN appears to be "a shell game perpetrated by the ACORN tax-exempt entities [that] appears to be no different than that conducted by the charities involved in the Jack Abramoff scandal."

"So again, you know, without a shred of proof, no documentation," Lewis said. "We have audits. We turn in our paperwork to the proper authority. Again, Senator Grassley's report was just that—another stretch of allegations of how to pound on ACORN and just paint a picture that, 'You must be doing that. If you're getting money, there's no way that you could keep it separately.' And it's just false."

ACORN lawyer Elizabeth Kingsley had worried about precisely that problem in her legendary 2008 legal memo. She wrote that her concerns fell into four major categories: "respect for corporate integrity, the necessary separation between different types of political work, the niceties of 501 (c) (3) tax compliance and accounting for those funds, and a big-picture question about organizational capacity." She added that there are "systemic institutional concerns."

Kingsley also warned of the danger posed by the ACORN affiliates' lack of proper documentation showing that the ACORN network has been following IRS rules on nonprofit behavior. There is too much overlap between various employees representing different affiliates and confusion about who is controlling which funds and this can only lead to trouble, she wrote. The attorney warned ACORN that "merely papering the transfer of money is not sufficient." The nonprofits have to be able to show that their funds were used for appropriate purposes, she wrote.

Following an anti-Karl Rove rant, Lewis smeared O'Keefe. Lewis said O'Keefe told the *Washington Post*, "They're registering too many minorities that usually vote Democratic. Somebody's got to stop them." In fact after the newspaper ran the September 18 cover story to which Lewis refers, the newspaper was forced to run a correction because O'Keefe said no such thing.

One reporter told this writer the day of the press club speech that he tried but failed to interview Lewis after the speech. "She ran away after the event like a bat out of hell," he said. Milbank explained why: "Lewis, in playing the victim, is her own worst enemy. Forget the film of the pimp and prostitute: Watching a film of Lewis's performance yesterday would probably be enough to cause lawmakers to cut off ACORN's federal funding."

ACORN'S MAN ON THE JUDICIARY COMMITTEE

Throughout the undercover video saga Congressman Jerrold Nadler (D-NY) remained a steady ally of ACORN. This is key because Nadler was chairman of the House Judiciary Committee's subcommittee on the Constitution, civil rights, and civil liberties in the last Congress. That panel could have investigated ACORN. If only its presiding officer wasn't in bed with the group.

Lincoln Anderson, a reporter for the *Villager*, an alternative newspaper in Manhattan's Greenwich Village, wrote that while he visited the office of ACORN's lawyer Arthur Z. Schwartz, a telephone call came in from Nadler. Nadler told Schwartz that the legislation defunding ACORN was an unconstitutional "bill of attainder" that unfairly punished ACORN without trial. "Schwartz said the congressmember, during the phone call, asked him why ACORN hasn't sued over this yet," Anderson reported.

Nadler's "bill of attainder" argument won praise from the Left. The congressman's newfound interest in the finer points of constitutional law earned him a fist bump from the *Village Voice*, a sure sign that he was up to no good.

How exactly is it appropriate for the chairman of a congressional subcommittee to be offering strategic advice to a group he was under growing pressure to probe? Nadler's spokesman, Ilan Kayatsky, refused to respond to this writer's requests for comment, except to send a snide email containing an accusation of bias.

Not long after Nadler urged ACORN to file a lawsuit challenging the law, ACORN filed a lawsuit challenging the law. In November, ACORN claimed to have a constitutional right to defraud the people of the United States. Actually, the lawsuit didn't use the word *fraud*, but that's what it amounts to because ACORN argues in the document that it has a right to taxpayer dollars.

In the action, ACORN plays the victim—as always. ACORN claimed the congressionally approved funding cutoff violated the Constitution's prohibition on bills of attainder, along with ACORN's free speech and due process rights. Of course, due process is a rather specific legal concept that applies to judicial proceedings, rather than the lawmaking process. A bill of attainder singles out an individual or group for punishment without trial.

Is it punishment for ACORN to be denied public funds? That implies the group has the right to receive those funds. Legal scholar Hans A. von Spakovsky of the Heritage Foundation flatly rejected the argument that the Constitution prevents Congress from doing the right thing. "The bill of attainder clause has never been read to prevent Congress from defunding an organization or a corporation whose employees engage in criminal conduct, and it has rarely been invoked by the modern Supreme Court."

According to ACORN the cutoff happened not because hidden-camera videos showed Americans the group's predilection for crime but because a vast right-wing conspiracy hoodwinked lawmakers. The legislation "was passed in large part due to a public relations campaign orchestrated by political forces that have persistently attacked and defamed the Plaintiff ACORN, its members, affiliates and allies (other Plaintiffs herein)," according to the legal complaint. ACORN's tormentors, it continued, are "motivated by their hostility toward the Plaintiffs' tireless commitment to registering voters, particularly those poor and working Americans who have been consistently disenfranchised and excluded from the American political system."

PRO-COMMUNIST LAW FIRM TAKES ACORN'S CASE

ACORN's selection of the Center for Constitutional Rights (CCR) to represent it in the lawsuit was revealing. Like ACORN, CCR lawyers agree with the Marxist critique of American society. Both groups were founded by 1960s radicals. Both groups are funded by radical philanthropist George Soros through his Open Society Institute. CCR wants to help make it easier for terrorists to attack the U.S. while ACORN hopes to spend the system into oblivion.

For more than four decades the leftist public interest law firm has protected the supposed constitutional rights of those who would destroy the United States. CCR has used what it calls "innovative impact litigation" to aggressively attack U.S. anti-Communist policy, the war on Islamist terror, and American businesses. The group was also involved in key Supreme Court cases in recent years that gave America's terrorist enemies access to the civilian legal system. Its website used to refer to the victory of Ho Chi Minh's Viet Cong as a "victory of the Vietnamese people."

CCR was co-founded by Willliam Kunstler who described himself as a "double agent" trying to "bring down the system through the system." Not surprisingly, the firm has represented members of violent terrorist groups including the Armed Forces of Puerto Rican National Liberation (FALN) and the Japanese Red Army. It also acted for Black Panther Party "Minister of Justice" H. Rap Brown, a convicted cop killer.[708]

Groups suspected of ties to Islamic terrorists fund CCR. Two organizations in Virginia, Safa Trust Inc. and the International Institute of Islamic Thought, each gave CCR donations of up to $99,999 in 2005. The Ohio branch of the Council on American-Islamic Relations (CAIR), gave CCR up to $2,499 in 2005. At least five of the Wahhabist group's employees and board members have been arrested, convicted, deported, or otherwise tied to terrorism-related charges and activities, according to analysts Daniel Pipes and Sharon Chadha.

In 2005, CAIR gave CCR president Michael Ratner its Civil Rights Award. Ratner is a Che Guevara admirer with both a political and financial interest in ACORN. As noted earlier, in 2005 ACORN signed an agreement with Forest City Ratner Companies LLC, a megabucks real estate development firm, pledging its support for the ambitious Atlantic Yards development in Brooklyn, that would become the new home of the New Jersey Nets basketball team. Ratner's brother Bruce is also principal owner of the Nets. Ratner is also an investor in the basketball team that would relocate to Atlantic Yards. His sister is left-wing commentator Ellen Ratner.

CCR's litigation prompted federal judge Nina Gershon to issue a bizarre ruling in late 2009. She agreed with ACORN's "bill of attainder" argument and ordered Congress to continue funding the group. Only in the through-the-looking-glass world of a leftist activist judge could cutting off taxpayer funding to an advocacy group be deemed punishment. The injunction itself appeared to be unconstitutional and an affront to the separation of powers. It seemed to rely on a novel, insidious legal doctrine known as "legislative due process." Simply put, groups have rights in the appropriations process. One of those so-called rights is to not be deprived of government funding without some kind of cause being shown. In other words, Congress no longer has the power of the purse regardless of what the Constitution says and appropriators should never vote again with first consulting the ACLU.

In a startlingly unusual victory for common sense, an appeals court slapped down Gershon. The Second Circuit Court of Appeals ruled in August 2010 that the "withholding of appropriations" was not punishment at all. "Congress's decision to withhold funds from ACORN and its affiliates constitutes neither imprisonment, banishment, nor death," the three-judge panel wrote. "In comparison to penalties levied against individuals, a temporary disqualification from funds or deprivation of property aimed at a corporation may be more an inconvenience than punishment."

MORE PROBLEMS IN THE HOUSE OF LABOR

A few weeks after the first undercover video surfaced, SEIU's Anna Burger shocked political observers when she announced her union severed ties with ACORN.

Burger, then SEIU's international secretary-treasurer, was asked about ACORN by Rep. Patrick McHenry (R-NC) during a September 30, 2009, hearing of the House Financial Services Committee. Called the "queen of labor" by some, Burger is an officer of George Soros's Democracy Alliance, the left-wing billionaire donors' collaborative that has steered funds to ACORN. She used to chair the powerful labor federation known as Change to Win.

Burger told McHenry, "SEIU has also cut all ties to ACORN." After the hearing she sent a letter to the committee showing that in 2008 SEIU paid $190,000 to ACORN for "Contributions (including General Support and ACORN Projects like Voter Registration)." The figure for 2009 was $25,000. SEIU paid ACORN $1.4 million in 2008 for "Contracted Services (including services such as the Organizing Apprenticeship Program and Childcare Worker Organizing Campaigns)." The figure for 2009 was $220,000.

SEIU spokeswoman Michelle Ringuette said in an interview that SEIU Locals 100 and 880, which were also part of the ACORN network, continued to exist as labor unions but are no longer affiliated with SEIU. Local 100 "simply couldn't meet requirements to be a stand alone union" because it was "not financially viable," she said. Local 100, headed by Wade Rathke, didn't appeal the disaffiliation decision, she said. Local 880, headed by ACORN insider Keith Kelleher, was absorbed into a larger collective bargaining unit.

That wasn't the end of ACORN's labor problems. Elizabeth Kingsley's legal memo indicated ACORN's pension funds were dipped into or moved around as a result of the embezzlement. This is a huge no-no. Pension funds are governed by strict rules. Employers cannot normally borrow from such funds, move them around, or tinker with them in any way. Without such strong legal protections, workers' life savings might be at risk.

Republican investigators on the House Oversight and Government Reform Committee also found that "ACORN plundered employee benefits and violated fiduciary responsibilities under ERISA by relieving corporate debts through prohibited loans to a related party." They added that SEIU Local 100 "under the direction of ACORN founder Wade Rathke—filed bogus reports with the Labor Department in order to conceal [the] embezzlement."[709]

Attorney F. Vincent Vernuccio, formerly a special assistant at the U.S. Department of Labor and editor of EFCAUpdate.org, said in an interview that it was "troubling" that debt between ACORN and funds that provide healthcare and pensions for employees was forgiven. "Forgiveness of the debt caused by the embezzlement may harm the participants and beneficiaries of the current ACORN healthcare and pension plans," he said. "If the money was not paid back it may put at risk the funding necessary for ACORN retirees or the healthcare of ACORN employees."

The looting of the employee benefit plans "shows the incestuous relationship between ACORN's many arms and the lack of care it exhibits for its employees' welfare," he said.

[FIFTEEN]

The Shadow Remaining: ACORN's Post-Mortem

IN 2010, ACORN took a cue from the French poet Charles Baude-laire. He wrote, "The greatest trick the Devil ever pulled was convincing the world he doesn't exist." ACORN figured out a way to try to convince America that it, like Saul Alinsky's favorite fallen angel, didn't exist. ACORN's fortunes tumbled following the release of the undercover child hooker videos. Its leaders desperately scrambled for a way to keep the organization afloat. They refused to give up their power. They came up with plan that would distract the media and the public while they quietly rebuilt ACORN. They faked ACORN's death so they could attend its funeral and could hear all the nice things its loved ones would say about the group. The tributes from radicals such as left-wing journalist Bill Moyers poured in. Leftist professor Peter Dreier's eulogy was typical: "No group was better at kicking ass" than ACORN.

In March 2010, Bertha Lewis said the group would shutter its state chapters and field offices on April 1. That's right: on April Fool's Day. After insulting the intelligence of Americans for decades by denying the group's criminal activities, Lewis decided to throw one more insult on the pile for good measure.

Investigators in Louisiana believed that for months Lewis had been involved in a "civil war" between the group's New York, New Orleans, and Washington, D.C. branches. She was also busy consolidating her power and hoarding ACORN's remaining assets. Investigators believe the group has about $20 million in cash spread out over 800 bank accounts and that ACORN affiliates hold $10 million in property.[710]

As Lewis apparently struggled to fend off rivals within the organization, ACORN leaders came to accept that the ACORN brand was tarnished. They had begun to feel this way after the unprecedented adverse publicity the group experienced in the 2008 election cycle. The bad PR of that period wasn't generated because ACORN was acting any differently than it ever had, but because the public and the media saw what community organizers like Barack Obama actually do. There was constant talk in the upper echelons of the organization about creating a new group with a new name. The embarrassing videos that scared away big individual and institutional donors on which the group had come to rely were the tipping point. Leaders decided to restructure and rebuild ACORN's congenitally corrupt empire of activism. Around the time Scott Harshbarger rolled out his report on ACORN's problems, the group's operatives were quietly filing incorporation forms in states across the country.

ACORN REBRANDING TABLE

ACORN Housing Corp. changed its name to **Affordable Housing Centers of America Inc.**
State-level chapters that have incorporated as *new* nonprofit corporations:
Arkansas: Arkansas Community Organizations
California: Alliance of Californians for Community Empowerment (ACCE)
Connecticut, Massachusetts, Rhode Island: New England United for Justice
District of Columbia, Maryland: Communities United, Communities United Training and Education Fund
Louisiana: A Community Voice
Minnesota: Minnesota Neighborhoods Organizing for Change

Missouri: Missourians Organizing for Reform & Empowerment (MORE)

New York: New York Communities for Change

Pennsylvania: Pennsylvania Neighborhoods for Social Justice (PNSJ) *and* Pennsylvania Communities Organizing for Change (PCOC)

Texas: Texas Organizing Project *and* Texas Organizing Project Education Fund

Washington: Organization United for Reform (OUR) Washington

Sources: author research; "ACORN Political Machine Tries to Reinvent Itself," U.S. House of Representatives, Committee on Oversight and Government Reform, April 1, 2010, available at http://republicans.oversight.house.gov/images/stories/Reports/20100401ACORNreport.pdf.

Under orders from the top, on December 3, 2009, Missourians Organizing for Reform and Empowerment Inc. (MORE) registered with nonprofit authorities in Missouri. Veteran ACORN organizer Jeff Ordower was identified as a co-founder.[711]

So far, MORE has been one of ACORN's most active renamed state chapters. The group is doing its part to sabotage the banking system by demanding a moratorium on mortgage foreclosures that banks need to carry out in order to remain solvent and in business. On July 21, 2010, the same day President Obama signed a sweeping financial regulatory bill into law, MORE incited a near-riot at a Chase bank office in a St. Louis suburb. Activists screamed "predatory lender, criminal offender!" and demanded banks not foreclose on defaulted mortgages.[712] MORE was also trying to shake Chase down for some more money. JPMorgan Chase Foundation has given ACORN affiliates at least $7.6 million since 1998.

On December 8, 2009, Amy Schur, a loyal 20-year-plus ACORN employee sources say has been willing to get her hands dirty for the cause, registered a new group with an innocuous-sounding name. Schur filed papers with the California secretary of state's office creating a "new" group called Alliance of Californians for Community Empowerment (ACCE). Schur became ACCE's executive director.

On behalf of ACCE and ACORN respectively, Schur and Lewis signed an "asset transfer and license agreement." ACCE wrote a check to ACORN for $9,000. According to the agreement, ACCE's payment was for ACORN's old computers and other office equipment. It also covered the rights to ACORN's databases which included "e-mail contact information for approximately 16,202 potential contributors residing in California."[713]

According to ACORN 8, Schur participated in the eight-year long embezzlement cover-up that led to Wade Rathke's ouster. ACORN insiders say Schur has intimate knowledge of how ACORN operates. Schur is corrupt and hopelessly tainted, Marcel Reid volunteered. "If there was true reform, why would Amy Schur be the head of ACCE?" she said in an interview.

A legitimate splinter group trying to make a clean break from the original group would presumably have the good sense not to operate out of the original group's office. Or not. ACCE's office address was shown in the registration as 3655 South Grand Ave., Suite 250, Los Angeles 90007. That address just so happened to be the address of California ACORN's headquarters too. Fannie Brown, who used to be a California state delegate on ACORN's national board, said it was the same old ACORN at work. "They started washing it a little bit and then they poured some bleach on it and kind of polished it up a little more to make it look good."[714]

On December 31, 2009, New York Communities for Change Inc. registered with the New York secretary of state's office. It reportedly has the same address as ACORN's headquarters in Brooklyn. On January 19, 2010, ACORN national president Maude Hurd, a Bostonian, followed through. Her "new" group, New England United for Justice Inc., registered with the secretary of the Commonwealth of Massachusetts. She became president.

By May 4, 2010, Communities United Inc. filed in the District of Columbia. The next day it held its first meeting at ACORN's office on 8th Street Southeast in the nation's capital. The same office continues to be the headquarters of Project Vote. "Communities United is just ACORN's way of thumbing their nose in the face of everyone," a source close to ACORN said in an interview. And so it went. ACORN chapters disappeared only to reappear with new names. The "new groups" had largely the same employees and many were located in the same offices.

ACORN ADMITS ITS DISSOLUTION IS A SHAM

"Just as criminals change their aliases, ACORN is changing its name," said Rep. Darrell Issa.

> But make no mistake about it, just because they change their name, doesn't mean anything has really changed at all. As this most recent presidential election has showed us, just because you profess change, doesn't mean you're going to change. The bottom line is, whatever they decide to call themselves, they are still the same corporation with the same board, staff and people. Ultimately, the real question is aside from their name, what is really going to change?[715]

A leaked February 22, 2010 email from ACORN's online director explained the group's rebranding hoax. "The truth is that it is hard for us to forsee [sic] any scenario where ACORN continues beyond the end of 2010 and some of us think it might not last that long," wrote Nathan Henderson-James, director of ACORN's online campaigns. "Last one to leave turn out the lights and wipe the server." Henderson-James sent the message to members of Townhouse, a left-wingers' discussion forum run by Matt Stoller, who was senior policy adviser to former Rep. Alan Grayson (D-FL).

Henderson-James, an ACORN employee since 1997, explained the subterfuge ACORN was using to dupe Americans into believing ACORN was shutting down. "It is definitely true that over the next week or so we should see a dozen or more organizations launched on the state level by staff who used to work for ACORN and leaders who developed their skills as ACORN members. These are not just simple name changes, but reimaginings of how best to organize low and moderate income constitiuencies [sic] without any of the legal problems and funding issues dogging ACORN, not to mention the brand damage."

It is a "tactically smart . . . reaction to the global situation that helps the work of building power for poor people to continue," he wrote. ACORN's ruse was designed to keep tax dollars and foundation grants flowing into its coffers. The plan was to keep the organization in business on a smaller scale temporarily before ramping up.

Despite dissolving its national infrastructure and laying off most its staff, ACORN continued to operate below the radar. On April 16, 2010, Lewis sent out an email to supporters assuring them that ACORN was "not dead!"

> We will continue to fight for working families with the support of members and supporters like you. We'll be here, on the web, and in the media. I'll be honest. We don't know what the future holds for ACORN—a lot of it depends on circumstances out of our control. But our ultimate success rests squarely in your hands—the hands of people who care about the future direction of our country and creating an America that ensures equity, justice, and freedom for all its people.[716]

The letter drew a strong rebuke from Rep. Steve King (R-IA), a leading ACORN critic. "ACORN is not going away," he said. "An all-out, full court press federal investigation is the only way to bring ACORN to heel." King urged the IRS and the Justice Department to jointly investigate ACORN and carry out a complete forensic analysis of its finances. There should be congressional probes and a special prosecutor appointed, he said. "People need to go to jail for criminal activities."[717]

King, a House Judiciary Committee member, previously called the ACORN saga "the largest corruption crisis in the history of America." "It's thousands of times bigger than Watergate because Watergate was only a little break-in by a couple of guys," he said. "By the time we pull

ACORN out by its roots America's going to understand just how big this is."[718]

A group of Republicans, including King and one of ACORN's most high profile critics in Congress, Rep. Michele Bachmann (R-MN), are demanding a probe of ACORN's ties to the Obama campaign. The *Politico* newspaper said Issa, despite his strong rhetoric, is not "enthusiastic about jumping back into the controversy" because "ACORN is out of business and most Democrats already have signed on to a bill barring federal funding of the group."[719]

The fact that ACORN settled a racketeering lawsuit in Ohio out of court and agreed to leave the state may put pressure on congressional leaders to launch a federal racketeering probe in 2011. In the settlement with the Buckeye Institute's 1851 Center for Constitutional Law ACORN agreed to "cease all Ohio activity" and surrender all its state business licenses.[720] If aggressive pro-life protesters who merely inconvenience abortion providers can be successfully sued under federal racketeering laws, why can't ACORN be criminally prosecuted for racketeering?

King's fears of ACORN's immortality seemed to be confirmed by John Atlas, who said ACORN plans to resurface under a new name after the 2010 elections. A new institution tentatively called the Community Action Support Center (CASC) will be created "to provide a range of training, technical assistance, and oversight services to the new community organizations." ACORN's Brian Kettenring will be interim executive director. Lewis plans to create a Black Leadership Institute. Steve Kest quit ACORN "but will work with the new community groups in a consulting and voluntary capacity." Kest later became a "senior fellow" at the Center for American Progress.

"The emerging community organizations will retain ACORN's commitment to building national power, and are beginning discussions toward a process to federate at some later date, presumably after the 2010 elections or in 2011," Atlas writes. The new groups' focus will be on localities and states. CASC "will support the continuation of organizing around jobs and low-wage work, bank lending and foreclosures, immigration, state fiscal crises, civic engagement, and green jobs and environmental justice." ACORN leaders are working on "voter engagement activities." They intend "to engage the surge voters of 2008 and turn them into permanent voters in 2010 and beyond."[721]

ACORN's fraud-prone Project Vote affiliate continues to operate. It ran a nationwide voter registration and get-out-the-vote drive during the 2010 election cycle. Despite its history of lawbreaking, it continues to operate undisturbed, doing business as usual. ACORN's housing bubble generator, ACORN Housing, changed its name to Affordable Housing Centers of America after the undercover video saga.

REWRITING HISTORY

In his email, Henderson-James acknowledged ACORN made mistakes, but claimed it was primarily a victim of dirty tricks perpetrated by the political right. "[W]e were all up against a 24-hour propoganda [sic] channel," apparently referring to the Fox News Channel, one of the few media outlets to closely follow the ACORN saga. Progressives didn't fight back hard enough "in a moment of extreme duress, orchestrated by propogand [sic] videos," he complains. The movement "stood by as ACORN got gutted, while we also handed the forces of pro-corporate politics a handy club to kick the shit out of anything that vaugely [sic] sounds progressive. And that comes with a license to go after the next group or groups that embody the progressive agenda. This went beyond ACORN. We were just a convienent [sic] target to make into a bogeyman. This was about everything progressives stood for. And when it came time to stand up, most of us didn't."

Henderson-James' views were echoed by radical intellectual Noam Chomsky. "The destruction of ACORN was a real, vicious, and vulgar attack on popular rights," he said. "Granting every charge that was made, it's miniscule as compared to the regular actions of public relations organizations of corporations and so on, and certainly government . . . If you went after mainstream organizations whether private or governmental on the basis of evidence like that, you'd throw them all out."

"Whatever the charges are against a few poorly paid employees that did something wrong, it's wrong, but in the balance of what happens every day, invisible," Chomsky said. "So it's just a harsh and brutal effort to destroy an organization that helps poor people." Asked which factor was most to blame for ACORN's downfall, he replied, "the failure of mainstream liberalism to defend it."

> They collapsed. They didn't want to take a principled position in defense of an organization where some minor infraction was discovered. But the point of the attack was to destroy an organization that helps the poor and that tries to improve democracy by giving people the opportunity to participate in elections. Of course people who hate democracy and think that the poor ought to be kicked in the face think that that organization should be destroyed.

Chomsky doubted a conspiracy was involved. "It was a crime of opportunity," he said. "I doubt that anyone planned it . . . There was a good chance to destroy an organization that is a nuisance because it helps the poor and it registers voters and so on."[722]

Unlike Chomsky, Marcel Reid blamed her end of the political spectrum. ACORN collapsed because progressives didn't come forward to help fix ACORN. "It's the left's fault because when it was time for them to police themselves they would not do it," she said. "They can't blame the right when they didn't clean up their own house."[723]

In his leaked email, Henderson-James also complained that federal lawmakers and the mainstream media didn't do enough to help ACORN, bemoaning "the breathtaking swiftness with which the Congress condemned us on the basis of what have been clearly shown by real journalists to be nothing but the purest propaganda."

Left-wingers have to promote a narrative "that says the attacks on ACORN were part of a concerted attempt to demobilize key progressive constituencies because they banded together to take power and threaten the status quo and that the legacy of ACORN deserves that regular people stand up for themselves and organize to take power, to pass public policies that create an America we all want to live in. One in which organizing is about average people making their lives and their communities and their workplaces better."

This left-wing spin "will be contested for a bit and you can be sure that it will be marked by serious right-wing triumphalism," he predicts. "Our side needs to make sure our narrative wins, using the kind of pushback that's taken place recently around [undercover video maker James] O'Keefe." Henderson-James cooed: "That's been beautiful."[724]

Henderson-James was referring to O'Keefe's arrest the month before for entering the New Orleans office of Sen. Mary Landrieu (D-LA) under false pretenses. Posing as telephone company workers, O'Keefe and three other young men hoped to prove that the senator's office was ignoring telephone calls from constituents angry about Democrats' national healthcare takeover plan. O'Keefe pleaded guilty to a misdemeanor and was sentenced to three years probation, a $1,500 fine, and 100 hours of community service. He acknowledged he "should have used other means."[725]

Although the distraction provided by O'Keefe's legal problems and other adverse publicity that he received gave the Left a few news cycles to advance the dishonest storyline that ACORN was a victim of a right-wing plot hatched by unscrupulous activists, the public wasn't fooled. Today ACORN remains synonymous with corruption in the public mind—and for good reason.

Henderson-James also encouraged ACORN supporters to help rewrite the history of the embattled group. "[T]here will be a fight over the narrative of ACORN's demise." The other side wants "a narrative about the corruption of popular organizations and how they are simply vehicles for the personal enrichment and power fantasies of their top staff members while pushing public policies that destroy Middle America." This argument must be fought, he argued, not because it's false but because it "gives people pushing a pro-corporate agenda a way to tar progressives and even non-progressive Democrats running for office with the ACORN brush."

Peter Dreier answered the call. He is leading a propaganda-masquerading-as-scholarship drive to encourage academics to help spread more lies about ACORN and other topics. Dreier is a politics professor and director of the urban and environmental policy program at Occidental College, which America's Community Organizer-in-Chief attended.[726] He's also a paid shill for ACORN. He wrote a gaseous, self-serving report claiming the media consistently botched its coverage of the pure-hearted angels at ACORN.[727]

To Dreier, ACORN can do no wrong—and no tactic is too loathsome. Dreier rewrote Pastor Martin Niemoller's famous statement about how Germans had failed to stand up to the Nazis. He tastelessly compared the victim-makers of ACORN to the persecuted Jews of the Third Reich. "First Big Business, Glenn Beck, Rush Limbaugh, Sean Hannity, Bill O'Reilly, Lou Dobbs, the Religious Right, the *Wall Street Journal*, Mitch McConnell, and Karl Rove came for ACORN, and the Democrats did not speak out—because they were not ACORN," an op-ed began.[728] It was Dreier's cute little way of calling ACORN's critics Nazis.

As ACORN's chickens came home to be roasted after the undercover videos surfaced, Dreier was on MSNBC's *Rachel Maddow Show* claiming ACORN was a victim of a massive conspiracy perpetrated by big business and the Republican Party. He even said the group, which did everything in its power to force banks to lend money to uncreditworthy borrowers, had tried to *prevent* the subprime mortgage crisis. Now that's chutzpah!

Dreier has a long radical pedigree. He previously worked with Saul Alinsky's Industrial Areas Foundation. He takes credit for writing the Community Housing Partnership Act, "legislation sponsored by Congressman Joseph Kennedy and Senator Frank Lautenberg, which became part of HUD's HOME program, created under the National Affordable Housing Act of 1990. This legislation provides federal funds to community-based non-profit housing development organizations"—like, maybe ACORN perhaps.[729] Dreier has been a player in the poverty industry for years. Who better to help ACORN airbrush its real history from the public record?

In May 2010, Dreier joined with fellow academics Donald Cohen, and Nelson Lichtenstein to distribute a request for proposals that seeks help "in an important project in the battle with conservative ideas." A propaganda effort was needed because history "shows that in almost every instance the opponents of needed social and economic change are 'crying wolf.'" It is critical "to construct a counter-narrative that demonstrates the falsity or exaggeration of such claims so that the first reaction of millions of people, as well as opinion leaders, will be 'There they go again!'" The repeated refrain "will undermine the credibility and arguments of the organizations and individuals who use such dire social and economic prognostications to thwart progressive reform."

ACORN is the odds-on favorite to be the subject of one of the first "Cry Wolf" projects to be published.

ACORN METASTASIZES OVERSEAS

Wade Rathke remains deeply involved with at least four of ACORN's affiliated nonprofits. He is still chief organizer of the United Labor Unions (ULU) Local 100 in Louisiana, Arkansas, and Texas, a position he has held since 1979. The local had been known as SEIU Local 100 until it was disaffiliated from SEIU in 2009. He is still listed as president and director of Affiliated Media Foundation Movement (AM/FM), an ACORN affiliate that produces news segments for eight alternative radio stations. Rathke remains publisher of ACORN's periodical, *Social Policy* magazine. That magazine used to be published by AISJ but is now published by Labor Neighbor Research and Training Center, another ACORN affiliate.

Rathke is trying to pollute the rest of the world with his destructive ideology. Like a modern-day Karl Marx in exile, he is doing his best to redistribute wealth all around the globe, spreading social justice and shakedown techniques. He uses the ACORN brand, which isn't tarnished abroad, in his international organizing efforts. He is in charge of ACORN's global outreach group, ACORN International, but changed its name in the U.S. to Community Organizations International (COI). Although both ACORN and ACORN International officially say the two organizations aren't connected,

ACORN insiders say Rathke is still working behind the scenes with some ACORN operatives.

Rathke maintains good relations with his friends in the Obama administration, which is quietly helping ACORN. In May 2010, the administration used U.S. government resources to help ACORN spread the gospel of left-wing community organizing in India. President Obama's ambassador to India, Timothy J. Roemer, lent his name and the prestige of the U.S. government to ACORN India's efforts at organizing rag-pickers in Mumbai (formerly known as Bombay). Roemer is a former Democratic congressman from Indiana.

Roemer met with rag pickers in Dharavi, a slum in the suburbs of Mumbai. The official caption accompanying a photo displayed on the U.S. embassy's website indicated Roemer was discussing "ACORN India's local waste management and recycling program." Roemer met with ACORN India representative Vikram Adige. The U.S. consulate in Mumbai, headed by Consul General Paul A. Flombsee, also co-sponsored a water conservation event on March 22 that year with ACORN India. Flomsbee was listed as the expected guest of honor at the event on ACORN India's website.

ACORN India reports to ACORN International, an umbrella organization for the many national organizations conducting ACORN's business outside the U.S. ACORN International is active in Argentina, Canada, Dominican Republic, Honduras, India, Kenya, Mexico, and Peru. It describes its mission as "building community groups in low income communities across the world to organize for power." ACORN India was created was to allow ACORN to apply its corporate shakedown techniques against Western corporations as they expand into rapidly developing markets such as India. Its website says the group defends the "socialist legacy" of Jawaharlal Nehru, India's leftist prime minister of India from 1947 to 1964. That "legacy" is "now in danger from the onslaught of the march of global corporatism."

"Countries like India are the next frontiers of significant market expansion for multi-national corporations; and these corporations are now starting to apply extreme pressure on the government of

India for unfettered access," according to ACORN India. "[The] Indian market is facing an onslaught of both foreign and domestic corporate retailers, the most notable of which is Wal-Mart."

THE DEMOCRACY ALLIANCE:
ACORN'S FAT CAT FRIENDS

The Democracy Alliance is a collection of socialist venture capitalists that funds ACORN and other left-wing groups that want to smash the American system. Leftist blogger Markos Moulitsas called it "a vast, Vast Left Wing Conspiracy to rival" the conservative movement.[730] The Alliance's founder, Democratic operative Rob Stein, thinks ACORN is a mainstream organization. He called ACORN, which received a grant of unknown size from the group in 2006, "a grassroots, tough-minded, liberal-left organization" and "a very responsible organization."

The Alliance is a secretive donors' collaborative to fund a permanent political infrastructure of nonprofit think tanks, media outlets, leadership schools, and activist groups to compete with the conservative movement. The group is registered in the District of Columbia as a taxable nonprofit. That status allows it to avoid having to publicly disclose its financial affairs. It is organizing state-level chapters in at least 19 states, and once-conservative Colorado, which hosts the Democracy Alliance's most successful state affiliate, turned Democrat blue. The group also funds the Secretary of State Project that helped to put in place the Minnesota secretary of state who helped Al Franken steal the 2008 U.S. Senate election. Alliance member Simon Rosenberg, founder of the New Democrat Network (NDN), said in 2008 that that the Alliance has already "channeled hundreds of millions of dollars into progressive organizations."

The Alliance's board is a microcosm of the modern left. In the top rungs are Rob McKay, a limousine liberal, SEIU's Anna Burger, San Francisco lawyer Steven Phillips, and Drummond Pike, a peacenik from the 1960s. Taco Bell heir McKay, its chairman, was born in conservative Orange County, California, and his parents were

Republicans. The vice chairman is Burger. Phillips is secretary and Pike, who created the Tides Foundation, is treasurer.

The Alliance has more than 100 donor-members, both individuals and organizations. However, it has not made available an official list of its "partners." Some of the more prominent members are ACORN benefactors Herb and Marion Sandler, Hollywood producer Norman Lear, and Gara LaMarche, CEO of the Atlantic Philanthropies. LaMarche used to be vice president at Soros's Open Society Institute. SEIU and AFL-CIO are institutional members.

Chief among the members of the Democracy Alliance is leftist troublemaker George Soros, a billionaire currency speculator who has funded the overthrow of several governments. He is the virtual owner of today's Democratic Party. Having purchased, rented, or placed a down payment on all the political influence up for sale in America, he announced plans in late 2009 to ramp up his war on markets worldwide by creating an "Institute for New Economic Thinking" (INET). "The system we have now has actually broken down, only we haven't quite recognized it and so you need to create a new one and this is the time to do it," Soros told the *Financial Times*.

Soros told *Der Spiegel* that European-style socialism "is exactly what we need now. I am against market fundamentalism. I think this propaganda that government involvement is always bad has been very successful—but also very harmful to our society." As preparation for INET, Soros gathered economists to plot his renewed drive for world statism. One of those economists is Joseph Stiglitz, a member of the socialist International. Stiglitz sits on SI's Commission on Global Financial Issues, which was created "to address from a social democratic perspective the ongoing global financial crisis." Of course to socialists a capitalist economy is by definition always in crisis.

Why Soros feels he's not having enough impact on the world is unclear. Soros helped finance the Czech Republic's 1989 "Velvet Revolution" that brought Vaclav Havel to power. He acknowledged having orchestrated coups in Croatia, Georgia, Slovakia, and Yugoslavia. He brought the financial systems of the United Kingdom and

Malaysia to their knees. In the U.S., his preferred candidate now lives in the White House, and interest groups and the bulk of the progressive political infrastructure kneel at his feet. Through his charity, the Open Society Institute, Soros funds ACORN and other influential groups.

Like ACORN, Soros is a lawbreaker. He is appealing his 2002 criminal conviction for insider trading to the European Court of Human Rights. A French court convicted Soros for his role in a 1998 battle to take over Societe Generale, one of France's largest banks. Soros was fined 2.2 million euros in the affair. The fine was later reduced to 940,000 euros.

The Democracy Alliance has at least 100 donor-members, both individuals and organizations. However, it has not made available an official list of its members. Here are some known Democracy Alliance members:

Naomi Aberly, philanthropist

Karen Ackerman, political director for AFL-CIO

AFL-CIO, an institutional member

Judith Avery, investor

Anne Avis, philanthropist

Fred Baron (died 2008), trial lawyer

Anne Bartley, heiress, step-daughter of Winthrop Rockefeller

Patricia Bauman, real estate investor

Joshua Bekenstein, managing director of Bain Capital

Daniel Berger, lawyer and writer

Lisa Blue, trial lawyer and widow of Fred Baron

Robert Bowditch, founded MB Management

Ann S. Bowers, widow of Intel co-founder Robert Noyce

Rutt Bridges, founded Advance Geophysical

Edgar Bronfman Jr., CEO of Warner Music Group

Joanie Bronfman, a Tides Foundation director

William Budinger, founded Rodel Inc.

Mark Buell and **Susie Tompkins Buell**, businessman; wife co-founded clothier Esprit

Anna Burger, was secretary-treasurer of SEIU

Julie Burton, consultant

Peter Buttenweiser, heir

Marcy Carsey, co-owner of independent studio Carsey-Werner Productions

Bob Clement, former congressman from Tennessee

John Cogan, economist

Noel Congdon, retired developer

Tom Congdon, retired energy executive

Lewis B. Cullman, financier

Quinn Delaney, philanthropist

David DesJardins, former software developer for Google

Robert H. Dugger, managing director of Tudor Investment Corp.

Albert J. Dwoskin, real estate developer

Robert Dyson, CEO of Dyson-Kissner-Moran Corp.

Stefan Edlis, retired plastics executive

Diane Feeney, vice chairman of Committee for Responsive Philanthropy

Ronald Feldman, art dealer

Lee and Amy Fikes, oil company president; wife is homemaker

Christopher Findlater, CEO of Cheyenne Exploration Co.

Richard and **Shari Foos**, entertainment entrepreneur; wife is therapist

David A. Friedman, philanthropist (and self-described centrist)

Gail Furman, psychologist

Chris Gabrieli, software entrepreneur
Tim Gill, created Quark software

Davidi Gilo, high-tech entrepreneur

Rob Glaser, heads RealNetworks

Steven M. Gluckstern, founded specialty reinsurance firm

James D. and **Suzanne Gollin**, fund manager; wife is philanthropist

Chad Griffin, managing partner of Griffin Schake

Louise Gund, philanthropist

Richard and **Lois Gunther**, philanthropists

John Haas, former chairman of chemical engineering company

Nick Hanauer, CEO of Pacific Coast Feather Co.

Paul Harstad, founded Harstad Strategic Research

Jonathan Heller and **Connie Cagampang** Heller, philanthropists

Lawrence and **Suzanne Hess**, philanthropists

Arnold Hiatt, former CEO of Stride Rite

Rampa Hormel, president of Global Environment Project Institute

Joseph Hornig, real estate developer

Joan Huffer, executive at Center on Budget and Policy Priorities

Blair Hull, financier

Megan Hull, consultant

Rachel Pritzker Hunter, heiress

John Hunting, office furniture heir

Robert Johnson, was partner at Impact Artist Management

Wayne Jordan, real estate developer

Joel Kanter, president of Windy City Inc.

Michael Kieschnick, founded Working Assets and Secretary of State Project

Livingston Kosberg, CEO of U.S. Physical Therapy Inc.

Ira Lechner, lawyer, chairman of Council for a Livable World

Barbara Lee, philanthropist (not the congresswoman)

Daniel Leeds, president of Fulcrum Investments LLC

Gara LaMarche, CEO of Atlantic Philanthropies, was vice president of Open Society Institute

Norman Lear, veteran television producer, founded People for the American Way

Daniel Lewis, member of Progressive Casualty Insurance Co. board, brother of Peter

Jonathan Lewis, consultant, son of Peter

Peter B. Lewis, founded Progressive Casualty Insurance Co.

Lawrence Linden, banker at Goldman Sachs

Arthur Lipson, investor

John and Rhonda Luongo, venture capitalist; wife is interior designer

Rodger McFarlane (died 2010), senior adviser to Tim Gill's foundation

Rob McKay, Taco Bell heir

Larry McNeil, executive director of SEIU's Institute for Change

Benjamin Miller, president of Western Development Corp.

Herb Miller, real estate developer

Mario Morino, philanthropist

Philip Murphy, former Goldman Sachs executive, former national finance chairman for DNC

Sanford Newman, founder of ACORN's Project Vote affiliate

Alan Patricof, co-founder of private equity firm Apax Partners

Anne Peretz, therapist

Leslie Peterson, former Wyoming Democratic Party chairman

Steven Phillips, attorney and political organizer, son-in-law of Herb and Marion Sandler

Drummond and **Liza Pike**, founded Tides Foundation; wife is philanthropist

Linda Pritzker, investor

Jared Polis, congressman from Colorado

Andy and **Deborah Rappaport**, husband is venture capitalist; wife is philanthropist

Rob Reiner, actor-director

William J. Roberts, executive at Atlantic Philanthropies

Charles Rodgers, president of New Community Fund

Simon Rosenberg, founded New Democrat Network

Paul Rudd, owner of Adaptive Analytics LLC

Deborah Sagner, philanthropist, social worker

Herb and **Marion Sandler**, co-founded Golden West Financial Corp.

Guy Saperstein, trial lawyer

SEIU, an institutional member

Stephen M. Silberstein, philanthropist

Bren Simon, real estate developer

George Soros, currency speculator

Jonathan Soros, son of George

William Soskin, lawyer

Marc Stanley, lawyer

Rob Stein, founded Democracy Alliance, was Clinton-era chief of staff at Department of Commerce

John Stocks, deputy executive director at National Education Association

Patricia Stryker, heiress

Stephen and **Ellen Susman**, lawyer; wife is journalist

Donald and **Emily Sussman**, financier; wife is philanthropist

Ted Trimpa, lawyer and former tobacco lobbyist

Cristina Uribe, political strategist

Michael Vachon, spokesman and political director for George Soros

Philippe and **Kate Villers**, founder of Computervision; wife is activist

Albert C. Yates, former president of Colorado State University

---

Sources: author research; internal ACORN documents; "The Democracy Alliance Does America," by Matthew Vadum and James Dellinger, *Foundation Watch*, December 2008.

ACORN could benefit if Democracy Alliance follows through on its plan to build a $150 million monument to leftism called the National Leadership Campus and wants taxpayers to subsidize part of it. But the group was rebuffed in 2009 by capital city officials. Reclusive insurance magnate Peter B. Lewis, a Soros friend and key member of the Democracy Alliance, had proposed building a massive progressive palace for housing liberal pressure groups at a Capitol Hill site. The other two principals in the project were Jonathan Lewis, who is Peter's son and also a liberal philanthropist and big Democratic donor, and Benjamin Miller, president of Western Development Corp.[731]

When contacted, the Democracy Alliance denied involvement in the project, but communications director Alexandra Visher said in an email that her organization "is committed to helping build the next generation of progressive leaders, and supports the concept for projects that aim to achieve that same goal." The denial seems implausible for a mountain of reasons, but whether or not the project was officially sanctioned by the organization is not terribly important in the scheme of things. That's because Democracy Alliance leaders, members, and groups receiving Alliance-approved grants were deeply involved in the planning process and they would have benefited had the project moved forward.

A June 2009 PowerPoint presentation by Scott + Yandura Consulting seemed to identify Democracy Alliance as a driving force behind the project. The briefing showed the Alliance, the secretive Tides Foundation, and one of the Alliance's institutional members, SEIU, were "supporters" of the project. It also listed a plethora of Alliance-approved grantees including Citizens for Responsibility and Ethics in Washington (CREW), Center for Community Change, Center for American Progress, and Media Matters for America, a left-wing character assassination squad that poses as a media watchdog. Consultant Paul Yandura said after the district rejected the proposal that his clients had not given up trying to develop a site in Washington. "We'll keep up the search privately."[732]

Liberal boy wonder George Stephanopoulos, now a TV talking

head, reportedly gave the Heritage Foundation building on Capitol Hill a one-finger salute while being driven past it during the 1993 Clinton inauguration festivities. With the help of Soros and Lewis, the next generation's Stephanopoulos may yet have the chance to do the same from the comfort of his taxpayer-subsidized office nearby. And ACORN's successor group will be there to claim its share of the loot.

EXPLOITING THE BAD ECONOMY

ACORN's allies say the bad economy gives them new opportunities to push America even farther down the road to socialism. "The banking crisis is the next big thing," George Goehl, executive director of National People's Action (NPA) said in June 2010. NPA is part of a nationwide campaign with SEIU, Jobs with Justice, Americans for Financial Reform, and other groups called the "Showdown in America," which consists largely of loud street protests. NPA and SEIU have also been using angry mobs to invade banks and terrorize bank executives in their homes.[733]

"The banking crisis is the way to build a big economic justice movement in this country," Goehl said.

> People are questioning capitalism. People are asking, Will this economy ever work for me or will it work for my kids? This is a once in a lifetime opportunity as progressives to engage millions of Americans in a big conversation around serious economic restructuring, not around eking out some victories around the margins, not about making life a little less worse for people, but about big time transformative change.

If you build a platform for revolution, they will come, Goehl said. "If we create a space for people to come out they want to come out. People are ready to move to the streets, some because they're angry, some because they want justice right now, and some because they're tired of hearing about the Tea Party coming out, and we as leaders in the progressive movement—we're failing if we don't create that room for people." Goehl said his comrades need to get involved in "mass political education at a different level than we've seen."

According to Heather Booth, executive director of Americans for Financial Reform, an economy-killing "financial speculation tax" was needed to curb the incentive for people to, well, participate in capitalism. "A big battle still needs to be waged to curb the incentive for speculation and to get *our* money back to fund jobs and health care, climate and more," she said. "This fight against Wall Street is part of an even larger fight over who matters in the society, over our values and our priorities, over whether or not we have corporate control in banking, whether BP can destroy the coast, whether the insurance companies can deny our health care, whether companies can dominate our politics saying that money is speech," Booth said.

Booth is an old hand at leftist astro-turfing operations. She's a disciple of Saul Alinsky and she founded the Midwest Academy, a training institute for radical community organizers. "Alinsky is to community organizing as Freud is to psychoanalysis," she has been quoted saying. According to former radical David Horowitz's online encyclopedia of the Left, DiscoverTheNetworks.org, "In the late 1960s and early 1970s, she supported the Weather Underground." What's worrisome is that Booth has strong ties to the Obama administration: She's a former training director for the DNC.[734]

Goehl and Booth may have their work cut out for them thanks to little noticed changes in the nation's welfare laws. President Obama and the Democratic-controlled Congress made it much easier for people like Wade Rathke who want to overload the system in order to bring about its demise.

That's because the spectacularly successful Clinton era welfare reforms that helped millions of Americans break free from crippling dependency on the public fisc were summarily executed in February 2010. Provisions buried deep in the stimulus package offer new financial incentives to states to increase their welfare caseloads. In other words, the seeds of the next welfare crisis have already been sown.

"They have completely overturned the fiscal and policy foundations of welfare reform," said Heritage Foundation senior research fellow Robert Rector.[735]

A 2009 study projected that the Obama administration would spend more on welfare in 2010 than the Bush administration spent on the Iraq war. Bush spent $622 billion on Iraq while Obama's welfare spend-a-thon in one year was expected to cost $888 billion, according to the Congressional Research Service. Meanwhile, Obama is calling for the biggest welfare spending increases in American history—amounting to $10.3 trillion over a decade, a Heritage Foundation study found.

The Clinton-era welfare reforms of 1996 dealt with just one program, Aid for Families with Dependent Children (AFDC). Recipients were required to work. Today 14 federal agencies administer 70 different welfare programs, according to Rector. "The average person says I thought we ended welfare. Well, it's a good thing we ended it, otherwise we'd be spending some real money," he quipped. "Medicaid, public housing, the Earned Income Tax Credit were not reformed."

About $16 trillion has been spent on the War on Poverty since it was launched. Adjusted for inflation, the U.S. has spent $6.4 trillion on every war it has fought. By 2014, annual spending on welfare programs is expected to hit $1 trillion. "One in seven in total federal and state dollars now goes to welfare. But this is a completely unknown story," he said. "No one knows Obama is spending $10 trillion on welfare."[736]

It's a crisis Cloward and Piven would love to take credit for and one that ACORN, in whatever form it takes in coming years, is poised to take advantage of.

Newt Gingrich isn't so sure ACORN will come out on top. "Obama is doing so much damage to the Left that by the time this cycle is over in another four to six years we may have very fundamentally different rules of engagement," he said in an interview. "I think you're about to see an enormous middle-class resurgence of people who are just fed up."

Acknowledgments

I WANT TO THANK the coffee growers of the world without whom this book might not have been possible.

Many people helped out. Jill Farrell and Tegan Millspaw of Judicial Watch shared their FOIAing expertise.

For their helpful advice and assistance, thanks to (in no particular order): Lee E. Goodman. Kirk T. Schroder, Rob Witwer, Christian Berg, Robert Stacy McCain, Andrew Breitbart, Brandon Darby, David Horowitz, Richard Poe, Casaday Nguyen, Franklin Raff, Richard Miniter, Vinnie Vernuccio, Katina Nordloh, Jeremy Lott, Neil Hrab, Robert Huberty, Matt Patterson, David Swindle, Seton Motley, Kerry Picket, and Trevor Loudon.

Thanks to David Hogberg, Ph.D., for his doctorial insights and to investigative reporter Kevin Mooney for his counsel. Thanks also to Steve Lock for his outstanding photography.

At Capital Research Center, thanks to CRC president Terrence Scanlon for kindly giving me some time off to finish the book, and to then-interns Elizabeth Klimp and Christopher Mylenbusch for their excellent research and transcription assistance. Thanks to the producers of "The Lottery" for giving me a screening of their powerful documentary film.

A special thanks to the legions of ACORN whistleblowers who came forward to provide critical information. Thanks also to the committee staff of Rep. Darrell Issa, the new chairman of the House Oversight and Government Reform Committee, for all their hard work.

For publishing my countless ACORN articles, my thanks go out to the fine folks at *American Spectator* (Wlady Pleszczynski and W. James Antle III), *Townhall* (Chris Field), Big Government (Mike Flynn), Big Journalism (Michael Walsh), NewsBusters (Matt Sheffield), *Washington Examiner* (Mark Tapscott, James Dellinger), *Washington Times* (David Mastio), Canada Free Press (Judi McLeod), and The Daily Caller (Megan Mulligan and Tucker Carlson).

Thanks to the good people at WND Books for all their help: Joseph and Elizabeth Farah, the shockingly patient book editor Megan Byrd, art director Mark Karis for outstanding cover art, John Perry for copy editing, and the sales and marketing staff.

In studying ACORN in recent years, I also drew upon the invaluable work of Nancy Armstrong, an intrepid researcher who blogged under the name MsPlacedDemocrat. Nancy died suddenly in July 2009.

Finally, special thanks go out to Hannah Giles and James O'Keefe: you two slew the beast. Of course, like the T-1000 android assassin in the movie *Terminator 2*, ACORN is slowly pulling itself back together even after being blown to bits.

But you two, Hannah and James, set back the cause of American radicalism by years. You both deserve medals.

APPENDIX A:
The 370 Faces of Acorn

N O ONE KNOWS for certain how many nonprofit affiliates, subsidiaries, political action committees, branch offices, and shell corporations ACORN controls. Here are the ones we know about:

1. Association of Community Organizations for Reform Now (ACORN)
2. ACORN National Office, Brooklyn, NY
3. ACORN Bronx, NY
4. ACORN Brooklyn, NY
5. ACORN Buffalo, NY
6. ACORN Hempstead, NY
7. ACORN Housing Corp., Brooklyn, NY
8. Project Vote, Brooklyn, NY
9. MHANY (Mutual Housing Association New York, Brooklyn), NY
10. ACORN National Office, Washington, D.C.
11. ACORN Washington, D.C.
12. ACORN Housing Corp., Washington, D.C.
13. ACORN Political, Washington, D.C.
14. AISJ (American Institute for Social Justice), Washington, D.C.
15. ACORN National Office, Little Rock, AR
16. ACORN Pine Bluff, AR
17. ACORN Housing Corp., Little Rock, AR
18. ACHC, Little Rock, AR
19. ANP Little Rock, AR
20. Project Vote, Little Rock, AR

21. KABF, Little Rock, AR

22. SEIU Local 100, Little Rock, AR

23. ACORN National Office, Phoenix, AZ

24. ACORN Glendale, AZ

25. ACORN Mesa, AZ

26. ACORN Tucson, AZ

27. ACORN Housing Corp., Phoenix, AZ

28. ACORN National Office, Dallas, TX

29. ACORN Arlington, TX

30. ACORN Dallas, TX

31. ACORN El Paso, TX

32. ACORN Ft. Worth, TX

33. ACORN Houston, TX

34. ACORN Irving, TX

35. ACORN San Antonio, TX

36. ACORN Research Dallas, TX

37. ACORN Housing Corp., Dallas, TX

38. ACORN Housing Corp., Houston, TX

39. ACORN Housing Corp., San Antonio, TX

40. AGAPE, Dallas, TX

41. SEIU Local 100, Corpus Christi, TX

42. SEIU Local 100, Dallas, TX

43. SEIU Local 100, Houston, TX

44. SEIU Local 100, San Antonio, TX

45. ACORN National Office, Boston, MA

46. ACORN Boston, MA

47. ACORN Brockton, MA

48. ACORN Springfield, MA

49. ACORN Housing Corp., Boston, MA

50. ACORN Housing Corp., Springfield, MA

51. ACORN National Office, New Orleans, LA

52. ACORN Baton Rouge, LA

53. ACORN Lake Charles, LA

54. ACORN New Orleans, LA

55. ACORN Housing Corp., New Orleans, LA

56. Louisiana ACORN Fair Housing Organization, New Orleans, LA
57. ALERT, New Orleans, LA
58. AISJ (American Institute for Social Justice), New Orleans, LA
59. SEIU Local 100, Baton Rouge, LA
60. SEIU Local 100, Lake Charles, LA
61. SEIU Local 100, New Orleans, LA
62. SEIU Local 100, Shreveport, LA
63. Hospitality, Hotels, and Restaurants Organizing Council (HOTROC), New Orleans, LA
64. ACORN Bay Point, CA
65. ACORN Fresno, CA
66. ACORN Los Angeles, CA
67. ACORN Oakland, CA
68. ACORN Sacramento, CA
69. ACORN San Bernardino, CA
70. ACORN San Diego, CA
71. ACORN San Francisco, CA
72. ACORN San Jose, CA
73. ACORN Santa Ana, CA
74. ACORN Housing Corp., Fresno, CA
75. ACORN Housing Corp., Los Angeles, CA
76. ACORN Housing Corp., Oakland, CA
77. ACORN Housing Corp., Sacramento, CA
78. ACORN Housing Corp., San Diego, CA
79. ACORN Housing Corp., San Jose, CA
80. ACORN Housing Corp., Santa Ana, CA
81. ACORN Aurora, CO
82. ACORN Denver, CO
83. ACORN Housing Corp., Denver, CO
84. ACORN Bridgeport, CT
85. ACORN Hartford, CT
86. ACORN Waterbury, CT
87. ACORN Housing Corp., Bridgeport, CT
88. ACORN Housing Corp., New Haven, CT
89. ACORN Wilmington, DE

90. ACORN Ft. Lauderdale, FL

91. ACORN Hialeah, FL

92. ACORN Jacksonville, FL

93. ACORN Lake Worth, FL

94. ACORN Miami, FL

95. ACORN Orlando, FL

96. ACORN St. Petersburg, FL

97. ACORN c/o the Progressive Center, Tallahassee, FL

98. ACORN Tampa, FL

99. ACORN Housing Corp., Miami, FL

100. ACORN Housing Corp., Orlando, FL

101. Floridians for All Miami, FL

102. ACORN Atlanta, GA

103. ACORN Housing Corp., Atlanta, GA

104. ACORN Honolulu, HI

105. ACORN Chicago, IL

106. ACORN Springfield, IL

107. ACORN Housing Corp., Chicago, IL

108. ACORN Housing Corp. of Illinois

109. SEIU Local 880, Chicago, IL

110. SEIU Local 880, East St. Louis, IL

111. SEIU Local 880, Harvey, IL

112. SEIU Local 880, Peoria, IL

113. SEIU Local 880, Rock Island, IL

114. SEIU Local 880, Springfield, IL

115. ACORN Indianapolis, IN

116. ACORN Iowa

117. Peace and Social Justice Center of South Central Kansas, Wichita, KS

118. ACORN Louisville, KY

119. ACORN Baltimore, MD

120. ACORN Hyattsville, MD

121. ACORN Housing Corp., Baltimore, MD

122. ACORN Detroit, MI

123. ACORN Housing Corp., Detroit, MI

124. Edison Neighborhood Center Kalamazoo, MI

125. ACORN St. Paul, MN

126. ACORN Housing Corp., St. Paul, MN

127. ACORN Financial Justice Center St. Paul, MN

128. ACORN Kansas City, MO

129. ACORN St. Louis, MO

130. ACORN Housing Corp., Kansas City, MO

131. ACORN Housing Corp., St. Louis, MO

132. SEIU LOCAL 880 East St. Louis, MO

133. SEIU LOCAL 880 St. Louis, MO

134. ACORN Jersey City, NJ

135. ACORN Newark, NJ

136. ACORN Paterson, NJ

137. ACORN Housing Corp., Jersey City, NJ

138. ACORN Albuquerque, NM

139. ACORN Las Cruces, NM

140. ACORN Housing Corp., Albuquerque, NM

141. ACORN Charlotte, NC

142. ACORN Cincinnati, OH

143. ACORN Cleveland, OH

144. ACORN Columbus, OH

145. ACORN Toledo, OH

146. Lagrange Village Council Toledo, OH

147. ACORN Portland, OR

148. ACORN Housing Corp., Portland, OR

149. ACORN Allentown, PA

150. ACORN Harrisburg, PA

151. ACORN Philadelphia, PA

152. ACORN Pittsburgh, PA

153. ACORN Housing Corp., Philadelphia, PA

154. ACORN Housing Corp., Philadelphia, PA

155. ACORN Housing Corp., Pittsburgh, PA

156. ACORN Providence, RI

157. ACORN Housing Corp., Providence, RI

158. ACORN Memphis, TN

159. ACORN Norfolk, VA
160. ACORN Richmond, VA
161. ACORN Burien, WA
162. ACORN Milwaukee, WI
163. ACORN Housing Corp., Milwaukee, WI
164. ACORN Beverly, LLC
165. ACORN Center for Housing Inc.
166. Arkansas Community Housing Corp.
167. ACORN Community Land Association Inc.
168. ACORN Community Land Association, Albuquerque, NM
169. ACORN Community Land Association of Baltimore, MD
170. ACORN Community Land Association of Louisiana, New Orleans, LA
171. ACORN Community Land Association of Pennsylvania Inc.
172. ACORN Community Land Association of Illinois
173. ACORN Community Labor Organizing Center Inc.
174. ACORN Fair Housing, A Project of American Institute, Washington, D.C.
175. Arkansas ACORN Fair Housing Inc.
176. New Mexico ACORN Fair Housing Albuquerque, NM
177. ACORN Fair Housing, Washington, D.C.
178. ACORN Housing 1 Associates, LP (limited partnership)
179. ACORN Housing 2 Associates, LP (limited partnership)
180. ACORN Housing 2 Inc.
181. ACORN Housing Affordable Loans, LLC
182. ACORN Housing Corp. Inc.
183. Desert Rose Homes, LLC
184. Franklin ACORN Housing Inc.
185. Mott Haven ACORN Housing Development Fund
186. Mutual Housing Association of New York Inc.
187. New Orleans Community Housing Organization Inc.
188. ACORN Community Land Association of Illinois
189. Massachusetts ACORN Housing Corp.
190. Broad Street Corp.
191. Elysian Fields Corp.

192. ACORN 2004 Housing Development Fund Corp.

193. ACORN 2005 Housing Development Fund Corp.

194. ACORN Dumont-Snediker Housing Development Fund Corp.

195. Dumont Avenue Housing Development Fund

196. Elysian Fields Partnership

197. Fifteenth Street Corp.

198. New York ACORN Housing Co. Inc.

199. Development Fund Corp.

200. New York Organizing and Support Center Inc.

201. Baltimore Organizing and Support Center Inc.

202. Chicago Organizing and Support Center Inc.

203. Houston Organizing and Support Center Inc.

204. 5301 McDougall Corp.

205. New Mexico Organizing and Support Center Inc.

206. New York Organizing and Support Center Inc.

207. Phoenix Organizing and Support Center Inc.

208. 385 Palmetto Street Housing Development Fund Corp.

209. Sixth Avenue Corp.

210. 4415 San Jacinto Street Corp.

211. St. Louis Organizing and Support Center Inc.

212. St. Louis Tax Reform Group Inc.

213. Greenwell Springs Corp.

214. Austin Organizing and Support Center Inc.

215. Boston Organizing and Support Center Inc.

216. American Home Day Care Workers Association Inc.

217. American Workers Association

218. Baton Rouge Association of School Employees Inc.

219. Hospitality Hotel and Restaurant Organizing Council

220. Illinois Home Child Care Workers Association Inc.

221. Labor Link Inc.

222. Labor Neighbor Research and Training Center Inc.

223. Missouri Home Child Care Workers Association Inc.

224. Middle South Home Day Care Workers Association Inc.

225. Wal-Mart Alliance for Reform Now Inc.

226. Wal-Mart Association for Reform Now

227. Working Families Association Inc.

228. Wal-Mart Workers Association Inc.

229. People Organizing Workfare Workers/ACORN/CWA Inc.

230. Texas United City-County Employees Inc.

231. Texas United School Employees Inc.

232. United Labor Foundation of Greater New Orleans Inc.

233. United Security Workers of America

234. Orleans Criminal Sheriffs

235. SEIU Local 100

236. SEIU Local 880

237. Arkansas Broadcasting Foundation Inc.

238. Agape Broadcasting Foundation Inc.

239. Affiliated Media Foundation Movement Inc.

240. Allied Media Projects Inc.

241. ACORN National Broadcasting Network Inc.

242. Alabama Radio Movement Inc. (Dissolved)

243. ACORN Television in Action for Communities Inc.

244. California Community Television Network

245. Flagstaff Broadcasting Foundation Inc.

246. Iowa ACORN Broadcasting Corp.

247. Maricopa Community Television Project Inc.

248. Montana Radio Network Inc.

249. Radio New Mexico Inc.

250. Shreveport Community Television Inc.

251. Crescent City Broadcasting Corp.

252. KABF Radio

253. KNON Radio

254. ACORN Institute Inc.

255. ACORN Institute Inc., Washington, D.C.

256. ACORN Institute, Dallas, TX

257. ACORN Institute Inc., New Orleans, LA

258. American Institute for Social Justice Inc.

259. Association for Rights of Citizens Inc.

260. New York Agency for Community Affairs Inc.

261. Pennsylvania Institute for Community Affairs Inc.

262. Project Vote/Voting for America Inc.

263. ACORN Tenant Union Training & Organizing Project Inc.

264. ACORN Law for Education Representation & Training Inc.

265. American Environmental Justice Project Inc.

266. ACORN International Inc.

267. Environmental Justice Training Project Inc.

268. Movement for Economic Justice, Education & Training Center Inc.

269. Missouri Tax Justice Research Project Inc.

270. ACORN Beneficial Association Inc.

271. ACORN Canada

272. ACORN Children's Beneficial Association Inc.

273. ACORN Campaign to Raise the Minimum Wage Inc.

274. ACORN Cultural Trust Inc.

275. ACORN Dual Language Community Academy

276. ACORN Fund Inc.

277. ACORN Foster Parents Inc.

278. ACORN Institute Canada

279. ACORN Political Action Committee Inc.

280. ACORN Tenants' Union Inc.

281. Community Training for Environmental Justice Inc.

282. Connecticut Working Families

283. Democracy for America

284. Hammurabi Fund Inc.

285. McLellan Multi-Family Corp.

286. Metro Technical Institute Inc.

287. New Party National Committee Inc.

288. Volunteers for America Inc.

289. Volunteers for California Inc.

290. Volunteers for Missouri Inc.

291. ACORN Management Corp.

292. Associated Regional Maintenance Systems

293. ACORN Associates Inc.

294. ACORN Associates Inc. Albuquerque, NM

295. ACORN Campaign Services Inc.

296. ACORN Services Inc.

297. Citizens Consulting Inc.

298. Chief Organizer Fund Inc.

299. Citizens Services Inc.

300. People's Equipment Resource Corp. Inc.

301. National Center for Jobs & Justice

302. Service Workers Action Team

303. Living Wage Resource Center

304. American Home Childcare Providers Association

305. Association for the Rights of Citizens Inc.

306. California Community Network

307. Child Care Providers for Action Franklin

308. Citizens Action Research Project

309. Citizens Campaign for Work, Living Wage & Labor Peace

310. Citizens for Future Progress

311. Citizens Campaign for Finance Reform

312. Floridians for All PAC

313. Greenville Community Charter School Inc.

314. Student Minimum Wage Action Campaign

315. Site Fighters

316. Social Policy

317. Southern Training Center

318. ACORN Votes

319. Communities Voting Together

320. Arkansas ACORN Political Action Committee

321. Arkansas New Party

322. California APAC (Political Action Committee)

323. Citizens for April Troope

324. Colorado Organizing and Support Center Inc.

325. Citizens Campaign for Fair Work

326. Citizens Services Society Inc.

327. Clean Government APAC

328. Community Voices Together

329. Community Real Estate Processing Inc.

330. Council Beneficial Association

331. Council Health Plan

332. Desert Rose Homeowners' Association

333. District of Columbia APAC

334. Friends of Wendy Foy

335. Illinois APAC

336. Illinois New Party

337. Institute for Worker Education

338. Jefferson Area Public Employees

339. Jefferson Area School Employees

340. Local 100 Health & Welfare Fund

341. Local 100 Political Action Committee

342. Local 100 Retirement Fund

343. Local 880 PAC

344. Local 880 Political PAC

345. Louisiana APAC

346. Maryland APAC

347. Massachusetts APAC

348. Missouri APAC

349. Mutual Housing Association of New York Neighborhood Restore

350. Neighbors for Arthelia Ray

351. Neighbors for Maria Torres

352. Neighbors for Ted Thomas

353. New Mexico APAC

354. New Orleans Campaign for Living Wage Committee

355. New York APAC

356. Oregon APAC

357. Orleans Criminal Sheriffs Workers Organization Inc.

358. Pennsylvania APAC

359. Progressive Houston

360. Progressive St. Louis

361. Rhode Island APAC

362. ACORN Housing 3 Inc.*

363. ACORN Housing 4 Inc.*

364. 1825 Atlantic ACORN Housing Inc.*

365. 730 Rockaway ACORN Housing Inc.*

366. ACORN Housing 3 Associates, LP (Limited Partnership)*
367. ACORN Housing 4 Associates, LP (Limited Partnership)*
368. Phoenix Estates, LLC*
369. New Jersey ACORN Housing Corp.*
370. MHANY 2003 Housing Development Fund Corp.*

---

* Identified as a related organization on IRS Form 990 for Tax Year 2008 for Mutual Housing Association of New York Inc., at http://www.guidestar.org/FinDocuments/2009/112/848/2009-112848938-05e57872-9.pdf (accessed Aug. 31, 2010).

Source: "Is ACORN Intentionally Structured As a Criminal Enterprise?" U.S. House of Representatives, Committee on Oversight and Government Reform, July 23, 2009, at http://republicans.oversight.house.gov/images/stories/Reports/20091118_ACORNREPORT.pdf: 74–81.

APPENDIX B:
SELECT ORGANIZATIONS, GOVERNMENT AGENCIES, GOVERNMENT PROGRAMS, AND LAWS

Action for Boston Community Development (ABCD)

AFDC (Aid to Families with Dependent Children)

ACORN 8

Advanta Corp.

AFSCME (American Federation of State, County and Municipal Employees)

All of Us or None

Alliance for Justice

Alliance for Worker Freedom

America Coming Together (ACT)

America's Servicing Co.

AARP (American Association of Retired Persons)

ACLU (American Civil Liberties Union)

AFL-CIO (American Federation of Labor—Congress of Industrial Organizations)

American Federation of State, County and Municipal Employees (AFSCME)

American Federation of Teachers (AFT)

American Institute for Economic Research

AIG (American International Group Inc.)

Americans for Financial Reform

AmeriCorps

Ameriquest

Apollo Alliance

Arca Foundation

Arkansas Power and Light (AP&L)

Arkay Foundation

Atlantic Philanthropies

Bank of America

Bank of America Charitable Foundation Inc.

Bank of New York

Barbra Streisand Foundation

Barclay's Bank of New York

Bauman Family Foundation

Beldon Fund

Ben & Jerry's Foundation

Beneficial Corp.

Black Panther Party

Eli & Edythe L. Broad Foundation

Cal Fed Bank

Campaign for America's Future

Capital One Bank

Capital One Foundation

Capital Research Center (CRC)

Carlyle Group

Carnegie Corp. of New York

Casa de Maryland

Annie E. Casey Foundation

Marguerite Casey Foundation

Catholic Campaign for Human Development (CCHD)

U.S. Census Bureau

Center for American Progress (CAP)

Center for American Progress Action Fund

Center for Community Change (CCC)

Center for Constitutional Rights (CCR)

Center for Neighborhood Enterprise (CNE)

Center for Public Integrity

Center for Reproductive Law and Policy (CRLP)

Center for Reproductive Rights

Center for Responsible Lending (CRL)

Center for Working Families (CWF)

Center on Budget and Policy Priorities (CBPP)

Chase Bank

Chemical Bank

Chicago Annenberg Challenge (CAC)

Children's Defense Fund (CDF)

CITGO

Citigroup Foundation

CitiMortgage

Citizen Action

Citizens Energy Corp.

Citizens for the Abolition of Poverty

Citizens for Responsibility and Ethics in Washington (CREW)

Citizens' Crusade Against Poverty

Citizens Organized for Public Service (COPS)

Civil Rights Act

Edna McConnell Clark Foundation

Clergy and Laity United for Economic Justice (CLUE)

Color of Change

Committees of Correspondence for Democracy and Socialism

Common Ground

Communist Party Marxist-Leninist

Communist Party USA (CPUSA)

CDBG (Community Development Block Grants)

Community Housing Partnership Act

Community Reinvestment Act (CRA)

Congressional Research Service (CRS)

Con Edison (Con Ed)

CORE (Congress of Racial Equality)

Congressional Progressive Caucus (CPC)

Corporation for National and Community Service (CNCS)

Council on American-Islamic Relations (CAIR)

Countrywide Financial

Cross City Campaign for Urban School Reform

Crossland Savings Bank

Nathan Cummings Foundation

Data and Field Services (DFS)

Davis, Miner, Barnhill & Galland

Developing Communities Project (DCP)

Democracy Alliance

"Democracy Restoration Act" (proposed)

DNC (Democratic National Committee)

Democratic Socialist Organizing Committee (DSOC)

Democratic Socialists of America (DSA)

Deutsche Bank Americas Foundation

DART (Direct Action and Research Training Institute)

Discount Foundation

EITC (Earned Income Tax Credit)

Economic Opportunity Act (EOA)

ERAP (Economic Research and Action Project)

Edison Schools Inc.

1851 Center for Constitutional Law

U.S. Election Assistance Commission (EAC)

"Employee Free Choice Act" (proposed) (EFCA—also known as "card check")

ERISA (Employee Retirement Income Security Act)

Employment Policies Institute (EPI)

U.S. Environmental Protection Agency (EPA)

U.S. Equal Employment Opportunity Commission (EEOC)

Exelon Corp.

Fannie Mae (FNMA—Federal National Mortgage Association)

FBI (Federal Bureau of Investigation)

FCC (Federal Communications Commission)

FDIC (Federal Deposit Insurance Corp.)

FEC (Federal Election Commission)

FEMA (Federal Emergency Management Agency)

Freddie Mac (FHLMC—Federal Home Loan Mortgage Corp.)

FHA (Federal Housing Administration)

Federal Reserve Board

FSLIC (Federal Savings and Loan Insurance Corp.)

FTC (Federal Trade Commission)

Fenton Communications

First American Title Insurance Co.

First Union

Fleet Bank

Ford Foundation

Forest City Ratner Companies LLC

Freedom of Information Act (FOIA)

Friends of the Earth

FALN (Fuerzas Armadas de Liberación Nacional Puertorriqueña—Armed Forces of Puerto Rican National Liberation)

FARC (Fuerzas Armadas Revolucionarias de Colombia—Revolutionary Armed Forces of Colombia)

Gamaliel Foundation

Bill & Melinda Gates Foundation

General Electric (GE)

GE Capital Mortgage Insurance Corp.

Gill Foundation

Golden West Financial Corp.

Grassroots School Improvement Campaign (GSIC)

Greenlining Institute

Greenpeace

H&R Block

Evelyn & Walter Haas Jr. Fund

Hamas

Harlem Success Academy

Harmon, Curran, Spielberg & Eisenberg

Harvard University

Haymarket People's Fund

Edward W. Hazen Foundation Inc.

Head Start

Health Care for America Now (HCAN)

Health Care for America Education Fund

U.S. Department of Health, Education, and Welfare (HEW)

U.S. Department of Health and Human Services (HHS)

Heritage Foundation

Hezbollah

Hip Hop Caucus

HKH Foundation

Home Depot Foundation

Homestead Act

Household Finance Corp.

Department of Housing Preservation and Development (New York City)

U.S. Department of Housing and Urban Development (HUD)

HSBC Finance

Human Rights Watch

India for unfettered access," according to ACORN India. "[The] Indian market is facing an onslaught of both foreign and domestic corporate retailers, the most notable of which is Wal-Mart."

THE DEMOCRACY ALLIANCE:
ACORN'S FAT CAT FRIENDS

The Democracy Alliance is a collection of socialist venture capitalists that funds ACORN and other left-wing groups that want to smash the American system. Leftist blogger Markos Moulitsas called it "a vast, Vast Left Wing Conspiracy to rival" the conservative movement.[730] The Alliance's founder, Democratic operative Rob Stein, thinks ACORN is a mainstream organization. He called ACORN, which received a grant of unknown size from the group in 2006, "a grassroots, tough-minded, liberal-left organization" and "a very responsible organization."

The Alliance is a secretive donors' collaborative to fund a permanent political infrastructure of nonprofit think tanks, media outlets, leadership schools, and activist groups to compete with the conservative movement. The group is registered in the District of Columbia as a taxable nonprofit. That status allows it to avoid having to publicly disclose its financial affairs. It is organizing state-level chapters in at least 19 states, and once-conservative Colorado, which hosts the Democracy Alliance's most successful state affiliate, turned Democrat blue. The group also funds the Secretary of State Project that helped to put in place the Minnesota secretary of state who helped Al Franken steal the 2008 U.S. Senate election. Alliance member Simon Rosenberg, founder of the New Democrat Network (NDN), said in 2008 that that the Alliance has already "channeled hundreds of millions of dollars into progressive organizations."

The Alliance's board is a microcosm of the modern left. In the top rungs are Rob McKay, a limousine liberal, SEIU's Anna Burger, San Francisco lawyer Steven Phillips, and Drummond Pike, a peacenik from the 1960s. Taco Bell heir McKay, its chairman, was born in conservative Orange County, California, and his parents were

Republicans. The vice chairman is Burger. Phillips is secretary and Pike, who created the Tides Foundation, is treasurer.

The Alliance has more than 100 donor-members, both individuals and organizations. However, it has not made available an official list of its "partners." Some of the more prominent members are ACORN benefactors Herb and Marion Sandler, Hollywood producer Norman Lear, and Gara LaMarche, CEO of the Atlantic Philanthropies. LaMarche used to be vice president at Soros's Open Society Institute. SEIU and AFL-CIO are institutional members.

Chief among the members of the Democracy Alliance is leftist troublemaker George Soros, a billionaire currency speculator who has funded the overthrow of several governments. He is the virtual owner of today's Democratic Party. Having purchased, rented, or placed a down payment on all the political influence up for sale in America, he announced plans in late 2009 to ramp up his war on markets worldwide by creating an "Institute for New Economic Thinking" (INET). "The system we have now has actually broken down, only we haven't quite recognized it and so you need to create a new one and this is the time to do it," Soros told the *Financial Times*.

Soros told *Der Spiegel* that European-style socialism "is exactly what we need now. I am against market fundamentalism. I think this propaganda that government involvement is always bad has been very successful—but also very harmful to our society." As preparation for INET, Soros gathered economists to plot his renewed drive for world statism. One of those economists is Joseph Stiglitz, a member of the socialist International. Stiglitz sits on SI's Commission on Global Financial Issues, which was created "to address from a social democratic perspective the ongoing global financial crisis." Of course to socialists a capitalist economy is by definition always in crisis.

Why Soros feels he's not having enough impact on the world is unclear. Soros helped finance the Czech Republic's 1989 "Velvet Revolution" that brought Vaclav Havel to power. He acknowledged having orchestrated coups in Croatia, Georgia, Slovakia, and Yugoslavia. He brought the financial systems of the United Kingdom and

Human Service Employees Registration and Voter Education Fund (Human SERVE)

Industrial Areas Foundation (IAF)

Industrial Workers of the World (IWW—also known as "Wobblies")

Institute for New Economic Thinking (INET)

International Institute of Islamic Thought

Investor Responsibility Research Center (IRRC)

Jackson Hewitt

Japanese Red Army (JRA)

Job Corps

Jobs with Justice (JwJ)

Judicial Watch

U.S. Department of Justice (DOJ)

Justice, Equality, Human (Dignity) and Tolerance Foundation (JEHT)

W.K. Kellogg Foundation

Edward M. Kennedy Serve America Act

Ku Klux Klan (KKK)

U.S. Department of Labor (DOL)

LawCash

Lear Family Foundation

Living Wage Resource Center

Lobbying Disclosure Act

M&T Charitable Foundation

Magna Bank

Make the Road New York

Manor Care

Media Matters for America

Media Matters Action Network

Mellon Bank

Middle South Utilities

Midwest Academy

Minnesota Majority

Missouri Progressive Vote Coalition (ProVote)

Mobilize.org

Mobilization for Youth (MFY)

Money Mart

JPMorgan Chase Foundation

Mothers for Adequate Welfare (MAW)

Charles Stewart Mott Foundation

Movement for Economic Justice (MEJ)

MoveOn Civic Action

MoveOn Political Action

National Abortion Rights Action League (NARAL)

National Affordable Housing Act

NAACP (National Association for the Advancement of Colored People)

National Bolivarian Militia

National Council of La Raza (also known simply as La Raza)

National Education Association (NEA)

National Endowment for the Arts (NEA)

National Judicial Conduct and Disability Law Project Inc.

National Labor Relations Board (NLRB)

National Legal and Policy Center (NLPC)

National Paint & Coatings Association (NPCA)

National People's Action (NPA)

National Right To Work

National Voter Registration Act (NVRA—also known as the Motor Voter law)

NationsBank

Needmor Fund

Neighborhood Assistance Corp. of America (NACA)

NeighborWorks (also known as Neighborhood Reinvestment Corp.)

New Black Panther Party

New Democrat Network (NDN)

New Party

NY Citizens Services Inc.

New York Community Trust

New York Times Co.

La Nueva Televisora del Sur (teleSUR—"The New Television Station of the South")

Liberty Tax Service

National Urban League (NUL)

National Welfare Rights Organization (NWRO)

Natural Resources Defense Council (NRDC)

Norwest Financial

October League

Office of the Comptroller of the Currency (OCC)

Office of Economic Opportunity (OEO)

Omidyar Network Fund Inc.

Open Society Institute (OSI)

Organizing for America (OFA)

Orkin Exterminating Co.

Outer Mission Residents Association, San Francisco (OMRA)

Organizers' Forum

Occupational Safety and Health Act (OSHA)

William Penn Foundation

PICO (People Improving Communities Through Organizing)

Peoples Hurricane Relief Fund

PDVSA (Petroleos de Venezuela SA)

Pew Charitable Trusts

Philadelphia Gas Works

Picower Foundation

Planned Parenthood Federation of America

PNC Bank

PNC Financial

PNC Foundation

Port Huron Statement

Pratt Institute Center for Community and Environmental Development

Progressive America Fund Inc.

Progressive Chicago

Protect Our Land Association (POLA)

Precinct Action Leaders (PAL)

ProPublica

Provident Bank Foundation Inc.

Public Service Enterprise Group Inc. (PSEG)

RainbowPUSH Coalition

Red Cross

RNC (Republican National Committee)

Republican National Lawyers Association (RNLA)

Z. Smith Reynolds Foundation

Robin Hood Foundation

Rockefeller Brothers Fund Inc.

Rockefeller Family Fund Inc.

Roosevelt Financial Group Inc.

Roseanne Foundation

Safa Trust Inc.

Salomon Smith Barney

San Diego Gas & Electric (SDG&E)

Sandler Foundation

Save Health and Property (SHAP)

Scott + Yandura Consulting

Secretary of State Project (SoS Project)

Securities and Exchange Commission (SEC)

SEIU (Service Employees International Union)

Sherwin-Williams

Sierra Club

Stephen M. Silberstein Foundation

Socialist International (SI)

Southern Poverty Law Center

S-CHIP (State Children's Health Insurance Program)

Students for a Democratic Society (SDS)

Site Fighters

Small Schools Workshop

Success Charter Network

Supplemental Nutrition Assistance Program (SNAP)

Student Nonviolent Coordinating Committee (SNCC)

Socialist Party

Socialist International (SI)

SEPTA (Southeastern Pennsylvania Transportation Authority)

Starbucks Foundation

Symbionese Liberation Army (SLA)

TCF Financial Corp.

Teamsters

Teamsters for a Corruption Free Union

Tides Center

Tides Foundation

Tulsa Urban Renewal Authority

Union Bank of California Foundation

United Auto Workers (UAW)

United Farm Workers (UFW)

United Federation of Teachers (UFT)

United Labor Unions (ULU)

United Mine Workers of America (UMW, UMWA)

United Missouri Bancshares (UMB)

United Nations (UN)

United Steelworkers (USW)

US Bancorp Foundation

United States Conference of Catholic Bishops (USCCB)

U.S. PIRG (U.S. Public Interest Research Group)

Vanguard Charitable Endowment Program

Vanguard Public Foundation

VISTA (Volunteers in Service to America—now known as Ameri-Corps VISTA)

Wachovia Bank

Wachovia Wells Fargo Foundation

Wal-Mart

Wallace Global Fund

Washington Interfaith Network (WIN)

Weatherman

Wells Fargo

Western Development Corp.

White House Council on Environmental Quality (CEQ)

The Woodlawn Organization

Woods Fund of Chicago

Workforce Development Institute (WDI)

Working Families Party (WFP)

World Savings Bank

WTO (World Trade Organization)

Weather Underground Organization (WUO)

Young Communist League

Young Democrats of America

Young Democratic Socialists (YDS)

APPENDIX C:
Wade Rathke's Blog Post about Brandon Darby

Common Ground Infiltrator

January 31, 2009, New Orleans

There was a brief squib on the wire that defied easy explanation. One of the co-founders of Common Ground, an agency that had sprung after Katrina first with a health center on the West Bank and then involved in some recovery work on the East Bank, was revealed to be an FBI-informer who had fingered some folks for mayhem designed for the Republican National Convention in 2008 in the Twin Cities. It seemed so, how should I say it, sixties?

We recognized the guy, Brandon Darby, though did not know him well. For awhile when the building was reopened on Elysian Fields where all of us worked it was one of the few hotspots in the downtown area and a staging point for work in the 9th and lower 9th ward. In the evenings some time Common Ground folks would stop by just to see what was happening. The organizers and I remember Brandon being with them a time or two, but nothing special.

Now it seems that there may have been a lot more or less to all of this, because as more of the story trickles out, it really gets weird.

Everyone seems to agree that Malik Rahim from New Orleans, who had been around the local scene before the storm, and I think even a candidate for Mayor at one point, if I remember right, founded Common Ground along with Darby and another friend of theirs from Austin named Scott Crow, both of whom seem to have been activists there and largely anarchists more than anything else. During the first year Darby even acted as executive director and as these things go seems to have been both in and out of New Orleans and the Common Ground crowd as they agreed or disagreed on one thing or another as happens.

Still this FBI informant thing is a little past the pale. One thing to disagree, but it's a whole different thing to rat on folks, or, even worse, as some now allege, to try and mousetrap people.

The local weekly in New Orleans, Gambit, ran a piece recently that quoted Lisa Fithian at length, which made me take another look at all of this. Lisa was a former organizer for SEIU's Justice for Janitors campaign, more than a decade ago. We had her speak about new tactics about 8 years ago at an Organizers' Forum dialogue because she was involved in some interesting and novel work with anti-globalism forces post-Seattle. She even had a moment of fame with a big story and a picture in the *New York Times* Sunday magazine sections a couple of years ago, though I don't remember the topic. I even did a double-take in Washington last week when I saw her at the immigration rally we were putting together after the inaugural, but I didn't get to speak. Anyway, I had not realized she was anywhere around New Orleans or Common Ground, but so she seems to have been and she was quoted in the Gambit story with a lot of theories that this guy was a provocateur and might have been doing that duty for the FBI in the post-Katrina days. She seemed to infer that some of the internal squabbles and problems that Common Ground had from time to time might have been this guy's mischief. She says they are making a bunch of FOIA requests to find out when Darby went over to the dark side, so to speak.

All of this is disconcerting. Why would an anti-hurricane group be infiltrated? Is that why they were coming by on a drop-in basis to the New Orleans ACORN operation then as well? Why in the age of Bush did we need to go back to the 60's and the Darth Vader times again?

I'm not sure exactly what may have happened. Darby is suddenly not talking, but this is all both sketchy and creepy, and I want there to be different rules of engagement in the Age of Obama.

Source: http://chieforganizer.org/2009/01/31/common-ground-infiltrator/.

APPENDIX D:
Bertha Lewis's Speech to Young Democratic Socialists, March 2010

BERTHA LEWIS: Yes, it's me. Notorious. First of all, let me just say, I would like to give my honor to all of you and give you all a hand because any group that says I'm young, I'm democratic, and I'm a socialist is alright with me. You know that's no light thing to do, to actually say I'm a socialist, basically.

You guys know that right now we are living in a time which is going to dwarf the McCarthy era. It is going to dwarf the internments during World War II. We are, right now, in a time that is going to dwarf the era of Jim Crow and segregation. We are in it, right now. This is not theoretical. This is not [a case of] well maybe it could be. This is for real. We're talking about this economic crisis. And, I was, like, crisis? What crisis? When did this crisis start? Me and mine have always been in a crisis. Always. It's nothing new. Always. For 10 years, my organization has been saying that the sky was falling. Predatory lending was going to bring us down. We all resented Bill Clinton. Jokingly, people call him the first black president. Come on now. How insulting is that? Especially when welfare reform is all about black people. And yes, H.R. 10, which some of you will go back with Bill Clinton, sitting behind his big desk, with a bunch of white guys around him, signing the abolishment of Glass-Steagall Act.

We are in this right now. These are very dangerous times. Don't let people say to you that there is a crisis. Yes, it's a crisis for them, but we've always been in a crisis. If you're poor, if you're working, and if you're a person of color in this country, it's like black folks used to say, 'When old *massa* sneeze, do we say we gotta cold?' And that's what's happening here. Wall Street sneezes and we have the swine flu. [unintelligible] or not. Culpable corporations, gee, they still have a lot of money. And none of these people are on the unemployment line. None of them are trying to get food stamps. There's still a lot of money out there. I mean, how blatant do they have to be? You know, we're going to have all these sort of talk shows about Wall Street bonuses, how can there even possibly be a bonus? How insane is this? A bonus? I mean, you know, people just go along as if it really is all about how big it is. This is one instance where size does not matter. There should be none. Not how big is your bonus or how tiny is your bonus, no bonus. None! None!

Hollywood. I'm so sick of Hollywood. How do we live in a universe in which a movie, a *movie*, can cost hundreds of millions of dollars, and then be talked about because it hit over the billion dollar mark? How insane is that? And yet there is an argument in Congress that healthcare is too sweeping and too expensive. How is it that we have a war that's going on and we have, in the month of January, more suicides having been committed by servicemen and women than all of the troops that were killed in Iraq and Afghanistan? Human beings gone. How is it that we can have a trillion, multi-trillion dollar industry called Hollywood and, with a straight face, say we can't afford healthcare? That's ridiculous. And yet, let's have the pundits debate it and talk about it and first year in high school, it's like when you get Logic 101, you gotta accept the premise.

Well, Young Democratic Socialists, again, the reason that I'm glad to be here today, always invite me every year and I will always come, is because you all did not accept the premise. Here, and folks know that we are the canary in the mine, other than this new reactionary era, and one of the things that really, really is shameful is the so-called progressive, liberal foundations in this country. When you want to talk about building institutions and organizing, and Joe's right, you've got to knock on a door. You actually have to meet up together. You actually have to make a strategy. And it's not just one march. That's mobilizing. And it's not just being for the right thing and asking people to do the right thing. That's advocacy.

What is dangerous is organizing, and the empire will strike back. Believe me: I know. And when they can't twist what you're doing, or demonize it, they will just make it up. I have to say that part of our problems on the Left, and those progressives, if you still want to call yourselves progressive 'cause you know Glenn Beck has already decided the next campaign is to demonize progressives, and to actually do a revisionism of the history of progressives, so you might want to say that you're young, you're democratic, and you're a progressive socialist. That'll be something because then, I think, again, you ought to just take them on and say, 'Yeah, I am, What of it?' Because that's how they're coming at them. The foundations, Rockefellers, Atlantic Philanthropies, Ford, all these big guys, these people, I don't know most people talk about . . . these are your enemies. These folks are part of the very fabric that keep all of this madness going in this capitalist country. As a community organization, part of our problem, which we learned, is you can't depend on the kindness of these strangers to support your program. You always had to say 'we're not really organizing, we're doing civic engagement.' And anytime you have to, kind of, soften up what you are actually doing, beware. Beware.

We understand that for 40 years our organization has been trying to do the right thing, organize for poor people, not just at soup kitchens and give out warm coats and empower folks but actually trying to build something where people have real power, that in fact, the very foundations that were supposed to be liberal and progressive and supposed to like poor people, the folks in charge, none of the folks in charge like poor people and like people of color—just let's be clear about that. They don't. They don't like us, and they don't like you either because you're young, you're democratic, you're socialist. These are the same folks who make their money through the exploitation of all of us in this country. These foundations, their boards consist of the captains of industry. So, *duh!* There we were for 40 years fighting against the same people who we were asking to give us a grant, and when the hammer came down, and the empire struck back, these folks were the first to run. They are the ones.

There's this unconstitutional defunding language which the constitutional lawyer President Obama signed. The last time there was this bill of attainder where a group of people were singled out, was these government employees that happened to be socialists. It was finally declared 'you cannot do that' because the Founding Fathers said you cannot hold down any group for infamy but our constitutional president, I guess he missed that class. Foundations in this country are just like corporations: they're huge, they control a lot of public opinion and if you are progressive in any way, they will be the first ones to come and crush you. So folks, really, as Jones says, that's a dirty little secret.

And that brings us to the attack on us, on ACORN and the Working Families Party and organization after organization. Ladies and gentlemen, people, if there's nothing else I can impart on you today, you should, yes, be afraid and pissed off and angry because it is us today—it is you tomorrow. And it probably is you today. Don't think that you are too small to be noticed. They are coming, and they are coming after you and they are going to be brutal and oppressive. They've already shown it to you. So when Jones says organize, get out into the street, you really have got to circle the wagons. This is not rhetoric or hyperbole. This is real. This is real. They will come after you, after your mother, after your father, after your sister and after your brother. Believe me.

When you heard about the Bush administration wire-tapping people, did you think that that didn't apply to you? Did you feel, this is the crisis, when we talk about economics, because it's always about the money, always about the money. We need the fundamental things: food, clothing, shelter, just so you can live—and what is being attacked? Your food, people you need to clothe yourself, and your shelter in the foreclosure crisis. And not only that: we're human beings. We have a body. Why do you want to be able to take care of your body? If this isn't blatant that there is a genocide of liberals and progressives and radicals, I don't know what is.

And then, we have the cowardly lions of the Democratic Party in Congress. Unbelievable. That is why we need a third party in this country. We need a third party, and it ain't for tea. We need a third party in this country. Because no matter what, one thing you can say about that dumbass Bush, and those Republicans: they didn't give a damn. Millions, billions of dollars, faith-based initiative. You got something to say about it? Didn't bother, didn't matter. Deregulation, no regulation. We don't care. It's a big party. We won. Our folks are in and we're going to reward our buddies. No problem. It didn't care.

Would you vote, would the Democrats vote, war? There's no reason to go to war but we going to make up one. Give me Karl Rove, right now, that bastard, oh yes, there were no WMDs but we knew it. We used it. We should have lied more. And it's no coincidence, this rise of this Tea Party so-called movement, bowel movement in my opinion, and this blatant uncovering and ripping off the mask of racism. I mean have you seen anything like this? I mean this used to be, what folks would talk about, like in Selma, Alabama, when there was a struggle for civil rights. Have you seen this? Absolutely. It's just like it's P.L. Some guy sends out an email to all his Republican friends for a fundraiser making a joke saying have you seen Tarzan's cheetah lately? Remember Cheetah? You used to see those old grainy Tarzan movies, Cheetah the Chimp. Oh yeah, Cheetah's doing quite well. She went to law school and now she's living in the White House. And there's a picture of Michelle Obama, you know, pursing her lips.

There's a picture of a chimpanzee next to her. And it's alright. And it's just not hidden or some fringe thing. This is the Tennessee Republican Party and it's alright. This should be frightening. So, here's what we have to do. Damn it, this particular organization, Young Democratic Socialists, you do whatever you can, in every way that you can, and all of you devote more time, to building this organization. I mean

that. Build it. We need more members, get out there, and do everything that you can to build this institution. And as you are building
it, make sure that you build it in a way in which you are self-sufficient.
Do not rely on the kindness of strangers. Do not rely on little, tiny,
itty-bitty, things of money. Make your own business. Make your own
exchanges.

But you build this organization because the reason we were cut
down is because we actually built our organization for poor people.
For poor people. There's no big organization for poor people in this
country. There's no organization to really protect working families
that has any power. There's no organization to protect children,
except if you want to privatize anything to do with our children. And
there certainly isn't any organization to protect old people 'cause it
ain't the AARP, that big insurance company of America. The reason
that you have to build your organization, and make it as big and as
powerful as you can, is because you need to get into real battles.

And here's what I think you need to do: And you need to make
sure that you get into this battle, the next big battle that's coming,
whether healthcare lives or dies. And I think it will limp along in some
[unintelligible] retarded, you know, I said it, retarded thing. Because
that's what it's going to be. This mish-mash bill. Immigration is the
next big battle. Immigration, immigration and immigration. And the
reason that this is so important is, you know, here's the secret. [*Begins
to whisper.*] We're getting ready to be a majority-minority country. Shhhhh. We'll be like South Africa. More black people than white people. Don't tell anybody. [*End of whispering.*] Get yourselves together.
Get strong. Get big. And get in this battle. Get in this battle because
again it's all about money. How this country works. All that we have in
this country, and the fact that this fear of a black planet, that's being
played out, in the United States today, the future of our country, is
people of color. And how that's going to change our psyche and our
economics. This is why folks are grabbing so hard to change the economic paradigm because we gettin' ready to have a majority country
of people of color. And the fear of a black planet is real.

So, we talk about jobs, jobs, jobs, think about what Joe talked about in terms of immigration. What kind of jobs and for who. Who are producing those jobs and for who? How many of those jobs? Will they be fair? Open? Jobs with benefits? Or, living wages? Or will we continue to accept the exploitation of immigrants? And my challenge to black folks and to people of color and civil rights folks is this: the face of immigration needs to be a lot blacker than it is because once they can frame the immigration debate is about Latinos, crossing some mythical border, when in fact we have second and third generation black folks, in this country, who come from immigrant families, but they're not standing up and marching with their Latino brothers and sisters and saying 'I am an immigrant, too.' Marcus Garvey would be ashamed of you. So, Young Democratic Socialists, join this immigration war. Black people, young black people, that have been put in the vast vat of African Americans, join. Don't march alongside. Don't march in the back. Be right out front. Because that will be the battle for our democracy. That will the battle for the kind of government that we have. That will be the economic battle of epic proportions. Immigration, self-sufficiency, and the people united.

Sources: "The Economic Crisis - YDS Winter Conference," Parts 4, 5, and 6, available at http://www.youtube.com/user/TheYDSUSA#p/u/11/vkQOhfbGDHM, http://www.youtube.com/user/TheYDSUSA#p/u/10/RbQIK1i8VUg, and http://www.youtube.com/user/TheYDSUSA#p/u/9/0_bou5bSWZM.

APPENDIX E:
Saul Alinsky's Rules from
Rules for Radicals

Saul Alinsky describes 24 rules in *Rules for Radicals*. Of those 24 rules, 13 are rules of "power tactics":

1. "Power is not only what you have but what the enemy thinks you have."
2. "Never go outside the experience of your people."
3. "Wherever possible go outside of the experience of the enemy."
4. "Make the enemy live up to their own book of rules."
5. "Ridicule is man's most potent weapon."
6. "A good tactic is one that your people enjoy."
7. "A tactic that drags on too long becomes a drag."
8. "Keep the pressure on, with different tactics and actions, and utilize all events of the period for your purpose."
9. "The threat is usually more terrifying than the thing itself."
10. "The major premise for tactics is the development of operations that will maintain a constant pressure upon the opposition."
11. "If you push a negative hard and deep enough it will break through into its counterside."

12. "The price of a successful attack is a constructive alternative."
13. "Pick the target, freeze it, personalize it, and polarize it."

The remaining 11 rules Alinsky describes are concerned with "the ethics of means and ends":

1. "One's concern with the ethics of means and ends varies inversely with one's personal interest in the issue . . . Accompanying this rule is the parallel one that one's concern with the ethics of means and ends varies inversely with one's distance from the scene of conflict."
2. "[T]he judgment of the ethics of means is dependent upon the political position of those sitting in judgment."
3. "[I]n war the end justifies almost any means."
4. "[J]udgment must be made in the context of the times in which the action occurred and not from any other chronological vantage point."
5. "[C]oncern with ethics increases with the number of means available and vice versa."
6. "[T]he less important the end to be desired, the more one can afford to engage in ethical evaluations of means."
7. "[G]enerally success or failure is a mighty determinant of ethics."
8. "[T]he morality of a means depends upon whether the means is being employed at a time of imminent defeat or imminent victory."
9. "[A]ny effective means is automatically judged by the opposition as being unethical."
10. "[Y]ou do what you can with what you have and clothe it with moral garments."
11. "[G]oals must be phrased in general terms like 'Liberty, Equality, Fraternity,' 'Of the Common Welfare,' 'Pursuit of Happiness,' or 'Bread and Peace.'"

Notes

PROLOGUE

1. Wade Rathke, "Common Ground Infiltrator," Chief Organizer blog, January 31, 2009, at http://chieforganizer.org/2009/01/31/common-ground-infiltrator/, accessed May 29, 2010. The entire blog post is available in Appendix C.

2. Author interview with Brandon Darby.

3. Employment Policies Institute, "The Real ACORN," October 2004 (updated version): 4. At http://epionline.org/studies/EPI_acorn_10-2004.pdf, accessed September 8, 2010.

4. Matthew Vadum, "Radical Awakening: From America Hater to Hero," Big Government, April 13, 2010 at http://biggovernment.com/mvadum/2010/04/13/exclusive-radical-awakening-from-america-hater-to-hero/. Big Government posted with permission the article of the same name that was published in *Townhall*, April 2010. Hartmann's statement came during an interview with the author on the "Thom Hartmann Program" on June 11, 2009. An audio recording is available at http://www.capitalresearch.org/podcast/mp3/p1244748628.mp3.

5. News release from U.S. Attorney's Office for the District of Minnesota, May 21, 2009, at http://www.justice.gov/usao/mn/major/major0363.pdf, accessed July 20, 2010.

6. *Glenn Beck Program*, Fox News Channel, June 22, 2009.

7. Matthew Vadum, "ACORN Allies Scheme to Distract from Corruption Allegations," American Spectator blog, May 27, 2009, at http://spectator.org/blog/2009/05/27/acorn-allies-scheme-to-distrac.

CHAPTER 1

8. "America's Suicide Attempt" is a chapter in *Modern Times: A History of the World From the 1920s to the 1990s*, by Paul Johnson (Phoenix, 1996).

9. Gary Delgado, *Organizing the Movement: The Roots and Growth of ACORN* (Temple University Press, 1986), ix.

10. "2010–2011 Board of Directors," Project Vote, at http://www.projectvote. org/our-board.html, accessed June 21, 2010.

11. "About Us," Social Policy website, at http://www.socialpolicy.org/index. php/about-us, accessed June 21, 2010.

12. Madeleine Adamson and Tim Sampson, "Celebrating Richard Cloward's Life and Work," *Social Policy*, June 22, 2001.

13. Delgado, *Organizing the Movement*, 40.

14. Frances Fox Piven and Richard A. Cloward, *Poor People's Movements: Why They Succeed, How They Fail* (Vintage Books, 1979), 266.

15. Kirkpatrick Sale, *SDS* (Vintage Books, 1973), 65–6, 70.

16. Premilla Nadasen, "Expanding the Boundaries of the Women's Movement: Black Feminism and the Struggle for Welfare Rights," *Feminist Studies*, June 2002.

17. "ACORN posters," ACORNstore.org, 2003, at http://web.archive.org/ web/20030729212637/acornstore.org/, accessed January 10, 2010. The numbered prints were offered for sale for $35. Prints signed by the artist cost $115 each.

18. Speech by John Atlas, "Tea Parties, Beck, Bachmann and Blarney" panel discussion at "America's Future Now!" conference, Washington, D.C., June 8, 2010.

19. Matthew Vadum, "ACORN's Federal Judge," American Spectator blog, March 17, 2009, at http://spectator.org/blog/2009/03/17/acorns-federal-judge.

20. U.S. House of Representatives, 111th Congress, Committee on Oversight and Government Reform, "Is ACORN Intentionally Structured As a Criminal Enterprise?" Staff Report, July 23, 2009. The report was updated November 18, 2009.

21. Phil Sutcliffe, "Springsteen: The Lost Four Years," *The Independent* (London), March 25, 1992. Bruce Springsteen gave $10,000 to ACORN's Project Vote affiliate.

22. John Atlas, *Seeds of Change: The Story of ACORN, America's Most Controversial Antipoverty Community Organizing Group* (Vanderbilt University Press, 2010), 10, 63.

23. "ACORN People's Platform," archived ACORN website, at http://web. archive.org/web/20010615002306/www.acorn.org/people%27s_plat form.html, accessed July 23, 2010.

24. Employment Policies Institute, "The Real ACORN," 2.

25. Ibid., 3.

26. Bruce Marks frequently describes himself as an "urban terrorist." In fact, he self-applies the description so often that a Nexis search of the terms "bruce marks" and "urban terrorist" on July 21, 2010, yielded 54 media hits. Marks has also been known to call himself a "banking terrorist."

27. Delgado, *Organizing the Movement*, 190–1.

28. Ron Grossman, "Strong Words at 64, Linguist Noam Chomsky Continues

to Say Things Not Everyone Wants to Hear," *Chicago Tribune*, January 1, 1993.

29. David Horowitz, "The Sick Mind of Noam Chomsky," *Front Page Magazine*, September 26, 2001, at http://97.74.65.51/readArticle. aspx?ARTID=24447, accessed August 12, 2010.

30. Takeshi Suzuki, "Lingua Frankly; Analyzing Responses to Bush's Rhetoric," *Daily Yomiuri* (Tokyo), December 2, 2002. Chomsky frequently complains that he has been misquoted so I am providing the quotation from the article: "A brief statement . . . taken from a U.S. Army manual . . . is that terror is the calculated use of violence or the threat of violence to attain political or religious ideological goals through intimidation, coercion, or instilling fear. That's terrorism. That's a fair enough definition. I think it is reasonable to accept that."

CHAPTER 2

31. Mona Charen, "ACORN, Obama, and the Mortgage Mess," Real Clear Politics, September 30, 2008, at http://www.realclearpolitics.com/articles/2008/09/acorn_obama_and_the_mortgage_m.html, accessed September 5, 2010.

32. Stanley Kurtz, "Inside Obama's Acorn," *National Review*, May 29, 2008, at http://www.nationalreview.com/articles/print/224610, accessed September 5, 2010.

33. Greg Pierce, "Protesters Disrupt Reinvestment Hearing; Acorn Housing Connection Denied," *Washington Times*, March 9, 1995.

34. "The Truth About ACORN," narrated by Megyn Kelly, Fox News Channel, aired October 2, 2009, at http://www.hulu.com/watch/103509/fox-news-specials-the-truth-about-acorn, accessed July 15, 2010.

35. Rachel O'Neal and Ray Pierce, "Protesters Crash Conference, Send Governor Fleeing; Upset about Welfare Reform," *Arkansas Democrat-Gazette*, April 29, 1998.

36. Rachel O'Neal, "Police Investigate ACORN Speech Protest; Group's State Chairman Calls Inquiry 'Retaliation'; KTHV-TV Subpoenaed for Videotape," *Arkansas Democrat-Gazette*, May 1, 1998.

37. David Horowitz, *Barack Obama's Rules for Revolution: The Alinsky Model* (David Horowitz Freedom Center, 2009), 47. At http://www.discoverthenetworks.org/Articles/Rules%20for%20Revolution%20(2).pdf.

38. Michelle Malkin, "Big Labor's Legacy of Violence," *Human Events*, September 3, 2010, at http://www.humanevents.com/article.php?id=38862, accessed September 5, 2010.

39. Nicholas N. Eberstadt, "Daniel Patrick Moynihan, Epidemiologist," in *Daniel Patrick Moynihan: The Intellectual In Public Life*, edited by Robert A. Katzmann (Johns Hopkins University Press, 2004), 60. Moynihan's essay, "Defining Deviancy Down" appeared in *The American Scholar*, Winter 1993.

NOTES

40. Transcript of "ACORN Scandals: What's Next?" a Judicial Watch panel discussion on December 17, 2009, at http://www.judicialwatch.org/files/documents/2009/acornpanel-transcript-12172009.pdf, accessed July 23, 2010. Note that the cover of the transcript provides an incorrect date for the panel.

41. The videos are available at http://biggovernment.com/acorn/.

42. Joe Conason, "In defense of ACORN," *Salon*, September 18, 2009, http://www.salon.com/news/opinion/joe_conason/2009/09/18/acorn, accessed August 22, 2010.

43. National Consortium for the Study of Terrorism and Responses to Terrorism, "Terrorist Organization Profile: Hezbollah," March 1, 2008, at http://www.start.umd.edu/start/data/tops/terrorist_organization_profile.asp?id=3101 accessed July 23, 2010.

44. Council on Foreign Relations, "Hamas," August 27, 2009, at http://www.cfr.org/publication/8968/hamas.html#, accessed July 23, 2010.

45. Jim Geraghty, "Sometimes, It's Okay to Tweet Ill of the Dead," National Review website, July 8, 2010, at http://www.nationalreview.com/campaign-spot/230831/sometimes-its-okay-tweet-ill-dead, accessed July 20, 2010.

46. Heidi J. Swarts, *Organizing Urban America* (University of Minnesota Press, 2008), 51.

47. Ibid., 36–9.

48. Delgado, *Organizing the Movement*, 200.

49. Ibid., 179.

50. Wade Rathke, "Tactical Tension," Chief Organizer blog, at http://chieforganizer.org/wp/wp-content/uploads/2009/05/tactical-tension.pdf, accessed July 31, 2010. The paper indicates it was published in the summer 2001 issue of *Social Policy*.

51. John Berlau, "Eco-Terrorism: When Violence Becomes An Environmentalist Tactic," *Organization Trends*, February 2007, at http://www.capital-research.org/pubs/pdf/v1186063844.pdf, accessed July 31, 2010. This article was adapted from Berlau's book, *Eco-Freaks: Environmentalism Is Hazardous to Your Health*, published in 2006 by Nelson Current.

52. Rathke, "Tactical Tension."

53. The subject of pirate democracy is discussed in several sources, including *The Invisible Hook: The Hidden Economics of Pirates*, by Peter T. Leeson (Princeton University Press, 2009).

54. "The Weather Underground," directed by Sam Green and Bill Siegel, Free History Project, 2003, at http://www.youtube.com/watch?v=LV7GSff4fIA.

55. David Freddoso, *The Case Against Barack Obama* (Regnery Publishing, 2008), 125.

56. Dinitia Smith, "No Regrets for a Love of Explosives; In a Memoir of Sorts, a War Protester Talks of Life With the Weathermen," *New York Times*, September 11, 2001.

57. "Larry Grathwohl on Ayers' Plan for American Re-education Camps and the Need to Kill Millions," posted October 29, 2008, at http://www.you tube.com/watch?v=HWMIwziGrAQ, accessed July 25, 2010. Grathwohl made the assertion in *No Place to Hide: The Strategy and Tactics of Terrorism (Part V)*, a 1982 documentary film directed by Dick Quincer. Grathwohl is author of *Bringing Down America*, an out-of-print book published by Arlington House in 1976. He infiltrated the Weather Underground and participated in internal discussions in which its leaders laid out plans to systematically liquidate those who resisted the communist revolution they aspired to create.

58. "'I Never Denounced' W.U. Violence: Ayers Compares Weather Underground to WikiLeaks," The Blaze, December 7, 2010, at http://www.theblaze.com/stories/bill-ayers-restrained-weather-underground-just-like-wikileaks-against-violent-us-i-never-denounced-wu-violence/, accessed December 7, 2010.

59. Michael Hauben, "Participatory Democracy From the 1960s and SDS into the Future On-line," at http://www.columbia.edu/~hauben/CS/netdemocracy-60s.txt, accessed July 25, 2010.

60. "Port Huron Statement of the Students for a Democratic Society," at http://coursesa.matrix.msu.edu/~hst306/documents/huron.html, accessed July 25, 2010. This is the full text of the Port Huron Statement, as provided by Tom Hayden.

61. Saul D. Alinsky, *Rules for Radicals* (Vintage Books, 1989), 63.

62. Ana Maria Ortiz and Matthew Vadum, "The American Friends of Hugo Chavez: Dial 1-800-4-TYRANT," *Organization Trends*, March 2008, at http://www.capitalresearch.org/pubs/pdf/v1204310378.pdf.

63. Jonathan Wolan, "Today's Topic: From the Front Porch to the White House," AP, July 2, 1979.

64. "Bolvian [sic] President Morales Delivers Unvarnished Truth of the Moment at Copenhagen Summit," Pacific Free Press, December 19, 2009.

65. Author interview with Marcel Reid.

66. Delgado, *Organizing the Movement*, 188.

67. Ibid., 55–6.

68. Ibid., 52–3. Delgado is sometimes referred to as a co-founder of ACORN. Although he was clearly an important influence on the nascent organization, this is overly generous to Delgado. In fact, Rathke hired Delgado to carry out his orders.

69. Ibid., 55–6.

70. Employment Policies Institute, "Rotten ACORN: America's Bad Seed," July 16, 2006, at http://www.rottenacorn.com/downloads/060728_badSeed.pdf, accessed July 15, 2010. The name of the conference was "Researching ACORN: Past, Present and Future."

71. Delgado, *Organizing the Movement*, 55–6.

72. Ibid., 150–1.

73. Ibid., 123, 132.

74. Ibid., 144–5. Stanley Kurtz has also unearthed several early documents showing ACORN leaders' reliance on socialist thinkers in his book *Radical-in-Chief* (Threshold Editions, 2010). He devotes a full chapter to ACORN.

75. Andre Gorz, *Reclaiming Work: Beyond the Wage-Based Society* (Blackwell Publishers Inc., 1998), 77–81.

76. Delgado, *Organizing the Movement*, 148.

77. Ibid., 172.

78. *Glenn Beck Program*, Fox News, May 6, 2009, transcript at http://www.foxnews.com/story/0,2933,519337,00.html, accessed July 1, 2010.

79. Matthew Vadum, "MSM Ignores 'Nonpartisan' ACORN Boss Bertha Lewis's Impassioned Endorsement of Obama," NewsBusters, October 29, 2008, at http://newsbusters.org/blogs/matthew-vadum/2008/10/29/msm-ignores-nonpartisan-acorn-boss-bertha-lewiss-impassioned-endorsem. The YouTube video dated October 22, 2008, is at http://www.youtube.com/watch?v=YfUEPeO2_pc, accessed July 22, 2010.

80. Chelsea Schilling, "Unearthed! Obama's Twisted ACORN Roots: Track Timeline of President's Ties to Group Immersed in Scandals," World Net Daily, September 18, 2009, at http://www.wnd.com/?pageId=110131, accessed July 31, 2010.

81. Leslie Wayne, "D.N.C. Sues McCain Over Campaign Loan," *New York Times*, The Caucus blog, June 24, 2008, at http://thecaucus.blogs.nytimes.com/2008/06/24/dnc-sues-mccain-over-campaign-loan/?scp=19&sq=mccain%20campaign%20finance%20violations%20democrats&st=cse, accessed May 18, 2009.

82. Jim Rutenberg, Marilyn W. Thompson, David D. Kirkpatrick and Stephen Labaton, "For McCain, Self-Confidence on Ethics Poses Its Own Risk," *New York Times*, February 21, 2008, at http://www.nytimes.com/2008/02/21/us/politics/21mccain.html?_r=1&pagewanted=all, accessed May 18, 2009. Matthew Vadum, "NYT Finally Admits It Spiked Obama/ACORN Corruption Story," News Busters, May 18, 2009, at http://newsbusters.org/blogs/matthew-vadum/2009/05/18/nyt-finally-admits-it-spiked-obama-acorn-corruption-story. For the record, Stephanie Strom sent me a letter dated May 19, 2009, protesting the blog post I wrote. I wrote that "Strom broke a number of important stories about ACORN and surely much of the information she used came from her trusted source Anita MonCrief." Strom wrote that I had made "two erroneous assumptions." The first was that MonCrief "was a source for all of the stories I have written about Acorn. In fact, Ms. MonCrief did not contact me until after I began following the story of embezzlement at Acorn in July 2008." The second assumption was "that I was aware of Ms. MonCrief's credibility problem from the outset of my interactions with her. In fact, I had no knowledge of the problem until after she had agreed to go on the

record in the third week of October 2008 and I had made arrangements to formally interview her. She called me back after those arrangements were made and told me that she had been fired for charging personal expenses to a corporate credit card."

83. Jim Hoft, "Breaking: Anita MonCrief to File FEC Charges Against Obama Administration," Big Government, July 24, 2010, at http://biggovernment.com/jhoft/2010/07/24/breaking-anita-moncrief-to-file-fec-charges-against-obama-administration/, accessed August 1, 2010. As of July 2010, MonCrief had posted the donor lists at http://emergingcorruption.com/?p=100.

84. "Representative Maxine Waters Discusses the Violence in Los Angeles," CBS News Transcripts, from CBS This Morning, aired May 5, 1992.

85. "ACORN Grassroots Democracy Campaign," May 12, 2008, at http://www.youtube.com/watch?v=cLCSnbN1lRI, accessed July 22, 2010.

86. Alex Isenstadt, "Senate Denies ACORN Funding," Politico, September 14, 2009, at http://www.politico.com/news/stories/0909/27153.html, accessed July 31, 2010.

87. Anita MonCrief, "Nadler, ACORN and the Working Families Party: No Credible Evidence?" Anita MonCrief blog, April 13, 2009, at http://anitamoncrief.blogspot.com/2009/04/nadler-acorn-and-working-families-party.html, accessed July 23, 2010. MonCrief is a former ACORN employee who had access to ACORN's financial data.

88. Atlas, Seeds of Change, 218.

89. Bill Clinton, Giving: How Each of Us Can Change the World (Knopf, 2007), 51, 79, 193.

90. "Sen. Clinton Speaks at ACORN's 2006 National Convention," US Fed News, July 10, 2006.

91. Joe Sciacca, "Protest Gives Menino a Feel for Life in Mayoral Hot Seat," Boston Herald, April 8, 1993.

92. Letter of appointment dated February 5, 2010 of Maude Hurd, City of Boston website, accessed June 21, 2010.

93. "ACORN to McCain: Have You Lost That Loving Feeling? Senator Allied with ACORN as Recently as 2006, Now Turns Cold Shoulder," U.S. Newswire, October 13, 2008.

94. Aaron Deslatte, "ACORN's Voter Signups Bother McCain, But Not Crist," by Aaron Deslatte, Orlando Sentinel, October 12, 2008, at http://articles.orlandosentinel.com/2008-10-12/news/capview12_1_acorn-mccain-crist, accessed July 31, 2010.

95. Solomon Moore, "States Restore Voting Rights for Ex-Convicts," New York Times, September 13, 2008.

96. "Governor Schwarzenegger Signs Legislation to Help Protect Homeowners from Foreclosure," States News Service, July 8, 2008.

97. Tad Vezner, "Pawlenty: Halt State Funds for ACORN Community Organizing Group," St. Paul Pioneer Press, September 16, 2009.

98. "Minnesota Adopts New Laws Addressing Mortgage Abuses," *Northwestern Financial Review*, June 1, 2007, at http://www.allbusiness.com/banking-finance/banking-lending-credit-services/8900316-1.html, accessed July 31, 2010.

99. David Kibbe, "State Rep. Quinn Pushed Through Lending Crackdown in '04," *Standard-Times* (New Bedford, Mass.), October 1, 2008, at http://www.southcoasttoday.com/apps/pbcs.dll/article?AID=/20081001/NEWS/810010391, accessed July 31, 2010.

CHAPTER 3

100. Matthew Vadum, "ACORN Still Owes $2.3 Million in Overdue Taxes," Big Government, November 16, 2009, at http://biggovernment.com/mvadum/2009/11/16/acorn-still-owes-2-3-million-in-overdue-taxes.

101. Matthew Vadum, "Bertha Lies," *American Spectator*, October 20, 2009, at http://spectator.org/archives/2009/10/20/bertha-lies.

102. Erica Payne, editor. *The Practical Progressive: How to Build a Twenty-first Century Political Movement* (Public Affairs, 2008), 53. The $50 million figure is provided in the ACORN entry written by Maude Hurd.

103. Wade Rathke, "Understanding ACORN: Sweat and Social Change," in *The People Shall Rule: ACORN, Community Organizing, and the Struggle for Economic Justice*, edited by Robert Fisher (Vanderbilt University Press, 2009), 52.

104. Peter Dreier and John Atlas, "ACORN Under the Microscope," *Huffington Post*, July 14, 2008, at http://www.huffingtonpost.com/peter-dreier/acorn-under-the-microscop_b_112491.html, accessed July 23, 2010.

105. Swarts, *Organizing Urban America*, 40, 80. Delgado, *Organizing the Movement*, 117.

106. *Glenn Beck Program*, Fox News Channel, May 18, 2009. The ACORN 8 group was helpful to this writer but not always. Often the group refused to comment.

107. Seth Colter Walls, "Fox News, GOP Tag-Team Obama with Voter Fraud Smear," *Huffington Post*, October 3, 2008, at http://www.huffingtonpost.com/2008/10/03/obama-camp-debunks-voter_n_131686.html, July 23, 2010.

108. "Complaint for Injunctive and Declaratory Relief" in *ACORN v. Edgar* (January 11, 1995), University of Michigan Law School, The Civil Rights Litigation Clearinghouse, at http://www.clearinghouse.net/chDocs/public/VR-IL-0042-0010.pdf, accessed July 24, 2010.

109. Chelsea Schilling, "Unearthed!"

110. Trevor Loudon, "Obama File 41: Obama Was a New Party Member—Documentary Evidence," New Zeal blog, October 23, 2008, at http://newzeal.blogspot.com/2008/10/obama-file-41-obama-was-new-party.html, accessed July 31, 2010.

111. Swarts, *Organizing Urban America*, 83.

112. Atlas, *Seeds of Change*, 133.

113. Trevor Loudon, "Obama File 101 Who's Been Fibbing Then? Evidence That Obama Was Deeply Involved in Socialist New Party 'Sister Organization,'" New Zeal blog, April 7, 2010, at http://newzeal.blogspot. com/2010/04/obama-file-101-whos-been-fibbing-then.html, accessed September 12, 2010.

114. The Foulkes article is available at http://www.capitalresearch.org/ blog/?p=1701.

115. Matthew Vadum, "ACORN: Who Funds the Weather Underground's Little Brother?" *Foundation Watch*, November 2008, at http://www.capitalresearch.org/pubs/pdf/v1225222922.pdf.

116. Stanley Kurtz, "Obama and Ayers Pushed Radicalism on Schools," *Wall Street Journal*, September 23, 2008, at http://online.wsj.com/article/NA_ WSJ_PUB:SB122212856075765367.html, August 1, 2010.

117. Aaron Klein and Brenda J. Elliott, *The Manchurian President* (WND Books, 2010), 119.

118. John Fund, "Acorn Who?" *Wall Street Journal*, September 21, 2009, at http:// online.wsj.com/article/NA_WSJ_PUB:SB10001424052970204488 30457442704163636038.html, accessed August 1, 2010.

119. "2008 Democratic Delegates," RealClearPolitics.com, at http://www.realclearpolitics.com/epolls/2008/president/democratic_delegate_count. html, accessed September 4, 2010.

120. Michelle Malkin, *Culture of Corruption: Obama and His Team of Tax Cheats, Crooks, and Cronies* (Regnery, 2010, updated paperback version), 268.

121. David M. Brown, "Obama to Amend Report on $800,000 in Spending," (Pittsburgh) *Tribune-Review*, August 22, 2008, at http://www. pittsburghlive.com/x/pittsburghtrib/news/election/s_584284.html, accessed September 4, 2010.

122. Sanford A. Newman, "Acorn Didn't Employ Obama in '92," *Wall Street Journal*, July 22, 2008.

123. "ACORN Accusations," FactCheck.org, October 18, 2008, at http://www. factcheck.org/elections-2008/acorn_accusations.html, accessed August 2, 2010.

124. "Voter Registration: Project Vote! Targets Urban Swing Areas," *The Hotline*, October 8, 1992.

125. U.S. government trademark records show that the trademark "Project Vote," serial number 76568057, registration number 2926255, was first used in commerce on April 1, 1994. The government database known as the Trademark Electronic Search System (TESS) may be accessed online at http://tess2.uspto.gov/.

126. Atlas, *Seeds of Change*, 101.

127. Stanley Kurtz, *Radical-in-Chief*, 230. For more information on the connections between Obama, ACORN, and Project Vote, see Kurtz's authoritative book, which deals with the subject exhaustively.

128. Matthew Vadum, "ACORN's Man in the White House," *American Spectator*, September 28, 2009, at http://spectator.org/archives/2009/09/28/acorns-man-in-the-white-house. RedState bloggers Erick Erickson and Moe Lane did an excellent job in various blog posts connecting the dots between Gaspard, ACORN, and President Obama.

129. Wade Rathke, "SEIU's Good Obama Bet," Chief Organizer blog, May 16, 2009, at http://chieforganizer.org/2009/05/16/seius-good-obama-bet/, accessed May 31, 2010.

130. Matthew Vadum, "The Politico Gets Played By ACORN," American Spectator blog, September 29, 2009, at http://spectator.org/blog/2009/09/29/the-politico-gets-played-by-ac.

131. Matthew Vadum, "ACORN's Big Spender," *American Spectator*, November 6, 2009, at http://spectator.org/archives/2009/11/06/acorns-big-spender.

132. Atlas, *Seeds of Change*, 239–240.

133. Jim Rutenberg, "Acorn's Woes Strain Its Ties to Democrats," *New York Times*, October 16, 2009.

134. *Roll Call*, April 28, 2009.

135. This writer filed a FOIA request with HUD on March 18, 2010. By letter dated November 22, 2010, HUD FOIA director Dolores W. Cole advised that "[a] search of Headquarters' records by knowledgeable staff failed to locate any records responsive to your request."

CHAPTER 4

136. Piven and Cloward, *Poor People's Movements*, 270–1.

137. Ibid., 271.

138. J. David Gillespie, *Politics at the Periphery: Third Parties in Two-Party America* (University of South Carolina Press, 1993), 188. Defenders of Harrington like to argue that he became less radical as he aged, moving from the Communist camp to the democratic socialist camp, as if the core beliefs of these two radicals groups were worlds apart. They're not. Similarly, defenders of the assassinated radical Malcolm X tried to rehabilitate his image by claiming he too was moving away from radicalism in his twilight years.

139. Frances Fox Piven and Richard A. Cloward, *Regulating the Poor: The Functions of Public Welfare* (Vintage Books, 1972), 46.

140. Kyle Olson, "Frances Fox Piven: Thomas Jefferson Would Be 'Stunned' at America Today (But Not For the Reason You Think)," Big Government, February 9, 2010, at http://biggovernment.com/kolson/2010/02/09/frances-fox-piven-thomas-jefferson-would-be-stunned-at-america-today-but-not-for-the-reason-you-think/, accessed July 17, 2010.

141. Speech by Frances Fox Piven, "The Weakness of Labor Unions and New Forms of Solidarity," Rosa Luxemburg Foundation's "Class in Crisis" conference, Berlin, Germany, June 19–20, 2009, at http://www.youtube.com/watch?v=cg5HQvNa1Ao, accessed June 23, 2010.

142. "Our Structure," Democratic Socialist of America website, at http://www.dsausa.org/about/structure.html, accessed July 27, 2010.

143. Trevor Loudon, "Proof at Last—Richard Cloward was a 'DSAer,'" New Zeal blog, July 26, 2010, http://newzeal.blogspot.com/2010/07/proof-at-last-richard-cloward-was-dsaer.html, accessed July 26, 2010. Frances Fox Piven has made no secret of her membership in DSA but until 2010, proof of her husband Richard Cloward's membership remained elusive. Loudon discovered proof in the form of a reference to Cloward's membership in the official DSA magazine, *Democratic Left.*

144. "Commissioner Ken Grossinger," District of Columbia Housing Authority website, at http://www.dchousing.org/commissioners/bio_ken_grossinger.htm, accessed August 6, 2010.

145. Ken Grossinger, "Richard A. Cloward: Scholar and Activist, 1926–2001," *Democratic Left*, December 2001.

146. Horowitz, *Barack Obama's Rules for Revolution: The Alinsky Model*, 4.

147. G. David Garson, "Economic Opportunity Act of 1964," at http://wps.prenhall.com/wps/media/objects/751/769950/Documents_Library/eoa1964.htm, accessed July 25, 2010.

148. Lillian B. Rubin, "Maximum Feasible Participation: The Origins, Implications, and Present Status," (abstract), *The ANNALS of the American Academy of Political and Social Science*, (September 1969), 385: 14–29, at http://ann.sagepub.com/content/385/1/14.abstract, accessed July 24, 2010.

149. "What Should Reaganites Do Now?" *Insight on the News*, December 22, 2003. In the article Phillips says OEO's budget in 1973 was $3 billion.

150. *New York Times*, March 15, 1973. The lawsuit, *Williams v. Phillips*, reported in law reports as 482 F.2d 669 and 157 U.S.App.D.C. 80, is referenced at http://openjurist.org/482/f2d/669/williams-v-j-phillips.

151. J.M. Lawrence, "Robert Coard, Fought for Justice as Head of ABCD," *Boston Globe*, November 4, 2009, at http://www.boston.com/bostonglobe/obituaries/articles/2009/11/04/robert_coard_fought_for_justice_as_head_of_abcd/, accessed July 25, 2010.

152. "Book TV," C-SPAN2, November 11, 2004, at http://www.theblaze.com/stories/piven-violence-is-okay-if-its-a-big-party-of-your-strategy/, accessed September 17, 2010. The video clip shows Piven at the University of Wisconsin and may be found at http://www.c-spanvideo.org/program/id/137874.

153. Frances Fox Piven, "The Weakness of Labor Unions and New Forms of Solidarity."

154. Piven and Cloward, *Regulating the Poor*, 67–8.

155. Frances Fox Piven, "The Weakness of Labor Unions and New Forms of Solidarity."

156. The information was contained in documents from the FBI's file on Cloward that were released to the author pursuant to a request he made under the Freedom of Information/Privacy Acts (FOIPA). The specific

FBI memorandum cited is dated July 23, 1965. The wording in the FBI document suggests the Cloward quotation, "The problems are being greatly exaggerated. The American people are more lawful today than ever before," may be a paraphrase rather than a direct quotation.

157. Gwendolyn Mink (editor), Richard Cloward, and Dorothy Trujillo, "Women and Welfare Reform—Women's Poverty, Women's Opportunities, and Women's Welfare," Part 7 of 17, Institute for Women's Policy Research, 1994.

158. Stephanie Flanders, "Richard Cloward, Welfare Rights Leader, Dies At 74," *New York Times*, August 23, 2001.

159. Grossinger, "Richard A. Cloward: Scholar and Activist, 1926–2001."

160. Stephanie Flanders, "Richard Cloward, Welfare Rights Leader, Dies at 74."

161. The information was contained in documents from the FBI's file on Cloward that were released to the author pursuant to a request he made under the Freedom of Information/Privacy Acts (FOIPA). The specific FBI memorandum cited is dated July 22, 1965.

162. Piven and Cloward, *Poor People's Movements*, 26.

163. Piven and Cloward, *Regulating the Poor*, 39–40.

164. Alice Widener, "In the East and West Ballrooms: A Special Report by Alice Widener on the Second Annual Conference of Socialist Scholars," *U.S.A. Magazine*, September 16, 1966.

165. Rogan, "Now It's Welfare Lib," *New York Times*, September 27, 1970.

166. Piven and Cloward, *Poor People's Movements*, 273.

167. Frances Fox Piven and Richard A. Cloward, "Low-Income People and the Political Process," in *The Breaking of the American Social Compact* (The New Press, 1997), 283–4. The paper was originally published in 1963, according to a note at page 284.

168. Rogan, "Now It's Welfare Lib."

169. Richard A. Cloward and Frances Fox Piven, "The Professional Bureaucracies: Benefit Systems as Influence Systems," in *Blacks and Bureaucracy: Readings in the Problems and Politics of Change*, edited by Virginia B. Ermer and John H. Strange (Thomas Y. Crowell Co., 1972), 222.

170. Adam Nossiter, "Suit: Welfare Recipients 'Humiliated'; Louisiana Officials Question Women Applicants on Sex Lives," *Atlanta Journal and Constitution*, April 5, 1991. The article indicates the Cloward and Piven quotation appears in their book, *Regulating the Poor*.

171. Piven and Cloward, *Regulating the Poor*, xiii, 3, 22.

172. Richard A. Cloward and Frances Fox Piven, "The Professional Bureaucracies," 213.

173. David Frum, "Guaranteed Annual Income Doomed to Fail," *The Financial Post* (Toronto, Canada), July 31, 1993 (Weekly Edition).

174. Richard Poe, "The Cloward-Piven Strategy," Discover The Networks, 2005, at http://www.discoverthenetworks.org/Articles/theclowardpivenstrategypoe.html, accessed June 20, 2010.

175. Rogan, "Now It's Welfare Lib."

176. Richard Cloward and Frances Fox Piven, "The Weight of the Poor: A Strategy to End Poverty," *The Nation*, May 2, 1966, at http://www.thenation.com/article/weight-poor-strategy-end-poverty, accessed June 20, 2010. Beware of Optical Character Recognition (OCR) technology, which appears to have been used to convert the original text into web-friendly text. There are some errors in the online version. For example, the online version speaks of "Saul Slinky," but the original refers to "Saul Alinsky." Also, Piven again called for a violent uprising in the Jan. 10/17, 2011 *Nation*: "So where are the angry crowds, the demonstrations, sit-ins and unruly mobs?"

177. Aaron Klein and Brenda J. Elliott noticed this unusual Trotsky-inspired wording and referenced it at page 110 of *The Manchurian President: Barack Obama's Ties to Communists, Socialists and Other Anti-American Extremists* (WND Books, 2010).

178. Robert Vincent Daniels, *A Documentary History of Communism in Russia: from Lenin to Gorbachev* (Vermont, 3rd edition, 1993), 95.

179. Leon Trotsky, *Dictatorship vs. Democracy: A Reply to Karl Kautsky*, Workers' Party of America, 1922, at http://www.marxists.org/archive/trotsky/1920/terrcomm/ch02.htm, accessed August 17, 2010. This book is an English translation of a book with the Russian language title of *Terrorism and Communism*.

180. Leon Trotsky, *Platform of the Joint Opposition*, 1927, at http://www.marxists.org/archive/trotsky/1927/opposition/ch08.htm, accessed June 16, 2010.

181. Leon Trotsky, *The Revolution Betrayed*, 1937, at http://www.marxists.org/archive/trotsky/1936/revbet/, accessed June 20, 2010.

182. Saul D. Alinsky, *Reveille for Radicals* (Vintage Books, 1989), 18.

183. Richard A. Cloward and Frances Fox Piven, "The Professional Bureaucracies," 206–7, 218.

184. Piven and Cloward, "Low-Income People and the Political Process."

185. Frances Fox Piven, "Militant Civil Servants in New York City," in *Blacks and Bureaucracy*, 146–152.

186. Frances Fox Piven and Richard A. Cloward, "The Case Against Urban Desegregation," in *The Breaking of the American Social Compact*, 128. The essay was originally published in 1966, according to a note at 128.

187. Ibid., 113, 125.

188. Ibid., 119, 124–5, 127–8.

189. Nexis searches suggest that I introduced Glenn Beck to "The Weight of the Poor" article and the Cloward-Piven Strategy when I appeared on his TV program to discuss ACORN on May 13, 2009. Beck seemed so fascinated by the implications and sheer deviousness of the strategy that our segment ran long and we used up some of the time of the next scheduled guest, Rep. Michele Bachmann, a Republican congresswoman representing Minnesota.

190. *Glenn Beck Program*, Fox News, May 28, 2009.

191. Kyle Olson, "Frances Fox Piven: Glenn Beck Seeks 'Foreign, Dark-Skinned, Intellectual' Scapegoats," Big Government, February 8, 2010, at http://biggovernment.com/kolson/2010/02/08/frances-fox-piven-glenn-beck-seeks-foreign-dark-skinned-intellectual-scapegoats/, accessed July 17, 2010.

192. Richard Kim, "The Mad Tea Party," *The Nation*, April 12, 2010, at http://www.thenation.com/article/mad-tea-party, accessed June 20, 2010. The "Cloward-Piven Strategy," was referenced in "Now It's Welfare Lib," by Richard Rogan, *New York Times*, September 27, 1970.

CHAPTER 5

193. "ACORN: A Summary of Recent Accomplishments," ACORN press release, May 2009.

194. Atlas, *Seeds of Change*, 184.

195. Matthew Vadum, "Wrathful Wade Rathke," *American Spectator*, July 16, 2009, at http://spectator.org/archives/2009/07/16/wrathful-wade-rathke; and "The Ultimate Organizer: An Interview With ACORN's Founder Wade Rathke," by intrepidliberal, July 12, 2009, DailyKos.com, at http://www.dailykos.com/storyonly/2009/7/12/752731/-The-Ultimate-Organizer:-An-Interview-With-ACORNs-Founder-Wade-Rathke, accessed July 15, 2009.

196. Alan Bjerga, "Food Stamps Went to Record 41.3 Million in June, USDA Says," Bloomberg, September 2, 2010, at http://www.businessweek.com/news/2010-09-02/food-stamps-went-to-record-41-3-million-in-june-usda-says.html, September 5, 2010.

197. David S. Broder, "Who Wants Votes From the Poor?" *Washington Post*, August 18, 1985.

198. Richard A. Cloward and Frances Fox Piven, "Toward a Class-Based Realignment of American Politics: A Movement Strategy," *Social Policy*, Winter 1983.

199. Frances Fox Piven and Richard A. Cloward, *The New Class War: Reagan's Attack on the Welfare State and Its Consequences* (Pantheon Books, 1982), 1.

200. Cloward and Piven, "Toward a Class-Based Realignment of American Politics."

201. Vernon Jarrett, "'Project Vote' Brings Power to the People," *Chicago Sun-Times*, August 11, 1992.

202. Robert Pear, "Drive to Sign Up Poor for Voting Meets Resistance," *New York Times*, April 15, 1984.

203. Cloward and Piven, "Toward a Class-Based Realignment of American Politics."

204. Ibid.

205. Ibid.

206. Ibid.

207. Robert Pear, "Drive to Sign Up Poor for Voting Meets Resistance."

208. Ibid.

209. Cloward and Piven, "Toward a Class-Based Realignment of American Politics."
210. Richard Poe, "The Cloward-Piven Strategy," Discover The Networks, 2005, at http://www.discoverthenetworks.org/Articles/theclowardpiven-strategypoe.html, accessed August 18, 2010; Frances Fox Piven, Lorraine C. Minnite, and Margaret Groarke, *Keeping Down the Black Vote: Race and the Demobilization of American Voters* (The New Press, 2009), 111–2.
211. John Fund, *Stealing Elections: How Voter Fraud Threatens Our Democracy* (Encounter Books, 2nd edition, 2008), 27–8.
212. Ibid.
213. Kyle Olson, "Frances Fox Piven: ACORN-style Mass Movement May Deepen Foreclosure Crisis, Forcing Government & Banks to Address Homeownership Rights," Big Government, February 10, 2010, at http://biggovernment.com/kolson/2010/02/10/frances-fox-piven-acorn-style-mass-movement-may-deepen-foreclosure-crisis-forcing-government-banks-to-address-homeownership-rights/, accessed July 17, 2010.
214. Nick Kotz and Mary Lynn Kotz, *A Passion for Equality: George Wiley and the Movement* (W.W. Norton & Co. Inc., New York, 1977), 246.
215. Ibid., 177.
216. Ibid., 304.
217. The letter from the FBI to the author was dated April 30, 2010. It indicated that "[r]ecords which may be responsive to your request were destroyed on May 4, 2009, and June 15, 1990. Since this material could not be reviewed, it is not known if it was responsive to your request."
218. Kotz and Kotz. *A Passion for Equality*, 292.
219. Ibid., 231.
220. Ibid., 232.
221. Ibid., 284.
222. "Amiri Baraka," Discover The Networks, at http://www.discoverthenetworks.org/individualProfile.asp?indid=2171, accessed July 27, 2010.
223. Kotz and Kotz. *A Passion for Equality*, 126.
224. Ibid., 256.
225. Ibid., 256–7.
226. Ibid., 252.
227. Ibid., 91.
228. Ibid., 181–5.
229. Ibid., 192–3.
230. Ibid., 246.
231. Ibid., 231.
232. Ibid., 199, 233.
233. Sol Stern, "ACORN's Nutty Regime for Cities," *City Journal*, Spring 2003.
234. Jason DeParle, "What Welfare-to-Work Really Means," *New York Times*, December 20, 1998.
235. Kotz and Kotz. *A Passion for Equality*, 233, 258, 260.

236. Ibid., 281.

237. Rogan, "Now It's Welfare Lib."

238. Sparer claimed to have joined the Communist Party USA in 1949 and to have left it in 1956. The information was contained in documents from the FBI's file on Cloward that were released to the author pursuant to a request he made under the Freedom of Information/Privacy Acts (FOIPA). The specific FBI memorandum cited is dated July 23, 1965.

239. David Frum, *How We Got Here: the 70's, the Decade that Brought You Modern Life—For Better or Worse* (Basic Books, 2000), 228–9.

240. The case is *Goldberg v. Kelly*, 397 U.S. 254. It is available at http://supreme. justia.com/us/397/254/case.html.

241. Martha F. Davis, *Brutal Need: Lawyers and the Welfare Rights Movement 1960–1973* (Yale University Press, 1993), 117.

242. Sarah Slavin, editor, *U.S. Women's Interest Groups: Institutional Profiles* (Greenwood, 1995), 430.

243. Kotz and Kotz, *A Passion for Equality*, 295, 298.

244. Atlas, *Seeds of Change*, 9–10.

245. "The Truth About ACORN," narrated by Megyn Kelly, Fox News Channel, aired October 2, 2009, available at http://www.hulu.com/watch/103509/fox-news-specials-the-truth-about-acorn, accessed July 15, 2010.

246. Kotz and Kotz, *A Passion for Equality*, 227–230.

247. Atlas, *Seeds of Change*, 12.

248. Ibid.

249. Ibid., 280.

250. Ibid., 227–230.

251. Atlas, *Seeds of Change*, 15–60.

252. Rathke, "Tactical Tension."

253. Atlas, *Seeds of Change*, 9, 17.

CHAPTER 6

254. Georgie Ann Geyer, "Saul Alinsky Could Rub People the Right Way, Too," *Tulsa World* (Oklahoma), April 15, 2007.

255. Wade Rathke, "Nick Von Hoffman on Alinsky," Chief Organizer blog, December 8, 2009, at http://chieforganizer.org/2009/12/08/nick-von-hoffman-on-alinsky/, accessed June 27, 2010.

256. Nicholas von Hoffman, *Radical: A Portrait of Saul Alinsky* (Nation Books, 2010), 150. The biography of Cohn that von Hoffman wrote was called *Citizen Cohn*, published by Doubleday in 1988. Radical leftists like von Hoffman have never forgiven America's patriotic Red hunters from the 1950s. For more on the Left's enduring hostility to Sen. Joseph McCarthy, see *Treason*, by Ann Coulter (Crown Forum, 2003).

257. Ibid., 194.

258. Sanford D. Horwitt, *Let Them Call Me Rebel: Saul Alinsky, His Life and Legacy* (Vintage Books, 1992), 6, 541.

259. Ibid., 19–20.
260. Ibid., 20–1.
261. Alinsky, *Reveille for Radicals*, 21.
262. Ibid., 18.
263. Alinsky, *Rules for Radicals*, 25.
264. Ibid., 44-5.
265. David Horowitz, "An Enemy Within," *Front Page Magazine*, September 19, 2001, at http://archive.frontpagemag.com/readArticle.aspx?ARTID=21218, accessed August 12, 2010.
266. Alinsky, *Rules for Radicals*, 158.
267. Ibid., 156.
268. Rathke, "Tactical Tension."
269. Alinsky, *Reveille for Radicals*, 38.
270. Jeff Zeleny, "Obama Weighs Quick Undoing of Bush Policy," *New York Times*, November 9, 2008, at http://www.nytimes.com/2008/11/10/us/politics/10obama.html?_r=1, accessed August 19, 2010.
271. Matthew Vadum, "Hillary Clinton: "Never Waste a Good Crisis," Capital Research Center blog, July 3, 2009, at http://www.capitalresearch.org/blog/2009/07/03/hillary-clinton-never-waste-a-good-crisis/. The Clinton comments, made during her visit to the European Parliament in Brussels on March 6, 2009, appear in "'Never Waste a Good Crisis'—Hillary Clinton," posted March 6, 2009 at http://www.youtube.com/watch?v=B62igfNu-T0, accessed July 3, 2009.
272. "Radical Saul Alinsky: Prophet of Power," *Time*, March 2, 1970, at http://www.time.com/time/magazine/article/0,9171,904228,00.html, accessed August 21, 2010.
273. Alinsky, *Reveille for Radicals*, 38. My former co-worker, James Dellinger, came up with the wonderful phrase "Social Justice League."
274. Ibid., 90.
275. Karl Marx, "Circular Letter to Bebel, Liebknect, Bracke, and Others," 1879, at 554 of *The Marx-Engels Reader*, 2nd edition (W.W. Norton & Co., 1978).
276. David Gilbert. *SDS/WUO: Students for a Democratic Society and the Weather Underground Organization* (Abraham Guillen Press and Arm the Spirit, 2002), 4. Weatherman Gilbert said this in a court statement in 1982 following his arrest.
277. Alinsky, *Rules for Radicals*, xvii, xxii.
278. Weather Underground, *Prairie Fire: The Politics of Revolutionary Anti-Imperialism* (Communications Co., 1974), 45, 145.
279. Alinsky, *Rules for Radicals*, 16, 185–6.
280. Alinsky, *Reveille for Radicals*, 91.
281. Abdon M. Pallasch. "Obama: God, Guns are Only Refuge of Bitter Pennsylvanians," *Chicago Sun-Times*, April 12, 2008, at http://www.suntimes.com/news/politics/obama/891685,CST-NWS-obama12.article, accessed July 28, 2010.

282. Alinsky, *Rules for Radicals*, 188–9.

283. Ibid., 150.

284. "Gordon Sherman of Midas Muffler," *New York Times*, May 16, 1987, at http://www.nytimes.com/1987/05/16/obituaries/gordon-sherman-of-midas-muffler.html, accessed August 20, 2010.

285. Alinsky, *Rules for Radicals*, 191.

286. Bill Ayers, *Fugitive Days: Memoirs of an Anti-War Activist* (Beacon Press, 2009), 265.

287. Alinsky, *Rules for Radicals*, xxi.

288. Alinsky, *Reveille for Radicals*, 228.

289. Horwitt, *Let Them Call Me Rebel*, 59–60.

290. Ibid., 39.

291. "Leon Despres," Zoom People Information, February 2010.

292. Trevor Loudon, "Obama File 85 Security Implications? Obama's Man Axelrod Was Mentored by Marxist Radicals," New Zeal blog, at http://newzeal.blogspot.com/2009/09/obama-file-85-security-implications.html, accessed August 22, 2010.

293. Horwitt, *Let Them Call Me Rebel*, xv.

294. Alinsky, *Rules for Radicals*, 18–9.

295. Ibid., 43.

296. Alinsky, *Reveille for Radicals*, 25.

297. Alinsky, *Rules for Radicals*, 44.

298. Alinsky, *Reveille for Radicals*, 90–1.

299. Horwitt, *Let Them Call Me Rebel*, 40–1.

300. Ibid., 244.

301. Horowitz, *Barack Obama's Rules for Revolution: The Alinsky Model*, 28.

302. "Obama's Radical Roots and Rules," *Investor's Business Daily*, August 14, 2008, at http://www.investors.com/NewsAndAnalysis/Article.aspx?id=495281#, accessed July 23, 2010.

303. Horowitz, *Barack Obama's Rules for Revolution*, 23.

304. "The Truth About ACORN," narrated by Megyn Kelly.

305. Elias Crim and Matthew Vadum, "Barack Obama: A Radical Leftist's Journey from Community Organizing to Politics," *Foundation Watch*, June 2008, http://www.capitalresearch.org/pubs/pdf/v1212187691.pdf.

306. David Alinsky, "Son Sees Father's Handiwork in Convention," *Boston Globe*, August 31, 2008, at http://www.boston.com/bostonglobe/editorial_opinion/letters/articles/2008/08/31/son_sees_fathers_handiwork_in_convention/, accessed July 18, 2010. This was a letter to the editor written by Alinsky's son.

307. William Dembski and Edward Sisson, "How Did Barack Obama's Community-organizer Training with the Radical IAF Organization Shape Him as a Leader?" *World* magazine, October 10, 2008, at http://www.worldmag.com/webextra/14535, accessed July 19, 2010. The book Ayers

praised is *Organizing the South Bronx*, by Jim Rooney (State University of New York Press, 1995).

308. John Judis, "Creation Myth: What Barack Obama Won't Tell You about His Community Organizing Past," *New Republic*, September 10, 2008, at http://www.tnr.com/article/creation-myth-0, accessed July 19, 2010.

309. Industrial Areas Foundation website, at http://www.industrialareasfoundation.org/locate_sw_wc.html, accessed July 17, 2010.

310. Peter Slevin, "For Clinton and Obama, a Common Ideological Touchstone," *Washington Post*, March 25, 2007, at http://www.washingtonpost.com/wp-dyn/content/article/2007/03/24/AR2007032401152.html.

311. Author interview with David Horowitz.

312. Joseph A. Morris, "Archidiocese Bankrolls Return of Religious Left," *Crain's Chicago Business*, May 22, 1995.

313. Horwitt, *Let Them Call Me Rebel*, 547.

314. Laurie Goodstein, "Harnessing the Force of Faith; Movement Spreads the Gospel of Community Power," *Washington Post*, February 6, 1994.

315. David A. Vise, "A Rising New Force in D.C. Wins First Lady's Attention," *Washington Post*, December 22, 1996.

316. "Henry Cisneros, CEO of City View, Supports the Work Done by the Affordable Housing Centers of America," Affordable Housing Centers of America website, at http://secure.ahcoa.org/resources/index/Cisneros.wmv, accessed August 19, 2010.

317. Alinsky, *Rules for Radicals*, xix.

318. Ibid., 116–9.

319. "ACORN Scandals: What's Next?"

320. Alinsky, *Rules for Radicals*, 107–113.

321. Ryan Lizza, "The Agitator," *New Republic*, March 19, 2007.

322. "Remarks of Senator Barack Obama: Super Tuesday, Chicago, IL, February 05, 2008," Organizing for America website, at http://www.barackobama.com/2008/02/05/remarks_of_senator_barack_obam_46.php, accessed August 21, 2010.

323. Alinsky, *Reveille for Radicals*, 55.

324. Delgado, *Organizing the Movement*, 77.

325. "Barack Obama and the History of Project Vote," March 21, 2008, at http://www.youtube.com/watch?v=Px1Ut433xPU, accessed May 26, 2010.

CHAPTER 7

326. Alinsky, *Reveille for Radicals*, 94.

327. Author interview with Marcel Reid.

328. "Radical Saul Alinsky: Prophet of Power," *Time*, March 2, 1970, at http://www.time.com/time/magazine/article/0,9171,904228,00.html, accessed August 21, 2010.

329. Horowitz, *Barack Obama's Rules for Revolution*, 19.
330. Alinsky, *Rules for Radicals*, 61.
331. Ibid., 113.
332. *The Democratic Promise: Saul Alinsky & His Legacy*, directed by Bob Hercules and Bruce Orenstein, (IndieFlix, 2000). Alinsky is shown in archival footage in this documentary film.
333. "THERE IS ONLY THE FIGHT...An Analysis of the Alinsky Model," by Hillary D. Rodham, May 2, 1969. This is Hillary Clinton's senior thesis from Wellesley College. The version the author of this book worked from lacked page numbers.
334. Alinsky, *Rules for Radicals*, 3.
335. Alinsky, *Reveille for Radicals*, 133–4.
336. The figure of 191 excludes variants of the word *power* such as *powerful*.
337. Alinsky, *Rules for Radicals*, 10.
338. Hillary D. Rodham, "THERE IS ONLY THE FIGHT..."
339. Alinsky, *Reveille for Radicals*, 53, 91.
340. Thomas Sowell. "Is U.S. Now On Slippery Slope to Tyranny?" *Investor's Business Daily*, June 22, 2010.
341. Alinsky, *Reveille for Radicals*, 18.
342. Alinsky, *Rules for Radicals*, 164.
343. James Madison, "Property," The Founders' Constitution, at http://press pubs.uchicago.edu/founders/documents/v1ch16s23.html, accessed August 23, 2010.
344. Abraham Lincoln, "The Perpetuation of Our Political Institutions," in *Life and Works of Abraham Lincoln: Early Speeches, 1832–1856, Including Legislative and Congressional Resolutions, Political Circulars, Notes, Etc.*, edited by Marion Mills Miller (The Current Literature Publishing Co., New York, 1907). Lincoln delivered the speech to the Young Men's Lyceum of Springfield, IL, on January 27, 1837.
345. "Washington's Farewell Address 1796," at http://avalon.law.yale.edu/18th_century/washing.asp, August 23, 2010.
346. James Madison, "Property."
347. Alinsky, *Rules for Radicals*, 3, 7.
348. Alinsky, *Reveille for Radicals*, ix.
349. Lizza, "The Agitator."
350. Alinsky, *Rules for Radicals*, 127.
351. Ibid., 126.
352. Karl Marx, "Circular Letter to Bebel, Liebknect, Bracke, and Others," 1879, 551 of *The Marx-Engels Reader*, 2nd edition (W.W. Norton & Co., 1978).
353. Alinsky, *Rules for Radicals*, 75.
354. Ibid., 127.
355. Ibid., 81.
356. Ibid., 127.

357. Ibid.
358. Ibid., 139–140.
359. Ibid.
360. Ibid., 141.
361. Ibid., 142–3.
362. Ibid., 128.
363. Horowitz, *Barack Obama's Rules for Revolution*, 32.
364. Rogan, "Now It's Welfare Lib."
365. Alinsky, *Rules for Radicals*, 128.
366. Ibid., 137–8.
367. Ibid., 128.
368. Ibid.
369. Ibid., 129.
370. Ibid.
371. Ibid.
372. Ibid., 130.
373. Ibid.
374. Gerald Astor, "The 'Apostle' and The 'Fool.'" *Look*, June 25, 1968: 34. Cited in "THERE IS ONLY THE FIGHT..." by Hillary D. Rodham.
375. Alinsky, *Rules for Radicals*, 133–4.
376. Ibid., 133.
377. Ibid., 100.
378. Ibid., 17.
379. Ibid., 26.
380. Ibid., 26–9.
381. Ibid., 35.
382. Ibid., 29.
383. Ibid., 129–130.
384. Ibid., 25.
385. Ibid., 30.
386. Ibid., 33.
387. Ibid., 34.
388. Ibid.
389. Ibid., 35.
390. Ibid.
391. Ibid., 43–4.
392. Ibid., 36–41.
393. Ibid., 44–5.
394. Ibid., 45.

CHAPTER 8

395. "ACORN Scandals: What's Next?"
396. Committee on Oversight and Government Reform. "Is ACORN Intentionally Structured As a Criminal Enterprise?"

397. Atlas, *Seeds of Change*, 219–220.

398. "ACORN Scandals: What's Next?"

399. "Acorn's Ally at the NLRB," *Wall Street Journal*, October 15, 2009, at http://online.wsj.com/article/SB10001424052748704107204574471393 545371128.html, accessed February 4, 2010.

400. Wade Rathke, "Becker to the NLRB," Chief Organizer blog, April 30, 2009, http://chieforganizer.org/2009/04/30/becker-to-the-nlrb/, accessed February 4, 2010.

401. Matthew Vadum, "Becker Lied to McCain," *American Spectator*, February 4, 2010, at http://spectator.org/archives/2010/02/04/becker-lied-to-mccain.

402. "ACORN Scandals: What's Next?"

403. Meghan Clyne, "ACORN & the Money Tree," *National Review*, October 31, 2004.

404. Charlotte Allen, "From Little ACORNs, Big Scandals Grow," *Weekly Standard*, November 3, 2008.

405. "ACORN Scandals: What's Next?"

406. Pablo Eisenberg, "After an Embezzlement, an Advocacy Group Seeks to Regain Trust," *Chronicle of Philanthropy*, October 2, 2008.

407. "The Corporate Democracy Act and Big Business Day: Rhetoric and Reality," Heritage Foundation backgrounder, March 11, 1980, at http://www.heritage.org/Research/Reports/1980/03/The-Corporate-Democracy-Act-and-Big-Business-Day-Rhetoric-and-Reality, accessed June 20, 2010.

408. Searches of the tax returns of the various ACORN affiliates were conducted in October 2008. The information was taken from the most recent publicly available tax returns available at guidestar.org, an online repository of IRS Form 990s.

409. PAC disclosure form, Michigan Department of State, Bureau of Elections, September 27, 2007, at http://miboecfr.nicusa.com/cgi-bin/cfr/show_img.cgi?doc_seq_no%3D290750%26com_id% 3D513537 %26total_images%3D1%26image_id%3D1%26doc_scanned%3D10/08/2007%26doc_date_proc%3D10/08/2007%26doc_type_code%3DSOA%26caller%3D%26last_match%3D%26cfr_com_id%3D%261%3D1, accessed Oct. 24, 2008.

410. "ACORN Scandals: What's Next?"

411. *Glenn Beck Program*, Fox News Channel, May 11, 2009, at http://www.foxnews.com/story/0,2933,519948,00.html, May 20 2009.

412. *Glenn Beck Program*, Fox News Channel, July 6, 2009.

413. Employment Policies Institute, "Rotten ACORN: America's Bad Seed," July 2006, at http://www.rottenacorn.com/downloads/060728_badSeed.pdf, accessed August 26, 2010.

414. Committee on Oversight and Government Reform, "Is ACORN Intentionally Structured As a Criminal Enterprise?"

415. This was the conclusion of Bob Cocchiaro, CPA, MBA, president of Cocchiaro & Associates, based on an examination of the Independent Auditor's Report of ACORN Housing Corp. Inc. and subsidiaries for the years ended June 30, 2007 and 2008, by Paciera, Gautreau & Priest LLC, dated January 12, 2010. The report was provided by HUD in 2010 further to the author's Freedom of Information Act request.

416. The tax returns, known as IRS Form 990s, of ACORN Housing, which changed its name recently to Affordable Housing Centers of America, may be viewed at guidestar.org. In some of the forms AISJ is referred to by its former name, Arkansas Institute for Social Justice.

417. Swarts, *Organizing Urban America*, 85.

418. Ann Mariano, "Advocates Stand Up for Poor, Homeless; Campaign to Move Families Into HUD Properties Takes Hold in D.C.," *Washington Post*, September 22, 1990.

419. Atlas, *Seeds of Change*, 67–8, 71.

420. The subsidiaries are identified in the Independent Auditor's Report of ACORN Housing Corp. Inc. and subsidiaries for the years ended June 30, 2007 and 2008, by Paciera, Gautreau & Priest LLC, dated January 12, 2010.

421. Swarts, *Organizing Urban America*, 85–86.

422. Kurtz, *Radical-in-Chief*, 233.

423. *Glenn Beck Program*, Fox News Channel, July 23, 2009.

424. Committee on Oversight and Government Reform. "Is ACORN Intentionally Structured As a Criminal Enterprise?"

425. "Report on the Activities of the Committee on Economic and Educational Opportunities During the 104th Congress," Report 104–875, U.S. Government Printing Office, January 2, 1997.

426. Employment Policies Institute, "The Real ACORN," 5.

427. "Report on the Activities of the Committee on Economic and Educational Opportunities During the 104th Congress."

428. Home page of website for Harmon, Curran, Spielberg & Eisenberg, at http://www.harmoncurran.com/?fuseaction=content.getMainPage, accessed August 27, 2010.

429. Trevor Loudon. "Obama File 89 Deepak Bhargava 'Advancing Change in the Age of Obama,'" New Zeal blog, October 7, 2009, at http://newzeal.blogspot.com/2009/10/obama-file-89-deepak-bhargava-advancing.html, accessed August 27, 2010.

430. "Our Clients," Harmon, Curran, Spielberg & Eisenberg website, at http://www.harmoncurran.com/?page=clients, accessed August 27, 2010.

431. The author wrote on this topic in "ACORN's Prophetic Lawyer," *American Spectator*, October 1, 2009, at http://spectator.org/archives/2009/10/01/acorns-prophetic-lawyer, and provided the Kingsley memo to the Big Government website at http://biggovernment.com/mvadum/2009/10/01/

exclusive-acorn-legal-memo-confirms-depths-of-troubles. The author was the first to publish the memo in its entirety.

432. Stephanie Strom, "Acorn Report Raises Issues of Legality," *New York Times*, October 22, 2008.

433. Ibid.

CHAPTER 9

434. ACORN Housing Corp. "To Each Their Home: Success Stories from the ACORN Housing Corporation," 1999, at http://capitalresearch.org/blog/wp-content/uploads/2008/10/toeachtheirhome.pdf. "Writing and production" credit is given on the final page of the document to ACORN stalwart Madeleine Adamson.

435. Atlas, *Seeds of Change*, 67.

436. Steven Malanga, "Obsessive Housing Disorder," *City Journal*, Spring 2009.

437. "Community Reinvestment Act (CRA) Fact Sheet," Council of Development Finance Agencies website, at http://www.cdfa.net/cdfa/cdfaweb.nsf/fbaad5956b2928b086256efa005c5f78/f133ad718f3081d4862571410077df1d/$FILE/CDFA%20Fact%20Sheet%20-%20CRA.pdf, accessed August 31, 2010.

438. Trevor Jensen, "Squire Lance: 1933–2010; Key Community Activist, Political Organizer," *Chicago Tribune* (Chicagoland Final Edition), April 15, 2010.

439. Swarts, *Organizing Urban America*, 77.

440. Neal R. Peirce and Jerry Hagstrom, "Watch Out, New Right, Here Come the 'Young Progressives,'" *National Journal*, December 30, 1978.

441. Kurtz, *Radical-in-Chief*, 235.

442. Atlas, *Seeds of Change*, 68.

443. Joe R. Feagin, "Excluding Blacks and Others From Housing: The Foundation of White Racism," *Cityscape: A Journal of Policy Development and Research* (Vol. 4., No. 3, 1999), 79–84.

444. Shannon McCaffrey, "Cuomo HUD Reports Criticized as Self-promotional," AP, February 21, 2001.

445. George Melloan, *The Great Money Binge: Spending Our Way to Socialism* (Threshold Editions, 2009), 55.

446. Howard Husock, "The Trillion-Dollar Bank Shakedown That Bodes Ill for Cities," *City Journal*, Winter 2000.

447. James Bovard, "Urban Bank Loan Shakedowns Targeted," *Washington Times*, January 19, 1999.

448. Michelle Minton, "The Community Reinvestment Act's Harmful Legacy: How It Hampers Access to Credit," Competitive Enterprise Institute, March 20, 2008, at http://cei.org/cei_files/fm/active/0/Michelle%20Minton%20-%20CRA%20-%20FINAL_WEB.pdf, accessed August 31, 2010.

449. Stan Liebowitz, "The Real Scandal: How Feds Invited the Mortgage Mess," *New York Post*, February 5, 2008.

450. Tami Luhby, "Scrutiny Looms for Bank Deals; Cash for Community Groups at Risk," *Crain's New York Business*, November 8, 1999.

451. ACORN Housing Corp., "To Each Their Home: Success Stories from the ACORN Housing Corporation."

452. Michael J. Rochon, "ACORN Takes Protests to Firms: Group Targets 2 Mortgage Lenders," *Philadelphia Tribune*, June 27, 2000.

453. Atlas, *Seeds of Change*, 69–70.

454. Ibid., 62–3.

455. Gregory D. Squires, "No Protest Without Progress," *Shelterforce Online*, March/April 2003, at http://www.nhi.org/online/issues/128/CRAat25.html, accessed September 1, 2010.

456. Randy Stoecker, "Has the Fight Gone Out of Organizing?" *Shelterforce Online*, Spring 2010, at http://www.shelterforce.org/article/1983/has_the_fight_gone_out_of_organizing/, accessed September 2, 2010. The information paraphrased was in the photo caption in the article.

457. Kurtz, *Radical-in-Chief*, 255.

458. "He's Frank, But Not Honest; Democrat Plays Race Card against Subprime Critics," *Orange County Register* (California), October 12, 2008.

459. Edward Pinto, "Yes, the CRA Is Toxic," *City Journal*, Autumn 2009.

460. ACORN Housing Corp., "To Each Their Home: Success Stories from the ACORN Housing Corporation."

461. Swarts, *Organizing Urban America*, 29.

462. Pinto, "Yes, the CRA Is Toxic."

463. For more information on "The Lottery," see http://www.imdb.com/title/tt1515935/.

464. "Q&A," hosted by Brian Lamb, guest Madeleine Sackler, broadcast June 24, 2010 on C-SPAN, at http://www.c-spanvideo.org/program/294243-1&buy, accessed July 16, 2010.

465. RiShawn Biddle, "The NEA Pays to Play: Buying Influence With ACORN and Other Leftwing Groups," *Labor Watch*, April 2010, at http://www.capitalresearch.org/pubs/pdf/v1270827381.pdf.

466. Alex Tiegen, "Documentary Focuses on School Choice War," *Sunshine State News*, June 8, 2010, at http://sunshinestatenews.com/story/new-doc-shed-light-school-choice-war, accessed July 16, 2010.

467. "Lessons Learned from the 2008 Election: Hearing Before the Subcommittee on the Constitution, Civil Rights, and Civil Liberties of the Committee on the Judiciary," (U.S. Government Printing Office, March 19, 2009), 76.

468. Transcript of hearing in *Moyer v. ACORN*, October 29, 2008, at http://www.docstoc.com/docs/5005886/Moyer-v-ACORN-transcript, August 30, 2010, 55–6. MonCrief's testimony was given before Judge Robert Simpson of the Commonwealth Court of Pennsylvania in Harrisburg.

469. Written statement of Anita MonCrief provided at a Republican-sponsored discussion of ACORN on Capitol Hill, December 1, 2009, at http://www.

judicialwatch.org/files/documents/2009/MonCrief_Testimony.pdf, accessed August 30, 2010.

470. Thomas Heath, "SEIU Presses Carlyle Group on Manor Care Deal," the Washbiz Blog of *Washington Post*, October 17, 2007, at http://voices.washingtonpost.com/washbizblog/2007/10/seiu_increases_public_pressure. html, accessed August 30, 2010.

471. Michael Clancy, "Protesters Pop In on the Carlyle Group," by Michael Clancy, *Village Voice*, September 19, 2007, at http://www.maketheroad. org/article.php?ID=400, accessed August 30, 2010.

CHAPTER 10

472. Erick Erickson, "A Review of ACORN CEO Bertha Lewis's Rolodex Suggests Strong White House Ties," Red State, September 22, 2009, at http://www.redstate.com/erick/2009/09/22/redstate-exclusive-a-review-of-acorn-ceo-bertha-lewiss-rolodex-suggests-strong-white-house-ties/, accessed May 31, 2010.

473. Matthew Vadum, "Radical Awakening: From America Hater to Hero," Big Government, at http://biggovernment.com/mvadum/2010/04/13/exclusive-radical-awakening-from-america-hater-to-hero/, accessed May 29, 2010; Big Government posted with permission the article of the same name that was published in *Townhall*, April 2010.

474. Alejandro Lazo, "Citgo Giving $1.5 Million to Maryland Charity," *Washington Post*, August 5, 2008, at http://www.washingtonpost.com/wp-dyn/content/article/2008/08/04/AR2008080401485.html?sub=AR, accessed August 5, 2008.

475. "Chavez Pushes Through State-control Decrees," AP, August 5, 2008.

476. "Why Cynthia Nixon Votes Working Families Party," at http://www.youtube.com/watch/?v=os7LOlv-l_M, October 22, 2010, accessed October 22, 2010.

477. Edward-Isaac Dovere, "Empty On Funding, ACORN Shutters Around the Country," City Hall News, February 22, 2010, at http://www.cityhallnews. com/newyork/article-1147-empty-on-funding-acorn-shutters-around-the-country.html, accessed September 5, 2010.

478. "25 People to Blame for the Financial Crisis," *Time* magazine, February 2009, at http://www.time.com/time/specials/packages/0,28757,1877351, 00.html, accessed August 27, 2010.

479. Sean Higgins, "The Irresponsible Center for Responsible Lending," *Organization Trends*, March 2010, at http://www.capitalresearch.org/pubs/pdf/v1268673474.pdf.

480. E. Scott Reckard, "Putting Their Money into the Right to Know; A Pair of Ex-bankers Are Launching ProPublica, a Nonprofit Investigative News Organization," *Los Angeles Times*, November 19, 2007 (Home Edition).

481. Joe Nocera, "Self-Made Philanthropists," *New York Times Magazine*, March 9, 2008.

482. *Glenn Beck Program*, Fox News Channel, June 3, 2009.

483. Sean Higgins, "The Irresponsible Center for Responsible Lending."

484. "ACORN Targets Wells Subsidiaries," *National Mortgage News*, May 12, 2003.

485. Dennis Domrzalski, "ACORN Files 14 Complaints against Wells Fargo Financial," *New Mexico Business Weekly*, November 28, 2003, at http://www.bizjournals.com/albuquerque/stories/2003/12/01/story8.html, accessed September 2, 2010.

486. "ACORN Announces Class Action Lawsuit Against Wells Fargo," Business Wire, June 28, 2004.

487. "ACORN Calls on Fed to Remove Wells Fargo CEO From Council; New Study Finds Racial Inequality in Wells' Subprime Lending," U.S. Newswire, August 30, 2005.

488. *Glenn Beck Program*, Fox News Channel, June 3, 2009.

489. Higgins, "The Irresponsible Center for Responsible Lending."

490. Center for Responsible Lending, "A Review of Wells Fargo's Subprime Lending," April 2004, at http://www.responsiblelending.org/mortgage-lending/research-analysis/ip004-Wells_Fargo-0404.pdf, accessed September 2, 2010.

491. Higgins, "The Irresponsible Center for Responsible Lending."

492. John J. Miller, "Giving Liberally," *National Review*, November 17, 2008, at http://www.heymiller.com/2009/06/giving-liberally/, accessed September 2, 2010.

493. Jess Wisloski, "Sealed with a Kiss: Ratner, Mayor, ACORN, Agree on Housing Plan," *Brooklyn Paper*, May 28, 2005, at http://www.brooklynpaper.com/stories/28/22/28_22nets1.html, July 9, 2009.

494. Roberto Santiago, "ACORN Hits Developer on Tenants," *Daily News* (New York), February 25, 2000.

495. Anita MonCrief, "ACORN and FCR: Did They Dupe Brooklyn?" Anita MonCrief's blog, January 5, 2009, at http://www.anitamoncrief.blogspot.com/2009/01/acorn-and-fcr-did-they-dupe-brooklyn.html, accessed July 9, 2009.

496. Eliot Brown, "After Rowdy Atlantic Yards Hearings, a Senate Bill to Punish Heckling," *New York Observer*, November 23, 2009.

497. CUNY TV's "Brian Lehrer Live," aired June 4, 2009, at http://livething.com/brianlehrertv/?p=198, accessed August 4, 2010.

498. Rich Calder, "Atlantic Yards Budget Balloons By Nearly A Billion," *New York Post*, June 23, 2009.

499. Niev Duffy, "ACORN's Fair Housing Fight in Working Class Communities: A Conversation with ACORN CEO Bertha Lewis," *Regional Labor Review*, Spring/Summer 2009, at http://www.hofstra.edu/pdf/Academics/Colleges/HCLAS/CLD/CLD_rlr_sprsum09.pdf, accessed July 9, 2009.

500. Kurtz, *Radical-in-Chief*, 231, 233.

501. ACORN Housing website home page as of August 20, 2007, at http://web.archive.org/web/20071011005438/www.acornhousing.org/index.php, accessed August 31, 2010.

502. "Our History," Affordable Housing Centers of America website, at http://www.ahcoa.org/about/history.cfm, accessed August 31, 2010.

503. John Berlau, "Trust-Funding Fannie and Freddie," *Human Events,* July 24, 2008, at http://www.humanevents.com/article.php?id=27666, accessed May 31, 2010.

504. Michelle Malkin, "The Left-wing Mortgage Counseling Racket," Michelle-Malkin.com, April 3, 2008, at http://michellemalkin.com/ 2008/04/03/the-left-wing-mortgage-counseling-racket/, accessed September 7, 2010.

505. Matthew Vadum, "ACORN Still Owes $2.3 Million in Overdue Taxes," Big Government, November 16, 2009, at http://biggovernment.com/mvadum/2009/11/16/acorn-still-owes-2-3-million-in-overdue-taxes. The complete list of tax liens is available at http://www.capitalresearch.org/blog/wp-content/uploads/2009/11/copy-of-acorntaxliens_masterlist_nov2009.xls.

506. "ACORN Holds Summer Summit with Banks and Thrifts," *ABA Banking Journal,* October 1, 1992, at http://www.allbusiness.com/finance/325691-1.html, accessed May 30, 2010.

507. Sol Stern, "ACORN's Nutty Regime for Cities."

508. Vanguard Charitable Endowment Program is a donor-directed, also known as a donor-advised, fund. Such funds distribute donors' money anonymously.

509. "Tides Foundation & Tides Center," ActivistCash.com, 2005, at http://www.discoverthenetworks.org/Articles/Tides%20Foundation.htm, August 28, 2010.

510. Matthew Vadum and Jeremy Lott, "In a Rotten Nutshell: Everything You've Ever Wanted to Know about ACORN," *Labor Watch,* November 2008, at http://capitalresearch.org/pubs/pdf/v1225223330.pdf.

511. Matthew Vadum, "De-funder of the Left," *American Spectator,* January 5, 2009, at http://spectator.org/archives/2009/01/05/de-funder-of-the-left.

512. Kevin Mooney, "Liberty Tax CEO recalls ACORN's 'Mongolian Horde,'" *Washington Examiner,* July 7, 2009, at http://www.washingtonexaminer.com/opinion/columns/OpEd-Contributor/Liberty-Tax-CEO-recalls-ACORN_s-_Mongolian-Horde_-7931814-50049047.html, accessed, July 19, 2009.

513. "The Truth About ACORN," Fox News Channel.

514. "Bank of America Agrees to Purchase Countrywide Financial Corp.," January 11, 2008, at http://www.sec.gov/Archives/edgar/data/25191/000089882208000054/exhibit991.htm, accessed August 28, 2010.

515. HSBC Finance "Prospectus Supplement (To Prospectus Dated December 5, 2006)" at http://www.sec.gov/Archives/edgar/data/1382691/000095013706013422/c10222bbe424b5.htm, accessed August 28, 2010.

516. "Pennsylvania PUC Approves Merger Between PECO Parent Exelon and N.J.'s PSEG," January 27, 2006, at http://www.sec.gov/Archives/

edgar/data/1168165/000095013706001049/c01976exv99.htm, accessed
August 28, 2010.

517. Rollins Inc., Form 10-Q, for quarter ended June 30, 2006, at http://
www.sec.gov/Archives/edgar/data/84839/000008483906000056/for-
m10q2q.htm, accessed August 28, 2010.

518. TCF Financial Corp., 1993 annual report via Nexis.

519. Roosevelt Financial Group Inc., 1993 annual report via Nexis.

520. Rob Wells, "Bank of New York Agrees to $750 Million Lending Plan," AP,
September 24, 1992.

521. Pay Doyle, "AG Office Queried about Diverted Funds," *Star Tribune* (Minneapolis), July 1, 2008 (Metro Edition).

522. Swarts, *Organizing Urban America*, 78.

523. Mark Skertic, "Household Settles Class-action Suits for $100 Million," *Chi-
cago Tribune*, November 26, 2003 (Chicago Final Edition).

524. Household Finance Corp., Form 8-K dated October 15, 2003 via Nexis.

525. *New York Times*, June 26, 2006.

526. Matthias Rieker, "Citi in Low-Income Lending Pact with Acorn," *American
Banker*, September 21, 2004.

527. Atlas, *Seeds of Change*, 218.

528. Kevin Mooney, "ACORN's 'Muscle for Money' Does the Bidding of SEIU,"
Washington Examiner, July 6, 2009, at http://www.washingtonexaminer.
com/opinion/columns/special-editorial-reports/EXAMINER-SPE-
CIAL-REPORT-ACORNs-Muscle-for-Money-does-the-bidding-of-
SEIU–50090352.html, at August 30, 2010; "Noisy Activists Invade Meeting
of Paint Industry Executives," AP, October 24, 2005; "The Truth About
ACORN," Fox News Channel.

529. "The Truth About ACORN," Fox News Channel.

530. Peter Krouse, "Sherwin-Williams Shareholders Hear That Company to
Continue Court Fight," *Plain Dealer* (Cleveland), April 20, 2006.

CHAPTER 11

531. R.A. Dyer, "ACORN Activists Re-emerge Here with a Determined Voice,"
Houston Chronicle, January 17, 1997.

532. Delgado, *Organizing the Movement*, 103, 115, 204.

533. "ACORN," *Houston Post*, May 7, 1979.

534. *Arkansas Democrat-Gazette*, September 2, 1987.

535. Atlas, *Seeds of Change*, 33, 36.

536. Delgado, *Organizing the Movement*, 123–4, 140.

537. Stern, "ACORN's Nutty Regime for Cities."

538. Delgado, *Organizing the Movement*, ix.

539. Kotz and Kotz, *A Passion for Equality*, 300.

540. Delgado, *Organizing the Movement*, 101.

541. Kevin Mooney, "ACORN's 'Muscle for Money' Does the Bidding of SEIU,"
Washington Examiner, July 6, 2009, at http://www.washingtonexaminer.

com/opinion/columns/special-editorial-reports/EXAMINER-SPE-
CIAL-REPORT-ACORNs-Muscle-for-Money-does-the-bidding-of-
SEIU–50090352.html, at August 30, 2010.

542. Delgado, *Organizing the Movement*, 92–4.

543. Rathke, "Tactical Tension."

544. Stern, "ACORN's Nutty Regime for Cities."

545. Ibid.

546. Valerie Bauman, "Protest of NY Senate Coup Becomes Physical," AP, June 11, 2009.

547. "Victories: Elections, Issues, Organizing," Working Families Party website, at http://www.workingfamiliesparty.org/about/victories/, accessed September 14, 2010.

548. James Bovard, "Urban Bank Loan Shakedowns Targeted," *Washington Times*, January 19, 1999 (Final Edition).

549. Brian Reilly, "Squatters' Move into HUD Home Leads to Arrests," *Washington Times*, August 29, 1990.

550. Lisabeth Weiner, "Acorn Demands Homes from FSLIC," *American Banker*, March 10, 1989.

551. *ACORN v. St. Louis County, Mo.*, No. 89–3011, U.S. Court of Appeals for the Eighth Circuit, 930 F.2d 591; 1991 U.S. App. LEXIS 5633, April 8, 1991.

552. *Dallas ACORN v. Dallas County, Texas, Hospital District*, No. 79–3967, U.S. Court of Appeals for the Fifth Circuit, 670 F.2d 629, March 19, 1982.

553. *San Diego Union-Tribune*, December 20, 2001.

554. Laura Vozzella, "ACORN More Subdued in Quest to Alter Council," *Baltimore Sun*, October 7, 2002; Stern, "ACORN's Nutty Regime for Cities"; *American Banker*, June 20, 1991.

555. Stern, "ACORN's Nutty Regime for Cities."

556. Ibid.

557. Ibid.

558. Ibid.

559. *Newsday*, July 29, 1993.

560. Nathaniel Scott, "ACORN Demands HUD Reform Housing Program," *Michigan Citizen*, July 13, 1991.

561. Christine Dugas, "Group Confronts FDIC Property," *Newsday*, November 6, 1992.

562. George Landau and Jim Gallagher, "UMB Exec Defiant at 'Blackmail'; ACORN Demanding More Loans for Poor," *St. Louis Post-Dispatch*, January 27, 1993.

563. "Bank Protest Toned Down," *St. Louis Post-Dispatch*, May 27, 1993.

564. Ayana Jones, "Union Pickets in Protest of SEPTA Fare Hike," *Philadelphia Tribune*, May 11, 2001.

565. "Group Pickets Mayor's Home over Budget," *St. Louis Post-Dispatch*, March 25, 1991.

566. Kim Bell, "Community Activists Strike Out for Minimum Wage Increase," *St. Louis Post-Dispatch*, October 28, 1996.

567. Akweli Parker, "Midday Protest Shuts PGW Office," *Philadelphia Inquirer*, February 3, 2001.

568. Michelle Malkin, "Document Drop: The Truth about ACORN's Foreclosure Poster Child," MichelleMalkin.com, February 23, 2009, at http://michellemalkin.com/2009/02/23/document-drop-the-truth-about-acorns-foreclosure-poster-child/, accessed September 6, 2010; Joshua Rhett Miller. "Arrest Made in Home Foreclosure Civil Disobedience Program," FoxNews.com, February 23, 2009, at http://www.foxnews.com/story/0,2933,498669,00.html, accessed September 6, 2010.

569. Atlas, *Seeds of Change*, 76, 93.

570. Ibid., 91, 93.

571. Ibid., 96.

572. Inter Press Service, September 17, 1985.

573. Steven Erlanger, "New York Turns Squatters Into Homeowners," *New York Times*, October 12, 1987.

574. "Last of Squatters Move From City-Owned Houses," AP, May 6, 1982.

575. United Press International, June 25, 1982.

576. Stuart Whatley, "ACORN Launches Home Defenders Campaign to Fight Foreclosures," *Huffington Post*, February 20, 2009, at http://www.huffingtonpost.com/2009/02/20/acorn-launches-home-defen_n_168269.html, accessed September 6, 2010.

577. Stanley Kurtz, "Spreading the Virus," *New York Post*, October 14, 2008.

578. Atlas, *Seeds of Change*, 69.

579. "Community Reinvestment Act: Hearings before the Subcommittee on Financial Institutions and Consumer Credit of the Committee on Banking and Financial Services, House of Representatives, One Hundred Fourth Congress, First Session, March 8, 9, 1995," (U.S. Government Printing Office, 1995, serial no. 104–8), 1–2.

580. Ibid., 2.

581. Ibid.

582. Ibid., 90.

583. Ibid.

584. Ibid., 744–751.

585. Kurtz, "Spreading the Virus."

586. David Hogberg, "NACA: Neighborhood Assistance Corporation of America: ACORN's Rival In Shakedown Tactics," *Organization Trends*, April 2009, at http://www.capitalresearch.org/pubs/pdf/v1238510994.pdf.

587. Jacqueline S. Gold, "Planned CRA Reform May Hit 1st Amendment Wall," *American Banker*, January 11, 2000.

588. Dean Anason, "Jesse Jackson Assails Gramm and ABA in Defense of CRA," *American Banker*, September 16, 1999.

589. Gold, "Planned CRA Reform May Hit 1st Amendment Wall."
590. Richard A. Oppel Jr., "Many Banks Make Money On Lending in Poor Areas," *New York Times*, October 22, 1999 (Late Edition—Final).
591. Stanton McManus, "Sunburn; A New Banking Law Is Set to Silence Consumer Advocates," *In These Times*, April 17, 2000.
592. "Test Program for Poor Seeking to Buy Homes," AP, February 25, 1993.
593. Verne Kopytoff, "Low-Income Mortgage Assistance," *San Francisco Chronicle*, July 27, 2000.
594. Marcy Gordon, "Mortgage Co. Enters Pilot Program," AP Online, July 26, 2000.
595. "Ameriquest, ACORN Partner on Pilot Lending Program; Mortgage Firm Commits $360 Million and Defines 'Best Practices'; 'Breakthrough' Agreement on Fair Lending Standards Unites Industry, Activists," PR Newswire, July 26, 2000.

CHAPTER 12

596. Richard Kirsch, "What Progressives Did Right to Win Healthcare," *The Nation*, August 9, 2010, at http://www.thenation.com/article/153947/what-progressives-did-right-win-health-care, accessed September 5, 2010.
597. Philip Klein, "How Liberal Activists Passed Obamacare," *Foundation Watch*, August 2010, at http://www.capitalresearch.org/pubs/pdf/v1280761786.pdf.
598. Delgado, *Organizing the Movement*, 104.
599. Swarts, *Organizing Urban America*, 81.
600. Jon Gertner, "What Is a Living Wage?" *New York Times*, January 15, 2006 (Late Edition—Final).
601. Swarts, *Organizing Urban America*, 83.
602. Vadum and Lott, "In a Rotten Nutshell: Everything You've Ever Wanted to Know about ACORN."
603. Don Loos, "ACORN and Big Labor: Two Peas in a Pod," Big Government, January 6. 2010, at http://biggovernment.com/dloos/2010/01/06/acorn-and-big-labor-two-peas-in-a-pod/, accessed July 29, 2010.
604. Edward-Isaac Dovere, "All in the Family Part 4," *City Hall News*, December 3, 2009, at http://www.cityhallnews.com/newyork/article-1049-all-in-the-family-part-4.html, accessed September 14, 2010.
605. "Activists Protest Outside AIG Execs' Homes," *USA Today*, March 23, 2009, at http://www.usatoday.com/money/industries/insurance/2009-03-20-aig-employees-security_N.htm, accessed September 14, 2010.
606. Eric Shawn, "'They Tried to Steal an Election,' N.Y. Voter Fraud Case Heats Up," FoxNews.com, October 20, 2009, at http://www.foxnews.com/politics/2009/10/20/tried-steal-election-ny-voter-fraud-case-heats/, accessed September 14, 2010.
607. "Victories: Elections, Issues, Organizing," Working Families Party website, at http://www.workingfamiliesparty.org/about/victories/, accessed September 14, 2010.

608. Sally Goldenberg, "Working Families 'Scam' to Boost Pals," *New York Post*, October 27, 2009, at http://www.nypost.com/f/print/news/local/item_ YEZ7jXNl4QhmHQg3BsjHCM, September 6, 2010.

609. Edward-Isaac Dovere, "Four Candidates Pour Cash Into Company with Apparent ACORN Ties," City Hall News, August 26, 2009, at http://www. cityhallnews.com/newyork/article-878-four-candidates-pour-cash-into-company-with-apparent-acorn-ties.html, September 13, 2010.

610. Edward-Isaac Dovere, "All in the Family Part 1," *City Hall News*, November 30, 2009, at http://www.cityhallnews.com/newyork/article-1043-all-in-the-family-part-1.html, accessed September 13, 2009.

611. Edward-Isaac Dovere, "All in the Family Part 3," *City Hall News*, December 2, 2009, at http://www.cityhallnews.com/newyork/article-1048-all-in-the-family-part-3.html, accessed September 13, 2010.

612. Gregory Hall, "Former Organizer Says ACORN Will Commit Fraud in Census Work," *Washington Examiner*, May 18, 2009.

613. Matthew Vadum, "ACORN's Labor Pains," *American Spectator*, August 7, 2009, at http://spectator.org/archives/2009/08/07/acorns-labor-pains.

614. Van Smith, "Do-Gooder Blues," *Baltimore City Paper*, July 26, 2006, at http:// www.citypaper.com/news/story.asp?id=12077, accessed May 27, 2010.

615. Appellants' Opening Brief, *ACORN v. State of California*, 1996: 10–11, as cited in "Rotten ACORN: America's Bad Seed," by Employment Policies Institute: 7, at http://www.rottenacorn.com/downloads/060728_bad-Seed.pdf, accessed May 30, 2010.

616. Richard B. Berman, "ACORN's Nutty View of Wages," *Washington Times*, February 16, 1996.

617. *EEOC v. ACORN*, 1995 U.S. Dist. LEXIS 2948; 67 Fair Empl. Prac. Cas. (BNA) 508.

618. "San Jose ACORN Campaign Closes," *Industrial Worker* (May 2002, Vol. 99), 5.

619. Charles Rabin, "Miami Workers Angry about Not Receiving Pay after Minimum Wage Increase," Knight Ridder Tribune Business News, November 17, 2004.

620. "King County, 2007–2008, Charter Review Commission, Public Hearing," (transcript) June 20, 2007, West Seattle, Washington: 19–20, at http:// your.kingcounty.gov/exec/charter/outreach/WestSeattletranscript.pdf, accessed September 8, 2010.

621. Stern, "ACORN's Nutty Regime for Cities."

622. Ibid.

623. Dennis Shirley, *Community Organizing for Urban School Reform* (University of Texas Press, 1st edition, 1997), 289.

624. Stern, "ACORN's Nutty Regime for Cities."

625. Kurtz, *Radical-in-Chief*, 235.

626. Miaya Pierce, "Acorn Goes to Washington," ACORN website, 2001, at http://web.archive.org/web/20011119051501/home.netcom.com/~mr_ zero/html/mind.html, accessed September 6, 2010.

627. Ben Block, "Expanded Coalitions Support U.S. Climate Bill," Worldwatch Institute, June 8, 2009, at http://www.worldwatch.org/node/6146, accessed September 9, 2010.

628. Patrice Hill, "'Green' Jobs No Longer Golden in Stimulus," *Washington Times*, September 9, 2010, at http://www.washingtontimes.com/news/2010/sep/9/green-jobs-no-longer-golden-in-stimulus/, accessed September 11, 2010.

629. Patrick Courrielche, "Explosive New Audio Reveals White House Using NEA to Push Partisan Agenda," Big Journalism, September 21, 2009, at http://bighollywood.breitbart.com/pcourrielche/2009/09/21/explosive-new-audio-reveals-white-house-using-nea-to-push-partisan-agenda/#more-227610, accessed September 8, 2010.

630. Phil Kerpen, "The Apollo Alliance: Unifying Activists on the Left," *Foundation Watch*, October 2009, at http://www.capitalresearch.org/pubs/pdf/v1254459150.pdf.

CHAPTER 13

631. Matthew Vadum, "Do Census Layoffs Clear the Way for Hiring of ACORN Workers?" Capital Research Center blog, July 2, 2009, at http://www.capitalresearch.org/blog/2009/07/02/do-census-layoffs-clear-the-way-for-hiring-of-acorn-workers/.

632. Hall, "Former Organizer Says ACORN Will Commit Fraud in Census Work."

633. Jeane MacIntosh, "1 Voter, 72 Registrations," *New York Post*, October 10, 2008.

634. Ginger Adams, Susan Edelman, and Melissa Klein, "7-Yr.-Old Gets an ACORN Vote," *New York Post*, October 12, 2008.

635. David Horowitz, *Barack Obama's Rules for Revolution: The Alinsky Model* (David Horowitz Freedom Center, 2009), 33, at http://www.discoverthenetworks.org/Articles/Rules%20for%20Revolution%20(2).pdf.

636. John Fund, *Stealing Elections: How Voter Fraud Threatens Our Democracy* (Encounter Books, 2nd edition, 2008), 53.

637. James Vaznis, "Supreme Court Upholds Voter ID Law," *Boston Globe*, April 29, 2008, at http://www.boston.com/news/nation/washington/articles/2008/04/29/supreme_court_upholds_voter_id_law/, accessed September 12, 2010.

638. "Feds to Probe Voter Registration Problems," KMBC, October 24, 2006, at http://www.kmbc.com/politics/10147706/detail.html, accessed September 7, 2010; "ACORN Workers Indicted For Alleged Voter Fraud," KMBC, November 1, 2006, at http://www.kmbc.com/r/10214492/detail.html, accessed September 7, 2010.

639. Frank Swoboda, "Calif. Fund-Raiser Pleads Guilty in Teamsters Election Case," *Washington Post*, August 18, 1998 (Final Edition); "Heather Booth," Discover The Networks, at http://www.discoverthenetworks.org/individualProfile.asp?indid=1641, accessed September 6, 2010; "$1 Million Scan-

dal Latest to Hit ACORN," Consumer Rights League, undated, at http://
www.consumersrightsleague.org/uploadedfiles/Latest%20Million%20
Dollar%20ACORN%20Scandal.pdf, September 6, 2010.

640. Bill Sammon, "Board Ex-Chairman Pleads Guilty," *Plain Dealer* (Cleveland, Ohio), December 19, 1992.

641. "Pro-Gambling Camp Pays Firms to Sign Up Voters," *St. Louis Post-Dispatch* (Missouri), October 20, 1994.

642. Fund, *Stealing Elections*, 47–8.

643. "Voter Purges Upheld in Bias Suit," *Philadelphia Daily News*, June 16, 1994.

644. Teresa James, "Caging Democracy: A 50-Year History of Partisan Challenges to Minority Voters," Project Vote, September 2007, 36.

645. Erica Payne, editor, *The Practical Progressive: How to Build a Twenty-first Century Political Movement* (Public Affairs, 2008), 272. This refers to the "Project Vote" entry.

646. Jeff Jacoby, "How to Stuff the Ballot Box," *St. Louis Post-Dispatch*, November 13, 1996.

647. "The Politics of Voter Fraud," Project Vote, undated: 5. The report is available at http://www.capitalresearch.org/blog/?p=1897.

648. Frances Fox Piven, Lorraine C. Minnite, and Margaret Groarke, *Keeping Down the Black Vote: Race and the Demobilization of American Voters* (The New Press, 2009), 164.

649. Richard Wolf, "Welfare Agencies See Wave of Voters," *USA Today*, July 21, 2010.

650. "A Promise Unfulfilled: The National Voter Registration Act in Public Assistance Agencies, 1995–2005," ACORN, Project Vote, and Demos, July 2005.

651. Delgado, *Organizing the Movement*, 222.

652. Zachary Roth, "Iglesias: 'I'm Astounded' By DOJ's ACORN Probe," TPM Muckraker, October 16, 2008, at http://tpmmuckraker.talkingpointsmemo.com/2008/10/iglesias_im_astounded_by_dojs.php, accessed September 13, 2010. A report on the firing of the U.S. attorneys by the DOJ is available at http://www.justice.gov/oig/special/s0809a/final.pdf.

653. J. Christian Adams, "Voter Fraud and Democracy: How Damaging Is DOJ's Failure to Enforce Voting Law?" Pajamas Media, August 4, 2010, at http://pajamasmedia.com/blog/voter-fraud-and-democracy-how-damaging-is-dojs-failure-to-enforce-voting-law/, accessed September 9, 2010.

654. J. Christian Adams, "Doing the DOJ's Job for Them: Demanding Valid Voter Rolls Before November," Pajamas Media, September 7, 2010, at http://pajamasmedia.com/blog/doing-the-dojs-job-for-them-demanding-valid-voter-rolls-before-november/, accessed September 9, 2010.

655. John Fund, "Falsified Registrations Become Votes," *Politico*, November 2, 2008, at http://dyn.politico.com/printstory.cfm?uuid=5FF874F9-18FE-70B2-A89977D364B3A669, accessed November 3, 2008.

656. Jesse Jackson Jr., "Attacks on ACORN Based Not on Facts, But on Fear of 1.3 Million Poor People Registering," *Huffington Post*, October 10, 2008, at http://www.huffingtonpost.com/rep-jesse-jackson-jr/attacks-on-acorn-based-no_b_133657.html, accessed October 12, 2008.

657. Michael Falcone and Michael Moss, "Group's Tally of New Voters Was Vastly Overstated," *New York Times*, October 24, 2008.

658. Transcript of hearing in *Moyer v. ACORN*, October 29, 2008, at http://www.docstoc.com/docs/5005886/Moyer-v-ACORN-transcript, August 30, 2010: 55–6. MonCrief's testimony was given before Judge Robert Simpson of the Commonwealth Court of Pennsylvania in Harrisburg.

659. Matthew Vadum, "ACORN Employees Tell FBI of Deliberate Election Fraud, According to New Documents," *The Daily Caller*, June 10, 2010. Judicial Watch made the documents available at http://www.judicial-watch.org/news/2010/jun/judicial-watch-obtains-new-fbi-documents-regarding-acorn-voter-fraud-investigation.

660. Fund, *Stealing Elections*, 52.

661. Fund, "Falsified Registrations Become Votes."

662. Mary Manning, "Criminal Charges Filed Against ACORN, Two Employees," *Las Vegas Sun*, May 4, 2009, at http://www.lasvegassun.com/news/2009/may/04/criminal-charges-filed-against-acorn-two-employees/, accessed May 4, 2009.

663. "Man Pleads Guilty in Voter Registration Scam," *Duluth News-Tribune*, December 8, 2004; "Voter Card Stash Brings Guilty Plea," by Mark Brunswick, *Star Tribune* (Minneapolis), December 7, 2004; "Voter Registration Cards Found in Car," by Patrick Sweeney, *Duluth News-Tribune*, October 8, 2004.

664. Holly Herman, "Bogus-forms Scheme Leads to Jail Term," *Reading Eagle* (Pennsylvania), March 6, 2008.

665. Chris Lawrence, "Ex-ACORN Worker: 'I Paid the Price' for Voter Registration Fraud," CNN.com. October 22, 2008.

666. Fund, *Stealing Elections*, 51.

667. "ACORN Workers In Fraud Case Say They Had Quota Pressure," June 5, 2009, at http://www.thepittsburghchannel.com/r/19471568/detail.html, accessed September 11, 2010.

668. "In Brief," *Spokesman Review* (Spokane, Wash.), October 30, 2007 (Metro Edition).

669. "King Country Removes 1,762 Voter Names It Says Were Fraudulent," AP, July 26, 2007.

670. "ACORN Hires Child Rapist, Thieves and Drug Dealers," *Election Journal*, video of KRQE news report posted at http://www.youtube.com/watch?v=EvJE3SMHRTs on August 5, 2008, accessed July 16, 2010.

671. Walter F. Roche Jr., "Zappala Charges ACORN Workers with Violating Election Laws," *Pittsburgh Tribune Review*, May 8, 2009.

672. Steven Hepker, "ACORN Worker Bound Over," *Jackson Citizen Patriot* (Michigan), October 28, 2008.

673. Patrick M. O'Connell and Jake Wagman, "Ex-ACORN Worker Indicted in Voter Fraud Case," *St. Louis Post-Dispatch* (Missouri), January 6, 2009.

674. Aaron Mackey, "Voter Registrations by Convict Queried," by Aaron Mackey, *Arizona Daily Star*, October 16, 2004.

675. Fund, *Stealing Elections*, 50.

676. Atlas, *Seeds of Change*, 207–8.

677. Matthew Vadum, "Fighting Frankenstein," *American Spectator*, April 14, 2009, at http://spectator.org/archives/2009/04/14/fighting-frankenstein.

678. Matthew Vadum, "SOS in Minnesota," *American Spectator*, November 7, 2008, at http://spectator.org/archives/2008/11/07/sos-in-minnesota.

679. "Watchdog Group Releases Report on Felon Voter Fraud," Minnesota Majority, June 29, 2010, at http://www.minnesotamajority.org/Portals/0/documents/2010-06-29PressRelease-ReportOnFelonVoters.pdf, accessed September 12, 2010.

680. Spencer Meads, "Did Fraud Enable Al Franken's 'Efficient Campaign'?" National Legal and Policy Center, July 26, 2010.

681. Aaron Klein, "Felonious Assault on U.S. Elections," World Net Daily, July 13, 2010, at www.wnd.com/?pageId=178833, accessed September 13, 2010.

682. Aaron Klein, "Kaboom! Look Who's Really Behind Plan to Steal Election," World Net Daily, July 19, 2010, at http://www.wnd.com/?pageId=181125, accessed September 13, 2010.

CHAPTER 14

683. Atlas, *Seeds of Change*, 160.

684. Ginger Adams Otis, "Hey, Big Spender! Lavish Life of ACORN 'Thief,'" *New York Post*, September 27, 2009, at http://www.nypost.com/p/news/local/item_ekp1paAPaHSUidBrZOKKEO, accessed May 30, 2010.

685. "The Truth About ACORN," Fox News Channel.

686. The board minutes are available at http://www.capitalresearch.org/blog/wp-content/uploads/2009/09/acorn_boardminutes_june202008.pdf.

687. Arthur Z. Schwartz letter dated June 11, 2009, at http://www.capitalresearch.org/blog/wp-content/uploads/2009/06/acorn_desist_letter_june112009.pdf.

688. Michelle Malkin, "Project Vote Sues Whistleblower," Michelle Malkin.com, June 22, 2009, at http://michellemalkin.com/2009/06/22/project-sues-whistleblower-obamacorn-bully-tactics-exposed/, accessed September 6, 2010.

689. David Hogberg, "The Gamaliel Foundation: Alinsky-Inspired Group Uses Stealth Tactics to Manipulate Church Congregations," *Foundation Watch*, July 2010, at http://capitalresearch.org/pubs.pdf/v1278370073.pdf.

690. The 2006 election cycle payment is disclosed in a contract between CSI and Donna Edwards. The contract was attached to a letter dated March 24, 2008, by ACORN lawyer Elizabeth Kingsley, to the FEC. It is available at http://eqs.nictusa.com/eqsdocsMUR/29044251014.pdf, accessed July 20, 2010.

691. Arca Foundation donated to Project Vote ($180,000 since 2004) and AISJ ($220,000 since 2001). Source: FoundationSearch.com.

692. Author interview with Zach Polett, June 8, 2010.

693. Author's attempt to interview Donna Edwards, June 7, 2010.

694. Rosalind S. Helderman, "Wynn Files Campaign Complaint; Incumbent Accuses Edwards of Violating Finance Laws," *Washington Post* (suburban edition), January 30, 2008.

695. The file number of the complaint Sherwood filed with the FEC was MUR 5970. The FEC announced it dismissed the case in a February 26, 2009, press release available at http://www.fec.gov/press/press2009/20090225MUR.shtml, accessed July 20, 2010.

696. Katrina vanden Heuvel, "Donna Edwards: A New Kind of Democrat," The Nation blog, February 13, 2008, at http://www.thenation.com/blog/donna-edwards-new-kind-democrat, accessed July 20, 2010.

697. "ACORN Grassroots Democracy Campaign," May 12, 2008, at http://www.youtube.com/watch?v=cLCSnbN1lRI, accessed July 22, 2010.

698. S.A. Miller, "Conyers Suggests Probe of ACORN," *Washington Times*, March 20, 2009, at http://www.washingtontimes.com/news/2009/mar/20/conyers-suggests-probe-of-acorn, accessed September 6, 2010.

699. Frank James, "ACORN, McCain's Not So Merry-go-round," The Swamp blog (*Chicago Tribune*), October 17, 2008, at http://www.swamppolitics.com/news/politics/blog/2008/10/acorn_fbi_mccain_republicans.html, accessed September 6, 2010.

700. Matthew Vadum, "Who Killed ACORN Probe?" *Washington Times*, June 28, 2009, at http://www.washingtontimes.com/news/2009/jun/28/who-killed-acorn-probe.

701. Hannah Giles, "The Truth Is Too Scandalous for YouTube," Townhall.com, September 23, 2008, at http://townhall.com/columnists/HannahGiles/2008/09/23/the_truth_is_too_scandalous_for_youtube, accessed July 12, 2010.

702. J. Linn Allen, "Undercover Testers to Seek Lending Bias," *Chicago Tribune*, May 7, 1993, North Sports Final Edition.

703. "REVEALED: ACORN, NBC Worked Together in 'Undercover Video Sting,'" Big Government, November 30, 2009, at http://Biggovernment.com/publius/2009/11/30/acorn-nbc-worked-together-in-undercover-video-sting/, accessed September 1, 2010.

704. Justin Pritchard, "How the ACORN 'Pimp and Hooker' Videos Came to Be," AP, September 23, 2009, at http://www.breitbart.com/article.php?id=D9ATAACG0, accessed July 12, 2010.

705. Michael McCray, "ACORN Layoffs Are Taxpayer Rip-offs," Big Government, October 22, 2009, at http://biggovernment.com/mmccray/2009/10/22/acorn-layoffs-are-taxpayer-rip-offs, accessed August 2, 2010.

706. Joe Garofoli, "Brown Won't Prosecute ACORN or Those Who Filmed," *San Francisco Chronicle*, April 2, 2010, at http://articles.sfgate.

com/2010-04-02/news/20832017_1_conservative-filmmakers-hannah-giles-community-organizing-group-acorn, accessed September 6, 2010.

707. "ACORN Scandals: What's Next?"

708. Marc Thiessen, *Courting Disaster: How the CIA Kept America Safe and How Barack Obama Is Inviting the Next Attack* (Regnery Press, 2010), 240–1.

709. "Is ACORN Intentionally Structured As a Criminal Enterprise?" 5.

CHAPTER 15

710. "ACORN Political Machine Tries to Reinvent Itself," House Oversight and Government Reform Committee, April 1, 2010, 3.

711. Judy Keen, "Vows to Pick Up Where ACORN Left Off Are Made," *USA Today*, at http://www.usatoday.com/news/washington/2010-03-24-acorn-vows_N.html, accessed September 5, 2010.

712. "ACORN Missouri Assaults Bank as President Obama Signs Bank Bailout Bill," Big Government, July 21, 2010, at http://biggovernment.com/capitolconfidential/2010/07/21/acorn-missouri-assaults-bank-as-president-obama-signs-bank-bailout-bill/, accessed July 21, 2010.

713. Copy of contract and check dated March 25, 2010 on file with author.

714. Author interview with Fannie Brown.

715. Press release from Rep. Darrell Issa, March 23, 2010.

716. Matthew Vadum, "'Dissolved' ACORN Still Hitting Up Supporters For Funds," Big Government, April 20, 2010, at http://biggovernment.com/mvadum/2010/04/20/dissolved-acorn-still-hitting-up-supporters-for-funds, accessed July 16, 2010. The email is embedded in the article.

717. Press release from Rep. Steve King, April 16, 2010.

718. Author interview with King.

719. Glenn Thrush, "GOP Plans Wave of White House Probes," *Politico*, August 27, 2010, at http://www.politico.com/news/stories/0810/41506.html, accessed August 28, 2010.

720. "ACORN Settles with 1851 Center, Folds Ohio Operation," 1851 Center website, March 11, 2010, at http://ohioconstitution.org/2010/03/11/acorn-settles-ohio-rico-case-folds-state-operation/, accessed August 1, 2010.

721. Atlas, *Seeds of Change*, 248–9.

722. Author interview with Noam Chomsky.

723. Author interview with Marcel Reid.

724. The email of Nathan Henderson-James dated February 22, 2010, is available at http://www.docstoc.com/docs/30906287/ACORN_NathanHenderson-JamesEmail. In subsequent email conversations with the author Henderson-James declined to comment on the record.

725. Ramon Antonio Vargas, "James O'Keefe and Friends Plead Guilty in Mary Landrieu Office Caper," (New Orleans) *Times-Picayune*, May 26, 2010, at http://www.nola.com/crime/index.ssf/2010/05/james_okeefe_and_friends_plead.html, accessed September 4, 2010.

726. Patrick Courrielche, "In Praise of Capitalism: How the 'Social Justice'

Left Uses Economic Incentives to Create Academic Propaganda," Big Government, June 8, 2010, at http://biggovernment.com/pcourri-elche/2010/06/08/in-praise-of-capitalism-how-the-social-justice-left-uses-economic-incentives-to-create-academic-propaganda/, accessed September 12, 2010.

727. Peter Dreier and Christopher R. Martin, "Manipulating the Public Agenda: Why ACORN Was in the News, and What the News Got Wrong," Occidental College website, at http://departments.oxy.edu/uepi/acornstudy/acornstudy.pdf, accessed September 12, 2010.

728. Peter Dreier, "First They Came For ACORN," *Huffington Post*, September 26, 2009, at http://www.huffingtonpost.com/peter-dreier-first-they-came-for-acorn_b_300941.html, accessed September 12, 2010.

729. "Peter Dreier," Occidental College website, at http://departments.oxy.edu/politics/faculty/dreier.htm, accessed September 1, 2010.

730. For more information on the Democracy Alliance, see "The Democracy Alliance Does America: The Soros-Founded Plutocrats' Club Forms State Chapters," by Matthew Vadum and James Dellinger, *Foundation Watch*, December 2008, at http://www.capitalresearch.org/pubs/pdf/v1228145204.pdf.

731. Ruth Samuelson, "National Leadership Campus: Insurance Philanthropist Peter Lewis's Grand Development Concept," *Washington City Paper*, June 17, 2009, at http://www.washingtoncitypaper.com/blogs/housingcom-plex/2009/06/17/national-leadership-campus-insurance-philanthropist-peter-lewiss-grand-development-concept/, accessed August 1, 2010.

732. Author interview with Paul Yandura.

733. Mandy Nagy (blogging as Liberty Chick), "SEIU Storms Private Residence, Terrorizes Teenage Son of Bank of America Exec," Big Government, May 20, 2010, at http://biggovernment.com/libertychick/2010/05/20/seiu-storms-private-residence-terrorizes-teenage-son-of-bank-of-america-exec/, September 4, 2010.

734. "Heather Booth," Discover The Networks, at http://www.discoverthenetworks.org/individualProfile.asp?indid=1641, accessed June 10, 2010.

735. Tony Allen-Mills, "Obama Warned Over 'Welfare Spendathon,'" *The Times* (UK), February 15, 2009, at http://www.timesonline.co.uk/tol/news/world/us_and_americas/article5733499.ece, accessed August 1, 2010.

736. Fred Lucas, "Obama Will Spend More on Welfare in the Next Year Than Bush Spent on Entire Iraq War, Study Reveals," CNS News, September 22, 2009, at http://www.cnsnews.com/news/article/54400, August 1, 2010.

Index

INDEX